The Stage 5

A sort of memoir

—◦◦◦—

Neville Phillips

Matador
9 De Montfort Mews
Leicester LE1 7FW, UK
Tel: (+44) 116 255 9311 / 9312
Email: books@troubador.co.uk
Web: www.troubador.co.uk/matador

ISBN 978 1906510 435

Typeset in 11pt Stempel Garamond by Troubador Publishing Ltd, Leicester, UK

Matador is an imprint of Troubador Publishing Ltd

ABOUT THE AUTHOR

1930: aged six, Neville Phillips was scuttling about the stage of the Opera House in Cape Town as a wolf in Peter Pan. Being a susceptible child he believed everything in the play was real and spent the rest of his childhood trying to fly.

1941: aged sixteen, he joined the South African Army as a gunner in the coastal artillery and with the 2nd Heavy Battery manned the guns guarding the strategic British Naval Base at Simon's Town.

Good fortune came his way when a chance letter from his mother to Field Marshall Smuts resulted in his being transferred to the newly formed Army Entertainment Unit, where he spent the next four years entertaining the allied forces in South Africa, Egypt, Libya and Italy.

1946: demobbed in London, he got to meet and work with some truly remarkable people, as well as writing for West End revues, pantomime, cabaret, and a musical starring Pat Kirkwood.

2008: aged eighty-four (and still waiting for the telephone to ring), he has written this memoir: a funny, informative and sometimes sad account of the times, places and people that played such an important part in the life of a gay young man eager for adventure and seriously struck by the stage.

There are also many amusing anecdotes about the famous, infamous, charming, charmless and sometimes downright loony people he met on the way.

For Jeremy who was once foolish enough to ask me what I did in the war and sent my mind spinning back through the years. He was in India and had just turned two when this story commences.

CONTENTS

PART ONE

"THE WAR AND I"

The life and loves of a gay young thespian staff sergeant in World War II

ONE

"My old flame,
I can't even think of his name,".... sang Mae West.
(I know what she meant.)

It was Cape Town, the sizzling hot January of 1941, the long summer holidays, I was sixteen years old and in love again. He was about four years older than me and his name was Lionel. I think it was Lionel. If it wasn't Lionel it should have been, he was definitely the Lionel type. Funny how someone can change the course of your life so irrevocably and yet you can't even think of their name. Very funny, if funny's the word.

The affliction lasted for about six devastating weeks and then ended as abruptly as it had begun, and not for a moment of its torturous duration did he have the slightest inkling that I was in love with him. That's how silly he was. Yes, his name must have been Lionel.

I don't know what he made of my constant fawning presence, for I had to be with him every moment it was humanly possible. He lived at Sea Point and I about a mile away at Clifton, but I had a bicycle. Perhaps he mistook my attention for hero worship (the sort of thing that occurred at public schools in Boys Own Annuals) and felt flattered by it, and being a bit lonely himself (he didn't seem to have any other friends) was glad of the company however soppy it may have seemed. Whatever suggestion Lionel made I agreed to with eager enthusiasm: swimming at Clifton or Camps Bay, climbing Lions Head or Table Mountain, going to the bioscope (that's what we called the cinema in South Africa then) or just walking and talking for hours on end. I suppose I did most of the talking, and it must have been almost entirely about the theatre for apart from Lionel that was all I really cared about. He must have been bored out of his mind at times but he never showed it. He was either very patient or not listening.

His uncle owned a fish and chip shop in the insalubrious suburb of Salt River where he occasionally helped out of an evening. When he did I would take the bus from Clifton into Cape Town, then a train out to Salt River just to stand at the counter and talk to him between customers. On a couple of very busy nights I was allowed to join him behind the counter and sprinkle salt and vinegar on the fish and chips before he wrapped them up in newspaper. Those were magical evenings. Of course, I always knew my future would be in England and on the stage, but there were the odd mad moments then when I could visualise Lionel and me together somewhere in a little fish and chip shop of our own.

He liked to play billiards which didn't interest me at all, but then no games did. With one ruse or another I had managed to get through school without ever playing rugby, football, cricket or even tennis. I had reluctantly joined in on a few games of rounders on the beach, but very reluctantly, for to be perfectly honest I couldn't see the point of games: they didn't seem to have a story, a theme, or even a passable sub-plot. The only ones ever to have taken my fancy, and you don't need to be Freud to realize why, were 'Postman's Knock' and 'Sardines' – both of which I would have loved to have played with Lionel, but no, he was the billiards type. So I would traipse along to the billiard room of a pub in Sea Point and sit in a corner for hours on end watching him knock silly little balls into pockets with a bunch of boisterous, beer swilling lewd minded layabouts. My God, the things one did for love!

One lazy afternoon, when they were all just slouched around between games smoking and telling dirty jokes, Lionel, whose timing was bizarre to say the least, suggested I recite for them a piece of Shakespeare that I had told him I had just memorised. I was horrified and, of course, I refused, but he was persistent, and let's face it, I was putty in his hands; anyway, by then I wanted to show them I wasn't just some kinky voyeur sitting there salivating over their sadistic treatment of billiard balls – I was a theatrical artiste to be reckoned with; so I stood up in the middle of the billiard room and gave them a very grand guignol rendition of Othello's violent smothering of Desdemona: "Put out the light, and then put out the light..." etc. I was expecting some sniggers and the odd ribald remark but they remained silent throughout, and when I had finished they asked me to do something else, so I did Fagin in the death cell: "To be 'anged by the neck till I'm dead...To be 'anged by the neck till I'm dead..." etc. And to round off I gave them my ever popular Uriah Heep: "I'm very 'umble, Mr. Copperfield. Very 'umble — Curse him, curse him, CURSE HIM!!!!" I realize now that my performance was grotesquely over the top, but I also realize that if it hadn't been I would not have had such an attentive, wide-open-mouthed audience.

On a hot, late January afternoon when I had tracked Lionel down to the little beach beside the Sea Point Pavilion where he sometimes liked to sunbathe (and so did I) he told me he was going to join the army. I felt a dagger in my heart. I was quite used to dying a little every time we said goodbye and I rode back to Clifton on my bicycle, but to have him marching out of my life forever was unthinkable. There and then I decided to enlist with him. Images from the film, 'Beau Geste,' floated before my eyes: He was Gary Cooper, of course, and I, Ray Milland or Robert Preston – I couldn't remember which had the nicer role. There was one small problem however, you had to be seventeen to join the South African army and for me that was still several months ahead. But the problem was not insoluble: I lied about my age at the recruiting office, and my mother, after some heavy persuasion, did likewise. She knew there was no chance of my being sent off immediately to fight in the desert. South African soldiers had to volunteer to leave the country, and they had to be eighteen before they could go, and we all knew the war would be over long before then. Lionel fancied the Ack Ack – the Anti Aircraft Artillery and so did I, but there wasn't one; so he then chose the Coastal Artillery and so did I, and luckily there was one; but I had no idea what was entailed.

I can remember very well the moment I knew I was no longer in love with Lionel. It was our first day in the army. We were standing in line in a large storeroom at the old Castle in Cape Town being kitted out with uniforms and rifles, and as I picked up my heavy kitbag I turned and looked at him and felt nothing – absolutely nothing. He wasn't even good looking any more. In fact, he was rather plain: skinny and gangly with a bad skin, and I couldn't think what I had ever seen in him. The feeling of nothing turned to dislike – intense dislike, and finally to anger that he had got me into this mess. I suppose I could have cried out, "Help! I'm only sixteen – get me out of here!" but like my mother I was never one for making a fuss.

How he felt about my sudden and complete abandonment of him I'll never know. Perhaps it was relief at not having to hear any more anecdotes about Bea Lillie, Ivor Novello or Lilian Baylis. Whatever he felt I didn't care, I hated him for destroying my career and ruining my life and I never wished to see him again, which apart from the odd cool nod on the parade ground I never did. And so that was Lionel out of my life… or was it Leonard?

We were stationed in the docks at Cape Town and trained to man the guns at the end of the quays that protected the harbour from enemy attack. To begin with I found army life very hard; I was younger than all the other recruits and much less prepared for the physical exertion that was required; the most strenuous thing I had done until then was a tap dance solo to 'Happy Feet.'

All day, every day, was spent marching up and down, doing rifle drill, and loading and unloading the guns with unwieldy hundred pound shells, while a ferocious sergeant major shrieked obscenities at us at the top of his voice. "He'll get nodules on his vocal chords," I thought, "and serve him right, using such language. I'm only glad my mother didn't decide to join up." What few hours we had away from the parade ground were spent cleaning rifles, polishing buttons and shining boots until one could almost see one's unhappy face in them.

It was tough going at first and I was very miserable, but slowly I got into the rhythm of it, and eventually felt quite pleased with myself for being able to cope as well as the others did. It is true I dropped a shell on a soldier's foot and he had to be invalided out of the army, but as he said when I went to visit him in the sick bay with some grapes, "Think nothing of it, man, I was wanting to get out anyway, you've done me a big favour. Have a grape." So what I had thought was a disaster turned out to be a blessing in disguise, which was a great relief for all concerned – well, for the two of us, anyway.

After several weeks of intensive training I was posted to the 2nd Heavy Battery, Queen's Battery at Simon's Town. It was situated on a hill above the harbour, its guns facing down to the sea, ready for any German U-boats that might suddenly appear. For over 150 years Simon's Town had been the South Atlantic High Command of the British Royal Navy. In 1941 it was of particular strategic importance as all ships bound for the Middle East, India and the Far East had to pass round the Cape, the Mediterranean being too dangerous owing to a heavy German and Italian naval presence there. Several British ships had been sunk in the Straits of Gibraltar. The ships always travelled in convoy with a strong naval escort, this meant that Simon's Town was now visited by many naval ships, and it brought thousands more naval personnel to the base.

It was a charming little town of old Dutch and English colonial architecture. Nice to look at but there was not a lot there for a sailor to do, so St George's Street was always bustling with seamen on their way to or from the station. Cape Town was a short train journey away with all the amenities a sailor might require. It was also renowned for its warm hospitality to visiting servicemen. Whenever troopships docked in Cape Town harbour the citizens of the city would wait at the gates and take as many soldiers as they could to their homes to feed and entertain them. Our house at Clifton was often full of British soldiers who we told to treat it as their home for as long as they could stay. As we lived on one of the most beautiful beaches in the world it was the perfect place for them to relax and unwind after their long, confined sea voyage. For a day or two the house echoed with cheerful talk and laughter; someone would play the piano and they would gather around and sing: 'Run Rabbit, Run', 'They Can't Black Out The Moon' or 'We'll Meet Again'. You wouldn't think any of them had a care in the world. Then suddenly the house would be silent again, and we would watch from our veranda as the convoy sailed past Clifton, on its way to...who knows where? Although brief the friendships we made, we remembered some of those soldiers for a long time afterwards and often wondered what became of them. I can remember fantasizing that one day when the war was over I would be touring with a play in England and one of them would see my name on a poster outside a theatre, come backstage and we would resume our brief wartime friendship. Yes, I was as soppy and sentimental as that then.

Although he only played a walk on part in my story I think it would be a pity to write about Simon's Town during the war and not mention its most celebrated personality. Today in a small square above the harbour stands a life sized bronze statue of him, and so much of a legend is he that passers by often stop to pat him on the head – for he wasn't a man but a dog, a massive Great Dane called Just Nuisance, or to give him his rightful title: Able Seaman Just Nuisance RN, the only animal ever to be officially enlisted with rank and number in the history of the British Royal Navy.

As a puppy he had belonged to a man who ran a rest home for seamen in Simon's Town. He was always made a great fuss of by the sailors there, and as time went by he began to think of himself as one of them. Finally the day came when he metaphorically slung his kitbag over his shoulder and swaggered off to live the carefree life of a jolly jack tar. He was permitted to pass through the dock gates at will, and was allowed aboard the British naval ships that were docked there, and where a meal could always be rustled up for him. Because of his habit of sunning himself on gangways and sleeping in front of doorways, his enormous bulk making it difficult for naval personnel to pass, he became known as Nuisance. The 'Just' part of his name came later.

His love of the navy did not extend to all ranks however. Officers and petty officers were totally ignored as were military personnel and all civilians. Only ratings with round caps and bell-bottom trousers did he empathise with. They were his friends and oppos and wherever they went he went too. I often saw him with a group of them on their way to the station. With them he would board the train and on arrival in Cape Town usually make his way up to the Union Jack Club where there was a permanent bed reserved for him and a meal whenever he wanted it. Then he would wander down to the Standard, a bar in Adderley Street frequented by the British Navy. He was the bar's favourite customer and his first drink was always on the house. In a large bowl, especially kept for him, the barman would pour a quart of Lion Lager knowing that when the news got around that Just Nuisance was there the navy would flock to the bar; flock they did, and he was as fond of his beer as any of them. Many a night he was seen staggering to the station to catch the last train to Simon's Town in the company of a few ratings equally unsteady on their feet. One cold night he was seen on the train stretched out on three seats with a sailor's greatcoat covering him while the sailor sat in the corner shivering.

The South African Railways Authorities began to complain about his travelling on their trains without a ticket and warned that unless he was restrained from doing so they would have him destroyed. This caused such uproar in Simon's Town and Cape Town that the Admiralty quickly stepped in, enlisting him as an official member of His Majesty King George VI's Royal Navy, and issuing him with a free train pass that was attached to his collar. As his certificate of enlistment was being drawn up, the petty officer filling in the document, when he came to the space marked 'CHRISTIAN NAME' said, "The dog doesn't have a Christian name, he's just 'Nuisance,' so in the space he wrote 'JUST', and that is how a Great Dane became: Able Seaman Just Nuisance R.N. He was also issued with a sailor's round cap. To keep it on there were ribbons that tied under the chin. But he was not enamoured with it and except for photographs and special parades it was seldom worn.

I have borrowed liberally from a delightful book by Terence Sisson entitled: 'Just Nuisance AB', (Published by W.J. Flesch & Partners (Pty) Ltd. Cape Town.) which is a collection of anecdotes and photographs from men who served with the Royal Navy in Simon's Town during the war and were personally acquainted with the amazing dog. Some of the adventures they tell of are quite astonishing. Once he was kidnapped by some drunken sailors (he was probably slightly inebriated himself at the time) and smuggled aboard the HMAS Australia. As the cruiser sailed from port and he noticed Table Mountain receding from view he quickly sobered up, leapt overboard and swam ashore. (There are several versions of this story. This is the one I chose.) Then on a couple of occasions he was spotted sitting beside the pilot in the cockpit of an Albacore aircraft of the Fleet Air Arm as it zoomed over the harbour on a patrol of the Cape coast. The anecdotes are both hilarious and touching, and the final ones I found deeply moving. Just Nuisance died on the 1st April 1944 on the very day of his birthday. He was exactly 7 years old. The Royal Naval Hospital's diagnosis was, 'paralysis of the sciatic nerve,' but there were a few regulars in the Standard Bar who thought it might be cirrhosis of the liver.

On the day of his funeral the whole of Simon's Town was in mourning. He was buried with full naval honours at Klaver Camp, above Simon's Town; his body was wrapped in a Royal Navy White Ensign and as he was lowered into the grave a lone bugle sounded and a volley was fired by a party of Royal Marines. More than a hundred sailors filed past the grave and there was hardly a dry eye amongst them. On his large impressive tombstone is written:

Great Dane
Just Nuisance
Able Seaman RN
1940 – 1944   (But this would mean he was only 4 years old?)
Died 1st April 1944
Age 7 years   (This must mean he was born in 1937. Strange
              that the Stonemason, especially, didn't notice
              the discrepancy.)

I have strayed quite far from the plot, I know, but I hope you have thought, as I do, that it was a detour worth taking. Mind you, it was not altogether without self interest, for although whenever our paths crossed (usually at railway stations) he completely ignored my presence, I always get this slightly smug feeling when I say, "Oh, yes, I was there, you know, I remember him well." And when I recently revisited Simon's Town to see the statue of him there was a distinct lump in my throat as I stroked his head and murmured, "Hello, sailor!"

I read in the Cape Times one morning that The Gwen Ffrangcon-Davies Marda Vanne Company were to appear at the Hoffmeyer Hall in Cape Town with two plays: 'Twelfth Night' and 'Quality Street'. I was determined on my next evening pass to go and see them. I knew about Gwen Ffrangcon-Davies from the many theatre books and magazines I had collected over the years. She had been a famous Juliet to John Gielgud's Romeo at the Old Vic, and had appeared with him in the long running 'Richard Of Bordeaux', also 'The Importance Of Being Earnest' and Michel St Denis' much acclaimed 'The Three Sisters.' Among her many other West End successes were 'The Barretts Of Wimpole Street' and 'Gaslight'.

Of Marda Vanne I knew less. She was an Afrikaner, the daughter of a Transvaal judge, Sir Willem van Hulsteyn, and she got married quite young to a man named Johannes Gerhardus Strijdom who later became the Prime Minister of South Africa; but she was not at his side when this happened, having abandoned the marriage early on to go on the stage. This, as you can imagine, caused quite a stir among the members of the Dutch Reformed Church who at the very word 'stage' were apt to fall to their knees and pray. After a hasty move to England her talent was soon recognised by Basil Dean, one of the leading directors of the day, and she went on to play many leading parts in the West End and on Broadway. It was at this time that she met Gwen Ffrancgon-Davies and their long and close friendship began.

At the beginning of the war when practically all the London theatres had closed (not the Windmill, of course) and no one was sure when they would reopen, Marda decided to return to her homeland, persuading Gwen to accompany her and start a theatre company of their own. This was the company that was now appearing at the Hoffmeyer Hall. There were whispers in the profession that Gwen had gone to South Africa to escape the war. Although I can see nothing wrong in not being bombed if you can avoid it, if the accusation had been true she would never have returned to England by sea in 1942, a time when German U-Boats were sinking passenger ships in the Atlantic and London was suffering its worst bombing to appear with John Gielgud in 'Macbeth', and then have to risk the hazardous sea voyage back. That doesn't strike me as cowardice, more like foolhardiness, especially when you decide to do THAT play!

The first play I saw was 'Twelfth Night'. It was a good production with an excellent cast of South African and English actors, and Marda Vanne gave a fine performance as Maria, but the moment Gwen Ffrangcon-Davies appeared as Olivia everything else faded from view. I thought she had the most beautiful voice I had ever heard, she spoke the verse to perfection, played the part with great wit, and she had the rare quality of making everything she said sound as if she had only just thought of it. I knew I was watching a great performance. The only time it had happened to me before was with Gracie Fields, who I had watched night after night from the gallery of the Cape Town Opera House; her signatures almost filled my autograph album; the others already in it were Sir Seymour Hicks, Molly Picon, Gordon Harker, Bebe Daniels and Ben Lyon, Forsythe, Semon and Farrel, and my friend Maurice who wrote: 'By hook or by crook I'll be last in this book.'

I then saw 'Quality Street', a slightly creaky romantic comedy by James Barrie that Gwen had appeared in in 1921, and although in the first act she played a girl more than half her age her voice was so light and lyrical and her acting so sublime that I was again mesmerised.

On the train back to Simon's Town that night I felt very frustrated. I knew I would never be a great actor, but just to be in the theatre, on a stage, where such miracles could happen would be enough for me. And now I would have to wait until this wretched war was over, thanks to Louis...or was it Leslie...No, I think it was Lionel.

On a cold, wet night in June as I was coming off guard duty, drenched and frozen, I heard cheers coming from the guardroom. I hurried in to be told that they had just heard on the wireless that Russia was at war with Germany. We were jubilant. Things were not going too well for the allies in the desert at that time, but now with a mighty military power like Russia attacking from the east surely it would all be over in a matter of weeks...but it wasn't. And it was still several months before America entered the war. We had to wait until the 7th of December and Pearl Harbour.

It was an afternoon in late August and a pale, watery sun was lighting me through the window as I sat all alone spit and polishing my boots and feeling a bit like Cinders when everyone else had gone to the ball and there wasn't even the chance of Buttons popping in to cheer one up. I had met no sympathetic souls at the camp. My hut mates and I seemed to have absolutely nothing in common. None of them had ever heard of Gwen Ffrangcon-Davies or even Marda Vanne, and I had no interest in their silly mindless activities. They were probably kicking a ball around the recreation field at that very moment.

So there I was spitting and polishing and thinking that at the rate the war was dragging on by the time it was over and I was eventually demobilised, the only parts I would still be able to play were old Adam in 'As You Like It' or Firs in 'The Cherry Orchard', when all of a sudden, in the guise of an orderly corporal, Buttons popped his head around the door and told me the Commanding Officer wanted to see me in his office immediately. I was flabbergasted. Why would the Commanding Officer want to see me? And why the tearing hurry? I couldn't recall having done anything very reprehensible since I had been at Simon's Town, and surely that little incident of the dropped shell on Gunner Grunewald's foot in Cape Town docks was long enough ago to be forgiven and forgotten. Buttons either couldn't or wouldn't tell me what it was about so I put on my cap and accompanied him to the office.

"At ease," said the Commanding Officer after I had executed what I thought was a simply stunning halt, leap to attention and salute. So pleased with it was I that I was tempted to do it again, but wisely thought better of it. There then unfolded a tale so extraordinarily Cinderella like that I had to surreptitiously pinch myself to make sure I wasn't dreaming.

My mother, unbeknownst to me, had written a letter to the Prime Minister, in which she said: 'Dear Field Marshal Smuts, I hate to bother you at a time like this, when I know you must be very busy with the war, but my friend Mrs. Millard tells me that at your instigation the army has formed an entertainment unit for the purpose of taking shows round the camps to entertain the troops. Her son, Maurice has already joined it.' Maurice and I had been close friends since early childhood. We were in the Young South African League together, and in 1936 toured the Union in a highly successful revue entitled 'Wee Chaps', in which he did his delightful Betty Boop and I my much acclaimed Mae West – but you don't have to take my word for it, this is what the critic of the Cape Argus had to say: 'One of the highlights of the evening was the clever skit on a well known film star by young Neville Phillips – "Come Up And See Me Sometime." Neville had all the appeal of the glamorous person whom he mimicked and he put his number over the footlights with convincing style.' If quoting the above review strikes you as pathetic and rather sad you must remember that one doesn't get notices like that every day. Incidentally, that same critic five years later asked me to his flat to read for a part in 'East Of Suez.' and seduced me on the sofa. I think I would have been offered the part, only when it finally came to be produced I was already in heavy artillery.

But I have digressed again. My mother's letter then went on to inform the Prime Minister of my many theatrical accomplishments: Eisteddfod Gold Medalist, elocution; 3rd Prize African Theatres National Talent Contest, film star impersonations; stage actor, regular broadcaster with the SABC, tap dancer and comedy sketch writer. In her humble opinion my talents would be of far greater service to the war effort if I was in the Entertainment Unit rather than the Coastal Artillery, and if the dear Field Marshal could possibly spare the time to see if such a transfer could be arranged she and I would be eternally grateful. Then after wishing him good luck with the war, she signed herself, 'yours humbly, Mrs. Clare Phillips, widow.'

In response to her plea a letter had arrived at Simon's Town that morning addressed to 'The Officer Commanding 2nd Heavy Battery, Queens Battery,' and was now lying open before him on his desk. It read as follows:

Re: No. 155980, Gunner Phillips, N.D.
A letter from Mrs. Phillips, mother of the above mentioned detail, has been forwarded to me for attention by Field Marshal Smuts's Private Secretary. Mrs. Phillips mentions in this letter that her son is desirous of joining the Entertainment Unit. If you are prepared to accede to her request would you please be good enough to give Gunner Phillips the necessary rail warrant to enable him to proceed to Pretoria to give me an audition.
Yours faithfully,
Myles Bourke. (signed) Major.
O.C. NO. 19 Reserve M.T. Coy.

After I had explained to the Commanding Officer what an audition was he graciously consented to my going to Pretoria to do one. I was to pack my kit immediately and leave on the night train for Johannesburg. Before I left he wished me good luck and said that my conduct as a gunner in the 2nd Heavy Battery had been exemplarily. No mention of ex Gunner Grunewald's foot, thank goodness. As I passed through the orderly room I waved Buttons a fond farewell. Cinders was going to the ball, after all!

On the train I found a compartment to myself and spent most of the thousand mile journey rehearsing things I might do for the audition, including a bit of quiet tap dancing.

In Johannesburg I changed trains for Pretoria where Staff Sergeant Terris was supposed to meet me at the station but forgot. There were a lot of things that Staff Sergeant Terris conveniently forgot, like the time he crept into my bed pretending he was drunk and had come to the wrong house by mistake. A likely story. I know all those houses looked alike but his wasn't even in the same row. I very nearly kicked him out.

I waited at the station for exactly twenty minutes then took a taxi down to Defence Headquarters only to find the offices were shut for the night. The guard at the gate suggested I took my problem to the Military Police Headquarters which was just around the corner; there, a very civil young duty officer offered me one of his cells for the night; I accepted his kind offer feeling it would be churlish to refuse and besides I hadn't enough money for a hotel. The cell contained a hard bunk, a rough blanket and a bucket in the corner, and what with the animal noises coming from some of the other cells and the strong smell of Jeyes Fluid I did not have a restful night.

In the morning when I got up to leave I found the door of my cell had been locked, and then to my horror I discovered that the staff from the night before had gone off duty and the new lot knew nothing about me. For about half an hour I pleaded through the bars with the other prisoners yelling at me to 'shut up' and worse. I even offered to perform something for them to prove that I was who I said I was, but they were a philistine bunch and didn't want to hear any Shakespeare or Noel Coward. Eventually someone found a scribbled note among the papers on the desk that explained my presence and I was released. After hurriedly washing and changing into a clean uniform, and hoping I wasn't smelling too much of Jeyes Fluid, I made my way back to DHQ which was now open and had a new guard at the gate who directed me to Artillery Row.

It was a row of small single storey houses that had been converted to army offices. Number 15 housed the administration of the UDF Entertainment Unit, officially called NO.19 Reserve M.T. Coy, although I never discovered why. Perhaps DHQ thought it sounded less frivolous. It was the last house in the row and beyond it there were several large huts belonging to the unit. These were the rehearsal rooms and workshops where the costumes, scenery and props were made. I could hear distinct sounds coming from a couple of the huts – sounds of music, singing, tap dancing – and suddenly my heart stood still! (Lorenz Hart. 1927) I closed my eyes and listened for a moment. "When I die," I thought to myself, "surely arriving in heaven will be just like this!"

To spare you the breathless suspense I shall deal with the audition straight away. It was taken by Lieutenant Leo Quayle, a handsome, fair haired man in his late twenties. He was the Unit's musical director and a brilliant musician who after the war became a celebrated orchestral conductor. For all I know he could have been the greatest conductor who ever drew breath, Toscanini, Sir Thomas Beecham and Geraldo rolled into one, but he knew nothing about putting a nervous auditionee at their ease. When we met he was wearing a vague, far away expression, and when the audition was over he was still wearing it. His mind was obviously miles away, probably mulling over a tricky bit of Mahler or Schoenberg, which might have been fascinating for him but was most unnerving for me. The audition would normally have been taken by the Production Officer, Captain Frank Rogaly. Now, he had it down to a fine art: oozing enthusiasm, warmth and appreciation, he would encourage a performer to really give of their best; but he was having a tooth filled that morning and Lieutenant Quayle, I fancy, was filling in for him.

I started off with what I hoped were some witty film star impersonations, they usually got a good laugh, but, no. In desperation I moved on to one of my Dickens monologues, with some extra loud shouting added in case he might be falling asleep. Then to finish with I borrowed a pair of tap shoes from Maurice (whose welcoming face was one of the first I saw on arrival) and did a frenetic tap dance to sixty four bars of 'Happy Feet.'

When I had finished, that expression still there, he thanked me politely and told me to remain where I was. I then saw him mentally put down his baton, step off the rostrum, acknowledge his applause and, with the cries of 'Maestro!' still ringing in his ears, sweep out of the Albert Hall, leaving me stranded somewhere in outer limbo, not knowing where I was going.

Almost immediately Maurice came hurrying in to see how I had fared, and then to assure me that it would be all right. He was followed by some friendly fellow members to whom he introduced me, but neither their names nor their faces registered as I sat there with my heart in my mouth and my fingers tightly crossed. The thought of being packed off on the afternoon train to spend the rest of the war in Simon's Town hurling heavy shells about, now that I had had this glimpse of Paradise, was too dreadful to contemplate. Maurice kept on telling me not to worry, he was sure I would get in, but remembering that look on Lieutenant Quayle's face I was not convinced. Of course, I didn't know then, as Maurice obviously did, just how untalented some of the members were.

About five minutes later, although it seemed much longer, Regimental Sergeant Major Brickman marched in to inform me that I had been accepted into the unit and if I went with him to his office the business of the transfer could be dealt with straight away. Maurice and I hugged each other and gave great whoops of delight; we then regaled everyone with the heart-warming story of our early touring days together in

'Wee Chaps', which even almost made RSM Brickman smile. Maurice then told him that there was a spare bed in the room he was in at the barracks and it would be nice if I could have it. With as much charm as you can expect an RSM to muster he agreed it was a nice idea and said that as soon as we had completed our business in the office Maurice could take me there and help me to settle in.

The barracks were up a short road behind DHQ. They consisted of several rows of houses similar to Artillery Row of which a few were occupied by the Entertainment Unit. (The female barracks were somewhere else.) Each room had three or four beds in it. There was an outside lavatory and washing facilities and there were showers nearby. The food in the mess was no better or worse than any other mess, but anyway we seldom went there except to gulp down a cup of coffee and grab some fruit to take to rehearsal with us. At DHQ there was a canteen that sold delicious freshly baked Cornish pasties and sausage rolls, several of which I daily devoured; also, five minutes down the road from Artillery Row were some cheap and cheerful Greek cafes where we mostly ate at night. There seemed to be no restrictions at the barracks where the unit was concerned; we could come and go as we pleased; as long as our quarters were kept tidy that was all that was required. Some of our members never stayed there at all but shared rented flats in Pretoria, which is what Maurice and I, another member called Ken Geyer (more of him later) and three of the girls from our show did for the final weeks of rehearsal before we went out on our first tour.

The difference between the rigid discipline of Simon's Town and the easygoing ways of the Entertainment Unit at first quite astonished me. After attending roll call on the parade ground in uniform each morning we would change into our rehearsal clothes and for the rest of the day all matters military were completely forgotten. For me it was like a dream come true. But whoever said 'Man is weak,' must have had someone rather like me in mind. I was not only weak, I was foolish as well. Not content with this fabulous new freedom I had acquired I had to start pushing the boundaries, wide as they were, even wider until my ridiculous behaviour began to be noticed by the Pretoria Military Police. My misdemeanours were mostly of a sartorial nature: walking in the street without a cap; having all the buttons of my tunic undone; and even more heinous, dancing around a seated statue of Paul Kruger in corduroy trousers and sandals (me, not him). It could have been worse, of course. I could have been sitting on his lap, naked.

It was lucky for me that the Major was such a generous, kind-hearted man. He could very easily have got rid of me, but I was having such a whale of a time I didn't stop to think of the consequences. Maurice tried to warn me a few times but I wouldn't listen. He was much more reserved than I was; really quite conservative in his ways;

where as I had always been a bit of an anarchist; I loathed conformity and fought against discipline of any sort, except, of course, in the theatre where I knew it had to be absolute.

This was also the time when I had just turned seventeen and my faux intellectual phase had begun (hence the corduroys and sandals). I can remember once we were travelling on the long train journey to South West Africa (formally German West Africa, and now Namibia) to do some shows at Windhoek and the naval base at Walvis Bay. Maurice and I had window seats opposite each other. He, as usual, was doing something useful with his hands, like making a wig or something, while I puffed at a Turkish cigarette through a long black holder and read Nietzsche aloud (someone had told me it was subversive stuff and I was determined not to appear humdrum). Maurice tolerated it for as long as he could, then he suddenly leant across, snatched the book and cigarette holder from me and flung them out of the window. I thought his behaviour was both childish and affected and told him so, and from that moment on our long and close friendship ceased to exist for at least a couple of hours. When I discovered Gertrude Stein I made sure not to read her aloud near an open window. Maurice always had his feet very firmly on the ground while I, all too often, was on my way to the moon on gossamer wings. Still, as different as we were, we made excellent touring companions. He kept me in check and I loosened him up a bit. It was 'Wee Chaps' all over again.

Before I introduce you to some of the beautiful and not so beautiful, talented and not so talented, bizarre and even more bizarre members of our mad little motley (oh, yes, we too had our share of madness, suicide and murder – after all, actors are only human), I think you should know a little more about the unit. It had almost three hundred members and by the time the war was over had produced twenty shows that toured South Africa, the Middle East and Italy, giving immense pleasure to millions of allied servicemen, which is more than can be said for ENSA (our British equivalent, except ENSA was not a military organisation).

The following is an extract from a souvenir brochure with photographs of all the shows that the Major later had printed:

'The idea of establishing an Entertainment Officer for the Union Defence Force was first mooted by the Adjutant-General, then Major-General F.H. Theron, who felt that entertainment was a real necessity in the battle against the boredom which inevitably exists in the military camps. This suggestion received the whole-hearted approval of Field-Marshal Smuts. As a result General Theron appointed Major Myles Bourke, the founder of the Pretoria

Repertory Theatre, as Chief Entertainment Officer for the UDF. He submitted a report suggesting the militarization of troop entertainment by the formation of an Entertainment Unit to consist of approximately eighteen concert parties, which would tour the camps in the union and the fighting areas. This suggestion was eventually accepted.

The foundations of this new and vital branch of the Union's Army were laid after long and difficult struggles. Potential recruits were interviewed at an office finally given to the Unit at Defence Headquarters. Six members of the 'Springbok Frolics', the popular Field Artillery production, who wished to join the Unit, were transferred after much trouble, and formed the first nucleus of the No. 19 Reserve M.T. Coy. After them others followed, but unfortunately, lack of suitable premises gave them nowhere to practice or rehearse. Major Bourke wanted a show produced as soon as possible, so he decided that they would use his home until proper rehearsal rooms were built. Fortunately it was summer time and the lawns were green and the trees in leaf. The scenes at the residence had to be seen, and heard, to be believed. Dancing and choruses on the large stoep; special ballet steps, leaps and jumps were practiced on the lawn; tap dancing in two empty garages; soulful 'Ave Maria' on a cello under the trees accompanied by a couple of saxophones practising scales or the latest swing music. From the vegetable garden came the strains of a violin playing 'Schubert's Serenade' and other lovely music, with the cocks and hens often joining in; while on the hillside at the back of the house the aloes and other queer prickly plants quivered to the sounds of Afrikaans liedjies and a variety of musical instruments. A little waterfall higher up burbled to the baritone's 'do ray mees,' and a dame comedian's naughty songs being learnt from a gramophone (Douglas Byng records).

After three months of intensive rehearsal in this unique setting the first show, called 'The Amuseliers,' was ready for presentation, and their first performance was given on Monday 21st March, 1941.

A few weeks later the unit moved from the office at DHQ to 15 Artillery Row where immediately the building of rehearsal rooms, a small theatre, storerooms and a carpenter's workshop was started: all necessary for the speedy production of shows.

Since the launching of the first unit, 15 more shows have been produced, which have visited nearly all the isolated military camps in the Union, whilst some have made extensive tours of the camps and casualty clearing stations in the forward areas of the Middle East. The unsolicited letters of appreciation and favourable comments prove, in some measure, how necessary a periodical tonic of entertainment is to the troops.

One thing is certain, without the Major the Entertainment Unit would never have seen the light of day. Although he had the full support of Field-Marshal Smuts and General Theron, there was a strong conservative element at DHQ that fought vigorously against the idea. But they weren't dealing with just any major: Myles Bourke was rich, influential and one of the most revered citizens of Pretoria. He was a great supporter of the arts; any cultural event in the city would certainly have his patronage; He founded the Pretoria Repertory Theatre; and when 'The Gwen Ffrancgon-Davies Marda Vanne Company' was born its two mothers were staying as guests in a cottage on his estate. One needn't ask the name of the midwife.

DHQ hated the unit. It resented our easy life style and the pleasure we derived from our work and was always trying to bring in restrictive rules and regulations to restrain us and dampen our spirits, but thanks to the power of the Major their mean, jealous little ploys were never imposed.

I suppose my silly brush-ups with the Pretoria Military Police were not exactly helping our cause, and on being summoned to his office for yet another admonishment the Major could be very stern with me. On one occasion I was demoted from staff sergeant to corporal, which meant a considerable reduction in pay. Fortunately after six months of good behaviour (I was much wilier by then) my former rank with pay was reinstated.

The worst thing about these meetings with the Major was not what he said but what he didn't say. He suffered from a mild form of sleeping sickness and would sometimes nod off in the middle of a conversation. He could be saying to me, "Now, Neville, unless you pull your socks up I will have to ..." Then his head would loll forward and I would be left wondering how on earth that sentence was going to end. Also what to do next? Which would be the bigger offence: a corporal shaking a major by the shoulders or marching out of his office without being dismissed? The only other alternative was to stand there until someone else came in, only hoping it wouldn't be the cleaning lady the following morning. Luckily it never came to that.

If the Major was the reason the Entertainment Unit existed, Captain Frank Rogaly was the reason it rolled along so merrily. Frank (no one ever called him Captain Rogaly) was one of the most delightful people you could ever wish to meet. He was vibrant, warm, witty and gay (in every sense of the word). The stage was in his blood: cut him and he would bleed revue or pantomime all over you. He was not a handsome man. To be quite frank Frank was quite plain. His nose and chin were ever so slightly on their way to resembling those of Mr. Punch, but with those twinkling eyes and that smile, bright as a row of footlights, he was always a joy to behold.

As Production Officer he was responsible for all the shows that went out. His was not a creative talent, he seldom came up with a really inspired idea; his brilliance lay in carefully choosing the right people and allowing them to try their wings and be innovative. He had impeccable taste and he knew instinctively what was right or wrong. Smut or vulgarity he would not tolerate. A Douglas Byng song sung by Freddie Neidham or a Max Miller routine done by Sid James – yes, that Sid James – was as blue as the material was ever allowed to be.

I think their wholesomeness was part of the success of our shows. The troops much preferred to see fresh faced young girls in pretty dresses singing sweet songs (talented or not) to the brassy looking half clad chorus girls that ENSA so often sent to the Middle East, plus a lewd comedian and a couple of novelty acts, such as one I remember where a blousy blonde of a certain age, tap dancing while she played the piano accordion, pretended to get her breasts trapped in the bellows each time she squeezed. Our shows were nothing like that. They were carefully devised, tastefully produced small revues. Some, of course, were better than others, but none sank to the insulting depths that ENSA was prepared to plummet. No wonder the British troops thought the initials stood for 'Every Night Something Awful.' The wonderful letters of appreciation we received after our shows I think proves what I have been saying.

'Springbok Frolics', a Field Artillery concert party, formed the first nucleus of the Entertainment Unit. The show had played to the public in a Johannesburg theatre for a couple of weeks in aid of the Red Cross and had been a sell out success. It was produced by Frank Rogaly who also appeared in it, giving himself a show stopping number: wearing the white uniform and peaked cap of a British naval officer, and backed by a chorus of sailors in navy blue, Frank, all teeth and smiles, sang: 'The Fleet's In Port Again.' This was accompanied by a rollicking hornpipe inspired routine in which Frank allowed himself a couple of very high kicks. The climax of the number, or the *coupe de theatre* as it turned out to be, came when the sailors danced down to the footlights and saluted the audience, and Frank, now standing back centre stage, smile brighter than ever, suddenly raced forward, leapt high in the air and while smartly saluting landed in the splits. The audience went wild. Johannesburg had never seen anything quite like it. Frank became the talk of the town. Months later people were still remembering the night they saw Frank Rogaly do the running splits.

This new and exciting, if somewhat bizarre, celebrity rather went to Frank's head and he began doing the splits all over the place. At a wonderful party, when all it needed was one extra little something to make it perfect, Frank would oblige and do the splits. At a deadly dull do, when the conversation had run out and everyone was growing more desperate by the second, Frank would save the day and do the splits. It wasn't long before the words 'Frank' and 'splits' became synonymous, and nobody who was anybody in Johannesburg society would dare to admit they had not witnessed the unique experience.

But, as with all the best things in life, the novelty wore off. Also, the Major may have had a word or two in his ear. Anyway, there wasn't going to be much future in it, so the splits were put on a shelf and only brought down on very rare occasions.

When a new show was in rehearsal he would pop in a couple of times during the day to see how it was going. When I say 'pop in' I mean the door would fly open and Frank would make a grand entrance (his jacket usually draped over his shoulders like a cape) followed by a wan faced corporal with a large box of Craven A. cigarettes in one hand and a lighter in the other. When Frank had bid us good morning or afternoon, as the case may be, he would make a slight gesture with his right hand and the corporal would step up smartly and proffer him the open box. Redolent of a character in a Noel Coward play he would take a cigarette, have it lit for him and blow a smoke ring in the air. The corporal would then step back and to the side so he would be well out of Frank's spotlight, had he had one.

"Right," Frank would say sitting down and crossing his legs, "Astonish me!" We would then show him what we had just been rehearsing, after which he would rise and say something like, "Lovely! It's going to be perfectly lovely – when you've got the hang of it. I'll look at it again in a couple of days." Or he might say, "That silly little step – I don't think the boys ought to do it – not all our audiences will have been Sadlers Wells balletomanes, you know." Another small gesture and the corporal would run to open the door so Frank could sweep out as spectacularly as he had swept in. We often wished, if he had been particularly pleased with us and was in an expansive mood, that he would honour us with the splits. But no, alas, the days of the splits had now gone – gone with the wind, as Margaret Mitchell so aptly put it ... although I don't recall Rhett Butler ever doing the splits. Mind you, it was a long book and I did skip a bit. I must read it again sometime and check up.

Maurice and I were both cast in an exciting new show called 'The Troopadours in "Speeding Along"', and with it we sped along for two and a quarter years, all over South Africa, Egypt, and up the North African coast as far as Tripoli, where with the Eighth Army we crossed to Sicily and then Italy. So attached to them had we become that Field Marshal Montgommery personally gave us permission to wear the Eighth Army flash on our sleeves.

'The Troopadours' was the most successful company the unit ever produced. I would like to be able to say that the success was mostly due to me. Or if I was going to be really generous, to Maurice and me – no, to me and Maurice – alas, that would not be true. As talented as most of the company were the real strength of the show was the extremely high quality of the music. We had five musicians. Three were refugees from Hitler's Germany: Thilo Runge, violinist; Erwin Lehrer, cellist; and Erwin Blumenreich, pianist. The first two had been distinguished members of the Berlin Philharmonic Orchestra, the third a fine classical pianist. Lieut. Frank Daly, the officer in charge of the show, had been playing his clarinet with jazz bands and in nightclubs for years and could coax the sweetest sounds out of the instrument. Al Marock was on drums and also played the guitar and banjo.

As if featuring classical music in an army entertainment wasn't brave enough we also had ballet (classical and modern) and even a spot of opera. The sketches too were of a rather sophisticated nature having come from smart West End revues. We even had a Dorothy Parker short story that I adapted as a sketch and performed with the lovely Cynthia Klette. From another of the sketches Cynthia and I did I can still remember these lines:

"Oh, maiden fair, wilt thou be my mistress?"

"Pray, sir, what is a mistress?"

"Something between a master and a mattress." Not very subtle but it never failed to get a laugh.

It is time now to introduce the rest of the company. As I have just mentioned her I shall start with Cynthia Klette. Klette had klass with a capital K! She was a Cape Town society beauty, elegant and soignee' with bright blue eyes and long blonde hair (she reminded me a bit of Constance Bennett in the 'Topper' films). Her photograph appeared constantly in the social sections of papers and magazines attending charity balls, the races and nightclubs, always escorted by some handsome, eligible, young bachelor. When she wasn't being social she sometimes acted and was a fine light comedienne. Her Amanda in 'Private Lives' at the Little Theatre in Cape Town was a great success.

The only reason I can imagine why she joined the Entertainment Unit (not that she stayed very long) was because all her escorts were away at the war, and instead of sitting at home knitting socks for the boys she decided her war work would be to let them see how beautiful she was, and how beautiful she was! Her singing voice was not that strong, but at a microphone putting over a Cole Porter lyric such as 'D'Lovely' she was delicious, delightful and delectable. Cynthia had a great sense of humour and was always full of fun and mischief, but one couldn't help feeling that touring with us she was ever so slightly slumming it.

Our dancers were Joan Kena and Pieter Geldenhuis. Joan was a beautiful American girl with raven black hair scraped back in a bun, large dark eyes and a vermillion mouth. It was a torrid Spanish look, in complete contrast to the smooth, blonde

Miss Klette. Her father was the American Minister for Plenipotentiary to South Africa which must have been the reason she had landed up in Pretoria, one of the dullest towns on earth. I wouldn't wish a weekend there on anyone – not even Lionel. We knew little about Joan except that she had been dancing in Paris until the German occupation. Rumour had it that she had left her lover and child behind but she never spoke of it to us. In fact, she never told us anything about herself. Joan was an enigma.

And Pieter wasn't exactly an open book. He was an Afrikaner, good looking with beautiful naturally blonde hair – the perfect foil for Joan's sultry dark looks. He had studied acting and dancing in London before the war, and was a member of the Gwen Ffrancgon-Davies Marda Vanne Company that I had seen in Cape Town earlier that year. I remembered being struck by his fine looks and silken fair hair. He was not a great dancer but he made a strong partner and could manage difficult lifts with ease, which was all that was really required. And he wore trousers. A male ballet dancer in tights would surely have broken the camel's back.

Pieter was slightly schizoid. One day he would talk about the wonderful times he had had in England and the marvellous people he had met there; the next day he would only converse in Afrikaans and rant about how brutally the British had treated his people in the Boer War, and we, by implication of our English parentage, were thought to be equal culprits. One never knew where one was with Pieter, but on his English days he was lovely.

He and Joan did a modern ballet *pas de deux* to Gershwin's 'Rhapsody in Blue.' with Frank Daly giving his all on the clarinet, which always went down extremely well. Joan's classical solo was an item called 'The Composer's Dream.' The composer (a cellist) sits at his instrument, head slumped forward, asleep. As he dreams he starts to play Handel's 'Lager', and a beautiful Giselle like vision floats on on her toes and does a romantic dream ballet. As the music ends she floats away into the darkness and the composer slumps over his cello again, asleep. Black Out! It may sound very corny but the music was played so beautifully and it was danced with such feeling that I never tired of watching it.

Another item I think Joan inspired, it certainly came via 'Coppelia', was 'The Magic Toy Shop.' A doddery old man with a stick brings a little girl into his shop and shows her his collection of toys. As she plays with them they come alive. I was Pinocchio, Joan did the Mexican hat dance, Maurice was a gollywog doing a ragtime cake walk to something by Ravel, Pieter was a tin soldier and there were two or three more dolls.

The opening too, I imagine, must have been Joan's idea, and now I come to think of it what a very weird idea it was. The scene is an all night court (very New York). A judge sits at his bench and admonishes a bunch of noisy nightclub revellers (girls in evening dress, boys in white tie and tails.) who are herded in by a comic cop with a truncheon played by Pieter (I suppose this had something to do with prohibition. I never thought to ask). I don't remember what the judge had to say but our response was to push him off his bench, knock the cop's cap off and then for everyone to sing Cole Porter's 'Anything Goes.' When we got to the Middle East we ditched this long and cumbersome opening for something much simpler.

Our singers were Harold Lake and Muff Evans (her name was Myfannwy but everyone called her Muff). Harold had a powerful baritone voice, and after the war spent some time in the opera chorus at Covent Garden. His solo in the show was the aria 'Figaro' from 'The Barber Of Seville.' Muff was just sixteen years old, with a pretty, fresh young face, sparkling eyes and a sweet soprano voice, and she sang romantic Deanna Durbin ballads with great charm.

We opened the second half with a very potted version of 'The Vagabond King'. Harold and Muff sang the love duets, 'Only A Rose', etc, while the rest of us dressed in rags as the Paris mob, stamped our feet and shook our fists as we snarled, "...and to hell with Burgundy!" My ragged trousers, with the help of Maurice's scissors, grew a little more ragged every night until quite an expanse of my right thigh was showing. I felt that there must be at least one or two in the audience each evening who might derive a little pleasure from it; minorities needed entertaining as much as anyone else, I was just doing my duty as an all round performer. However, Pieter had noticed what I was up to, and on one of his Afrikaans days reported it to Frank Daly, so I had to borrow needle and thread from Maurice and stitch up the tear.

Konni Hirsch was another German Jewish refugee. He and his mother had arrived from Munich in 1936. I had met him a few times in Cape Town doing charity shows and found him quite affable. His speciality was imitating musical instruments at the microphone. In The Troopadours that was a bit like taking anthracite to Newcastle, but he was good at it and the audiences liked him, and when he was being Louis Armstrong's trumpet, playing something really hot like 'Jeepers Creepers' with strong backing from the band, they lapped it up.

People kept telling Konni that he reminded them of Vic Oliver of whom he had never heard. The Unit managed to find some records of the comedian at work, which he learnt off pat, and when he had mastered the vocal inflections and timing it was difficult to tell them apart. After he had become confident performing the material he started adding jokes of his own. He was particularly popular with British troops, Vic Oliver being one of their favourite comedians, and the fact that he was married to Sir Winston Churchill's daughter Sarah at the time was no disadvantage for him, or Konni.

Maurice and I became good friends with Konni and we went about a lot together. It was while walking with him down a street in Tripoli that I first met Noel Coward. He was coming down the steps of his hotel and, thanks to Konni's nerve (I would have been far too shy myself), we introduced ourselves to him. He was most charming. He said he had heard all about The Troopadours and the sterling work we were doing, and he only wished he had time to see the show for himself. We felt extremely flattered, and I walked away on air.

Noel Coward had been my idol since I was a small child. I had all his records and knew them off by heart, he was one of my film star impersonations, and I had played young Joey in a radio production of 'Cavalcade'. Once, when I was about ten, I made my mother buy me a white dotted navy blue cravat like the one I had seen him wearing in a photograph. I remember we were standing in Adderley Street waiting to board a bus when two men, getting off it, clocked my cravat and gave each other funny looks; I just stared at them with disdain and remarked to my mother what common folk they were allowing on the buses these days. I also asked her to buy me a Sulka silk dressing gown but she balked at that.

Lynette Crossley-Kerr, who came to be called Tessie, was a rather big girl with an attractive voice. We didn't know quite what to do with her until someone suggested she sang a Tessie O'Shea number, 'Two Ton Tessie From Tennessee'. I don't think she ever really enjoyed doing it but it solved the problem: once the audience had seen her making fun of her size they were prepared to accept her doing other things; and she was funny again in the toy shop scene as a large Shirley Temple doll singing, 'On The Good Ship Lollypop'.

Then there were the Kempens, Steve and Joan, husband and wife champion ballroom dancers. Before their marriage she, as Joan Strange, had been a successful dancer in stage shows. She also sang very well, and with her fine features, shoulder length auburn hair and lovely long legs was quite out of the ordinary. I always thought she would one day make a name for herself in musicals. She certainly had the talent and the looks for it.

Steve in civilian life was a bank clerk, and a duller bank clerk I am sure it would have been hard to find. He was not bad looking though, and on a dance floor he was something else altogether! That could be the only reason why Joan had married him; if there was another none of us ever saw it. Together they concocted an Astaire-Rogers type routine that was very effective. It started with Joan, all dressed up and nowhere to go, sitting beside her radio wistfully singing, 'Aint Missbehavin'; suddenly her dream lover appears in white tie and tails, he takes her in his arms and they dance for a few refrains with changing rhythms and tempos, building up to a fast twirly finish. The audiences loved it.

That just leaves Maurice and me. Maurice did several clever things during the show. His main item came just before the finale. Konni announced that we had a famous guest star with us that evening who had just flown in from Moscow, the great Russian opera singer, Madame Millardavia. On swept Maurice looking very glamorous in a black satin dress, strings of pearls, long white gloves, a white ostrich feather fan, long false eyelashes and a wig of red upswept hair (the whole shebang made by Maurice's own fair hands). On his entrance most of the audience thought he was a glamorous woman. With a good fake soprano voice he then proceeded to murder 'Il Bacio.' He started off quite straight, then things began to go wrong. First of all his bust started to slide down, then his dress kept slipping off one shoulder, the false eyelashes came unstuck, his wig went slightly askew, the feather fan got caught in his teeth, he had concealed in his cheek a wad of chewed up paper which he now spat out, he then began to scratch himself, found a flea, threw it to the ground and stamped on it to a loud sound effect made by wooden clappers that he had designed himself. The song ended with him being almost strangled by his pearls and losing his wig. The troops went wild, and not only the troops: when he auditioned the act for them in London the American comedians Olsen and Johnson snapped him up for their famous zany revue, 'Hellzapoppin' and with them he toured for several years, playing in many countries. The Olsen family, or it might have been the Johnson family, rather adopted him as a son and when the show was resting he stayed with them on their Californian ranch. When 'Hellsapoppin' finally closed Maurice moved to Hollywood where he acted in television for a short while, then became a costumier.

By that time we had lost contact with each other, but my mother wrote to say Mrs. Millard had told her that Maurice was now making all Red Skelton's bird costumes. I was intrigued to know how many bird costumes Red Skelton might require. I got Maurice's address and wrote to him, we resumed our old friendship and from then on we kept in regular touch. Maurice married twice, first to a showgirl from 'Hellsapoppin', then to Thelma White who had once starred in 'The Ziegfeld Follies'. She was many years older than him but they were devoted to each other, and when he died in 1999, after several years of ill health, Thelma was desolate. I wrote to her. She replied sending me photographs of herself with Maurice. I wrote again. There was no reply. I then heard from Maurice's sister Betty in South Africa that she had been moved to an actors' retirement home. Betty didn't know the address. And that was the last she heard of her. Then in the *Guardian* newspaper on the 27th of January 2005 I read an obituary for Thelma White who had died on the 11th of January, aged 94.

Me: I acted in all the sketches, sang and danced in the ensemble numbers and did my 'In Town Tonight' film star impersonations. I must admit that by then they were a bit out of date, some of them hadn't made a film for years, but the new ones weren't as interesting or as easy to do and I relied on people having good memories and remaining loyal fans; and if some of them had never heard of Tallulah Bankhead that was their loss, not hers or mine. It is not without some embarrassment that I tell you how I finished the act. With a monocle in my eye and my lower lip jutting out I gave them my George Arliss reciting Shakespeare's immortal lines, 'This royal throne of kings, this scepter'd isle, this earth of majesty, this seat of Mars, this other Eden, demi-Paradise...' (then as the band playing, 'There'll Always Be An England' got louder and louder) '...this blessed plot, this earth, this realm, this ENGLAND!!!!'

I know, I know, I feel deeply ashamed. But in my defence I must say that audiences at that time loved a bit of patriotism. So who was I to deny their pleasures? Indeed, I felt humbly grateful to them, being allowed to show so much British phlegm. It also saved my bacon.

At the very first performance of 'Speeding Along' the show sped on for well over three hours. We met the following morning and made drastic cuts; whole scenes and sketches were jettisoned, some of our favourites among them, and still the show was too long. We made further snips with our scissors and, though much lessened, the problem still remained. With so much music in the show, and we didn't want to lose it, there just wasn't enough performance cake for everyone to have their fair slice. The brutal truth was we didn't need such a large company. Heads ought to roll. But whose? Luckily before the tumbril trundled up the problem solved itself.

The Kempens started to have marital problems; they wouldn't converse and barely smiled at each other on the stage. One morning we woke to find them gone. They had been recalled to Pretoria and we never saw hair nor hide nor heard of them ever again. So much for my prediction that Joan would make a name for herself in musicals. Without them the show was the perfect length and we gave a great sigh of relief.

Then Miss Kena decided to make her exit, and far less discreetly. We had been on the road for about three months and were travelling on the night train to Cape Town to give some performances in the area. Maurice, Konni, Pieter and I were sharing a compartment. We were on our bunks, just getting off to sleep, when we heard shrieks coming from the next compartment. We ran out into the corridor to be met by Muff, Tessie and Cynthia all screaming at the same time, "Joan...Joan...it's Joan...she's jumped out of the window!" After we had peered into the compartment to make sure she wasn't there we pulled the communication cord and the train ground to a halt. The guard appeared and the girls, now quite hysterical, told him what had happened: they were lying on their bunks, all chatting away, that is all except Joan who had been silent for some time. She had been drinking quite heavily. Suddenly she slipped out of her bunk and threw herself out of the open window. The guard hurried away and nothing happened for a couple of minutes, then the train slowly began to move in reverse until a voice shouted that they could see a body beside the lines and the train stopped again.

Amazingly, Joan was still alive. What condition she was in we didn't know, and like the Kempens we never saw hair nor hide of her again. But some time later I heard that she had married a Cape Town impresario called Willie Powell, a man with whom I had had unpleasant dealings as a small child.

Willie was producing a lavish summer revue in which there was a sketch where a father tries to tell his son the facts of life, and he wanted me to play the son, and there were other things for me to do in the show. I can remember very excitedly going to a lawyer's office with my mother to sign my first stage contract. I was to get £3 a week, which was a lot of money then. My brother, a fully fledged electrician, only earned a pound or two more. It was a big cast and we rehearsed for several weeks. About ten days before we were due to open at the Muzenberg Pavillion our leading lady, a well known Afrikaner actress, gassed herself in her garage. A replacement was quickly found and rehearsed, then the day before the opening Willie vanished, and after all those weeks of rehearsal none of us received a penny. It then transpired that there had not been anything in his bank account for a very long time and that he owed money to people all over the town. Our only conclusion was that he must have been slightly mad, and with him it had taken the form of impresarioitis.

And so Willie had surfaced again, and so had Joan, and they were now husband and wife. What a cosy little couple they must have made.

In replacing Joan Kena we were extraordinarily lucky. Joyce van Geems was a Cape Town girl with a slightly eastern look. She had an olive complexion, large soulful eyes and glossy black hair. She had been dancing with the Ballet Russes de Monte Carlo since the age of fourteen and for four years had toured with them around the capitals of Europe. She was considered a very promising dancer and Leonide Massine had created a solo dance especially for her. It was a Russian peasant dance that started quietly and soulfully, then slowly built to an exciting climax of fast multi pirouettes. She would dance it with The Troopadours.

The Ballet Russes were in Paris when war broke out. They went to South America, Joyce with them. Anxious about the war, her parents insisted she came home and reluctantly she did. Apart from the odd engagement there wasn't a lot for Joyce to do in Cape Town (I suppose she could have taught but that wasn't in her character) so when Frank Rogaly invited her to join the Entertainment Unit she gladly accepted.

By the time she came to us she was slightly overweight for a ballet dancer. It must have been glandular for she had the appetite of a bird and never touched alcohol. What would have been a drawback for most dancers, because of Joyce's superb technique and depth of feeling, hardly mattered at all. It meant a little more work for Pieter but he wasn't fazed by it and he much preferred Joyce to Joan.

I can't believe there could be anybody who didn't like Joyce. She was sweet and natural, and (strange though it seems, having toured around Europe for four years with a ballet company) had remained a complete innocent. A staunch Roman Catholic, she attended Mass whenever possible. And it goes without saying, she was still a virgin. But then so were Muff and Tessie and a new girl to the company called Georgie. I have never seen so much purity lumped together on one stage. I felt it was my duty to even the scales a bit, and in my own quiet way I believe I did.

The fourth and last, but not least, to go was Cynthia. Having toured for six months she felt she had played Lady Bountiful to the troops for quite long enough. Cape Town society was pining for her, and surely there must be a handsome young escort or two back home on leave. It amazed me how easy it was for women to get discharged from the army. All it seemed to need was the right doctor's certificate. Miss Klette certainly knew the right doctors (she knew all the right people). For a man it was much harder. The only way I knew was to have someone drop a hundred pound shell on your foot.

Cynthia was replaced by a charming dark haired girl called Doris White. She had an attractive, slightly comedic face that reminded me a bit of Martha Raye. She played the sketches quite well and had a better singing voice but of course she was not in the same klass as Klette. But then no one could be. She really was a one off.

Then there was Georgie Greaves, a pretty girl who came in to replace Joan Strange (we needed another girl for the line up). She could sing a bit but she was really there to look good in the ensemble numbers. Although Georgie was part of the virgin circle she was quite a feisty character and had a wicked sense of humour. We got on very well together. One day she offered me some advice to improve my act. She suggested that I changed my intro music from the 'In Town Tonight' theme to 'The Dead March'. I pretended to laugh it off but it made me think, and not long after I ditched the act for a comic monologue I had written in the form of a lecture entitled, 'Head-Shrinking For Beginners'. Without the band playing 'There'll Always Be An England' the ending did not have the same emotional impact on the audience but they found it funny and I felt it was nearer to the legit work that I really wanted to do. I always wished that the Unit would produce plays but they never did.

In the Middle East Georgie abandoned the virgin circle when she met and fell passionately in love with a young airman. They became engaged and were going to be married on his next leave in Cairo. But his plane got shot down over Italy. Although she disguised her grief very well Georgie never got over the tragedy and some years later she committed suicide.

So The Troopadours company was once again in good nick and ready for the long tour ahead. The show would be a tremendous success, but for me it was never quite as glamorous as at the beginning when we had those three knockouts, Kena, Klette and Strange.

So, what was happening in my personal life? Well, it was happening, it was personal and it was lively. Abstinence and I never made good bed fellows. I left that sort of thing to the virgin circle, they were much happier dealing with celibacy than I was. Also, contrary to what I had been taught, I discovered that you can have your cake and eat it: it might mean a bit of indigestion and a pantry full of stale gateau but at least someone's been to tea.

One morning, when 'Speeding Along' was still in the early stage of production, I was changing into my rehearsal clothes (shirt, shorts and sandals) when a tall, devastatingly handsome young man entered the changing room. I took one look at him and in true Mills & Boon fashion fell instantly in love. To my utter astonishment the feeling was mutual and we plunged into a passionate affair that was to run for over a year. Being in different shows, we couldn't be together as much as we wanted, but when we did meet we made up for it. We were absolutely besotted with one another and although we tried to keep it a secret our feelings were so strong that it was impossible to hide them completely, and soon everyone knew.

The Major tried to separate us by sending the Montagues off in one direction and the Capulets in another, but as someone even wiser than the Major once said, "Love will find a way," and with days off and weekends free, and with very special thanks to the Telephone & Telegraph Company, South African Railways, friendly motorists and rides on the back of army trucks we somehow always managed to meet. Luckily we didn't have that dotty old Friar Laurence ballsing things up for us.

His name was Cecil, he was twenty, half English half Dutch and he sang Afrikaans folk songs in a show called 'The Montagues' – no, I mean 'The Ballyhoos.' As I think I may have already said, he was not bad looking. His hair was brown, his eyes blue, his mouth full and wide, showing beautiful, white, even teeth, and there was a dimple in his cheek when he smiled that I found quite irresistible. He was not awfully bright, but then you can't have everything, and we didn't travel miles and miles through bush, veld and desert to discuss the poems of W.H. Auden.

Whenever I hear 'Desert Island Disks' on the radio and the theme tune 'A Sleepy Lagoon' starts to play my mind goes racing back to Pietermaritzberg. It was there, around lunch time on a Saturday, that The Troopadours' caravan rolled up to a hotel where we were to stay for the next few days while performing at army camps in the area. As we entered the lobby I could hear the strains of 'A Sleepy Lagoon' coming from a radio. I was humming along with it quietly to myself when I heard the receptionist say, "Is there a Neville Phillips in the company? There's someone on the telephone for him." The company raised a quizzical eyebrow. They were right, of course, it was Cecil. The Ballyhoos were having a few days out and he had hot footed it down to Pietermaritzberg and taken a double room in a small hotel on the other side of town where he now was waiting for me to join him as soon as I could. I tried hard to conceal my excitement as I casually informed my eager listening audience that it was my Great Aunt Albania on the telephone and that she had invited me to spend the afternoon and evening with her at her at her lovely home on the outskirts of the town. I don't believe I fooled a soul. The company's next call was at 9 o'clock on Monday morning and until then our time was our own, so after I had unpacked, showered, sprinkled after-shave all over myself and put on a clean uniform I hurried across town to that heavenly little hovel of a hotel room where Cecil and I remained for the entire weekend, emerging only when in need of sustenance.

On Sunday night we were having dinner in the almost deserted dining room, it was only 8 o'clock but already everyone had been and gone except for a pair of slow coaches. They were two little old ladies who, between taking dainty mouthfuls of a violent pink blacmange, stole glances in our direction and then whispered to each other. Over coffee they grew bolder and actually smiled our way. We smiled back and in no time at all conversation was in full swing. They said they had been thinking how nice it was to see two soldiers being so friendly to one another. I explained that we were actually long lost brothers who had only just met again having been separated as babes by a dramatic shipwreck in the Aegean Sea. They were overjoyed at our reunion and insisted on buying us double brandies. When they got up to leave I could see that it had made their night for them. We didn't need potted tales from Shakespeare to make ours.

Durban was very nearly our Waterloo. It was a hot summer, and in Natal the humidity can be horrendous (you put on a shirt and five minutes later it is soaking wet) so we were glad to be staying on the sea front in quite a posh hotel. The company didn't always stay in hotels, posh or otherwise. We were often put up in army camps but if we were doing a lot of one night stands it was more practical for us to stay somewhere central rather than change quarters every day; and anyway not all the camps were equipped to accommodate females; and I am sure we were given very special concessions. But why am I worrying about the Government's war expenditure for the year 1942?

As I was saying, before I went off on that tangent about the Natal climate, Durban was very nearly our Waterloo. Maurice and I were sharing a room, as we usually did, and we had decided that afternoon to go and see Marlene Dietrich and Charles Boyer in 'The Garden Of Allah' at a nicely air conditioned cinema. We were just leaving the room when the telephone rang. It was Cecil. The Ballyhoos had arrived in Durban to await sea passage to Egypt. He could not wait to see me and I could not wait to see him so Maurice went to The Garden Of Allah on his own, leaving us the room to ourselves for the afternoon.

Cecil was sure that no one from the company had seen him enter the hotel. But he was wrong (it was probably Pieter on an Afrikaans day), for no sooner were we undressed than there was a knock on the door. It was Frank Daly who said he wanted to talk to me about something. Quickly, as though I had been playing Feadeau Farce all my life, I bundled Cecil into the small clothes closet and flung his uniform and boots in after him. Then having wrapped a towel around myself I feigned a sleepy voice and yawned as I opened the door. "What is it?" I asked. "I was just falling asleep." Frank hurried past me, his eyes darting about the room, he was definitely expecting to see Cecil there. I sat on my bed and yawned again. "What is it, Frank?" I asked. He sat on Maurice's bed and tried to think of something plausible to say. "Er.. that new song of Georgie's," he said, "that.. er.. 'Last Call To Arms', how do you think it's going?"

"It'll be fine," I said, "when she's more at ease with it. Of course, it won't sound quite the same as when Frank Sinatra sang it in that film with the Tommy Dorsey band.

"I suppose not," he said gloomily. Irony had never been his forte. There was a long pause during which I yawned and scratched myself languidly. Then he thought of something else to say, "Hot, isn't it?"

"Isn't it just," I said.

"Killing," he said.

"Killing," I said, thinking of Cecil in that stifling closet trying to hold his breath. Frank glanced at the closet a couple of times then looked at me to see if I would react. I didn't, although inside I was starting to panic. How much longer could Cecil survive in that death chamber? Eventually He got up to go. I could see he was still suspicious but if he had opened the closet door and found no one there he would have looked an awful fool and he wasn't prepared for that to happen.

Poor old Frank, his timing was just out. If he had delayed his exit by a mere ten seconds he would have seen Cecil, scarlet faced and covered in sweat, tumble out of the closet and lie naked at his feet in a dead faint.

And then what would have happened? Fortunately we shall never know.

While The Ballyhoos toured the Middle East and The Troopadours continued to tour South Africa Cecil and I wrote constantly to each other, long long letters avowing eternal love and yearning for the day when we would be together again, never more to part. From the bazaars of Cairo and Alexandria he sent me perfume, incense, amber, a carved ivory cigarette holder, a small fillagree box, a ring with a sphinx on it...I sent him some photographs of myself. Well, it's hard to find exotica in the Woolworths of Potchefstroom and Koffiefontein.

As the year wore on, hardly perceptibly to begin with, our letters grew less frequent, less fervent, and finally they became almost bland; and when the day arrived that we had waited for so long, and we were actually standing there facing one another, it felt as though we were strangers. The world had not stood still for us, it had moved on and it had taken us with it. Everything had altered. We were now two different people. We tried to pretend it hadn't happened but it was no good, the spark had gone, the affair was over. We would always remember it with great affection, it was the first big love affair of both our lives, but like all good things it had come to an end... and then I met the Baron!

Axel von Strahl was his name. His father was German, his mother Swedish. He went to school in Germany and had been a member of the Hitler Youth. He once showed me a photograph of himself with a group of them in lederhosen and I instantly understood the lure of Fascism. His parents separated. His mother returned to Sweden, his father took the post of German Consul in Cape Town and brought Axel to South Africa with him.

At the outbreak of war the Consul changed his allegiance to the allies (he had never embraced Nazism) and gave them much useful information concerning Hitler's secret plans for the eventual annexation of southern Africa; also detailed information about the strong pro-German movement that existed in the Union. The authorities trusted him implicitly and gave him a useful post in Pretoria. Axel joined the South African Army and became a corporal in the Intelligence Corps (rather risky I would have thought considering his dodgy background). The office where he worked was in Artillery Row, a couple of houses down from us, and he was always around the place chatting up the girls with whom he had tremendous success. He was about twenty two or three, tall, dark and very good looking in an aristocratic, slightly decadent way; and there was something just a little brutal about his smile that sent the women wild. To my certain knowledge he had had affairs with at least four girls in the unit. They had fallen madly in love with him and he had treated them abominably. So imagine my complete surprise when the following occurred:

About four weeks before The Troopadours were due to travel north, early on a

Friday evening (it was still light) a group of us were sitting in the yard of our house at the barracks, there was Maurice, Konni, Harold and a few members of a show called The Bandoliers, and we were all in the carefree, relaxed mood one is with a free weekend ahead. Suddenly I noticed Axel was standing in the yard (one of The Bandoliers must have brought him) and he seemed to be looking my way. It wasn't long before he had wandered across and was talking to me. I thought he was fascinating with his suave, European manner, and knowing he had a title did not leave me entirely unimpressed. His conversation was charming and witty, and as he talked I began to get the distinct impression, slightly to begin with but then very strongly, that he was making a pass at me. It was a ridiculous idea, I had to be imagining it. After all, he had had most of the eligible females on Artillery Row. But no, the look he was giving me could not be interpreted in any other way. I was growing flustered and wondering what to do when out of the blue he said, "What are you doing this weekend?"

"Joburg," I said, "staying at the Carlton."

"So am I," he said. "Shall we go together?"

Well, you could have knocked me down with a feather from one of Maurice's Red Skelton bird costumes!

We met at the station the next morning and were waiting for the 9 o'clock train when Frank Daly passed by. I couldn't resist showing off the sort of company I was keeping these days. "Lieutenant Daly," I said, "may I introduce my friend, the Baron von Strahl."

Frank looked startled for a moment, then calmly his eyes moved down to the stripes on Axel's sleeve. After a brief pause he murmured, "At ease, corporal," and passed on. I felt utterly humiliated, but I had learned my lesson and I would never introduce Axel in that affected way again.

The weekend was both highly pleasurable and educational: with Cecil it had always been romantic and passionate, with Axel it was cool sophisticated sensuality and a well hoed technique that left me dazzled and dazed. On Sunday night we were on our way to the station to catch the last train back to Pretoria when Axel suddenly stopped in the street, turned to me and said, "Fuck the train". Back to the Carlton we went for another spectacular night. During a post coital cigarette he taught me the German words to 'Falling In Love Again,' and for the next few days I went around singing in a low husky voice, "Ich bin von kopf bis fuss auf liebe eingestellt, und das ist meine welt..." until Maurice chucked one of his tap shoes at me.

On Monday morning when it was time for us to rise to catch the early train that would get us to Pretoria in time for roll call, Axel again said, "Fuck the train", and when we eventually arrived back, heavily hung over and totally exhausted, it was already lunch time. We went straight to see the medic at DHQ and told him we had both had food poisoning. He didn't believe us, but I don't remember anything serious happening because of it.

The next three weekends were equally *wunderbar*. And then it was *auf wieder-sehn*. To my despair and everyone else's delight The Troopadours were sent to Durban to wait for a ship. I missed Axel dreadfully and wrote to him almost every day. He sent me one long lyrical love letter full of quotations from Goethe, Schiller, Wedekind and Schnitzler that I read over and over again until I had savoured every nuance. But my favourite part was where he said he'd fallen in love again, he'd never wanted to, what was he to do? I thought I was going to treasure that letter forever.

To my delight and everyone else's disappointment we were told that our ship was not due for another month, so The Troopadours had to return to Pretoria. I telegraphed Axel to tell him when I was arriving, and that night he took me to a squalid little hotel on the scruffier side of town where no one we knew would see us. I wondered what the sudden secrecy was about, but in the hurly burly of the night's revelry I forgot to ask. For me it was as perfect as ever, so imagine my surprise (yes, surprised again! I really ought to learn) when from then on he became completely incommunicado. I tried phoning him, sending him messages, telegrams saying, 'Hail to thee, blithe spirit', but there was no response. Then a very kind friend felt it was their duty to inform me that he was now very heavily involved with a beautiful blonde singer called Dorothy who had just joined the unit. She hadn't much of a voice, I was told, but then that wasn't her major talent. I tried to contact him a few more times and then I decided to broach this so called Dorothy.

She laughed out loud in my face. "Oh, yes," she said, "Axel has told me how you keep pestering him, and how you won't understand that he's not interested in that sort of thing. You're on a losing wicket, I'm afraid. I wish you'd stop it."

I asked her if she knew we had been sleeping together.

Her laugh got shriller, "He said you might say something like that. Can't you see what a fool you're making of yourself. For God's sake leave the poor heterosexual man alone."

It was time for the denouement! The enlightenment of so called Dorothy! From my breast pocket I slowly drew out a letter (as I imagined Bette Davis might do if she had a breast pocket), took my time unfolding it, let her see it was Axel's handwriting and signature, and then read her some choice extracts, sparing her Goethe & Co, but none of the personal stuff, and I particularly emphasised the bit where he said he'd fallen in love again, he'd never wanted to, what was he to do? I watched so called Dorothy's pretty pink face turn ashen. Perhaps he had already written those very words to her.

Before you could say, "*Ein, zwei, drei*", he was around at the barracks demanding his letter back and threatening me with all sorts of Kafkaesque tortures if I dared to show it to anyone else. It had served its purpose and I didn't want the silly thing anymore so I gave it to him. And that, I thought, would be the last I would ever see of Axel. But I was wrong.

Fifteen months later, we were back from the Middle East, The Troopadours had been disbanded and we were all waiting to be cast in new shows. It was a Saturday afternoon and I was sitting in the lounge of the Carlton reading a book and about to order tea when I sensed a presence looming large before me. I looked up and there was Axel smiling at me as if nothing untoward had ever happened.

"May I?" he said, gesturing to the chair beside me.

"Please do," I replied. By then I had become deeply involved with someone I had met in Cairo, who was to change the course of my life even more irrevocably than Lionel had done. I was happy, at ease with myself and perhaps feeling a little smug. Nothing Axel might do could upset me now – so I thought. "Would you like some tea?" I asked.

"Actually," he said, "I am just about to go and have tea with a friend. He's an art dealer who has a lovely flat right at the top of Anstey's Building. It has a superb view and is full of wonderful paintings. Why don't you come with me? He's a charming man, I know he would be delighted to meet you."

The thought of the view and the paintings interested me so I said yes. Axel was right, the view was superb, the paintings were wonderful and the art dealer was delighted to meet me. He was a short, fat, bald man with a middle European accent. As we sat on the sofa talking about a Cape Town artist we both knew called Freida Locke, Axel quietly left the room. I thought he had gone to the loo. When after about ten minutes he hadn't returned I began to wonder what was happening. I did not have to wonder for long. Suddenly a firm hand gripped my groin and another slid around my waist. "What the hell are you doing?" I said, fighting him off. He looked as surprised by my reaction as I had been by his crude attack.

"I thought..." he said.

"You thought what?"

It then came out that he had been paying Axel money to procure young men for him. That very afternoon while I was looking at his pictures he had slipped him another tenner; and then, when he had vanished like that, he took it for granted that I was in on the arrangement. I was furious with Axel. He was furious with Axel. He was also cross with me; I had wasted his entire afternoon and cost him ten pounds to boot. With the minimum of politeness we parted company. I couldn't make up my mind whether Axel was just in need of a tenner or whether he was getting his own back for my showing his letter to so called Dorothy. Perhaps he was killing two birds with one stone. I had the sneaky feeling that Axel might quite like killing birds. Well, that, I thought, was definitely the last I had seen of him. Wrong again.

About four years later in London I was meeting some friends for tea at the SF Grill, a café in Denman Street (just behind Piccadilly Circus) where young actors met in the afternoon; some looking for work, some showing off that they were in work; and there was always a sprinkling of Rank Starlets there: Diana Dors, Maxwell Reed, Joan Collins… The three friends I was meeting were all ex unit members who, like me, had come to England to seek fame and fortune on the stage. They were Olga Lowe, her husband John Tore, and a stunning looking twenty year old Lithuanian called Larry Skikne who had just changed his name to Laurence Harvey, and would soon be a famous film star in Hollywood, having carefully climbed the ladder of success, wrong by wrong.

On the banquette beside Olga sat a man, his face completely concealed by a newspaper. I thought he was on his own at the next table until Olga said, "Look who's here." The newspaper was lowered and there was Axel smiling his devilish smile at me. Olga and John had become very matey with him in Pretoria. They had both found him extremely attractive and great fun to be with. But then so had everyone else in Pretoria. They must have been the only two he had not done the dirty on – unless one or even both of them had a guilty secret they were keeping to themselves. He was looking as handsome as ever, and quite prosperous with his Saville Row suit, gold wristwatch and rings; and he let it drop in conversation that he had a flat in Shepheards Market. He must have come into some family inheritance, I thought. He can't have made that sort of money from pimping in Johannesburg. His conversation was as witty and wicked as ever. He told us scurrilous stories about people in high office that had us all roaring with laughter. And then suddenly he was on his feet, bidding us goodbye and was gone, never to be seen again. In the flesh, that is.

A couple of years later on a Sunday morning Olga rang and asked if I had seen The News Of The World. I hurried out and bought a copy, opened it and there, smiling at me from the page, was Axel under the heading: 'JEWEL THIEF BARON. The scourge of Mayfair.' He was in Wormwood Scrubs having been convicted of multiple jewel thefts. Many a Mayfair lady (and I'm sure the odd gent or two) had been his victims, and he had got away with it until his over inflated arrogance and conceit had led him to do something so crassly stupid that I still can hardly believe it possible.

There was a very special opera production at Covent Garden for which it was almost impossible to get tickets. Axel managed (no, I don't want to know how) to acquire two and gave them as a present to a wealthy couple he had just met who had expressed a keen desire to see the production. While they were watching the performance he stripped their Mayfair flat of all its valuables, and when they were asked by the police if there was anyone they might possibly suspect they replied in unison, "The Baron, of course!"

Another two or three years later Olga heard from someone who had heard from someone else that Axel was dead. That was all we knew. How he had died, and where, and what he was doing to whom at the time we never found out. I sometimes feel that he isn't dead at all. There was something rather Harry Lime about Axel, and I wouldn't be surprised to turn a corner one day and see him standing in a doorway smiling his wicked decadent smile again.

A couple of nights before our ship left Durban I met a charming American in a bar and we spent a most delightful evening together. He was with the American Ambulance Corps (a voluntary and fairly elite association) and was on his way to drive ambulances in the western desert. His ship was docked in the harbour and was part of the convoy that ours would be joining.

His name was Stephan Cole, he was in the theatre and had just left a successful play at the Plymouth Theatre on Broadway to join the AAC, much to the chagrin of the play's leading lady, Tallulah Bankhead with whom he had worked on several previous plays. She always insisted on having him as her stage manager, partly because he was good at his job and partly because he was fun to party with. Tallulah loved to party, and when she partied everyone around had to party, and as she liked to party every night, and as Stephan, by the very nature of his work, was always around, and as it looked as if the play was in for a very long run, he decided to sneak away to the war and get a bit of rest.

The play he had just left, in which he also acted, was 'The Skin Of Our Teeth.' by Thornton Wilder. It had a cast of forty that included Frederic March and the very young Montgommery Clift. He told me all about this wonderfully wacky play with its strange scenic effects (at one point the scenery starts to fall down; at another, for no reason, it vanishes into the flies). I would see it in Cairo, performed by amateurs, and then in 1946 at the Piccadilly Theatre in London starring Vivien Leigh. I loved it then, it was my first exposure to the theatre of the absurd, but I am not sure how it would fare today. Since then we have had Beckett, Eunesco and Albee.

Stephan and I lunched together the next day and he regaled me with more stories about Tallulah. He had once shared a house with her and her then husband, and late one night when Stephan and she were sitting alone in a night club (everyone else had escaped, including her then husband) she showed him a small mother of pearl handled revolver that she had purchased that afternoon. When he asked her what she intended to do with it she said, "Shoot the bastard in the balls, darling. It'll be the one place where he'll know he's been shot." She then either lost it (in a powder room or taxi) or else her aim had been lousy, because after they were divorced the bastard still had his full quota of genitalia.

Stephan said that if I ever came to New York I should look him up, and I would have loved to have done so, but by the time I made it there it was 1983, four decades later, and I felt I had left it too late. He probably wouldn't remember who I was. He might even be dead?

A few years ago I read a biography of Tallulah Bankhead and Stephan's name appeared in it a few times. After the war he worked with her on several more shows, and then (this was the final mention of him) they had a tremendous bust up. It didn't say what it was about but it ended acrimoniously and he vowed never to speak to her again – and he never did. And that is all I know about Stephan Cole, which is sad because I would very much like to have had him as a friend.

On March the 1st 1943 The Troopadours set sail for Egypt on the MS Salandia. Also on board was another unit show called The Bandoliers. The voyage was not without incident. Rounding the Horn of Africa we had a U Boat alert and every vessel in the convoy switched off its engines. We then spent an eerie couple of hours watching the ships drifting silently on the wide empty sea. The alert over and all engines going again we continued our journey.

The harbour at Aden was a wonderful sight: our ships were surrounded by little boats with Arabs in them holding up brightly coloured cloths and shiny jewellery, while small boys dived into the sea to retrieve coins soldiers threw from the decks. We were allowed ashore and both The Troopadours and The Bandoliers companies were invited to visit Government House. Of course they only really wanted the girls, but the Major had made it a strict rule that the company was never separated. Wherever the girls went the boys went too. This was a very wise rule. It would have been untenable if, after a show, half the company were invited to an officer's mess and the other half not. Also Frank Daly never allowed anyone to go on ahead. The girls sat and waited until the boys had finished packing the trucks, then we all arrived together and left together. The offer of a drive back in an officer's car was never accepted. Not that the poor sod would have got very far with a Troopadours girl. Those not in the virgin circle (if any) were respectable to the point of prudishness. At a four letter word they all blanched. I think it would be true to say that the only person in the company who came anywhere near to behaving like a slut was me.

Government House was situated at the top of a hill overlooking the harbour. We were all sitting there sipping something cool and admiring the magnificent view when the urgent message arrived that the convoy was ready to depart and we were keeping it waiting. We hurried down the hill as fast as we could and were given filthy looks as we boarded the ship. Our officers got the brunt of it but we were all considered to have behaved recklessly. This was most unfair. On being invited to Government House we naturally assumed that whoever had invited us had sought permission first. For the rest of the voyage we were treated rather like pariahs and if we had then been attacked by a U Boat I have no doubt who would have been blamed.

We docked at Port Tewfic, and it was late afternoon by the time The Troopadous climbed into the back of a large army truck and set off for the South African Camp at Helwan, a few miles outside Cairo. Leaving Port Tewfic we drove through the town of Suez, and I was fascinated by the exotic atmosphere: the crowds in flowing gallabias, Arabic music blaring from radios, men, wearing tarbushes, sitting outside cafes playing cards and smoking hookahs, the smell of mint tea and coffee, donkey and bullock carts holding up the traffic, car horns hooting, black veiled women carrying freshly baked bread, children and dogs darting everywhere. It was all so new to me, and quite the most vibrant scene I had ever witnessed. It made Saturday night in Johannesburg seem like a wake.

Driving along the desert road in the dark, I suddenly sniffed a strange and intriguing smell. As we drove on it grew stronger and stronger…it was the smell of Cairo. I don't know if anyone has ever tried to describe it. I think it would be impossible to really do so. But somewhere in there is the scent of jasmine, oleanders, roses, ripe fruit, camel and buffalo dung, incense, rotting vegetation, petrol fumes, hashish, musk, massed humanity and I don't know what else. It was the most exciting and intoxicating smell I have ever known and one I could never forget. So, before I had even seen it, I had been drugged and seduced by Cairo!

But before we put the MS Salandia behind us for good I must tell you about a couple of shipboard romances that took place during the voyage: one poignant, the other tragic.

Muff Evans, now just turned seventeen and starry eyed, fell for the sexy charms of Gordon Mulholland, a good looking young comedian in The Bandoliers. Maurice and I had known Gordon since childhood when all three of us were in 'Wee Chaps' together. He was a bit older than us, and a sadistic little bully. One afternoon, while touring in the Transvaal, we encountered a freak storm of locusts. The sky grew black with them, and they covered the tram lines causing a tram to slide down a hill and crash. Gordon knew how petrified I was of the ugly flying insects and was determined to put some down the back of my shirt. I spent the entire afternoon in a chemist shop hiding from him. Luckily when he started to think about girls the bullying stopped. He didn't have time for both and the girls took precedence, they also became his life long preoccupation. As a teenager he was already known in Cape Town as Casanova Mulholland. So his little flirtation with Muff we did not take seriously. For him it was just a dalliance, another chance to show off The Mulholland magnetism, nothing more. Muff, however, was under the impression that they had become engaged; in her besotted state she must have misunderstood something that he had said, because knowing Gordon as well as I did I knew he would in no way commit himself to a permanent relationship with someone as simple and naïve as Muff then was. His was far too voracious an appetite for such a dainty little *hors d'oevre*. And I was right; as soon as the ship docked he was off after the first available bit of skirt, leaving Muff…well, a little bewildered, to say the least.

After the war he spent a brief spell in London, during which he appeared in a musical at the Hippodrome Theatre called 'High Button Shoes'. Also in the cast was another ex unit member, who would one day be known as that loveable old cockney, Sid, of the 'Carry On' films. And in the chorus was ever such a pretty girl they both fancied called Audrey Hepburn.

Gordon returned to South Africa and made a name for himself as a leading actor in musical theatre, light comedy and farce. His reputation with the ladies was equally impressive. As he got older they got younger. Muff would often laugh about this – a slightly brittle laugh. He married twice, once to a fan dancer from the Windmill Theatre (there's exotica for you). Muff never married. Gordon was her first love and I think really the only one. They remained good friends and she always spoke of him with great affection, though sometimes I thought behind it I could sense just a hint of bitterness.

The second shipboard romance I spoke of should not have been allowed to happen. Some of us tried to stop it; in hindsight we should have tried harder, but we hoped, as is usually the case, it would have run its course by the end of the voyage, and certainly none of us then could have foreseen how it would really end.

Sweet, loveable, still amazingly unworldly Joyce van Geems for the first time in her life fell in love, and to her great misfortune it was with a tap dancer in The Bandoliers called Ken Geyer. I suppose he wasn't bad looking in a slightly coarse featured way but there was something very serpentine about him; he was tall and slithery with snake hips, snake eyes and a snake mentality (sly, furtive and dangerous). As some of us already knew he was an inveterate liar. Maurice and I and three of The Troopadours girls had shared a flat with him in Pretoria for a few weeks before our first tour and we discovered then that for him the line between reality and fantasy hardly existed.

He came from a wealthy Afrikaner family, his father owned a coal mine in Springs, and they lived in a large house with lots of servants. The reason none of us were ever invited to his home was because he was not on speaking terms with his family, his having joined the army against their wishes. Well, that was what we all believed until someone visiting Springs discovered that old man Geyer was a poorly paid employee at the mine, not far above a black worker, and the 'Tara' like mansion Ken had described in such detail to us was a meagre little dwelling with a corrugated tin roof in the poor white section of the town. Mr. And Mrs. Geyer had not seen their son for a long while; in fact, not since he had run away from home having stolen money from them. Unfortunately by the time we learnt this it was too late. The snake had already mesmerised its victim and was not going to let it go.

When I saw that Joyce was falling in love with him I tried to warn her, as did a few of the others, but she wouldn't listen. In her eyes he was Romeo personified. The fact that he was gay and aggressively promiscuous with it she refused to believe. In her naivety she probably didn't even comprehend fully what we were telling her – and that was after four years in the Russian Ballet. Didn't I say she was an innocent? Even while wooing her on the ship Ken was on the look out for available men. On a couple of mornings he boasted to me of the wonderful sex he had had the night before with a member of the ship's crew in a lifeboat on the top deck. I don't know whether it was true or not but it certainly gave me a few pangs of jealousy. Since we had been at sea I had not had a single adventure and I was beginning to feel like one of those pieces of luggage that has a label stuck on it saying, 'Not Wanted On Voyage'.

But my real concern was for Joyce. I couldn't see how she was going to come out of it unscathed. I knew with her strong religious beliefs there would be no hanky panky before marriage, but I also knew that though this would have deterred most shipboard Romeos it would not concern Ken unduly; for after holding hands at the deck rail all evening and him promising her all sorts of wonderful things, they would part with a tender goodnight kiss, she to retire to her cabin and dream about her prince charming while the said prince raced hotfoot up to the top deck and jumped into a lifeboat full of randy sailors. Yes, I was jealous. I was extremely jealous!

Exactly what was going on in Ken's mind at that time it was impossible to know. A thought I had was that he perhaps imagined after the war they would become a famous dancing couple like the Castles or the De Marcos or the Astaires and go twirling around the world from one glittering city to another as he had seen portrayed in many a Hollywood movie. Whatever he imagined, Joyce was the key to the world he so desperately sought and he wasn't going to let it slip out of his fingers.

So we were saddened but not surprised when the second shipboard romance didn't end with the voyage. In Egypt it continued to flourish and even when they were apart for a long time, as when we spent the summer travelling up the north African coast and then the whole winter in Italy, almost every day Joyce could be seen writing to Ken. Our two companies crossed paths a couple more times in the Middle East and when they did the pair were inseparable.

In May 1944 both shows returned to Pretoria and were disbanded. After a few weeks leave we were back in Artillery Row waiting to be cast in new productions. Ken and Joyce went into The Sundowners. Maurice joined them (our close friendship had suffered a temporary but severe blow during our leave in Cape Town, which I shall come to later on), Konni and I joined The Boomerangs with John Tore and Olga Lowe, and in a very short while we were back in Cairo.

It was there in the summer of 1945 that Olga was matron of honour at the Roman Catholic wedding of Mr. and Mrs. Ken Geyer. By then Joyce had slimmed down tremendously and with her dark limpid eyes and long black hair she reminded me very much of Dorothy Lamour. In those days we spent most of our spare time in cinemas so film stars were quite prominent in our consciousness.

The Geyers in married life seemed to me less like a husband and wife than a fixated child playing with a precious doll. Ken designed all her clothes (inspired by the musical films of Alice Faye and Betty Grable), dressed her up in them, took her onto a dance floor and showed her off. At the Auberge des Pyramid in Cairo (one of King Farouk's favourite night haunts) all eyes would be on them as they danced the rhumba and samba, Ken basking in the reflected glamour that Joyce so naturally exuded.

The end of the war did not mean our work was over – far from it, we were busier then than ever. It took many months for all the allied forces to be repatriated and while they sat in desert camps waiting for transportation they easily became bored and restless and this sometimes even led to rioting, so entertainment then was of vital importance.

By January 1946, however, the situation had been more or less resolved and at long last we were able to hang up our army issue tap shoes and slip on a pair of civvies. Those of us younger ones who intended to continue in the business all came to London, except Konni who went to New York where his father was an eminent surgeon (London wasn't big enough for two Vic Olivers, I suppose) but he didn't like it there and soon returned to Cape Town where his mother lived.

I was the first to arrive. I had arranged to be demobilised in London, as did John, Olga and Maurice (now late of The Sundowners) who followed soon after. Then, having first returned to South Africa, came Harold Lake, Muff Evans (who gave up singing and became a beautician for Elizabeth Arden in Bond Street), Sid James,

Gordon Mulholland, Larry Skikne (who became Laurence Harvey), Alfred Rodrigues (who joined the Royal Ballet and became a successful choreographer and director), Harry Rabinowitz (our brilliant musical arranger who made a name for himself in films and television as a musical conductor), Dennis Mitchell (officer in charge of our Cairo office, who arranged all our Middle East itineraries. He was to become famous as an innovative producer of documentary films for the BBC). A few others followed, dipped a toe in the big pond, found it too cold and deep and hurried back to warmer shallower puddles.

It will always remain a mystery why Ken and Joyce didn't join the exodus to London. There was not a lot going for a dancer in Johannesburg at that time, they would have stood a far better chance of finding work in England. The only reason I can think of (of course Ken might have had a more devious one of his own) was that they were waiting for Frank Rogaly's big post war revue to happen. For years Frank had talked about the spectacular show he was going to produce when the war was over using all the best talent from the unit; it would have a grand title, something like, 'South Africa On Parade'; and if it was the great success he envisaged the Major might take it on a flag waving tour of the world, ending up in London! If ever there was a cock-eyed optimist it was Frank. Mind you, we were all pretty starry eyed about the future then and believed almost anything was possible.

In due course the revue was produced and although most of the creative talent Frank would have wanted to use in it had migrated the Geyers were still there and their dancing was prominently featured in the show. Ken must have been gambling on it being the smash hit Frank was so sure it would be because by then their funds were running low. The monies they had received from the government upon demobilisation plus Joyce's careful savings had gone on keeping up the life style expected of a rich coal mine owner's son.

To Frank's deep dismay and Ken's dire distress 'South Africa On Parade' folded after a few weeks and the Major's plans for a flag waving world tour were quickly forgotten. Without their regular army pay to fall back on and cabaret work being scarce and poorly remunerated Ken was in real trouble.

Having borrowed money from everyone he knew, he now started down the slippery slope of trickery and deceit. He got people to invest in a sure fire scheme that turned out to be a sure fire scam (Gordon Mulholland got his fingers burnt on this one); he then began forging signatures on cheques and tricking the gullible into cashing dud ones of his own; he even stole money from the wallets and handbags of friends.

Only now, it was thought, with the police about to pounce, did the sleeping beauty open her eyes and see the prince as he really was. If this makes her seem over incredulous you must remember that she adored him, trusted him implicitly and what a consummate and intrepid liar he was. When she discovered the depth of the deception their lives together had been she knew the marriage was over.

On that Friday afternoon when the fraud squad came knocking on their door they were already driving down to Cape Town where Joyce's family lived; she was very close to her parents and young brother and would have wanted to be with them at this most difficult time for her.

On the Sunday morning after Joyce had attended Mass, as she always did, Ken picked her up in the car and drove to a quiet spot on Milnerton Beach where they could talk things through without any disturbance. While she lay on the sand with a towel covering her face (Joyce always sunbathed this way, she didn't want her face any darker than it naturally was) Ken put a revolver to her temple and pulled the trigger. He then tried to do the same to himself but must have botched it somewhat, because his body was found several yards down the beach in a grotesque contortion with a trail of blood snaking back to where Joyce lay. Both the serpent and it's victim were dead.

Some said it was a suicide pact, but I don't agree. Joyce was too deeply religious to commit what she would have believed to be a mortal sin. And, anyway, weren't they saying she was about to leave him? What I think happened is this: Ken knew his time was up; he was going to prison for a long time; he had lost his one asset, Joyce; there would be nothing for him to look forward to, so he decided to exit with a grand flourish, taking his beautiful ballerina doll with him. He might even have been trying to emulate the famous Mayerling tragedy – that was the theatrically grandiose way his fantasist mind worked: it would be headlines in all the papers; their names would be on everyone's lips; it was a sort of fame, in a way, and the only sort he was ever going to achieve. Well, that's what I think happened.

I was sitting on the top of a number 52 bus travelling down Kensington Church Street (I had been rehearsing a play in Notting Hill Gate) when I opened the evening paper and saw an item at the foot of the page headed: 'Double Death On Cape Town Beach'. It was only a paragraph and simply stated their names, cause of death and where it happened. My sudden gasp and subsequent distress so startled the woman sitting beside me that I hurried off the bus and, finding the nearest pub, ordered a large brandy – then another – and another...

Should you think that was how the tragic story ended you would be mistaken. As if the van Geems had not had enough sorrow inflicted upon them, it was at this very time that the new Apartheid Laws came into practice; and as Mr. van Geems was of mixed blood, he was partly Malay, the family were forced to leave their home in a white suburb and move far out to a coloured area that was little more than a shanty town. This, following the blow of his daughter's death, was more than Mr. van Geems' mind could take and returning home one afternoon on the train he flung open the carriage door and leapt to his death. Mrs. van Geems died shortly afterwards from the shock and horror of it all. And what became of Joyce's young brother nobody seemed to know. He simply got swept away in the evil tide of Apartheid.

I once had tea with the van Geems family in their pleasant little home in Observatory, and a nicer, more law abiding and God fearing family it would be hard to find. Then suddenly, in one fell swoop, as if a ghostly tornado had struck that little house, everything in it was gone!

So much for those prayers of thanks Joyce gave every day to her Lord.

—⁓—

Cairo in 1943 must have been the most exciting place on earth. Everyone travelling to or from the Far East or engaged in the North African Campaign passed through Cairo. The city throbbed with life. The bars, restaurants and nightclubs were packed with servicemen on leave (for some it would be their last) all determined to live life to the full. Every night there was a party somewhere, and for an eighteen year old, not considered unattractive, gay hedonist such as myself, it was like entering paradise.

There were many who disliked Cairo, including some of the Entertainment Unit, they noticed only the heat and dust, the dirt and flies, the crippled beggars, the street vendors pestering them to buy fly-whisks, dirty postcards and Spanish Fly, the hordes of children tugging at their sleeve and pleading for *Baksheesh*. All that was deeply disturbing but there was another side. What they failed to notice was the beauty, the antiquity, the grandeur, the exotic sensuality and the seductiveness of the oldest city in the world. As you might have gathered I had fallen in love with Cairo.

We were stationed at the South African camp at Helwan, fifteen miles south of Cairo. It was a short journey by train and there were always gharries and taxis waiting at the camp gates and at the station to ferry one back and forth. But mostly we got lifts from the military vehicles that constantly to'd and fro'd from the city.

Helwan Camp was a great sprawling affair, in the centre of which were some shops, a laundry and a large open-air cinema. Shortly after arrival we noticed that 'Gone With The Wind' was being shown that night and some of us decided we would like to see it again. At that particular showing the projectionist got the reels of film muddled and after we had witnessed Melanie's very touching death she suddenly bounced on again fit as a fiddle. For those who had not seen the film before it must have been a most bewildering experience.

We were at the camp for just over three weeks, getting our equipment together, rehearsing a new opening chorus, updating a couple of the girls' songs and learning how to assemble the mobile stage that we would be using in the desert. We would travel with four trucks: the first would carry the company; the second and third the mobile stage, costumes, scenery, piano and other musical instruments and the fourth the generator that would provide electricity for the lights and microphone. The four drivers doubled as stage hands and we had two young wardrobe mistresses, one possibly and the other definitely affiliated to the virgin circle.

Whenever we had some free time we scooted off to Cairo, and on our weekends we stayed at Springbok House, a hostel for the South African forces in the very centre of the city, close to all the shops, restaurants and cinemas which we found very handy. We also did a lot of sightseeing: the Pyramids; the Sphinx; The Citadel and the white alabaster Mosque of Mohammed Ali with their wonderful panoramic views of the city; the old Coptic Church where Moses was supposed to have been found in the reeds; the Jewish Synagogue where Joseph and Mary were said to have hidden before their flight from Egypt; the Khan el-Khalili bazaar in the Mouski where we drank countless cups of mint tea and Turkish coffee while haggling with jewellers, tailors and perfume dealers. We also found time to visit Groppi's Garden Tea Room in the afternoons and watch some of Cairo's most elegant women in their fashionable finery conducting discreet liaisons over tea and cakes. At night we sat under the stars in open-air cinemas watching the latest films from Hollywood.

It was our third weekend at Springbok House, and early on Sunday evening transport was picking us up to take us back to Helwan from where we would leave the following morning for Alexandria, where our tour would commence. We still had over an hour before transport was due so Maurice and I decided to nip out and have a little stroll around the neighbourhood. Had we not done so my life would have turned out quite differently to the way it did. Or even if we had done so and turned left on leaving the building instead of right I would not be the same person I am today. Spooky, isn't it?

Passing a dusty looking old hall we saw there was an exhibition inside of paintings of Egypt by members of the British Army. Entrance was free so we decided to take a gander. As might be expected the subjects were mainly the Pyramids, the Sphinx, feluccas on the Nile, desert sunsets and lots of camels and they were all rather chocolate boxy.

There was one other person in the hall, a nice looking young British army lieutenant, and as the three of us moved around the hall together we struck up a friendly conversation. It was his last night in Cairo too; he was returning to his regiment in the desert the following morning. As we talked I began to sense that he might be gay, and then I began to sense that he had begun to sense that I might not be as normal as blueberry pie myself. What he and Maurice had begun to sense of each other I had no idea. When we had looked at as many camels as we cared to and were about to leave he asked us if we would like to have a drink with him. We declined graciously, explaining that we had transport picking us up nearby in just over half an hour.

"That still leaves time for a quick drink," he said. "I know of quite a nice little place just around the corner."

He was half right, it was just around the corner but it certainly was not quite a nice little place. It was an Aladin's cave full of the most gorgeous looking men I had ever seen, all in uniforms of different nationality and rank. I could hardly believe my eyes.

The place was called the Taverne Francaise and was a bar with a small restaurant attached which served quite tolerable French food. The restaurant had a mixed clientele of a theatrical nature. ENSA personnel used it, I once saw Alice Delycia lunching there, and Josephine Baker dining with a group of Free French Legionaires. The bar though was entirely gay and I had never seen so many handsome men in such close and amiable proximity. I suppose there must have been a few duds amongst them, but with so much beauty about they failed to be noticed. As I looked around I began to feel like a greedy child let loose in a sweet shop not knowing which delicious bonbon to try first.

"Time to go," said Maurice primly.

We gulped down our beers, bid our charming host goodbye and good luck and hurried back to Springbok House – but not before I had made a mental note of exactly where the Taverne Francaise was situated. I intended to return there as soon as possible, although, of course, I had no idea then how important a part it was going to play in my life.

I suppose you must be wondering how Maurice fits into all of this. To be perfectly honest I am not quite sure. I imagine that he was not as highly sexed as some of us. He would take a girl out to dinner or the pictures but it never seemed to go any further. He was equally at ease in gay society but didn't pursue that line either. I sometimes thought that if he had to choose between a bit of fun with a boy or girl and watching an Alice Faye movie Alice Faye would win hands down. He married twice, it is true, but then he was brought up in a strict Welsh Methodist home where conformity was the rule, and I am sure that Welsh witch of a mother of his had a lot to answer for (more of her wicked Welsh witchery later).

Alexandria is Egypt's second oldest city. It was founded by Alexander the Great (although he never lived to see it) and for a long period of its history was the fashionable capital of the world. It had many famous buildings and monuments: the Royal Palace of Ptolemy the First, the Great Lighthouse, the famous Library which held more than a million precious manuscripts of ancient civilizations. Alas, none of the antiquity has survived.

During the 19th century the city was given a complete make over by French architects, and that was more or less how we found it in 1943. There were many ornate villas, wide boulevards, public gardens and a grand Corniche that ran crescent like around the Eastern Harbour. Some of the buildings on it had spectacular roof gardens filled with exotic blooms. I once was lucky enough to visit one, the scent of the flowers was glorious and the view quite sublime. Off white sandy beaches we would bathe for hours in the wonderfully warm Mediterranean Sea, so unlike the icy Atlantic that I was used to. After the show at night we would take leisurely gharry rides along the sea front, and sitting on the terrace of a French or Greek restaurant with a chilled drink in one's hand and a cool breeze blowing in off the sea was a most agreeable experience.

Alexandria was so very different to Cairo. One could almost imagine one was in a Greek city (I had not yet been in one but I could almost imagine it), whereas Cairo was unmistakably Arab.

Our first performances were to be at the Globe Theatre, a charming, fully equipped small theatre attached to the Union Jack Club where the British Navy, when ashore, came to relax. The men of The Troopadours were to lodge there too, the girls at the YWCA. The club had a large, very adequate restaurant that was open from early morning until late at night. One paid for one's meals with little tickets, of which we were given whole handfuls, so whenever we felt slightly peckish we would pop in for eggs and chips, ice cream or a milk shake.

We were to open on Thursday night. The show that was playing until Wednesday was a play called, 'French For Love', which had had a short run in London at the beginning of the war starring the famous French actress, Alice Delysia, the star of many Cochran revues. I was delighted to see that she was playing the part again and we all went to see it.

The play was a sort of 'French Without Tears' meets 'Colette'. A young English student in the south of France falls for an older, much wiser French woman. It was not a very good play but it was wonderful to see the delectable Alice Delysia live on a stage. Also in the cast was someone I would work with one day called Noel Howlett.

Our opening night was a triumph and it continued to be so for the rest of the week. I don't think we ever played to better audiences. They consisted mainly of Royal

Navy personnel, but there were civilians there as well and it made for a very good mix. They got all the humour, enjoyed the ballets and appreciated the fine talents of our musicians. We were very sad to leave the Globe Theatre.

A word about the differences we found in audiences. The finest undoubtedly was the British Royal Navy; we never struck a dud one. Then came the Royal Air Force, the British Army and after that the Colonies, in no particular order except that the South Africans were especially pleased to see South African girls on the stage; it reminded them of the ones they had left back home. The worst audiences, and we dreaded playing them, were the Americans. English humour did not appeal to them at all; they hated the classical music – Erwin Lerher playing his cello was more than once told to "Swing it, Pop"; and whenever possible we cut the ballet *pas de deuxs*.

I suppose the reason the British audiences were the best was because they had a great tradition of theatre. Most of them might not have seen a play but they had probably been to a Music Hall or a Pantomime so they knew what live performance was about.

Alexandria at that time was extremely humid, and with the heat of the stage lights and all the quick changes we had to do we sweated a great deal and most of us ended up with a prickly heat rash, which was most uncomfortable and undignified. Still, playing the Globe Theatre, Alexandria, was an experience I would never forget

Next stop on our tour was Mersa Matruh, a charming little seaside town 180 miles to the west of Alexandria, which, in its time, had been host to many a famous name: Alexander the Great and Cleopatra to name but two – on separate occasions, of course.

On our way there we passed El-Alamein, the scene of one of the fiercest battles of World War Two. Rommel, in command of the German and Italian armies, was only 60 miles from Alexandria, when the British Eighth Army, commanded by Montgommery, repulsed him and, after months of agonising stalemate, assumed the offensive and drove him back through Libya and Tunisia. This was the turning point of the war for the allies.

It was an eerie sight: the detritus of battle was everywhere; as far as the eye could see were burnt out tanks and vehicles, abandoned military equipment and soldiers' personal belongings. We had to remain on the desert road – signs all along it warned of land mines – but there was enough *objet trouvé* on the side of the road to keep the keenest war trophy collector happy. I had just discovered a round metal badge with Mussolini's profile on it when Maurice noticed, a short way ahead, glinting in the sunlight, a trail of hundreds upon hundreds of small silver and bronze coloured pieces of metal which must have fallen out of the back of a fleeing truck; half of them were bronze coloured and half silver, otherwise they were identical: two and three quarter inches long and one and a half inches wide, flat and shaped like a hand; on one side was an Islamic design, on the other some writing in Arabic which, when translated into English, read: 'I am against the English dictator'; and there was a small hole at the wrist end of the hand so it could be threaded and hung.

These were representations of Fatimah's hand, which in Egypt is a symbol of good luck and wards off the evil eye; one sees them everywhere: over doorways, worn as jewellery, adorning the bridles of gharry horses, dangling from the driving mirrors of taxis. Fatimah was Mohammed's daughter, but why one of her hands should have assumed such symbolic significance I have never discovered.

These replicas of her hand that we had stumbled upon were obviously made to be handed out to the citizens of Cairo as tokens of friendship when Mussolini, who had flown to Derna bringing a white charger with him, entered the city in triumph.

How smart, I thought. What style. The allies would never have come up with anything like that – nor the Germans – it could only have been an Italian idea; if there was one thing the Italians had in abundance it was panache! For good luck we all took a few of Fatimah's pretty little hands. I still have one on my key ring today, and on the whole it seems to have done its job pretty well.

Arriving at Mersa Matruh was truly a wonderful experience. We had been travelling for hours in scorching heat through the monotonous grey sand and brush of the desert and were feeling hot, sticky and tired, when suddenly driving over the crest of a hill we saw beneath us, sparkling in the sunlight, the beautiful azure blue Mediterranean Sea fringed by miles of sugar-white sand. We drove to the edge of the beach, leapt out of the trucks, ran across the sand discarding our clothes as we went and, in just our underpants, raced into the beckoning sea. The girls being of a more prudish nature had to wait until they had unpacked their bathing costumes.

There was one large and imposing white Art Deco building on the beach; it was a hotel and one of its claims to fame was that Edward and Mrs. Simpson had stayed there while on a Mediterranean cruise. The hotel was deserted, as were all the little houses in the town; the residents having fled ahead of Rommel's army and not yet sure whether it was safe to return.

We stayed in the hotel; each of us had a room to ourselves with a balcony facing the sea. I can't remember anyone complaining.

We gave several performances at the YMCA hall in the town and the audiences were most receptive; then we played a couple of camps a short distance up the coast; but we still had time most days to swim or do a bit of sight seeing; we saw Cleopatra's Bath, a hollow carved out in the rocks and filled with sea water, where the Egyptian queen was said to have come to bathe; we also visited the Temple of Jupiter-Amun at Siwa.

Returning to Alexandria, we did a few shows in the area; and we revisited the Globe Theatre where we saw a RAF concert party that had a brilliant young comedian in it called Alfred Marks; then we travelled east to Port Said; Ismailia, where we boated and swam in the lovely salt lakes; then down the Suez Canal to Suez and Port Tewfic; and then back to Helwan and, luckily just in time to catch one of the last performances at the Cairo Opera House of the ENSA revue, 'Spring Party', starring Beatrice Lillie, Leslie Henson, Dorothy Dickson, Vivien Leigh, Nicholas Phipps, Kay Young (at the time married to Michael Wilding) and Richard Hayden; the production was directed by John Guilgud. Surely no touring revue had ever before boasted such distinguished names. Perhaps ENSA was trying to make amends for all the tacky little shows it had been sending to the Middle East.

It was very exciting seeing all those famous performers on the stage together, but one couldn't help feeling that the show had been thrown together in rather a hurry; everyone having dug deep into their trunk for something from an old show that they thought might just do.

Bea Lillie (who must surely have been the greatest comedienne of the 20th century) chose material far more suited to the Café de Paris than a troop show, and it was sad to see her wonderful iconoclastic wit going way over their heads.

Dorothy Dickson sang, 'I Don't Want To Set The World On Fire', while standing at an ironing board. I couldn't see the point of this; if the joke was that she was going to leave the iron on and actually set the world on fire then the joke was too subtle for me.

Vivien Leigh, looking absolutely ravishing in a costume from the film, sang, 'I'm Scarlet O'Hara, the terror of Tara...' a rather lame little lyric that must have been run up for her at the last moment; but it didn't matter a jot, it was quite enough to see Scarlet O'Hara alive on a stage! In the second half, looking equally stunning, she just came out and recited, 'You Are Old, Father William', a poem not exactly known for belly laughs or a funny pay off; it left everyone feeling slightly bewildered.

Kay Young sang a couple of popular ballads quite charmingly, but it was the men who came off the best with their broader style of humour.

Leslie Henson did a very funny turn sitting at a grand piano; then he and Nicholas Phipps performed the ever popular sketch, 'The Green Eye Of The Little Yellow God', which went down a treat; as did Richard Haydn's famous monologue on fish noises.

The show ended with the company singing Noel Coward's, 'The Party's Over Now' (the finale of his 1932 revue, 'Words And Music'). I love this song and would be happy if every show finished with it. Stephen Fry possibly agrees with me; he used it to end his delightful film, 'Bright Young Things' (in which I was delighted to play a small part).

It was also a great delight to see inside the Cairo Opera House with its white, crimson and gold interior (sadly destroyed by fire in 1971). It was built in 1869, made entirely of wood, mud and plaster and was completed in a matter of weeks – just in time for the first performance of 'Aida', which Giuseppi Verdi had been commissioned to write for its inauguration, to celebrate the opening of the Suez Canal.

It was lovely seeing inside that historic building, where before the war, the Comedie Francaise and the Paris Opera paid regular visits; and I could just imagine that first night of 'Aida' with the Empress Eugenie and half the royalty of Europe sitting in those gilded boxes in their opulent splendour, their myriad sparkling jewels almost blinding the poor opera singers on the stage. But the really amazing thing about the Cairo Opera House was that such a hastily constructed, jerry built, rickety old fire hazard of a building actually survived as a working theatre for over a hundred years. Fatimah had a hand in it, I'm sure.

Back in Helwan we were told that we could have ten days leave before starting our major tour of the western desert, which might last for several months. Everyone in The Troopadours except me decided they wanted to visit Jeruselem. I decided I wanted to visit the Taverne Francaise. They all tried to persuade me to join them, especially Frank Daly who didn't trust me an inch, but they couldn't force me to go, and I was adamant; I told them I just wanted to sit in a quiet garden somewhere and think; no one said anything but I saw them giving each other old fashioned looks. Having waved them off I booked myself into Springbok House, and before you could say, 'Taverne Francaise' the ten days were over and my heart was about to break again.

At the start my days had a sort of routine: in the morning I would go sightseeing or visit the bazaars; the afternoon I spent swimming and sun bathing at the open air swimming pool in the Ezbekieh Gardens; after that I might take tea in Groppi's garden or an iced coffee at the Brazillian Coffee Store; then, after a short rest, I would shower, slap on a bit of aftershave and make my way to the Taverne Francaise where I made one or two most agreeable acquaintances.

Then, on the evening of July the 4th, while I was sitting at the bar sipping my first refreshing lager of the evening, a young GI, dark of hair, handsome of face and lean of limb came and sat on the stool beside me. After a short while he started a conversation; he told me that the 4th of July was not only Independence Day but also his birthday, and he would be honoured if I would help him celebrate by having a drink with him. I saw no reason to refuse, after all, Boston was long enough ago not to rankle anymore.

His name was Bill, he came from Nashville Tennessee and he spoke with the most seductive southern drawl. His father owned a chain of gas stations and Bill ran one of them. In time he would inherit the lot; I was most impressed. When I told him what my line of business was he gawped; he had never seen a live actor before; I believe he thought they existed only on celluloid.

A few celebratory drinks later, and after a fairly meaningful pause, he looked me straight in the eye and asked, "Do you know the score?" I had never heard the expression before but I thought, 'If it means what I think it means I am not going to miss out on this,' so I looked him straight back in the eye and gave him a very positive, "Yes!" I had made the right decision, because it wasn't much later that we were sitting in a hotel bedroom a couple of streets away continuing the celebration with a bag of samosas and a bottle of Southern Comfort. There followed a night of sheer delight; neither of us got much sleep but then that wasn't the plan.

Early the next morning when Bill had to leave for his camp on the outskirts of Cairo (he worked in the MT stores during the day but his nights were always free), as he was about to go he asked me if I would meet him again that night. I was overjoyed; the thought that I might not see him again had been distressing me all the while I was watching him dress. We met again that night, and then every night until my leave was over. I had fallen madly in love with Bill, and he with me.

One day he managed to get a full day's pass and we spent the precious time together. He took me to a US Services Club, the luxury of which made all our clubs look like the poor house; there was everything there that an American male might desire; and the nylons, Hershey Bars and chewing gum even provided them with female company; this and the fact that they earned more than three times as much as a British soldier was a cause of much resentment among the other allied forces.

As Bill and I sat on a sumptuous sofa dunking doughnuts in our coffee and listening to the latest hit tunes on the American Forces Radio we heard a song that we thought particularly poignant; the lyric began: 'You must remember this, a kiss is still a kiss, a sigh is just a sigh....' Soon, through the film, 'Casablanca', the whole world would be singing it, but for us that day, sitting there, dunking doughnuts, it was our song alone.

In the afternoon we went to see, 'Thank Your Lucky Stars', a Warner Brothers musical in which Bette Davis sang Frank Loesser's witty lyric: 'They're Either Too Young Or Too Old'; this was to become his first hit.

In the evening we had a meal in an open air restaurant beside the Nile that had little coloured glass lanterns hanging from the trees. In this most romantic setting Bill asked me to go and live in Nashville with him and help him run his father's gas stations. Like Lionel and the fish and chip shop I knew it would never really happen, but it was a lovely daydream and I enjoyed having it: I saw myself manning the pumps with great agility and aplomb and telling all the customers to have a nice day; then at night I would do a bit of Summer Stock at the local theatre; there must surely be one? Bill was appalled, he said that any further acting would be out of the question; he even asked me not to let his father know that I had ever been on a stage. I readily agreed, after all, the war was by no means over, there would be plenty of time to renegotiate; and anyway, I was sure that deep down he knew as well as I did that the whole idea was just a beautiful fantasy.

Suddenly the idyll was over. The 15th of July was my nineteenth birthday and our last night together; we had met on his birthday and we were parting on mine. The Troopadours were leaving for the Western Desert the next morning and there was no knowing when we would be back. Bill managed to borrow a flat from a Greek friend for the night, and lying there together with a full moon streaming in on us through the open French windows and the scent of jasmine wafting up from the garden below it was the most bitter-sweet night I had ever known; and next day as our caravan trundled west along the desert road and I sat staring out of the back of the truck, sadly singing to myself, "You must remember this, a kiss is still a kiss..." I thought my heart was going to break – but it didn't.

We wrote to each other a few times, but as all letters were censored we had to be very circumspect and they ended up being plain dull and boring. In December he wrote to say he was sending me a Christmas present; I then heard from our Cairo office that a large parcel had arrived for me which seemed to contain a box of some sort; as it was too bulky to send on they would keep it there until my return. I spent hours wondering what the mysterious present might be; It turned out to be a make up box that he had had made for me: it was wooden with a sliding lid and a tin handle; inside it were a couple of Mickey Spillane paperbacks, a collection of American Classic Plays, a book of three one act plays from 'Tonight At Eight Thirty' by Noel Coward (for someone totally ignorant of the theatre he had certainly done his homework), several packets of Lucky Strike, chewing gum and, of all strange things, a pipe. I wondered if this and the Mickey Spillanes were there to put anyone off the scent who might have watched him pack. I would use the make up box for most of my stage career in England, and the pipe came in very handy when I started doing weekly rep. Bill and I met again about eight months later, but that is another story entirely.

The battle of Tobruk had left the town in a battered state; it had been badly bombed by German Stukas and the buildings still standing were pock marked with bullet holes; the harbour was full of the debris of sunken allied ships and the wreckage protruding from the water took on the sinister appearance of sharks and strange sea monsters.

I have two vivid memories of Tobruk; the first being that George Formby joined us as a guest artist for several nights. I was a great fan of his as a child and had quite a few of his records; I even attempted to impersonate him once, singing, 'When I'm Cleaning Windows'. The fact that I mimed playing the ukulele I thought would not matter, but it did matter so I went back to doing Zazu Pitts instead. I had seen all his films, but then I had seen the films of most of the British music hall stars of the 30s; I loved them, they were cheaply made, poorly scripted, badly lit and crudely photographed but there was something endearing in their naïve tackiness that was a nice contrast to our main fare of Hollywood gloss. My favourites were Lucan and McShane as Old Mother Riley and her daughter Kitty, The Crazy Gang, Will Hay, Cicely Courteneidge and Jack Hulbert (not strictly music hall but near enough) and the queen of them all, Gracie Fields.

It was interesting meeting George and his wife, Beryl; she did all the talking, he just smiled, signed autographs and sang. He seemed more like her gormless son than her husband, and she behaved more like his bossy mother than his wife. The Troopadours did the first half of the show and George did the second. Having to precede a famous star on the stage for almost an hour is not an enviable task. When an audience has come along especially to see a favourite performer they don't want anyone else hogging the spotlight for half the evening. They were perfectly polite to us but we could sense they were waiting for us to finish so George could come on and give them some of his much loved cheeky songs – cheeky but never coarse, that was his secret, he was always George, the lovable Lancashire lad! The troops adored him and would have had him go on all night, but Beryl knew when enough was enough.

Seeing the way they worked together was fascinating. Beryl would stand in the wings with several banjos and ukuleles lined up, each tuned for a particular song, and when George came shambling off to multitudinous applause she would snatch the instrument from him, thrust another into his hands and enunciate clearly the title of his next song; he would then shamble back on and when the applause had subsided do as Beryl had bid. She was a vital part of the act, and I wondered how he would ever manage to perform without her.

In London after the war I had the good fortune to get to know Kay Walsh, a most beautiful woman and superb actress who told me about a film she had made with George Formby in the late 30s called, 'Keep Fit'. Beryl had got it into her head that Kay was lusting after George (she imagined this about all his leading ladies) which was very far from the truth; Kay at the time was very happily living with, and would soon be married to, a handsome young film editor who was to become the great director David Lean.

Beryl had gone through the script with a fine toothcomb, altering any scenes where the two of them were in close proximity; on a park bench they sat three feet apart upon her stipulation. The one scene she couldn't get changed, although she tried her damnedest, was the fade out kiss. When it came to shoot the scene she placed herself beside the camera in Kay's direct eye line and gave her a grim warning off stare. Kay said Beryl's warning was quite unnecessary – having her mouth full of George's tombstone teeth was enough to do the trick.

When the Formbys had moved on we went back to doing our full show and once again the audiences were most receptive. The moral being: never be a warm up to a star act!

My other memory of Tobruk, though not as starry, remains equally vivid. After the show one night a Leading Seaman of the British Royal Navy invited me back to his quarters to drink some navy rum with him. Not having tried the stuff before and being of a curious nature I accepted his kind invitation. He had a small room to himself in a partially bombed building beside the harbour, where from his window I could see in the moonlight those sinister shapes glistening above the water. There were no chairs in his room so we had to sit on his bed where I, not knowing the strength of it, drank far more navy rum than I should have. Upon our arrival he had shown me a photograph of his wife and two small children which I duly admired (this was to let me know that he was really straight, I suppose), he then carefully put them away and I could see he was preparing to forget about them for a convenient spell. It was after I had drained my second mug of navy rum and he was moving closer to me on the bed that the room started to go around and I began to feel violently sick. I got out just in time, and what might have been an entertaining divertissement turned out to be a night of retching in the desert sand.

The next morning I suffered the worst hangover of my life. As I lay on a camp bed in a tent wishing I could quietly die, Maurice fiddling with his wireless set got on to the American Forces Radio and we heard the young Frank Sinatra giving a concert in New York to an audience of screaming bobbysoxers. The song that particularly appealed to me (it was by Cole Porter, I didn't know that then, but I suppose I should have guessed) was called, 'You'd Be So Nice To Come Home To'. I never tire of hearing it, although whenever I do I am ever so slightly taken back to that dreadful morning lying on a camp bed in a tent in Tobruk wishing I was dead.

Incidentally, I never saw that Leading Seaman again.

Muff kept an itinerary of all the places The Troopadours played in North Africa, many of which I do not recollect at all. Names such as Katatba, Barce, Derna, Gazala, El Adem and Misurata mean nothing to me now. On the other hand the name Appolonia means a great deal. Unless my memory has been playing tricks with me it was as close to paradise as anywhere I have ever seen. Established in the 6th century BC it was the port to the great city of Cyrene, built on a hill twelve miles south, and it remained so for over a Millennium; by the 7th century AD it had surpassed Cyrene as the major city of the region.

By 1943 it was just a ruin, but one of staggering beauty; still standing were the eastern, central and western basilicas, the remains of a Byzantine church and a Greek theatre superbly positioned on a hill so that it had the Mediterranean as a backdrop. On the beach, half hidden by fine white sand lay marble fluted Corinthian columns, statues and mosaics. It reminded me of a Chirico painting. Everywhere one looked there was classical antiquity.

We did our show in an army hall with stage and dressing room backing onto the beach; one literally stepped out of the dressing room door onto the sand. In less than thirty seconds one could be in the sea, and on those hot August days we seemed to spend as much time in the cool waveless water as on dry land. After the show we would quickly remove our costumes and make up, slip on our bathing suits and run into the calm rippling water and just lie there until we had thoroughly cooled off. Later, reclining on rugs and cushions on the flat roof of a hospitable British army officer's house, we would drink Tunisian and Tripolitanian wine (it tasted of rusty nails and turned our teeth black, but we got used to it), and gaze up at the magnificent night sky. I could think of nowhere more perfect to be with someone one loved, and only wished that Bill could have been there to share it with me, that really would have made it paradise. I was determined to return there one day when the war was over. For one reason and another it has not been possible, but, who knows, I might still make it; although, I suppose, like everywhere else it will have changed out of all recognition. Perhaps I should keep it as a perfect memory.

We then moved on to Benghazi, 115 miles up the west coast from Appolonia. Like Tobruk it had been badly damaged during the fighting. Upon arrival we were told that Jack Benny was doing a show that night for American troops and if we wanted to we were welcome to attend. We jumped at the offer and joined an audience of thousands of GIs sitting on the desert sand facing a mobile stage (similar to our own) which was bare except for a black backcloth, a piano, a microphone and some floodlights.

The comedian had with him three guest artistes and a piano accompanist. The first was the beautiful English actress Anna Lee who didn't do much except look enchanting and feed him some gags. Then there was Larry Adler, the famous harmonica player (I had seen him perform at the Alhambra Theatre in Cape Town) and finally Winnie Shaw, who had sung some memorable songs in Warner Brothers musicals of the early 1930s; the two I remember best were, 'The Lady In Red', and,

'The Lullaby Of Broadway.' That night in the desert she introduced to us a brand new song that we would soon be hearing a lot of; it was Harold Arlen's, 'That Old Black Magic'.

Watching Jack Benny perform was a revelation; his timing was sublime; I doubt if anyone could hold a pause as long as he could; and his expressions of smugness, surprise, suspicion and disdain were wondrous to behold. The vast audience that night simply lapped him up.

I would see him to much greater advantage a few years later at the London Palladium (a large theatre but with a very intimate atmosphere) where his every subtle nuance could be appreciated and relished. He had with him in the London show three girl singers who called themselves, 'The Andrews Sisters'. When he pointed out to them that there was already a famous singing sister act called, 'The Andrews Sisters', their reply was a brusque, "We know what we're doin'". Then trying to curry favour with him they complimented him on his youthful appearance; he preened with narcissistic pride, and, tossing an imaginary boyish lock, invited them to guess his age.

"Twenty seven," said one of the girls. His eyes lit up, "A little older than that," he said coyly. "Try again." Having looked more closely at his face she now came up with, "Seventy three?" There then scudded across his face a veritable Thesaurus of looks: shock, horror, disbelief, hurt, pain, despair, huff, pique, insult and several other telling expressions, ending up with a long hard stare of contempt for these despicable little impostors trying to pass themselves off as the lovely Andrews Sisters. The cheek! The very idea! Who did they think they were, The Andrews Sisters?

This bit of silent business seemed to go on for minutes, much to the delight of the Palladium audience who were laughing so much I thought they might do themselves an injury and certainly dampen a few theatre seats.

Jack Benny became my favourite stage comedian. My favourite in films will always be that mean, cheating, curmudgeonly, wife, child and dog hating, gin sodden genius of a writer/comic, W.C. Fields. What I wouldn't give to have seen him on the stage performing one of his vaudeville sketches, and in particular, "The Fatal Glass Of Beer."

The Troopadours stayed in Benghazi for just over a week doing shows at various camps to large, enthusiastic audiences; and what with the fine compliments being paid to us after the shows we were beginning to feel a little smug. That feeling did not last long. Our next performance we were told would be at an American camp, and with unhappy memories of a couple of such outings our hearts began to sink – and they had every good reason to, for it turned out to be the unhappiest memory of them all.

Even before the show had begun we could tell that some of the audience were drunk; their voices were loud and raucous, and their language foul. The barracking started quite early on, and when Joyce did her first ballet solo, 'The Composer's Dream', they blew up condoms like balloons and bounced them onto the stage with entreaties to, "Take 'em off!" Joyce carried on valiantly but when she came off there were tears in her eyes. She was also curious as to where all those balloons had come from?

In the interval the officer in charge of entertainments at the camp came around to apologise for the bad behaviour and to assure us that the rowdier element had been removed. Quite a few others had gone of their own accord: the PX obviously having attractions more to their taste than our weird little offering. By now we knew the show was unsalvalvageable, so cutting the more delicate numbers we hurried through the second half not waiting for laughter or applause (well, the war was only going to last for another couple of years) and as we belted out the last notes of the finale, 'Everybody Sing', Mafeking could not have been more relieved.

It was customary after a show at an army camp to be invited to the officers' or sergeants' mess for a drink; this was both an expression of hospitality and so that the men, some having been starved of female company for months, could meet and talk to some nice young ladies (in our case nice enough to take home to mother); at this particular performance however no such invitation was forthcoming, for which we were immensely grateful; conversation about the show could have been rather embarrassing. We just got our stuff together as quickly as possible and, returning the entertainment officer's wan smile and wave, fled the camp. The nightmare was over!

I am in no way trying to compare our talents with the genius of Jack Benny or the celebrity of his guests, merely trying to understand how the audience reaction to our two shows could have been so diametrically opposite. This is my conclusion: Jack Benny was a famous American star of films and radio who they all knew and loved, and he had come all the way to North Africa bringing some famous guests with him to pay them a personal visit; whereas The Troopadours were a group of unknown foreign servicemen and women arriving out of the desert unannounced, talking with funny accents and performing material that seemed obscure to most of them… oh, yes, and it was also our luck to get the drunks! I think it was as simple as that.

Outside Benghazi, close to an army camp where we played, there was a deep cave that led down to a large underground lake which we visited. We were told it was the legendry River Lethe; in Greek mythology it is one of the rivers of Hades, and whoever drinks the water will forget everything they have ever said or done. The word means, 'oblivion'. In Musollini's day it was quite a tourist attraction. In little wooden boats, lit only by torchlight, we paddled across the dark, mysterious water, our voices and the sound of the paddles echoing in that vast open space. It was a very eerie experience.

According to Muff's itinerary we arrived in Tripoli on September 6th, having just played Misurata, of which, as I have said, I can remember nothing. Tripoli, the capital and major port of Tripolitania, was founded by the Phoenicians in the 7th century BC; since then it had been occupied by, among others, the Greeks, Romans, Arabs, Spanish, Turks and Italians. It had an imposing Spanish fort on the sea front and beside it a long palm tree lined promenade where it was fashionable to stroll in the cool of the evening. The city had architecture of various periods and cultures, the last being Italian. For the exposition of 1937 Mussolini had erected some neo fascist pavilions, and it was in one of these where we were housed during our stay there. We played in the comfort of the well equipped Teatro Miramare to large audiences of 8th Army personnel awaiting transport to Italy where the allied invasion had already begun.

(On July the 9th and 10th the British 8th, American 7th and Canadian 1st Armies invaded Sicily. By August the 17th after heavy combat and many casualties the island was secured, the axis troops having retreated across the Messina Straits to Italy. On September the 3rd British and Canadian troops crossed over to Calabria and made a successful beach landing at Taranto, then over the next few days further allied landings were made at Paestum and Salerno. German resistance was fierce and the allies suffered 12,500 casualties before the beach heads were firmly secured. No Italian troops took part in the battles; like petulant children when a game isn't going their way they decided to call it a day.)

This is where I begin to lose faith in Muff's itinerary. Nowhere in it does she mention the ancient city of Sabratha (twelve miles to the west of Tripoli) that has the largest and most magnificent Roman theatre in Africa (170 AD) which we not only visited but where we also gave a performance (and I have the snapshots to prove it). The theatre was in a remarkable state of preservation due to the work of Italian archaeologists in the 1920s. It had a spectacular three tier facade consisting of alcoves and 108 marble Corinthian columns, wonderful statues and carved panels; and the acoustics were perfect – from high up at the back of the auditorium you could hear every word spoken on the stage (would that the designers of London's Royal National Theatre had possessed such technical expertise). We could have performed much of the show without a microphone, except by now it was an integral part of the performance.

It felt a little incongruous doing "Speeding Along" on that vast awesome stage that had witnessed the plays of Euripides, Sophocoles, Plautus and Seneca; but we played to a full and enthusiastic house that night, and we consoled ourselves that the boys were enjoying themselves more with what we were giving them than they would be sitting through five hours of Clytemnestra with an all male cast wearing masks.

It was in Tripoli, as I have previously stated, where Konni and I bumped into Noel Coward. As I stood stiffly to attention gawping at my great idol little did I know that seven years later I would be performing in one of his West End productions. It was a musical called, 'Ace Of Clubs' starring the lovely Pat Kirkwood; her understudy, by the way, was the yet unknown June Whitfield; and there was a pretty dark haired girl in the chorus whose boyfriend waited for her every night at the stage door; her name was Vivien Merchant and his was Harold Pinter.

I had a very small part and also understudied, it was in no way prestigious, but I was glad of the work just then, I was going through a lean period and the salary, meagre though it was, was very welcome. On Christmas Eve the producer of the show, Tom Arnold, gave every member of the cast an unexpected Christmas present; arriving for the show that night we discovered that the closing notice had gone up and by the first week of January we would all be out of work. The performance that evening was not a particularly joyous one, and at the end of it we all wished Mr. Tom Arnold a very merry Christmas! I only discovered later that Noel Coward himself had put up two thirds of the backing for the show and the decision to take it off then was his. Incidentally, a few years later he would be sitting in the stalls of a West End theatre watching the lovely Pat Kirkwood starring in a musical that I and a couple of colleagues had written. 'Well, that's show business for you,' as Mrs. Abraham Lincoln was wont to say. But I am digressing again.

On the evening of November 2nd (if Muff's itinerary can be trusted any longer), with soldiers of the 8th Army we boarded one of several large landing barges and in the dark of night crossed the Mediterranean, via Malta, to Augusta on the south east coast of Sicily. We arrived early in the morning, it was still dark, nothing could be seen, but in the morning mist we could smell the scent of pine trees, wild herbs and wood fires. It was my first smell of Europe and it was most intriguing.

Having landed and been reunited with our transport we set off for Messina, a port on the north east tip of the island from where a couple of days later we would cross over to Reggio di Calabria at the toe of Italy. Driving through the Sicilian countryside we were staggered by it's immense beauty. In Taomina, where we stopped to admire the breathtaking view, Harold Lake came out with his famous remark – one he was going to regret for a very long time; gazing down at the superb vista he said, "It reminds me of Durban Race Course". After that, and until we eventually got bored with it, whenever we came across something really spectacular, such as the Teatro San Carlo, the ruins of Pompeii or smouldering Versuvius, someone would say it reminded them of Durban Race Course.

As soon as the allied forces set foot on their shores the Italians laid down their arms and declared an armistice. Hitler, infuriated by this capitulation, rushed German troops down to occupy the land and continue the fight without them; and from then on, like an audience at one of their operas, they just sat back and watched as their country was torn asunder in long and bloody battles. It is true that the Neapolitans rose up and attacked their German occupiers, but only when they knew the allies were about to enter the city.

Naples had been heavily bombed, the port area was quite decimated and there were large craters all over the town; even after we had arrived German planes continued to bomb the city.

The people were in dire distress. The Germans had planted booby traps all over, causing injury to many civilians; they had no soap or water and most of them were starving. In the streets women were openly selling themselves to soldiers for tins of bully beef and spam. Gonorrhoea and syphilis were rife and, as the Germans before leaving had destroyed the city's water supply and other vital amenities, cholera, typhus, dysentery, diphtheria and hepatitis were equally rampant. I would fall foul of two of these, but more of that later.

We were housed in the ENSA hostel located in part of a large ornate baroque building in the centre of the city and run by two very capable ladies. The first was Mrs. Vernon who, with her husband, had translated plays from the French for the London stage. I would meet her again in the early 1950s and discover that she was the aunt of the brilliant young Sandy Wilson of 'The Boy Friend' fame.

The second lady (if the word 'lady' can possibly be used to describe her) was the famous novelist, Niaomi Jacobs who dressed like a man, had her hair cut like a man, walked and talked like a man and even smoked her cigars like one (she was the real old fashioned stereotype of a butch lesbian). We were all rather intimidated by her until we discovered how kind and helpful she could be.

We had the luxury of performing in the beautiful Beliti Theatre, and the extra luxury of having the theatre's resident pit orchestra play a rousing overture before we began and *entr'acte* music during the interval. It made us feel very important and grand.

But by far the most exciting thing about being in Naples at that time was that the San Carlo Opera was allowed to reopen and give afternoon performances, and one on Sunday mornings especially for the armed forces. Thus, in one of the most beautiful opera houses in the world, I was able to experience exquisite singing in lavish productions of 'Madame Butterfly', 'Tosca', 'The Barber Of Seville', 'La Traviata' and 'Rigoletto'. It was my first exposure to opera on the grand scale and I was simply knocked out by it. The contrast of the squalor in the streets outside and the sumptuousness on the stage (God knows how they managed to achieve it) was almost unbelievable.

We now toured some of the towns in the Bay of Naples renowned for their legendry beauty. We started off in Amalfi where we set up our mobile stage on the beach and gave a couple of well received performances. We stayed in what had once been an ancient monastery built into the side of the mountain; it was turned into a hotel before the war, and they were proud to tell us that Greta Garbo and Leopold Stokowsky had stayed there.

Maurice and I shared a room that would once have been a monk's cell; its small window looked out onto a terrace of lemon trees full of ripe fruit; we hurried out and picked as many as we could carry and Maurice made us all delicious lemonade.

We then played Sorrento and again stayed at what before the war would have been a luxurious hotel. It was situated near the end of a steep cliff overlooking the sea and had an old fashioned iron lift (rusty and out of order) to take its guests to the tiny beach way down below. While on holiday in Ravello a few years ago I revisited the hotel and found it had returned to its pre war elegance, and the lift was once more working.

Next we toured Castelmare, then Herculanium and Salerno (where the 8th Army had made a spectacular landing on September the 9th), and then it was *arrivaderci* to the Bay of Naples and a long drive across Italy to the eastern port of Bari. As we drove through little mountain villages children came running after our trucks with outstretched hands crying, *"Pani! Pani!"* We had a large supply of army biscuits among our emergency rations and we proceeded to throw these to the children; like screeching seagulls they pursued us, snatching, scrabbling and squabbling over the biscuits. It was so pathetic seeing their hungry little faces that by the time we got to our destination our entire emergency rations had gone.

While playing in Bari we were able to replenish them, but when we reached Foggia they had all gone again. I suppose we could have been disciplined for it, but we didn't care, we felt those desperate children needed emergency rations far more than we ever would.

Foggia was a rather ugly industrial town that had had its share of battering. The front exterior of the theatre were we were to play had been slightly damaged by a bomb, but the rest of it was in good nick, and here, because of a nightly curfew, we gave afternoon performances for a couple of weeks to packed, enthusiastic audiences. Again we were housed in an ENSA hostel, and also staying there were some British actors who were touring in a light comedy entitled, 'Lover's Leap.' There was a brilliant actress in the company called Barbara Leake with whom I became friendly. (We would work together one day at the New Lindsey Theatre in Notting Hill Gate, and I would see her give some remarkable character performances in the West End; one I particularly remember was her 'Correspondent' in Somerset Maugham's, 'Home And Beauty,' starring Brenda Bruce at Wyndhams Theatre).

After our fortnight's run in Foggia we had a couple of days free and I spent both afternoons going to see, 'Lover's Leap' which had followed us into the theatre. How I envied those actors. I had been with The Troopadours now for almost two years and 'Speeding Along' was ever so slightly beginning to pall. I longed to act again in a straight play, and as I sat there I began fantasising that one of the actors would become ill, or get run over, or something, and being the only other actor in the hostel who had done straight plays, they would ask me to take over; the South African Army would be magnanimous and release me; and when the tour was over and the company returned to England they would take me with them, and then my exciting life on the British stage would begin! As I am sure you have realized nothing remotely like this happened.

At the second performance of, 'Lover's Leap' I found myself sitting next to a young American soldier, and before the play started we got into conversation. He loved the theatre and had been to many plays. Just before leaving America he had seen a strange new play by William Saroyan called, 'The Beautiful People.' I had never heard of William Saroyan but from what he told me about the play my appetite was whetted, and as soon as I could I began to read his work. On arrival in England in February 1946 one of the first plays I would see was Saroyan's 'The Time Of Your Life' at the Lyric Theatre, Hammersmith. It was a wonderful production by Peter Glenville and had a superb cast of twenty nine players including: Walter Crisham, Irene Worth, Margaret Johnston, Frederick Valk, Eileen Herlie, Miriam Karlin and Prudence Hyman.

I very nearly didn't get to see the play. When I arrived at the Lyric for the Saturday night performance I was told that my ticket had been for the matinee that day, then to my horror I discovered that the house was full and it was the last night of the run. I must have looked terribly distraught because they very kindly allowed me to stand at the back of the stalls. It was a glorious evening and I felt sure that my young American soldier friend in Foggia would have thought so too. I wonder whatever became of him? He was really quite good looking... there I go meandering again.

Walking down the street in Foggia one morning I noticed a small group of people gathered silently outside a barber's shop that had had its windows blown in. I went across, curious as to what they were staring at, and peering into the gloom saw the body of a man dangling on the end of a rope. It was a most chilling experience. I wondered if because his shop had been destroyed he had lost hope and taken his own life, or whether he had been too friendly with the Germans and the Partisans had assassinated him; this sort of thing was happening all the time we were told.

And it was in Foggia that we added a new number to the show: 'Lili Marlene' was constantly being played on the radio and soldiers were whistling it in the streets so we decided to do a production number using the song. It started with the band playing the tune softly while I recited the lyric; then Muff came on and sang the second refrain; Joyce and Pieter then danced a short ballet in which Lili Marlene and a soldier meet underneath the lamplight, make love and then sadly part; the music then grew marshal and loud and we all sang a rousing final refrain. It always went down well, and though I think we made a good job of it, its real success, I am sure, was its topicality.

We now moved north west to Campobasso, situated in the lower Abruzzi, and there, while playing in a charming little theatre on the side of a hill, I began to feel a bit seedy, then bilious, then extreme nausea, and finally I turned a vibrant shade of yellow all over. I had contracted yellow jaundice, which is very infectious, and was taken to an army hospital just up the hill from the theatre and put in a ward which, to my surprise, was chock-a-block with vibrant yellow soldiers: it was an epidemic! Jaundice is a very depressing illness and as I lay there day after day in that heavy yellow atmosphere I felt that life had lost all meaning for me. Then one morning I felt a little chirpier, I noticed the sun was shining, everyone was a little less yellow and I began to wonder if life perhaps did have some meaning, after all; and then the beautiful day arrived when I was no longer infectious and my yellowness had completely gone – and by then so had The Troopadours.

When I was fit enough to walk about but had not yet been discharged from the hospital I was allowed to go down the hill to the theatre where Geraldo and his Orchestra were now playing. They put on a terrific show and his singers were great; one I particularly admired was Dorothy Carliss who had a warm honey like voice; she sang ballads with great feeling, and also did a highly spirited rendition of 'Ragtime Cowboy Joe', which I would do as a duet with Olga Lowe in another show later.

By the time I rejoined The Troopadours they had moved north east to Vasto. On the parallel map of Italy we were now well to the north of Rome, and yet it would take another five months before the allies entered the city. Much of the fighting took place in the Abruzzi mountains; we could sometimes hear the gun fire in the distance and now and then a German plane would fly over; on a couple of occasions we had to get up in the middle of the night, put on our tin helmets and go down to an underground shelter, where, to while away the tedium, we would vie as to who could wear their helmet at the most fetching angle. Beautiful Joyce usually won.

I really should not have returned to the show as soon as I did; the yellow jaundice had left me feeling terribly weak; but I didn't want anyone to think I was malingering, and as Frank Daly was keen for me to return I returned. I found it a great strain though, especially the energetic dancing involved in our 'South American' first act finale which ended with a frenetic Conga. On a couple of nights I almost fell over.

In Vasto we stayed in a palace. The Troopadours men slept in the palace ballroom; it was vast and the walls, high ceiling and tall double doors were decorated with frescos and ornate gold mouldings. With its many chandeliers, gilt chairs, flowers and flunkies it must have looked magnificent, but now it was completely empty except for our few camp beds, kit bags and Maurice's paraphernalia which included a wind up gramophone, several albums of records (mostly of Bing Crosby and The Andrews Sisters), a primus stove, kettle, coffee pot, saucepan and a few other of life's little luxuries. As at one time or another we all benefited from these, we were more than happy to help him lug them around the place.

It was an extremely hard winter, and at night, with icy draughts blowing through the ballroom and no heating whatsoever, it felt like camping in the open without a tent! We actually took our baths in the open, in large wooden vats in the palace courtyard – although I can't recall any of the girls doing so.

Also stationed at the palace were two charming young English officers with whom some of us became quite friendly. They were very knowledgeable about the London stage and knew several well known actors. I was fascinated to hear about the two Hermiones (Baddeley and Gingold) and the wonderfully wicked sketches they did in their revues. (I would get to know these ladies quite well, and actually write material for both of them, but at that time they were just magical names to me.)

One day our officer friends invited us to join them for a black market plate of spaghetti after the show. Our acceptance was instant and unanimous; for months we had been living on nothing but bully beef (in its many manifestations) and the odd tin of Spam scrounged from the Americans (who seemed to have no lack of culinary variety). Actually I am sure we were better off with our bully beef than we would have been with a continuous diet of Spam – that grey sweaty pork substance would surely have got us down.

That night after the show we climbed four flights of unlit stairs to a shabby little flat where, in the family's cramped living room, we were each given a single plate of spaghetti accompanied by a dollop of delicious tomato sauce and a small sprinkling of grated cheese. I thought it was the most delicious meal I had ever eaten, and as I lifted the final strand on my fork, knowing there could be no second helping, I almost cried; I could have gone on eating it all night.

When people talk about the most memorable meal of their lives and names like

'La Tour D'Agent' and 'Grand Vefour' come up I always think of a shabby little flat in Vasto and a single plate of spaghetti. To this day (much to the irritation of my gourmet friends) Spaghetti Napoletana has remained my favourite dish.

We spent Christmas in Vasto, and on Christmas morning the girls visited a large casualty hospital and went around the wards talking to wounded soldiers; the visit was greatly appreciated and when they returned we could see how moved they had been by the experience.

And it was in Vasto (as stated in an early chapter) that Field Marshal Montgommery personally gave us permission to wear the Eighth Army flash on our sleeves. The news of this was not as joyfully received at DHQ as we had expected, and on returning to Pretoria we were made to remove them. It was explained to us that it was a British Army insignia and we were not in the British Army. We saw the reasoning of it but as we sat there unpicking the stitches we felt their action was rather petty and not untinged with envy.

On the afternoon of December the 30th Montgommery borrowed our stage and our microphone to give his farewell speech to the Eighth Army. He was returning to England to help plan the Normandy landings (but, of course, we didn't know that then). The theatre was packed to bursting point with officers and men, and there were crowds standing outside. We were kindly allowed to watch from the wings. It was a brilliant speech superbly delivered and everyone was deeply moved by it: he had been their leader in the long and victorious desert campaign and now he was leaving them. It was a sad occasion.

Over fifty years later I saw a television documentary on Montgommery that had film footage of his Vasto speech and felt great nostalgia to see him standing at OUR microphone, in front of OUR slightly creased silver tabs, and knowing that I was standing only a few feet away, just nineteen years old.

We gave one more performance then packed the trucks and early the next morning drove to Atessa, a tiny town in the Abruzzi mountains just seven miles behind the front line. Being high up we could now hear the gun fire more clearly. That day, New Years Eve, we gave two performances in a perfect little jewel of a theatre perched above the town. The auditorium was horseshoe shaped and had three levels of boxes stretching all the way around. It was like a miniature opera house and quite exquisite. Its only flaw, apart from there being no heating, was that a German shell had left a hole in the roof just above the stage and as we performed snow gently fell on us; it was a pretty effect but rather hard on the girls with their bare shoulders and skimpy dresses; but being the hardened pros they had now become they soldiered on without complaint.

They were housed down in the valley in a farm house where some South African Engineers were billeted; there was not enough room for us all so the men slept in the theatre. Maurice and I made ourselves as comfortable as possible in a box on the second level with lots of blankets and taking turns with his hot water bottle. In the morning we found the door of the box wouldn't open; snow had fallen heavily during the night and had blown in through a broken window in the passage right opposite our box and piled up against the door; and there we were trapped until a ladder could be found so we could climb down into the stalls.

Because of large snow drifts the girls could not get up to the theatre and that day's performance had to be cancelled. We were virtually snowed in; fortunately we had not been too profligate with our emergency rations of late so there was something for us to eat; and thanks to Maurice's primus stove regular cups of tea were had by all. To keep ourselves warm we put a large piece of corrugated tin on the stage and built a fire on it; we burned anything that would provide heat: coat hangers, music stands, chairs and tables; and while we spent New Years Day huddled together around a fire the girls were having an adventure: an officer in the South African Engineers had driven them to the Sangro and Aventino Rivers and two and a half miles past the front line to wish the 13th Field Corps a happy new year. When they told us about it the next day, rather smugly we thought, we were all very envious. On January the 2nd we woke to find the sun shining brightly, the girls were able to get up to the theatre and in the warm sunshine we threw snow balls at each other and made a snowman: for some of us it was our first experience of snow.

We did one more show and then returned to Foggia where we rested at the ENSA hostel for a few days; then it was back to Naples and another week at the Beliti Theatre where again the resident theatre orchestra played an overture. As we were about to commence the performance on the 24th (says Muff), the overture was just finishing and we were getting into place for the opening number, smoke flooded the stage. At first we thought the theatre was on fire, but then we were told that a German air raid was imminent and a smoke screen had been thrown over the city. When the curtain rose all we could see was a hazy glow where the footlights normally shone; worse still, the audience could see nothing at all, and with the smoke deadening the sound (the way pea-souper fogs once did in London) little could be heard above the coughing that came from both sides of the footlights. We were told to carry on with the show, and the audience to remain in their seats until the air raid was over. It was the most bizarre performance we ever gave, and the only nice thing about the evening was that no bomb fell on us.

And then I started to feel seedy again. At first I thought it was something to do with the yellow jaundice and my still being weak, but then it got worse: I began to get a terribly sore throat and a temperature, and then on the sunny morning of Februrary the 2nd (thanks, Muff) while visiting the ruins of Pompeii I suddenly felt desperately ill and returned to the truck to wait for the others. Back in the ENSA hostel I went straight to bed and a doctor was summoned. This time it was diphtheria and I was rushed to an army hospital and put in the large and very full Diphtheria Ward. If anyone ever tells you, as they did me, that you can't catch diphtheria twice don't you believe them: I had it the first time when I was five years old and almost died of it. It is a most unpleasant, lengthy and deadly boring illness, and second time round it is doubly deadly boring. Large, blunt-needled, hypodermics full of serum are painfully injected into one's rump at regular intervals; then one has to lie flat on one's back for six weeks; sitting up or any other violent action, because of the strength of the medica-tion, can seriously affect the heart. Eventually one is allowed one pillow, then two, then slowly one starts to exercise muscles that have not been used for weeks. Lying still, and even unable to read, all one can do is listen to the radio that is constantly on: 'ITMA', 'Hi Gang', the Billy Cotton Band Show'… and on the American Forces Radio, 'The Jack Benny Show', 'Burns and Allen', 'Charlie McCarthy (a ventriloquist's dummy that would inspire a British dummy called Archie Andrews to follow in its footsteps and have a radio show of its own), and songs from the American hit parade: one I instantly fell in love with was, 'People Will Say We're In Love' from a new show that had just opened on Broadway called, 'Oklahoma!'

By now The Troopadours were 'Speeding Along' in Bari and I was feeling very alone, so I was most grateful when Mrs. Vernon and Niaomi Jacobs (separately) came to visit me with fruit and chocolates. It was not part of their duty to do so, they did it purely out of the kindness of their hearts and I appreciated it very much.

The Anzio Landing took place on January 22nd 1944. The Germans were taken by surprise and there was practically no resistance to begin with; they had sent their troops south expecting the landing to take place there; however, they soon returned and the battle for Anzio dragged on for four months. Near the end of February the British sustained a heavy slew of casualties and beds were urgently needed for the wounded. Our ward was instantly cleared and got ready for their arrival. Ambulances took us on stretchers to an airfield and there in small planes we were stacked on racks, one above the other, several to a plane and flown to the lower slopes of Mount Vesuvius where a village school had been converted to a convalescent hospital. I was given a bed beside a large window through which I could see Vesuvius smouldering in the distance. It had a big stone window sill about three feet wide, and spring having come so early that year – the days were quite warm – I would lever myself up onto the sill (I was unable to walk) and sit there soaking in the sunshine. Each day before lunch we were given a bottle of Guinness to help build up our strength, and the highlight of my day was sitting on the window sill in the sun sipping my Guinness while reading the short stories of Somerset Maugham.

On March 19th I suddenly heard a mighty rumble, looked out of the window and saw Vesuvius erupt; it was the most awesome sight: molten lava spurting straight up into the air, and it continued like that throughout the night. I am surprised that none of us seemed threatened by it at the time. We thought, I suppose, that it was a regular occurrence: the volcano woke up, showed off a little and then went back to sleep. There had been nine eruptions in the last century alone. What we didn't know was that this one was the most violent since the destruction of Pompeii and Herculaneum; and also what we didn't know was that on the other side of the mountain lava was trickling down towards villages on the upper slopes.

The next day the sky went black as ash gathered in a vast cloud above us; suddenly the cloud burst and it rained mud the colour of Fullers Earth; I saw an old woman walking down the road, and a man with a horse and cart turn grey before my eyes; everything turned grey. When the mud dried it became a light grey ash and lay several inches deep: there was not a speck of colour to be seen. I was reminded of this sight when I saw Antonioni's film, 'The Red Desert' in which he painted an entire street and everything in it one colour.

The eruption continued at full force for over five days, and when it had subsided most of the town of San Sebastiano had been swept away. We only heard about it the next day, and as wise old sayings go there is a lot to be said for, 'Where ignorance is bliss...'

For the final stage of my recovery I was sent to a large hospital in Bari where I was taught how to walk again. After weeks in bed the muscles atrophy and it takes a long time and special exercises to get them back into full use. To begin with, just like a baby, you take a couple of steps towards someone who is ready to catch you should you fall; each day more steps are taken, and then finally that wonderful feeling when you can walk around the room all on your own. When I was surer on my feet I was taught how to make a bed with hospital corners, and from then on my job every morning was to go around the wards with another new walker and do just that.

I still had one big worry though, my left eye had developed a terrible squint; the doctors gave me eye exercises to do and said they thought the condition would probably correct itself. I sincerely hoped they were right. The chance of a producer looking for a young juvenile actor with an enormous squint was highly unlikely; and I dreaded to think what the reaction would be at the Taverne Francaise, and especially from Bill, when I swanned in with a twinkle in one eye and a squint in the other.

I did my eye exercises regularly each day, sometimes I did them while I was making beds; I am not sure that some of the patients didn't think I was winking at them. As the doctors predicted the eye righted itself – and not a moment too soon, for I was told I could be discharged and return to my unit: The Troopadours had long since flown back to Cairo and I was to join them there.

On my last night in Bari I went to the Opera House to see Cyril Richard and Madge Elliot in their His Majesty's Theatre production of 'The Merry Widow.' It was a gorgeous show and on the plane the next morning I couldn't get the Lehar tunes out of my head.

If asked what my overriding memory of Bari would be I would have to say, "Rice pudding." Every single meal at the hospital was concluded with a disgusting lumpy rice concoction that they had the nerve to call rice pudding; no matter how much jam one added to it it still remained disgusting; I felt sick just looking at it, and it has put me off rice served as a pudding for the rest of my life; friends say, "Ah, but you haven't tasted MY rice pudding, it's made with cream, etc."; well, I have gone so far once or twice as to try their rice puddings, but no, the memory of Bari overrides it all, and superbly made as it may be, not another spoonful will ever cross my lips.

The plane landed in Malta to refuel then flew across the Mediterranean to Tripoli, turned left and headed straight for Cairo. The turbulence caused by the heat of the desert sand was quite frightening; we rose and fell, bumped and shuddered, and a couple of times I wondered if the poor old Dakota was actually going to make it.

We reached Cairo in the late afternoon and I went straight to the unit office to report to Dennis Mitchell and collect my mysterious belated Christmas present from Bill. I was informed that The Troopadours were once more touring the camps in the Suez zone and would be away for several more days; and I was instructed to catch the early evening shuttle-bus to Helwan and there to remain resting until their return. I didn't tell Dennis Mitchell but I had plans of my own for the evening and forgetting about shuttle-buses I booked myself into Springbok House.

I had no idea how to contact Bill or even where he was, I just hoped, with luck, that he might turn up at the Taverne Francaise; and as strange coincidence would have it I bumped into him turning a corner in quite another part of town. He was no longer the Bill that I remembered; he seemed to have coarsened and there was something a little shifty about his eyes. He said he was pleased to see me and we went to the Taverne for a reunion drink; then on to another bar where he had arranged to meet some new acquaintances of his who I did not take to one little bit. There were three of them: Egyptian, fleshy and flashy with a lot of gold accessories, with one this went as far as a front tooth. I couldn't help feeling there was something rather dodgy about them; and suddenly there sprang to my mind an incident from the previous summer when two members of the Entertainment Unit (no one from The Troopadours I hasten to add) were apprehended stealing tyres and other motor equipment from the MT stores at Helwan to sell on the Cairo black market. Come to think of it, wasn't Bill's job something to do with MT stores? Oh, dear; I put the idea right out of my head.

We spent the night at a small hotel where he seemed to be a regular guest: it was not the same as that unforgettable night of July 15th 1943, but then, I suppose, it was silly of me to imagine it could be. In the morning I took the train to Helwan to establish my residency there for Dennis Mitchell's benefit, but returned to Cairo the following afternoon, and it was then that Bill did an Axel von Strahl on me… no, let me get this in the right order: it would be some months later on my return to Pretoria that Axel would do a Bill on me.

A wealthy Greek who owned one of the biggest open air nightclubs in Cairo invited Bill to his apartment for a meal and asked me to come along too. As Bill had suddenly to see someone somewhere about something he told me to go on ahead and he would follow and, of course, he never did. I suppose I should have guessed what might happen, perhaps I even had a slight inkling of it, but I thought it unlikely and anyway I wasn't a child, I would be able to handle it. I was not able to handle it: before we were anywhere near dessert I was being chased around the dining room table. Although my leg muscles were not yet back to their full strength I was still more agile than my lumbering, overweight pursuer and I managed to make it to the front door before he did. I had left my cap and a Penguin copy of 'The 6,000 Beards of Athos' in the hall but I considered that a small sacrifice compared to the alternative.

Exit Bill! I never wanted to see him again, and apart from a few glimpses of him in bars talking to shady looking characters I never did.

When I returned to Cairo the following year with a new show he was no longer on the scene. No one knew where or when he had gone. I couldn't help wondering if perhaps he was languishing in some military penitentiary having been caught flogging US Army jeeps to his black market buddies. I would never know what became of him; I didn't really care but I was still curious.

As they say, 'Idle hands play the devil's xylophone'…or words to that effect, and while I was waiting for the company to return from Suez I had a brief fling with a passionate Greek called George. I did not take it at all seriously and when it began to get heavy I broke it off. He turned violent and swore on his mother's eyes that he would scar my face with a razor. He never did, and whenever I saw a blind woman in Cairo after that I would wonder if she might be George's mother.

The Troopadours returned and we had a happy reunion; then one day Dennis Mitchell came out to Helwan with the exciting news that we had been invited to appear for a week at the Esbekeer Theatre in Cairo. It was managed by ENSA and only the most prestigious productions were ever asked to perform there. We felt both thrilled and honoured. The theatre was open to the general public and Cairo audiences were known to be quite sophisticated so we looked forward to it enormously. Many distinguished people were invited to the first night including the British Ambassador and his wife, Lord and Lady Killearn, to whom we were introduced on the stage after the show. It was a highly successful week and a wonderful climax to our stay in Egypt. And during that week something else happened that would change my life forever.

Across the street from Springbok House was a small bar mostly frequented by South African soldiers staying at the hostel, and there an hour or two before the show I would go with the others or on my own to have an ice cold lager; just one, I was very strict about that. I had learnt my lesson the hard way. It was in that very bar the year before that Bill and I met for a drink before I had to go off and do a show at a nearby camp. He was there first and when I arrived I found several glasses of beer already lined up for me. I stupidly drank them all and thought I was quite all right. It was only when I was on the stage and heard myself slurring words that I knew I was drunk and started to panic. It was a terrifying experience and I swore never to drink before a show again, except for one small beer and at least an hour before the performance.

On the evening of April 22nd to be precise (and I can be precise because the 23rd is St George's Day and I remember very well what happened on that day) I crossed over from Springbok House for my single ice cold pre theatre lager and got into conversation with a couple of British officers who were standing at the bar: one was an army major and the other a RAF flight lieutenant. They had been drawn to the bar by the length (or lack of it) of the South African soldiers' shorts. The South African Army wore their shorts far shorter than any other army, revealing a lot of sun tanned leg and even a bit of muscular thigh, which to gentlemen of a certain kind is like honey to a bee; and not to mix metaphors these two were definitely bees. Busy bees. I knew I was not their type, they fancied the big brawny Afrikaaner, but their conversation was droll and they were fun to be with. When the flight lieutenant asked me if I was in Cairo on leave I explained, with the least conceit possible, that I was an actor and was performing nightly in a revue called, 'Speeding Along' at the Esbekeer Theatre. The major, whose name was Mathew, and seemed to know something about revue, asked me what sort of material we had in the show, and when I mentioned a Herbert Farjeon sketch that I was doing he turned to his friend and exclaimed, "That was in Denis' show, 'Spread It Abroad' at the Saville." I had no idea who Denis was but I knew all about, 'Spread It Abroad'.

In 1936 when I was twelve years old my friend Doreen Norrish, who thought she was going to be an actress when she grew up, went with her mother to England to visit relations and while in London was taken to see, 'Spread It Abroad' which she absolutely adored, and on returning to Cape Town would often show me the programme and describe in detail each item. The hit number of the show, of which by now she knew all the lyrics, was, 'These Foolish Things' sung and danced by Dorothy Dickson and Walter Crisham. The star comedians were Nelson Keys and Ivy St Hellier; also in the company in her first West End revue was Hermione Gingold; and among the gentlemen of the chorus were the debonair young Michael Wilding and a sturdy lad called Cyril Butcher who became Beverley Nichols' lifetime companion. I know this is straying from the plot again but I think the account of how they met is worth the telling.

Beverley, already a rich and famous novelist, thought it was time he had someone to share his glamorous life with him and set about it in the following unique way: he went to see all the musical comedies and revues in London and methodically went down the programmes with a pen ticking off all possible candidates from the male chorus; after much consideration and the lengthy process of elimination he eventually decided upon Cyril and invited him to supper at the Savoy. Cyril accepted, supped, went back for a digestif and stayed for the rest of his life. I hope you agree that little diversion was worth the journey.

The 'Denis' Mathew had referred to was an old friend of his who had produced, 'Spread It Abroad' and other shows in London (today the producer is called the director and what used to be called the management is now called the producer. This swapping about of names came to the British theatre from America just after the war). Denis Freeman was his name; he was an Englishman serving in the French Army as a lieutenant and was stationed in Cairo where he worked at the French Legation on diplomatic business. Mathew was having dinner with him that very night and he said he would tell him I was doing the Farjeon sketch; then suddenly he had an idea and asked me if I would like to meet him. I said I would, very much.

"Tell you what," he said, "after your show tonight why don't you go to the Taverne Francaise, and when we've finished dinner I'll get him to come along and we can all have a drink together. How's that?" "Perfect," I said, drained my glass, bid them a fond farewell and crossed back to Springbok House where I knew Maurice and Konni were waiting for me to go with them to the theatre.

I was looking forward to this meeting. I had never met a real West End producer before, and one who had originally produced a sketch I was now doing made it of particular interest to me. I wondered if he might give me a new slant on interpretation, although after playing it one way for two and a quarter years that might be a little unsettling. The bar was fairly crowded when I arrived; I looked around carefully but Mathew was nowhere to be seen. Perhaps they weren't coming; he might have forgotten all about it.

While ordering a lager a handsome young New Zealander at the bar smiled at me. I smiled back. We spoke. It was his last night of leave in Cairo and he was staying in a small hotel nearby. This information I thought smacked slightly of an invitation. I explained that I was supposed to be meeting some friends for a drink and it would be very nice if he would stay and meet them. My reply I hoped smacked slightly of an acceptance. I was hedging my bets: it would be too frustrating if they didn't turn up and I watched this gorgeous creature going off with someone else.

Just then they arrived, Mathew and two other men: a civilian called Peter who worked at the British Council and a tall slim man in French lieutenant's uniform with that attractive French military cap called a Kepi, and wearing a glass in his right eye. The monocle had no frame or cord, it was simply a circular piece of glass wedged between his cheek and eyebrow that seemed to be part of his face; it never needed adjusting and he was known to sleep with it there. His features were strong and angular and he reminded me rather of Conrad Veidt, and I wondered if the German star had somehow influenced his choice of a monocle instead of glasses, which he would otherwise have had to wear. This was Denis Freeman and he had charm by the bucket full. He was most attentive to the New Zealander and myself; asked me questions about the revue and seemed genuinely interested in my answers. He said he would try to come and see the show. The strength of his personality quite overawed me.

When the bar started to fill up, as it always did at that time of night, and the noise made it difficult to hold a proper conversation, Denis suggested that we carry on the party at his place.

"A friend of mine who works at the British Military Hospital managed to get his hands on some purified alcohol," he told us, "and I have made the most delicious vodka with it. Don't worry, it's very smooth, you won't go blind."

We all agreed we would like to try his vodka and, cramming ourselves into a single gharry, crossed to Gazera and then over the English Bridge to the Midan Abdel Monim where he had a flat that was the entire ground floor of a double story building (the French teacher and his wife who lived above were so seldom seen that it was suspected they might be vampires). The flat was surrounded by a spacious garden full of sweet smelling flowers that Denis lovingly tended himself with the assistance his cook/gardener, Mahommed, who slept in a hut at the end of the garden. The flat itself was large and exotically furnished with Persian carpets, wall hangings and tiles, Coptic icons, ancient Egyptian and Greek object d'art and piles of books everywhere; it had a wonderful atmosphere to it. Denis also pointed out that it had three entrances, one at the front, one at the back and one at the side, also five windows and several large bushes so it was perfectly appointed should there ever be a raid.

When he was in the mood (and many shared my opinion) he could be the best company imaginable, and that night with the vodka flowing he was in the mood. His stories of the goings on in Cairo society (mostly irreverent) had us enthralled, and his theatrical anecdotes (for my benefit, I felt) were both fresh and excruciatingly funny. I thought he was the most fascinating man I had ever met. All too soon the party was over and it was time for us to leave. As we walked to the garden gate, out of ear shot of the others, he said to me that the next day (it was that already) was his birthday, which he shared with St George, and he was having a few friends to lunch; Mathew was coming and he would be delighted if I did too. I accepted with alacrity, and in the gharry crossing back over the bridges I arranged to meet Mathew in the morning and help him choose a birthday present (it was actually Denis's fortieth birthday but he led us to believe it was his thirty seventh). When we had said our goodnights to Mathew and Peter, the New Zealander and I went back to his hotel and spent a most agreeable few hours together, although once or twice my mind did stray to that intriguing French lieutenant with the glass in his eye. In the morning before we parted he told me that Denis' vodka party and my coming back with him had made it the best night of his leave. He was so young and sexy and good looking it seemed a shame that we probably would never meet again.

In the Khan EL Khali Bazaars Mathew bought Denis a heavy Turkish silver plate with a laced edge; it was very beautiful and even after the haggling cost him a lot. I was very nervous about this luncheon party; I had no idea what to expect; what sort of people would be there and how well would a South African staff sergeant fit in. As it turned out I need not have worried, everyone was charming and polite; although I did notice one or two of them eyed me with curiosity.

There were eight to lunch, Denis, Mathew, me and five others:

Joyce Murchie, who was known to everyone as Joy because that is what she gave them (after the war she and I would have many joyous travel adventures together). She had just returned from Yuglosavia where she had been with Randolph Churchill and Evelyn Wagh to liase with the Partisans (Randolph thought that Evelyn being a catholic might help). She wasn't sure how successful the meetings had been but she thought they might possibly have cleaned Bosnia out of Slivovitz.

Bobby Pratt-Barlow was a short, dapper man with white hair and a neat little moustache, and today he was wearing his usual ensemble of baby blue shirt, shorts and calf length socks, a thick intricately worked Turkish gold belt and several gold chains around his neck. He was extremely wealthy and owned a palace in Taomina that bestowed upon its owner the title of Duke. Bobby was biding his time at Shepheards Hotel until the authorities allowed him to return to Sicily. Before the war visitors to the palace were sometimes surprised to find that the entire palace staff, the head butler included, were all under the age of thirteen. At the first signs of puberty they were relieved of their duties and retired on a small pension. The locals thought this slightly eccentric but as their teenage children were all bringing home pensions it was not to be sniffed at.

Eileen Stead had a highly powered secretarial job at British GHQ.

Kosta was a distinguished Greek artist and photographer.

Miss. Elizabeth Glynne, who was working at the British Library in Cairo, would one day become the famous cookery writer, Mrs. Elizabeth David; and after the war Denis and I would share a house in Chelsea with her for a couple of years.

The conversation was sophisticated and erudite and I could not contribute to it much, but I was happy to just sit and listen to them. It was a completely new world to me. Now and then Denis or Mathew would draw me into the conversation asking questions about the theatre in South Africa and where I had most enjoyed touring. It was kind of them but I didn't need their help. I was perfectly at ease, and intrigued by the sort of conversation I had only experienced before in Evelyn Wagh novels. The meal was excellent as was all Mahommed's cooking, which he chose to do on a small cylinder gas stove outside the kitchen door.

After lunch, when everyone was leaving for their afternoon siesta, Denis asked me if I would care to stay on for a bit; I said I would, and before any of the others had got to bed, we had. My initial attraction to him had not been particularly sexual (unlike the others where physicality had been the predominant factor); I had simply been dazzled by his immense personality; but now, lying together in complete silence and perfect harmony I felt very differently about him: we seemed to gel, to merge, everything felt so right, we were one, this was it!... and I thought to myself, "Oh, dear, here I go again."

I had to leave soon for the theatre, and I spent that night (for a change) at Springbok House. The next evening, as he said he would, Denis came to the show and took me home afterwards and there began between us a deep indelible relationship that, apart from some forced separations, would last for eighteen and a half years.

I suppose you are wondering, as I did, what an Englishman was doing in the

French Army. Well, he had always been a Francophile, his mother was partly French, and when war broke out he was living in Paris in a flat on the Isle de Cité working on a film script he had been commissioned to write (an adaptation from a French operette) for Deanna Durbin. The project was instantly abandoned. When most of the English living in Paris returned home he stayed and drove ambulances conveying the wounded to casualty hospitals. For his bravery at this time, of which he never spoke, he was later awarded the highly prized *Croix de Guerre*.

When France fell he was one of the last people to leave Bordeaux and wrote a book about his escape entitled, 'The Road To Bordeaux' which became a best seller and went into several editions. A section of the book entitled, 'Panic' describes how civilians fleeing from the advancing Germans so choked up the roads that the French army was immobilised.

With his permission the British Government printed this section in a pamphlet as a warning in case of invasion; and he was asked to go to strategic towns and lecture the citizens on the danger of panic behaviour.

As he had suffered from weakness of the lungs since childhood (an inherent family complaint) the British Army would probably not have accepted him, but he didn't even apply; he had become so emotionally involved with France that he offered his services to General de Gaulle's Free French Army and was immediately sent to the Middle East.

In the desert he was attached for a while to the French Foreign Legion, which he found most interesting. With the identical food rations that the British Army had their cooks produced the most imaginative and delicious meals. That's the French for you! There was one incident though that deeply upset him and he could never forget: as an officer he had to sit in on the trial of two Legionnaires who were lovers and had been charged with committing the act of buggery. They were found guilty and executed. He never got over the horror of this.

He then fell ill with Amoebic Dysentery and almost died; they got him to a hospital in Alexandria just in time. When he had more or less recovered the canny French realised how useful he would be as a go-between between them, and the British and gave him a diplomatic post of sorts at the French Legation in Cairo. It was a fascinating job: the British and French didn't trust each other an inch and were convinced that the other was up to something devious. He was always having to tell the French that what they thought had been a terrible slight was due purely to British muddle mindedness and insensitivity; and then he would have to tell his friends at the British Embassy that contrary to the rumour they had just heard the French were not planning to sabotage some scheme of theirs. Denis enjoyed the job, but with such silliness going on on both sides it could be a little frustrating.

When Laurence Olivier's film of 'Henry V' was given a gala showing in Cairo the entire French contingent walked out in a huff and accused the British of making a film, the entire purpose of which was to vilify the French Nation. He had his time cut out trying to persuade them this was not so. Despite all his hard work the French continued to be suspicious and touchy and the British thoughtless and arrogant.

But in this way he got to meet some of the most important people in Cairo: diplomatic, military and civilian, and with all that charm of his he soon became part of the social scene.

And it was a glimpse of this world that I had during my last days in Cairo. The Troopadours tour was over and we were waiting to be flown back to Pretoria. Most men in public life who have a lover half their age, be they male or female, are inclined to keep them hidden away, but not so, Denis. Whenever possible and within reason he took me everywhere and introduced me to everyone: the British set, so many of whom seemed to have titles, French writers and artists, Greek poets and communists and some of the grandest and wealthiest Egyptians and Copts. We spent our nights in restaurants, nightclubs and, of course, the theatre where we saw the Crakow Ballet, the Greek National Theatre's presentation of 'Twelfth Night' and an American amateur production of 'The Skin Of Our Teeth'.

One night we dined at the Auberge des Pigeon, a lovely garden restaurant beside the Nile with lantern hung trees. The speciality was roast pigeon, and as I lifted my knife and fork to start a wild cat sprang down from the branch above me, grabbed the pigeon in its teeth and vanished into the bushes. The waiter just shrugged his shoulders and went off to fetch me another.

And then there was the night I was taken to see the Sphinx by the light of the full moon. We didn't approach it the usual way, along the Giza Road where you find it tucked off down to the left and dwarfed by the mighty pyramids; we drove across the desert through the Valley of the Dead and came to it straight on. To begin with it was a small white stone in the distance, and then it grew bigger and bigger and finally we were standing in front of it with the full moon shining down on its face. It was a most romantic experience. I have only seen the Taj Mahal by daylight but even by moonlight I am sure it can't hold a candle to the Sphinx.

But now it was time for The Troopadours to 'Speed Along' home. I felt utterly distraught at having to leave Denis and the exciting new world he had shown me. He was equally miserable at our parting but seemed more optimistic about the future than I was. He said he was sure we would be together again soon, but I was not; after my two illnesses, not to mention my slightly raffish behaviour (which must have got back to the Major's ears) I couldn't see them sending me back to Cairo in a hurry. Perhaps after the war...whenever that might be...we might possibly meet again...maybe in London...when I managed to get there...if he still remembered me. The prospect was far from rosy, and when I left the flat for the last time I felt quite desolate. The dream, I thought, was over...

But I wasn't counting on Denis' determination, his tenacity, his charm, his guile, his immense powers of persuasion. How could I possibly know he was going to work a miracle!

Pretoria was even more deadly dead than I remembered. I walked around like a zombie, an extremely snobbish zombie looking down my nose at everything and everybody. I must have been the most obnoxious company. I missed Denis desperately, and where was Joy Murchie's infectious laugh? The Patrick Kinross and Eddie Gaythorne Hardy wit? The Butrus Ghali charm? Cinders was definitely back in Baron Hardup's kitchen and nobody was going to come knocking on the door with a glass slipper in his hand. This time I would be stuck there until the war was over.

We were given twenty eight days leave and those of us from Cape Town – Maurice, Konni, Tessie and Gordon Mulholland, who had also just returned from the Middle East – travelled down on the train together. It was winter in the Cape, cold, wet and windy and there seemed nothing else to do but go to the cinema. One morning when we had all met for coffee in town someone, borrowing a line from Mickey Rooney, said, "Let's do a show." And we all cried, "Right here!" Armed with an article that had appeared the night before in the Cape Argus, giving a glowing account of our travels in North Africa and Italy with the Eighth Army, we approached the Managing Director of African Consolidated Theatres, Jack Stodel (for whom Maurice and I had both worked in our youth) with the idea of us doing a half hour or so stage show before the main picture at one of their cinemas. Influenced by the article, I am sure, for it would make good publicity, he offered us a week's engagement at the Alhambra, Cape Town's largest and most prestigious theatre; and then a week of one night stands at suburban cinemas.

Maurice was to do his, 'El Bacio', Konni his musical instrument impersonations, Gordon his Tommy Trinder style patter act and Tessie (now Lynette once more) would sing a popular modern ballad. I was the only one sticking out my neck by doing something completely new and perhaps rather risky. Before leaving Cairo, Denis had given me a monologue he had written especially for me. It was the sort of character the young John Mills would have played: a young cockney soldier on leave goes to visit his friend, Len's mother with a message from her son. It starts with him knocking on the front door (imaginary, straight out front) and it being opened by Len's (imaginary) mother. He gives her Len's message and tells her of some of the jokey things they have been up to, only to discover that Len has been killed in action. She had received his personal effects that morning. It ends with her giving him Len's wristwatch. It sounds terribly sentimental, and it was, but wartime audiences lapped up that sort of sentiment. My main worry was that it might be too intimate for as big a theatre as the Alhambra was; but at nineteen one doesn't have the sort of nerves that affect actors later on so I was ready to give it a go.

Maurice's mother, Nancy (the Welsh Witch), liked to let us poorer folk know that the Millards had money, she also liked us to know how very generous they were being with it. My mother was fond of Nancy and, being the kind soul she was, didn't notice that she was being patronised, but I did. Ted Millard was a placid man who sought a quiet life; he saw to the business side of things and let his extrovert wife get on with the rest.

On the Monday afternoon of our opening night my mother and I had been invited to the Millards' new home in Rondebosh, which had a large garden and tennis court they wanted us to admire. Nancy was going to give us high tea before we set off for the theatre; and after the show (we weren't staying for the film) they were taking us across the street to the Del Monico for a light supper; and then with two or three of Maurice's sister's young friends she had invited along (one a pretty but boring girl who kept throwing herself at me) we might even go dancing at the Bohemian Club. "And I don't want any arguments," she told us, "the evening is on us."

Ted and Nancy had not always been rich, they had started married life very humbly as dairy farmers at Tredegar in Wales. Nancy had always suffered from a weak chest and after a serious bout of TB they thought it advisable to move to a warmer climate. They chose South Africa and arrived in Cape Town with little money and no idea what they would do for a living. Their first home was a humble flat in Sea Point, and one evening there Nancy had a craving for fish and chips. They went out to look for some and discovered that there was none to be had anywhere. This gave them an idea and they opened their first shop right there in Sea Point. It flourished. They opened another and another and soon they had a whole chain of fish and chip shops. They also made potato crisps which they packaged in grease proof paper bags (unknown in Cape Town until then) and sold to shops, cafes and bars; and as the years went by they became quite rich. They had four children: a girl, a boy, a girl and a boy. Maurice was the second born and the only one with any artistic leanings, but he leant enough to make up for the whole family.

After the high tea, when we were being taken to admire the tennis court one more time, a servant came running out to tell me I was wanted on the telephone. Everyone was very curious (remember this was Cape Town, not Cairo). I hurried to the phone.

"Hello," I said, "who is it?"

"Me, of course," said Denis. "I am at the Mount Nelson Hotel, how soon can you get here?"

I was flabbergasted. After spluttering for a while I managed to say how glad I was to hear him. "What are you doing here?" I asked.

"I've come to see you, of course," he said. "How soon can you get here?"

I then had to explain to him that I was just about to leave for the theatre to do a show, and actually to perform the monologue he had written for me.

"All right," he said, "I'll come to the show. I'll see you backstage afterwards."

When I put the phone down I was in a state of complete numbness. How was I going to explain him away? How was I going to spend the night with him instead of at home? I don't know if I looked as traumatised as I felt when I told them, with as much nonchalance as possible, that a friend of mine from Cairo, who I told to look me up if he ever found himself in this neck of the woods, was here, and was coming to the theatre tonight.

"How nice," said Nancy. "Your young friend must join us for supper at the Del Monico, and if he likes dancing he could come on with us to the Bohemian Club, there are enough girls to go round. Do you know where he's staying?"

"The Mount Nelson," I said without thinking.

"Ah," she said, and as soon as I heard her say, "Ah," I remembered she had a rather waspish male friend who worked as a receptionist at the Mount Nelson Hotel and he was always regaling her with lurid stories about the goings on of the hotel guests. I saw Maurice pale before my eyes. Later when we were alone he said, "You can't go to the Mount Nelson."

"What can I do?" I said. "He's flown all the way from Cairo to see me."

"I don't know what you can do, but you can't possibly stay at the Mount Nelson. Wilfred works there."

I didn't realise it then but Maurice was thinking of his own skin, not mine. For the next couple of hours before the performance I remained in a cataclysmic trance. I had no idea what was going to happen. It was out of my control. I couldn't possibly not stay with Denis, on the other hand there would be all hell to pay if I did. I took the cowardly way out and decided not to think about it, just leave it all to fate.

Right up until the moment I walked on to the stage I felt nothing, then suddenly knowing Denis was out front I began to feel nervous. What if he thought I was dreadful? What if it altered his feelings about me? What if he didn't come around and instead took the first plane back to Egypt? That would solve the problem, of course, but at what a price.

The audience remained perfectly still throughout the monologue and then applauded warmly. I could tell they had been stirred by it. We finished the show, all of us standing in line in uniform, singing a chorus of, 'Lili Marlene' and we were very well received.

Back in the dressing room that we all shared I sat at my place waiting in a sort of doom-laden daze. Maurice had moved his stuff far away from me, he wasn't going to get involved in whatever it was that was going to happen, he knew the Welsh Witch too well for that. First to arrive were the Millard party with my mother, and they were very complimentary to everyone. Then there was a knock on the door. "Come in," shouted Konni. The door opened and there stood Denis looking very handsome and grand in his French officer's uniform with *kepi* and the glass in his eye. Everyone gawped as he, in Gallic fashion, kissed me on both cheeks and then did the same to Maurice and Konni who he had met in Cairo. I introduced him to everyone I knew.

Then Nancy spoke up, "Some of us are going over to the Del Monico to have something to eat and we would be more than happy if you would join us." He looked at me, saw my helpless expression and accepted her kind invitation.

Nancy sat at one end of the table, Ted at the other, Denis was on her left, I beside him and my mother beside me. Maurice and the girls sat on the other side. Denis and I had not yet spoken to one another, except for him to congratulate me on my performance which I felt was not thoroughly deserved; I knew I could do it much better. Nancy dominated the conversation, and most of it was trying to find out as much about Denis as she could. He knew what she was up to; he wasn't in the diplomatic business for nothing, and proceeded to charm and flatter her outrageously. On discovering that their dairy farm had been on the Tredegar estate he lost no time in telling them that Lord Tredegar was one of his closest friends (a lie. He did know him but rather disliked him) and how much he admired his magnificent home with all those remarkable pictures and statues. This put Nancy at a thorough disadvantage, they had obviously never been on social terms with his lordship, they were simply tenants on his estate. She quickly changed the subject.

"I can see the young folk are itching to dance," she said at the end of a very tricky meal, "so we're all off to the Bohemian Club, and even us old folk might care to shuffle about a bit."

Another desperate look from Denis. Another desperate look from me. We were trapped.

"We've got the van outside so we can pile you all in," she said, and this she endeavoured to do, but there were too many of us, so Maurice very wisely offered to walk with a couple of the girls – the nightclub was only a few streets away. Sitting there all cramped together in the back of a greasy van smelling of fried fish I dared not look Denis in the eye. At the club as soon as we were settled at a table the pretty but boring girl I mentioned earlier asked me if I would like to dance with her. As we fox trotted around I saw Nancy suggest to Denis that they might join us. Passing on the floor our eyes met and I could see that he had had quite enough of the Bohemian Club and the whole Millard charade. When the music stopped and we all returned to our table, as I went to sit down he took me firmly by the arm and announced that we had to go, there was something we must discuss, he thanked the Millards for supper, bid my mother a gracious 'goodnight' and swept me off, out of the club, onto the street, into a cab and up to his room at the Mount Nelson Hotel. He had done a very foolish thing. As I have said before, this was Cape Town not Cairo, and he didn't know how dangerous the Welsh Witch could be. Also I was wondering who would see my mother home, and what might she be thinking?

When it was time for us to talk he told me how he had managed to get down to see me. A kind friend of his, Lord Jeffrey Amherst, who was a wing commander in Cairo, touched by our sad plight, arranged for him to be flown down to South Africa so that he could give a series of lectures and broadcasts on the Free French Army, the brave Resistance Movement, the treachery of the Vichy Government and the great suffering of the ordinary French people. Such propaganda was badly needed at a time when France was being held in low esteem. He would be based in Johannesburg, knowing I was nearby; but on discovering that I was on leave in Cape Town he flew straight down and arranged to give his first broadcast there on the Tuesday evening.

By the time we awoke the next morning the Welsh Witch had already worked her wicked spell. The telephone rang; it was the hotel manager; he asked Denis to come and see him in his office. He told him that not only was it not allowed for two people to share a single room, it was also particularly objectionable for an officer to do so with a soldier from the ranks, and he asked him to leave. Denis didn't bother to tell me what his reply was but knowing his way with words I can't believe the manager didn't come off the worst. He moved to a small hotel in Wale Street where this time he took a double room, but already it was too late. Nancy had upset my mother dreadfully with her homophobic ranting; and had got my two brothers, (both much older than me) into a frenzied state where they were threatening if I stayed with him again to do something really drastic. I was frightened that in their rage they might attack him physically or even involve the police. Sitting in the hotel room watching the rain run down the windowpane we had to accept that the present situation was impossible.

Denis decided to leave that night after his broadcast, and asked me to join him in Johannesbug as soon as my theatre engagement was over. I said I would. Before we parted we went to tea at the Mount Nelson Hotel. An old and dear friend of his, Lady something or other, whose family owned the Union Castle Line, which in turn owned the Mount Nelson, happened to be staying there at the time and on hearing of Denis' humiliating treatment sought to make amends by inviting us to take tea with her that afternoon in the hotel lounge. We sat at the most prominent table in the room and she went out of her way to let the staff, including the manager and, I am sure, the Welsh Witch's accomplice, see how highly she regarded her guests. It was a very gracious thing to do and it slightly took the nasty taste out of our mouths.

I knew that going to Johannesburg for the rest of my leave would cause trouble. My mother wanted me to spend my birthday at home with family and friends (not that the Millards would have turned up) but I had promised to spend it with Denis, and it was with him that I wanted to be.

I slipped quietly out of Cape Town, relieved to get away from that small narrow-minded suburban atmosphere. I was sad that I had caused my mother so much distress, but it couldn't be avoided; and it made me angry that I was supposed to feel I was doing something wrong; I was also upset that my oldest friend, Maurice, when told to have nothing more to do with me meekly acquiesced and outside of the dressing room avoided me completely. Of course he knew his mother far better than I did, but it was not the way to treat a friend and this act of disloyalty would rebound on him later on. I have never felt guilty about being gay. I had been perfectly at ease with my sexuality since at the age of twelve I fell head over heels in love with a wee chap in 'Wee Chaps' called Vernon. Ah, pretty freckle-nosed little Vernon, where are you now? If still alive, possibly sitting in a sunny retirement home with your dear old missus, surrounded by photographs of all your wonderful grandchildren, and never giving a single thought to the first passionate lover in your life, ME! Ah, the treachery of the heart.

On the cold, crisp, sunny morning of my twentieth birthday the train pulled into Johannesburg station. It was still very early but I saw no point in hanging about and went straight to the Carlton Hotel and asked for Denis.

"Would you be Mr. Phillips?" asked the receptionist.

I said I would, and indeed I was.

"In that case," he suggested, "you might care to inspect your suite first."

I think I managed to disguise my surprise as I told him it being so early that might be the better idea. I had only ever stayed on the third and fourth floors before where the cheap rooms were, but this morning the lift went gliding up to the sixth where the rich folk dwell. I was shown into a small but tastefully furnished suite that consisted of a sitting room, bedroom and bathroom; and surprise, surprise, Denis was only two doors away. I said it would do very nicely, thank you, and gave the porter a sixth floor tip. After I had bathed, shaved and dressed (practically all I would ever do there apart from rumpling the sheets to satisfy the maids) I knocked on Denis' door.

It was like being back in Cairo, the horrors of Cape Town were fast fading away. For my birthday he had bought me a beautiful gold wristwatch with tiny rubies marking each five minutes on the face; and for my other wrist a heavy gold chain identity bracelet. I was beginning to feel 'kept' and I rather enjoyed the feeling. For the evening he had a tremendous surprise in store. It was the opening night at the Standard Theatre of the Gwen Ffrancgon-Davies Marda Vanne production of 'Blythe Spirit' which Noel Coward had to give them special permission to do, as it was still running successfully in the West End. Denis knew Gwen and Marda, having worked with them in his early days as a drama producer at the BBC; and since his arrival in Johannesburg had also met the two men in the play, Rolf Lefebvre and Sigfried Mynhardt. After the performance there was to be a party on the stage to which we had been invited. He had taken a box with four seats in it and had asked the French Military Attaché' and his wife to join us. We met first for drinks in Denis' suite; the Standard Theatre was just around the corner from the Carlton. I don't know what they made of my presence but they behaved in a perfectly charming manner and drank a birthday toast to me in champagne.

We got to the theatre about five minutes before the curtain rose, and as we entered our box I could sense that the entire stalls audience were watching us: two tall distinguished French officers, one with a monocle, a beautiful woman in elegant evening dress and a khaki clad staff sergeant. When we were seated I glanced down at the stalls and saw the Major and Mrs. Bourke, Frank Rogaly and a couple of other officers from the unit staring up at me with a look of incredulity on their faces. Were they cats they would have dropped dead right then and there. As my eyes met theirs I gave each a little nod of acknowledgement. This was the best birthday present I had ever had and the play hadn't even started; but even when it had I noticed Frank glance up a couple of times with puzzled eyes.

What should have been a first class production was let down by the extremely coarse and unsubtle acting of Marda Vanne in the role of Madame Arcati; as soon as she came on it became clear that light comedy was not her forte.

Margaret Inglis made a charming, languid and petulant Elvera, and Rolf Lefebvre was first rate as Charles (this part less expertly played can seem over wordy). But undoubtedly the star of the evening was Gwen who, as Ruth, gave a dazzling display of technical brilliance, managing to get a laugh on almost all her lines, and also on some that were not her own. It was ever such a slightly naughty performance but one that was magical to watch. I could always tell when Elvera had a good line coming up because Ruth would start plumping the cushions on the sofa or toying with a chiffon handkerchief or flicking something from her eyelashes. No cheeky young actress was going to steal the play from her – as if that was possible!

At the party afterwards Denis introduced us to Gwen and Marda. I had met them briefly once before when the Major had brought them to the unit to watch The Troopadours in rehearsal, but I felt that this was not the ideal moment to try jogging their memories. I also met Rolf Lefebvre and Sigried Mynhardt, both of whom I took to instantly and we soon became good friends; many happy hours would I spend in the delightful flat they shared with Rolf's sister, Peggy, and a very funny lady called Joss Pollard who Siggy eventually married.

Then I introduced Denis to the Major and Frank and he went to work on them straight away, congratulating them on their magnificent achievement and saying how highly their shows were thought of in the Middle East. He charmed them, he flattered them and in a matter of days they were his bosom friends. The Major entertained him at his home in Pretoria and Frank dined with us often at the Carlton, he was also given an open invitation to stay if he ever came to Egypt.

Denis had already done the groundwork on Dennis Mitchell in Cairo, entertaining him lavishly and allowing him and his girlfriend to stay at his flat at weekends. Well, tit does call for tat and the Major was soon being urged to send another show up as soon as possible as the troops were becoming restless and entertainment was badly needed. Denis would reiterate this very subtly at his meetings with Frank and the Major, and thus the seeds were sown: before very long it was announced that a new show for the Middle East would be got together immediately. Denis offered to help compile the material and was even persuaded by Frank to produce some of the items. I don't think my name ever arose but it was taken for granted by everyone in the unit that I would be in the show, and I was.

You mustn't think he spent all his time at the Entertainment Unit, far from it. He kept to a very busy schedule of lecturing at army camps during the day and at town halls in the evening. He also made some very moving broadcasts about the plight of the French people and their need to be freed from the tyranny of Nazi occupation. As you can imagine, Johannesburg society was intrigued by this strange charismatic foreigner in their midst and wasted no time in inviting him to their homes, and whether they liked it or not I often accompanied him. This was another whole new set of people I was being acquainted with; I had met some of them peripherally at parties but now I was seeing them on their own home ground and I found it fascinating. Some were delightful, some ghastly, but all had one thing in common that kept them apart from the rest of us and that was money.

From what you have read you are probably under the impression that Denis was moneyed too. This was not so. He had no private income, every penny he had was earned by the sweat of his high and extremely talented brow; and the lavish entertaining he was now doing at the Carlton was making quite an inroad on his resources. What started off as one or two friends dropping in around six o'clock for a drink ended up as a regular soiree where you could meet some of the most interesting people in Johannesburg. A few, thinking he was loaded, presumed rather on his generosity. One of those was the young Prince Alexander of Yugoslavia, who was educated in England and was serving in South Africa with the RAF. Arriving back at the hotel from a lecture, hot and tired after a long car journey, Denis found several people sitting in his suite with glasses in their hands and the Prince playing host to them. He was furious and when they were alone he admonished him for his unprincely behaviour, saying he wouldn't dream of acting in that louche manner in London so why was he doing it here? Alexander apologised profusely and seemed genuinely contrite. Denis forgave him and after a short cooling off period he was back in the fold.

The one person who was never invited to the Carlton was Maurice. Denis had not forgiven him for the cowardly way he had abandoned me in Cape Town. Poor old Maurice, it must have been quite a shock for him returning to the unit to find everyone from the Major down treating Denis like the new Messiah. We would become good friends again, but it would take some time.

All too soon the Carlton days of wine and roses were over. Denis had to return to Egypt and I to the barracks in Pretoria. At the end of my leave I had exchanged my sixth floor suite for a humble fourth floor room that I never used but it meant I could come and go at the hotel without any questions being asked. Now I would go back to my old routine of just hiring a room at weekends when I required one. The morning we said goodbye and Denis left the hotel for the airport we were both quite wretched, but I did not feel the hopelessness I had when leaving the flat in Cairo; for if things went according to plan I would be back there soon, and, anyway, we felt the bond between us was now strong enough to stand any separation; and even though some jealous friends would do their best to break it up the bond remained rock solid. The Major and Frank went to the airport to see him off, and as a farewell present the Major gave him a large, beautiful, soft tiger cat rug that would grace the bed for many a year.

The new show was called, 'The Boomerangs', which I thought made us sound like an Aboriginal troupe. I suppose the name could signify 'a return', but I doubt if that was on Frank's mind when the title struck him. The officer of the company was John Tore, and his wife, Olga Lowe, was the leading lady. There were no leading ladies in the unit shows but Olga still managed to be one. Konni was also in the show.

When I first met John Tore I was in my early teens and he a few years older. We were appearing together in a concert party on the open-air roof of the Sea Point Pavilion. He wore a black magician's cloak and did wonderful conjuring tricks; I did wonderful film star impersonations (people then knew who Eric Blore and Edna May Oliver were). He would sometimes come to our house in Clifton for Sunday lunch (on Sundays we kept open house) and play the piano. He played by ear and was always composing tunes. His idol was Ivor Novello, who he slightly resembled, and his melodies were in a similar romantic style.

His name then was Arthur Nimr and he was Lebanese, his parents having emigrated to Rhodesia when he was a small boy. Arthur didn't like the name of Arthur and changed it to John, and when he took up Spanish dancing he changed Nimr to Toré.

It was only after The Boomerangs had arrived in Egypt that he discovered his uncle (his father's brother) was the eminent Dr. Feres Nimr Pasha, founder of the Cairo newspaper 'el Makkatam', and that his cousin, Amy, was Lady Smart, wife of Sir Walter Smart, the oriental councillor at the British Embassy. Lady Smart was known to be one of the biggest social snobs in Cairo, so you can imagine her reaction when her newly acquired first cousin and his wife turned out to be common theatricals from the colonies.

John, who always had his eye on the main chance, saw the possible advantage of having a wealthy Pasha for an uncle and tried to ingratiate himself into the old man's affections. But cousin Amy was having none of it: an invitation to tea at the Maadi mansion, followed by a stroll around the garden with her father and her, was as close as the relationship was allowed to get. Denis would derive much pleasure at smart Embassy parties watching the smart Lady Smart smart each time he mentioned her clever singing and dancing cousins in The Boomerangs.

John and Olga were demobilised in London as I was. With Maurice they arrived shortly after me, and together we all scanned the pages of 'The Stage' in search of theatrical employment. Olga did a bit of cabaret work, but there was very little of it in those austere post war days when the theatre began at six o'clock and the last bus was at ten. Apart from a few sleazy nightclubs in Soho and one or two Mayfair restaurants, late night in London was about as lively as late night in Pretoria.

John got some small parts in films playing Italian waiters and Maltese gangsters, and he appeared in two prestigious West End plays: 'Daphne Laureola' at the

Wyndhams Theatre starring Edith Evans and a new young Australian actor called Peter Finch; and 'The White Devil' at the Duchess Theatre starring Robert Helpman and the radiant young Claire Bloom. He also had several weeks work as a dancer on the film, 'The Red Shoes'. But his heart was not in performing, he wanted to write a romantic Ivor Novello style musical, so he and Olga sat down in their little flat above the Turkish Baths in Jermyn Street and did just that. Olga provided most of the words for which she selflessly took no credit.

Influenced by the folksy success of 'Oklahoma!' they set their musical in South Africa during the gold rush days and called it 'Golden City.' They had surprisingly little trouble in getting it accepted, and it was given a lavish production at the Adelphi Theatre, directed by Michael Benthall and choreographed by Robert Helpman, with magnificent sets and costumes by Audrey Cruddas.

Unfortunately London audiences at that time only wanted to see the big vibrant Broadway hits (the vitality of these American imports was something quite new and refreshing to them) and charming though 'Golden City' was it just couldn't compete with, 'Oklahoma!', 'Annie Get Your Gun' and 'Brigadoon', and sadly the show only had a modest run.

Undaunted, John was in the middle of writing another musical when out of the blue and without any warning whatsoever he dropped dead of a heart attack. Olga would soldier on as a performer, and at the age of eighty was acting with the Peter Hall Company at the Old Vic Theatre in a season of classical plays.

Even before joining the Entertainment Unit Olga had had quite a colourful stage career. At the age of twelve in a Johannesburg pantomime she had done a tap dance duet with Sid James who was several years her senior. Their costumes had been put together in rather a hurry and as they were doing the 'Buck and Wing' step a vital seam in Sid's trousers came unstitched, and, as he was wearing no underpants, his entire set of genitalia popped out and jiggled about in time to the music. When Olga saw what it was that the audience were laughing at she burst into tears and fled the stage. She would always feel guilty at such unprofessional behaviour, but to give the poor girl her due she was only twelve and had never seen anything quite like it before.

Strangely enough, it was on a stage with Sid again that she would have an even greater traumatic experience – and this one would not have a funny side to it. Always in need of money for his gambling activities, Sid agreed to go on a lengthy tour of the British provinces in a rickety old farce, and he offered Olga a part in it. For her role she had to pad out her breasts to a ridiculous size so that on her entrance Sid would do a double take and stand gawping at them with his mouth open. This was the first big laugh of the evening (and the humour continued in this vein throughout).

One night during the tour, after the boobs had come on followed by Olga and Sid had done his double take and gawp, he fell backwards onto the sofa and remained there motionless. This got a tremendous laugh from the audience, and the longer he remained motionless the louder the laughter grew.

"Stop playing silly buggers, Sid," hissed Olga out of the side of her mouth after some time had elapsed and he still had not said his first line. But he was not playing silly buggers, he had suffered a massive stroke and was lying in a coma. When she realised it was no joke Olga made her way down to the Prompt Corner adlibbing as she went – just saying any silly thing that came into her head. "Bring down the curtain," she then called into the wings; but the man whose duty it was to do so had only just taken the curtain up and knowing it would be twenty minutes before he was required to bring it down again was sitting in the pub next door enjoying a pint. Still adlibbing madly Olga now crossed to the OP and again pleaded for help, but there was no one there either. The Stage Manager, who after seeing the curtain up had slipped off to his office for a couple of minutes, now returned and hearing Olga's wild babbling peered on to see what was happening. Grasping the situation he brought the curtain down himself. This was greeted with much laughter and applause by the audience. Seeing that Sid was unconscious he rushed out in front of the curtain and asked if there was a doctor in the house. This got the biggest laugh of all. There was a doctor in the house and after a while he sensed that this was not part of the play and hurried backstage. Sid died in the ambulance on the way to the hospital.

I don't think Sid liked me. When we occasionally met in London he was never very friendly. I always had the feeling he was a bit homophobic. He certainly didn't like Kenneth Williams: mind you, that was another cup of vinegar entirely. I can remember him being quite chummy with Frank Rogaly: Frank, though, held a position of power in the unit so he might have been just playing his cards carefully. If he had wanted to, I always thought Sid could have been a fine straight actor; he had done some good drama in Johannesburg before coming to London; and shortly after his arrival I saw him give a powerful performance in a Jean Paul Sartre play directed by Peter Brook. But he didn't want to be a great actor; there were only three things that he really cared about: gambling, booze and women, and he had his fair share of all of them. If he was happy with that, so be it, but I still think it was a sad waste of a talent.

Shortly after her first traumatic experience with Sid, Olga, accompanied by her mother set sail for England to further her dancing studies. She sadly grew too tall to be a dancer; however, with her lovely Nefertiti like features, beautiful black hair, slender figure and new long luscious legs she had no trouble getting work as a showgirl, and was very soon appearing in 'Midnight Follies' at the Dorchester Hotel in Park Lane.

This was followed by a spectacular revue at the Prince Edward Theatre. She once showed me a photograph of herself in one of the scenes from the show; in it she is walking down the long trunk of a giant bejewelled elephant, looking quite stunning in a headdress of ostrich feathers, lots of beads and very little else.

In 1939 the famous Follies Bergere Theatre in Paris decided to take one of its revues on a tour of the Americas, and came to London in search of beautiful showgirls: Olga was exactly what they were looking for.

The tour began in the United States where they successfully played several of the major cities. Olga particularly enjoyed going to Hollywood and seeing where her favourite film stars lived. They then headed south and were playing in Rio de Janeiro when war broke out in Europe. The show closed and everyone was sent home. Olga's parents, as Mr. and Mrs. van Geems were doing, insisted that their daughter return to South Africa and, like Joyce, Olga obeyed their wishes.

It was a great wrench to leave Rio where she was having the time of her life on the beach at Copacabana surrounded by handsome, young, adoring Brazilians. She had also made a couple of close female friends: one was a cabaret singer who performed bright Brazilian songs with tremendous brio; Olga, whose Portuguese was now fluent, learnt some of them, thinking they might come in useful one day.

That day came a lot sooner than she expected, for by the time she had returned home and joined the Entertainment Unit her cabaret singer friend had become the famous Hollywood film star, Carmen Miranda; and who knew better how to do an impression of her than Olga?

Over the years there would be countless crude imitations of the star by both men and women (Ken Geyer to name but one), all based on the camp caricature that Hollywood had made of her, piling bananas and pineapples on her head and giving her would-be-cute little ditties to sing in fractured English. Olga wouldn't do this. She sang the Brazilian songs the way Carmen had done them in Rio. The others got all the laughs but she gave us the true spirit of Carmen.

A few years after the war Carmen Miranda came to London to appear at the Palladium and they renewed their friendship. Olga was shocked at how thin and frail she had become. She didn't know it but Carmen had cancer and in a matter of months would be dead.

Olga worked with many famous people in her time. One of her favourites (both on and off) was Harpo Marx who twice nightly chased her around the stage with a pair of scissors, snipping away at her dress. The highlight of her career in musicals I would say, and I think she might agree, was singing the Gypsy Rose Lee send up, 'Zip' in the first London production of 'Pal Joey'.

The flight from Pretoria to Cairo by Dakota took two days with three stops for refuelling: Bulowayo, Entebbe on Lake Victoria (where we spent the night), and Khartoum in the Sudan, where the moment the plane door was opened hot air rushed in scorching our throats and lungs. We arrived at Heliopolis Airport late in the afternoon and were met by Dennis Mitchell who introduced us to the driver of our transport. He then drove off in his car and we followed. To everyone's surprise, and my particular delight, instead of going straight out to Helwan we drove into Cairo and stopped at the gate of number 16 Midan Abdel Monim where Denis was waiting for us with food and drink.

It was wonderful seeing him again and to be back in that garden I thought I had seen for the last time; but it pained me to think how short this visit must be. So it was to my further surprise and delight that when The Boomerangs departed for Helwan they left me behind. Some of the less sophisticated members of the company may have wondered what was happening, but I am sure they soon cottoned on.

I was given permission to stay in Cairo and drive to Helwan each day for rehearsals or whatever. I think it sometimes annoyed John that although he was the officer in charge I seemed to be way above his control. But I never flaunted my position; I was as reticent about it as I could possibly be.

In Helwan we did a full dress rehearsal for Dennis and Denis and it was decided that before we opened at the Globe Theatre in Alexandria a few rough edges needed to be smoothed away. Also, as this was one of the last shows to be coming up from Pretoria, we were to have some extra scenery and, at Denis' suggestion, a white false proscenium with an arched entrance on each side and a set of white tabs. This would give the show a bright, fresh, elegant look.

Neil Menzies who worked at the unit base in Helwan and was an artist of sorts was given the job of designing and constructing the new scenery. I disliked Neil intensely. He had pretended to be a friend but was anything but that: jealous of my close relationship with Denis, whose affection he secretly craved, he had done his cunning best to separate us and very nearly succeeded. This is how it happened:

I was in Cape Town on a final short leave before The Boomerangs headed north; and Neil, down on leave from Egypt, happened to be there at the same time; and we both knew an artist who lived in a beautiful old Cape Dutch house in Bree Street (alas, long since demolished and turned into an office block). The artist's name was Freida Locke and she was a fine lyrical painter; trained at the Slade, she mainly painted landscapes: her old Dutch buildings, harbour scenes and deserted fair grounds were extremely potent and evocative (one or two hang in the city's art gallery today). She was a most fascinating woman; somewhere in her forties and not conventionally beautiful, but vibrant and gypsy-like with large, dark eyes, a mane of black hair, tanned skin and lots of Arabic jewellery. She had the freest spirit of anyone I had ever met: she lived her life as she wanted to and didn't give a damn what people thought. For anyone drawn to the Arts, Bree Street was a sort of Mecca; the most interesting people gathered there; and though she was broke more often than not there always seemed to be a party going on.

When not painting she sometimes helped out as a puppeteer with the John Wright Puppet Theatre (woe betide anyone touching one of his precious wooden children). After the war John Wright would come to London and beget his famous and long lasting 'Little Angel Theatre' in Islington.

The respectable citizens of Cape Town thought Freida Locke was beyond the pale. "Indians and even blacks go to that house!" my brother told me with a look of horror on his face when he learnt I was spending most of my time there. I had to make it quite clear to my family that I was now an adult and would keep the sort of company that I, and not the suburban likes of Mrs. Millard, wished. I found Freida's wild bohemian spirit exciting and terribly seductive, and she must have seen something attractive in me because I shared her bed with her for several nights and she was a most enthusiastic lover.

She had a lodger staying in the house, a young man from Johannesburg who was in Cape Town studying ballet with the eminent teacher, Dulcie Howes; his name was John Cranko, and he would one day be an internationally famous choreographer. While Freida was away in Stellenbosch and Paarl for a couple of nights, pulling puppet strings, John and I somehow got together and pulled a few of our own. When she returned and found the bedroom arrangements had gone slightly askew all hell broke loose, and I made a hasty retreat to my loving family in Clifton. I felt guilty that I had caused a rift between John and Freida, but I needn't have worried, for they had made it up by the next day, and when I left Cape Town they came to the station together to see me off, each bearing a farewell gift. Freida's was an utterly useless but pretty little black and gold stud with a tiny pearl in the centre that I have fondly kept to this day. John was more practical, he gave me an ivory back-scratcher that performed its duty for many a year, and then somehow sadly got lost – as did our friendship.

Neil Menzies came to Freida's house a few times while I was there, then flew back to Cairo and gave Denis a fully detailed report on my wicked, wanton ways. Whereupon I received a letter, many paged and white hot with fury; shortly followed by a beautiful, desolate, heartbroken poem (that I still have) accusing me of betrayal, shallowness and not really caring for him at all. This was completely untrue, I loved him as much as ever and longed to be with him, but we were several thousand miles apart and I was young and healthy and only human and (forgive the repetition) I thought you could have your cake and eat it.

He swore he had been faithful to me since we met, which I thought was admirable and I loved him for it, but if there had been an unknown brief encounter or two during our long separation I would have quite understood. Well, from where I was standing I would have to, wouldn't I? Eventually, after many letters between us, I was forgiven my errant ways; although when we met again in Cairo I felt there was still a slight coolness towards me. However, we soon thawed it out. And Neil, thinking he had played the trump card and finding it was only the joker, was now right out of the game. His big mistake, as any old fool could have told him, was to underestimate the power of youth.

Now, I am not going to introduce you to all the members of the company as I did with The Troopadours – that would be too monotonous – but there are a couple I would like to mention. The first is Gloria Curich, a dumpy little lady who stood about four and a half feet high (almost a midget) and was quite a feisty little comedienne. Wearing acrobat's tights and singing Noel Coward's 'The Wife Of An Acrobat', she was both funny and touching. Gloria had an elder sister called Joan who was in another unit show. She was six foot tall and thin as a beanpole. Seeing the sisters standing side by side in uniform on the parade ground was a sight no one liked to miss.

Gloria came to England after the war but Olga was the only one of us to see her. She unfortunately chose to knock on John and Olga's door in Jermyn Street early and unannounced on the very day of the opening night of 'Golden City'. Olga, busy taking in good luck telegrams and flowers and having a thousand and one things to think about, rather brusquely sent her away. She contacted no one else and that was the last we heard of little Gloria.

The other member I would like to tell you about was a very weird lady indeed. Nell Wheeler was her name. She was in her thirties and not altogether unattractive, but very prim, spinsterish and remote; and I sometimes thought she might be a little mad. Not the qualities most suited to a romantic ballad singer, you might think. But to compensate for, and override such drawbacks, she had the most magnificent pure bell-like soprano voice. In the first half, wearing a beautiful decollete ball dress of silvery blue, she sang, 'Spring In My Heart', quite exquisitely; and in the second half she gave a very religioso rendition of, 'Ave Maria'. For this item Frank Rogaly had gone to town and not only dressed her as a nun, but given her a painted cut-out depicting the stained glass window of a church. All of this rather went to Nell's head and she started acting like a nun. In the back of the truck, on our way to do a show, we would watch her sitting in the corner, eyes closed, hands clasped, praying; and on the stage she had taken to finishing the song on her knees, crossing herself. Then one memorable night, way out in the desert, playing to a large audience of soldiers sitting under the stars she suddenly stopped singing, thrust her arms out towards them and cried, "Boys, I have a message for you from God: Bless you all!" upon which she sank to her knees and making copious signs of the cross began blessing them all. The tabs were hastily drawn on her, and, still mumbling and crossing, she was dragged from the stage, bundled into a car and driven away. What the boys made of their blessing from God we didn't wait to find out. That was Nell's last performance with The Boomerangs, and, like one or two unit members before her, we never saw hair nor hide nor heard of her ever again.

It was lovely being back at the Globe Theatre in Alexandria, and we were thrilled at the wonderful way the show was received. I was doing a monologue that Denis had written for me before I left Egypt the year before. It was called, 'Growing Up', and was the story of a young man's first love affair told in four telephone conversations. 1: tentative and shy. 2: soppy and sentimental. 3: suspicious and slightly sardonic. 4: the brush off, in which he pretends to have a wild party going on by clinking glasses, doing funny voices and other background noises. I knew it was not the ideal material for the sort of show we had, the humour was too gentle and the young man a bit too posh, but I insisted on doing it, and I can truthfully say that even with our toughest audiences I always managed to get away with it.

This time in Alexandria I did not stay at the Union Jack Club but in the sumptuous home of King Farouk's English dentist, where Denis joined me at the weekend. And while I was there I had a small gold filling removed from a tooth and replaced by one of natural colour for which the kind dentist didn't charge me a single Piastre – which is more than King Farouk could boast. Returning to Ismailia was another great pleasure. As with The Troopadours we spent much of the day swimming and boating on the beautiful salt lakes, and then in the evening we had our lovely new show to look forward to. We were having a wonderful time.

After touring a few more camps in the Canal Zone we returned to Cairo to play a season at the ENSA Garrison Theatre (also known as the Esbekeer). The distinguished British actor, Nigel Patrick was now the colonel in charge of ENSA in the Middle East, and he wore his rank with all the reticence of Hannibal crossing the Alps on an elephant. At our first meeting with him we were treated to a splendid display of arrogance and condescension. I knew what he was thinking: we were just a bunch of inferior colonial amateurs, a far cry from his world of the smart West End theatre; whereas, apart from the occasional visit of a stage luminary, our show was of a much higher standard than practically anything ENSA had to offer. Thanks to the Major's and Frank's insistence on excellence and good taste, plus Denis' knowledge of revue and directorial expertise we now had a really classy little show. Artistically The Troopadours was far superior with its fine classical music and ballet, but for witty material and stylish production The Boomerangs was tops.

The first night was a great success, much to the surprise and chagrin of the ENSA colonel I imagine. After the show we were invited to a party at the actor, Noel Howlett's flat, nearby (in London I would get to know Noel well and we would act together in a play. Also in it would be Barbara Leake, the clever actress I had met in Foggia). When we got up to the flat we found Noel on the landing trying frantically to open the front door. The key refused to turn in the lock. He tried several more times and then we all had a go, but with no success. By now the stairs below were filling up with guests arriving for the party and all wanting to know what the hold up was. In desperation Noel decided to break the glass panel in the door and try to open it from the inside. A couple of burly lads came to his assistance and smashed the glass for him: only to reveal an Egyptian family cowering in the hall with a look of terror on their faces. We were on the wrong floor.

My twenty-first birthday party in the garden of number 16 Midan Abdel Monim was a marvellous affair. Months later Cairo society was still talking about it. Not because it was my birthday (only a few knew that), nor that it was marvellous (it did go on till dawn), but because it was so unique: it was the first party since the war began where everyone wore mufti. As it was going to be a very mixed party of civilians and men and women from the various services, Denis saw the difficulties that might arise if uniform was worn. The British forces were particularly class bound. Officers and other ranks never mixed socially; to invite them together in uniform would not make for a comfortable evening. The South Africans, Australians, and New Zealanders were much more democratic; but even among officers there could be a certain amount of snobbery and rank rivalry; so Denis hit upon a ploy and with brilliant diplomacy he managed to pull it off. He first went to the British and told them that the other nationals had all agreed to mufti being worn. Thinking they were the odd man out, and with rules and regulations much relaxed since the end of the war, they too, though rather reluctantly, gave their consent. He then continued the ploy with the South Africans, and so on, until everyone had agreed. And that was the party they were still talking about, where Cairo's elete, the staffs of embassies, high ranking officers at GHQ and soldiers, sailors and airmen of all ranks and nationalities mingled in perfect harmony: brigadier and lance corporal, Greek princess and Bloemfontein contortionist rubbed shoulders that night as equals, and a great time was had by all.

We had a dance floor in the garden and two bands (one South African, one RAF) that played alternately through the night. The trees were strung with little coloured lights, and also hanging from their branches and on bushes were countless strings of jasmine blossom that scented the air with their sweet perfume. Rugs and cushions were scattered about the lawn where guests could recline with their drinks and gaze up at the stars. Denis made a vast amount of his famous bathtub vodka and there was not a drop left over. Mahommed, assisted by other cooks from the Midan, produced a magnificent array of exotic food. And Bobby Pratt-Barlow, also wanting to help, gave himself the task of finding six of the tiniest little ink black Nubian boys who he dressed in gold lame turbans and loincloths and painted their fingernails, toenails and nipples with gold paint. These adorable little creatures moved among the guests with trays of cigarettes. Apparently they were so enamoured with their gold paint that they refused to have it removed, and went on proudly showing it off until it sadly wore away.

Around four o'clock in the morning when the bands had stopped playing and the odd inebriated guest had tinkled away at the piano, someone from the British Embassy who wrote revue numbers entertained a small group of us with a few of his songs. One of them that was currently being performed in the revue, 'Sweet and Low' at the Ambassadors Theatre in London, had a lyric that began:

'Beg your parding, Mister Harding,
Is my kitting in your garding?'

I don't remember how it continued but I know we laughed a lot at it. Mind you, by then we had all had a fair amount of vodka and wine. By dawn most of the guests had gone, but when the sun rose there were still a few in the garden, curled up asleep on the rugs and cushions. After Mahommed had given them breakfast with a lot of strong black coffee they finally staggered off, shielding their eyes from the merciless Egyptian sunlight.

I have been to several twenty first birthday parties in my time, and some of them were quite posh affairs, but I can honestly say without bias of any sort, that for a magical night to remember none of them have come anywhere near to mine.

The summer of 1945 was the happiest summer that I could remember. It was wonderful being back in Egypt, and although we worked extremely hard the audiences enjoyed the show and we enjoyed doing it. What free time I had was spent with Denis, going to interesting places and meeting a lot of fascinating people; and then there were the nights we spent at home alone, or with one or two friends, and after dinner on the terrace in the warm night air, the sky ablaze with moon and stars, and with the soft sound of Arabic music coming from somewhere in the distance we would sit and talk; and sometimes we would bring out the old portable gramophone, wind it up and listen to Billie Holliday, Benny Goodman and Jean Sablon.

This was the time when everyone was discussing the future, where they would go and what they would do now that the war was over. I was in the process of trying to arrange that I could be demobilized in England and Denis was hoping to leave the French Army at more or less the same time so we could arrive in London together. For me it was the most exciting prospect. All my life I had dreamed of going to London and now it seemed as if it was actually going to happen. I had no knowledge whatsoever of British politics: I knew that Winston Churchill was the Prime Minister, and as he was the great hero of the war I imagined he would continue to be Prime Minister, but at the General Election of 1945 Labour had a landslide victory over the Conservatives and Clement Attlee took his place. This caused quite a stir among the British in Cairo. Denis, who had always leaned to the left, as many intellectuals did (though not as far as the Communist Party), was delighted with the result, but many conservative friends were horrified and dreaded the thought of returning to a socialist Britain. As far as I was concerned, as long as the theatres stayed open and flourished with exciting new plays, musicals and revues, all was fine by me.

One night near the end of the year Elizabeth David came to dinner and told us, rather glumly, that she was going to join her husband in India. In August of the previous year, on the rebound from a disastrous love affair, she had decided to renounce bohemia and embrace respectability and security by marrying Lieutenant-Colonel Anthony David of the Indian Army, whose two great passions, besides lovely ladies, were polo and horse racing, both of which the intellectually minded Elizabeth abhorred. He had recently been posted to New Delhi where he now wanted her to join him, and very reluctantly she had agreed to do so. She would later say that she cried from the moment she arrived in India till the moment she left. But more of Tony and Elizabeth later.

As the year drew on the troops began to get restless. The war had been over since August and there they still were, sitting in their desert camps with nothing to do, just waiting to go home. With each day their boredom and anger grew stronger so entertainment was of vital importance. There had already been some riots; in fact, the night before we played to South African troops at Helwan Camp they had burnt down the open-air cinema and stoned all the windows of the Egyptian shops in the camp (this really was cutting off their noses to spite their faces). We were naturally rather nervous as to how the show would be received, but to our surprise they were quite a receptive audience. Still, I breathed a great sigh of relief when I had finished my monologue, 'Growing Up', and nothing had been thrown at me.

The Boomerangs gave their final performance on January the 10th and then waited to be flown back to South Africa; all except John, Olga, myself and Maurice of The Sundowners who had to wait for transportation to England.

Denis had found a superb tailor in Cairo who made suits of a quality that could be worn in Saville Row without embarrassment. I had two suits made: one light grey flannel, the other dark blue serge, both double breasted. (Meeting Laurence Olivier on the set of 'Hamlet' at Denham Film Studios in 1947 he showed more interest in my grey flannel suit than he did in me. "That's a very smart suit," he said, "where did you get it?" When he learned that he would have to go all the way to Cairo his face fell and I was not offered the part of the Player Queen that I had gone to see him about. He said that (short as I was, 5ft 7ins standing upright, as I was then doing) I was too tall for the part. The actor playing the Player King was about my height so the Player Queen would need to be smaller. Well, that was the reason he gave, but I wondered if he wasn't just jealous and cross about the grey flannel suit). I had had my final fittings for the suits and was told by the tailor that they would be ready in a week or so, and then everything happened at once!

The eminent French novelist and critic, Andre Gide, who had written extensively about North Africa in the 1890s decided, now the French were able to travel abroad once more, to revisit Egypt and turned up in Cairo demanding VIP treatment. For one or two reasons, plus the fact that he had read most of the great man's works, Denis was given the job of looking after him during his stay. Although quite elderly (77) he was as feisty as ever and insisted on going everywhere and seeing everything, which included a journey up the Nile to Luxor, Aswan, Abu Simbel, Wadi Halfa and beyond. He told Denis, "The further south you go the darker and more beautiful they become." He was determined to see a ceremony that took place on an island in the Blue Nile where the boys danced. As foreigners were forbidden to witness the ceremony they took a felucca and sailed as close to the island as possible, Gide with a pair of binoculars clasped to his eyes. He saw the boys dance and was thrilled by the spectacle.

In the middle of all of this I was suddenly told, without any sort of warning, that I must catch the early morning train for Alexandria the next day and board a ship that would take me on the first part of my journey. I was in a panic. My departure had come far sooner than expected, and what with Denis tearing all over the desert with randy old Gide we had not discussed the possibility of this happening. Where was I to go in London? What was I to do? I rushed around to the French Legation, told them I was leaving in the morning and that it was imperative that I speak to Denis on the telephone that day. They treated me with great sympathy. Denis, they told me, was staying at the Cataract Hotel in Aswan where they would leave a message for him to ring the Legation at 6 o'clock that evening. I was there waiting when precisely on the dot (God bless the Egyptian Telephone Company) the phone rang and it was Denis. He told me to go to his mother's flat: number 5, Alexandra Court, Queens Gate, Kensington, she would be expecting me, and to remain there until he arrived, which he thought would not be very long now; and he said he would collect my suits from the tailor and bring them with him. There were too many people about to say anything personal so we just wished each other good luck. It was fortunate that this hadn't happened a day later as Gide and he would then have been on a felucca sailing up to Wadi Halfa.

At the train window watching Egypt slip by and disappear behind me I was close to tears. I was leaving the place where I had known the most happiness. I wondered if I would ever see Cairo again – I never would, not the Cairo I knew. I have visited the city a couple of times since and enjoyed my stay. There remains a lot to be seen: the Pyramids and Sphinx are still there; Cairo Museum is full of fabulous treasures, and the Khan el-Khalili bazaars are much as they were, but gone are all the exciting cafes, bars and nightclubs where I spent so many glorious hours. The handsome Midan Abdel Monim with its fashionable houses and spacious gardens is no more: in its place is an ugly mass of grey concrete dwellings. Shepheards Hotel (burnt down in 1952) is a multi-storey car park. Glamorous Groppi's Tea Room has become a shabby café with plastic tablecloths. The stately Pyramid Road to Giza with its fine mansions and smart nightclubs is now just a sprawling stretch of hideous built up concrete, right to the very edge of the Pyramids. And try as hard as I may, and I did try very hard, I was unable to locate, even approximately, where that magic cave, the Taverne Francaise once stood. I still possess a little green cardboard train ticket with the words, 'Cairo Alexandria' on it. It is in a drawer with some old papers and when I occasionally come across it I think of that sad morning when I said goodbye to my beloved Cairo.

In Alexandria harbour I boarded a rusty old tub of a ship called, 'Ville D'Oran'. With two thousand troops crammed on board it resembled nothing as much as a giant tin of khaki clad sardines. We each had a numbered hammock slung about a foot apart, so getting in or out when the adjacent hammocks were occupied required some acrobatic skill. There were two other South Africans on board, both much older and bigger than me, but because I held the highest rank as staff sergeant, the others being sergeant and corporal, I was put in charge of them. We all thought this was hilarious. They were both charming men which was lucky for me, for had they turned out to be bolshy or belligerent drunks I don't know what I would have done.

We remained in port for two nights, and then at 9.15 am on Saturday the 26th of January we sailed for France. Until then I had imagined that the Mediterranean was always azure blue and beautifully calm, but how wrong I was. The Bay of Biscay I am sure has nothing on the stormy seas we encountered. The ship rocked. The ship rolled.

Sometimes I thought it was going to turn right over. No one was allowed on deck for fear of being swept overboard by the large waves that washed over it. I doubt if any of the two thousand passengers were not sick. There were buckets of vomit everywhere and the stench was unbelievable. Meal times were the worst; no sooner had a mouthfull of food been swallowed than it made a spectacular reappearance. For anyone wanting to lose weight I can thoroughly recommend such a cruise. While we all lay groaning in our hammocks I noticed a large rat run across the beam in front of me and I wondered if perhaps it had decided to leave the ship, knowing something about it that we did not. The hellish voyage continued like this for three whole days, but if you told me I had got it wrong and it was actually three whole years I would be prepared to believe you.

At 7.30 am on a bitter cold Tuesday morning the smelly old tub limped into the French port of Toulon and nobody could get off it fast enough. We were taken in trucks to a transit camp outside the pretty little town of Hyeres. Braving the icy wind (it had recently been snowing) my two South African pals and I decided to explore the town and very soon found ourselves in a cosy little bar with a blazing log fire, and there we remained consuming a vast amount of Cognac to settle our stomachs, and then to warm us up, and then to have one or two for the road. The next day, Wednesday, we had free so we went to visit the charming villages of La Crau and Valette du Var, the former where we had coffee and croissants and the latter where we lunched on *Jambon du Pays, Tarte A' L'oignon*, cheese and wine.

At 10.30 that night, sardine like again, we were packed onto a troop train with hard wooden seats and no heating, and then in great discomfort journeyed for forty-one hours across France to Dieppe. When the train came to a halt, as it did every now and then, soldiers would leap off and relieve themselves beside the tracks. At one such stop on the following day my South African corporal jumped out and was gone for a long time. I was beginning to wonder what sort of trouble I would be in if I lost one of my charges, when, just as the train was about to start, he sprang on board with two long batons of French bread, some cheese and a couple of bottles of wine. I decided that the anxiety he had caused me had been well worth it. We passed Paris at 2 o'clock in the morning but saw nothing in the darkness, and at 3 o'clock on Friday afternoon we finally reached Dieppe, where again we were transported by trucks to a transit camp on the outskirts of town.

Late that afternoon my now close bosom buddies and I (had we not been pressed together tightly for forty one hours?) set off to see the town and found a delightful café in a square that served the most scrumptious *Croque-Monsieurs*, mouth-watering pastries and coffee, and proceeded to make pigs of ourselves. Saturday and Sunday we were free to explore Dieppe with its beautiful old buildings (captured so superbly by the painters, Monet and Sickert), and discover little restaurants by the harbour where I had *Moules Mariniere* and *Bouillabaisse* for the first time, and also enjoyed some wonderfully fresh oysters.

Over those two days I got to know quite a bit about my companions. The sergeant was a tall, lanky man in his early 30s, rather quiet and reserved. While studying in England in 1939, he had become engaged to an English girl. They were then separated by the war, and now after six years apart he was going to see her again. He didn't say so, but I could see he was slightly anxious as to how the reunion would go. The corporal was a Hollander, slightly older and of brawny, peasant build, who had immigrated to South Africa in the late 1930s. His elderly parents lived on a farm near Arnhem, they had suffered a lot during the war and he was now going to see how they were. I didn't tell them my full story, only that I wanted to act and there was no better place for that than London.

But inwardly I had qualms. I knew nothing about Denis' mother with whom I was going to stay, except from what some of his friends had told me: that she could be quite a formidable lady; and that she dabbled in the occult; Tarot cards were seldom out of her hands and she insisted on telling everyone's fortune. A favourite story of hers was how, when reading the cards of a pretty young lady from a Cochran chorus, she told her that soon she would sign a paper that would take her to work in a large building, and shortly afterwards there arrived an enormous bouquet of red roses with a card that simply read, 'Bless You! Anna Neagle – Shepheards Bush Studios.' Hermione Gingold wrote a very funny revue number based on her, called, 'Only A Medium Medium.' Her jokes about séances, Indian spirit guides and ectoplasm did not amuse Mrs. Freeman one little bit, and Miss. Gingold had to steer clear of her for quite a while.

Marie Freeman knew many people in the Arts: painters, musicians, dancers. Romola Nijinsky (wife of the great Russian dancer Vaslav Nijinsky, who was in a Swiss sanatorium at the time suffering from schizophrenia) came to tea one afternoon with their daughter Kyra, and asked Marie if she might leave the child with her for a short while. Marie said she would be delighted, thinking that it would be for an hour or two. Little did she realize that Romola was about to sail for New York with a girlfriend and that she would have Kyra on her hands for almost a year. Kyra was a lumpy girl with a very heavy footstep that caused the neighbours in the flat below to complain about the thumping noises she made. The fact that she was the great Nijinsky's daughter did not placate them at all.

The dichotomy of being a devout Roman Catholic and a staunch believer in the occult posed no problems for Mrs. Freeman. The Church had more or less condoned it. For didn't that nice priest at the Brompton Oratory say it would be quite all right for her to tell the Tarot cards as long as she also told them at the Oratory's Annual Garden Fete? And hadn't she obliged by doing so, sitting all afternoon in a hot stuffy tent dressed as a gypsy?

Sunday morning Mass at the fashionable Brompton Oratory was *de rigeur*. But she was always late in getting herself ready. With angry sighs she would storm about the flat, mutter oaths to herself sotto voce, and on leaving viciously slam the front door. Denis would say she must be the only Christian who went to meet her God every Sunday with the word 'Fuck' on her lips.

So this was the woman with whom I was about to stay. How, I wondered, was she going to react to a young South African soldier she had never met before suddenly moving in on her for... God knows how long it might be before Denis arrived. I only hoped that Joy Murchie's description of her as a megalomaniacal monster of a mother who would kill to keep her son's affections all to herself might be a slight exaggeration. Well, we would just have to wait and see.

In the early morning of Monday the 4th of February 1946 we embarked on a ship called, 'Isle of Thanet', and at 11 o'clock set sail across the Channel for Newhaven. It was a grey, drizzly day with a cold wind and a choppy sea but I was determined to stand at the rail and see England appear on the horizon, and when it did it was a most moving experience. And then, as I saw the white cliffs rising up, I softly sang to myself,

'There'll be blue birds over
The white cliffs of Dover...'

I knew it was Newhaven, not Dover, but Newhaven didn't rhyme or scan with 'over', and anyway Dover was only a short way up the coast, and if I was going to be really pedantic there wouldn't be any blue birds there either. My heart was pounding as the ship glided into port. At last! This was where I had wanted to be ever since I could remember! The excitement was immense! But with that excitement there was also a feeling of trepidation... What would England have in store for me?

Aged 6 months.(I'm the jolly one on the right.)

Aged 4, with my father, on one of his rare visits.

My mother, 1926.

Aged 10, loitering on
the rocks below our
house at Clifton.

Aged 15, giving my
'Fagin in the death
cell' monologue —
scary stuff!

The Troopadours original cast.
From left, standing: Konni Hirsch, Lynettte (Tessie) Crossley-Kerr, Erwin Lehrer, 2/Lieut Frank Daly,
Thilo Runge, Pieter Geldenhuis (as policeman), Al Marrock, Harold Lake (as judge).
Sitting: Myfannwy (Muff) Evans, Maurice Millard, Cynthia Klette, me, Joan Keena, Erwin Blumenreich,
Steve and Joan Kempen.

At the barracks in Pretoria, caught unawares by the camera.

Capt. Frank Rogaly. Cut him and he would bleed revue and pantomime all over you.

Joyce van Geems and Pieter Geldenhuis dancing to 'Rhapsody in Blue'.

The evil Ken Geyer as Carmen Miranda and Maurice Millard as Topsy at the Alhambra Theatre, Cape Town.

The Troopadours head north.

Doris White and me in the sketch, 'The Charge of the Late Brigade'.

Mersa Matruh. From left: G. Dobbins (our wardrobe mistress), Tessie, Joyce, Georgie,, me and Muff.
Sitting: Doris and Maurice.

Tabruk, with our guest artist George Formby and his wife, Beryl.

At the Globe Theatre, Alexandria ('One Night in Rio').

Marjorie Gilby and me in 'Moment Romantique'.

Olga Lowe and me in my version of 'Caesar and Cleopatra'.

Marjorie and me doing a Dorothy Parker short story that I adapted as a sketch.

John, Olga and me on the beach at Suez.

Doing the monologue 'Growing Up' that Denis wrote for me.

China Town. Olga looking aghast on the left, John and me fighting furiously on the right.

Me in Cairo, 1944.

Lieut Freeman of the Free French Army.

C. Denis Freeman in Cairo, 1944.

The nightmare ship, Ville D'Oran!

The Roman theatre at Sabratha, Libya, 1943.

*On almost the same spot 63 years later in 2006.
Many ghosts!*

*Hyers, France with my two South African
charges.*

PART TWO

"THE CURTAIN RISES"

It also sticks and sometimes falls

This is not about great success or dismal failure
but something in between – a sort of muddling along
and meeting interesting people on the way.

TWO

It was a cold, wet night when the train pulled into Victoria Station. Clambering aboard an army truck, I hoped for the last time, I grabbed a place at the back, impatient to get my first glimpse of London. A friendly cockney soldier sitting opposite kept me informed as to exactly where we were:

"Just passing the back of Buckingham Palace"…"This is Hyde Park Corner"…"Now were going up Park Lane"…

Park Lane! I knew it well from novels, plays, films and songs: 'All Park Lane in a shimmering gown', as Noel Coward was wont to sing. I craned my neck hoping I might catch a glimpse of one of his Mayfair ladies, bejewelled and befurred, sweeping down the steps of a plush hotel to a waiting Rolls Royce or Bentley. But no, there were no Mayfair ladies, no Rolls Royces or Bentleys – not even an Austin Seven or a Morris Eight. Nor could I see glittering chandeliers shining through the drawing-room windows of the Georgian houses we passed. There was hardly a light anywhere; the empty street looked shabby and dark (London had not seen a lick of paint or had any of its stonework cleaned for over six years and all the buildings were now coated with black soot and grime; also it would be some time before the bright lights came on again. Austere wartime conditions still prevailed). All the same, it was Park Lane, that famous thoroughfare so prized on the Monopoly board, and just knowing that I was on it somewhere gave me a distinct feeling of achievement.

"We're going round Marble Arch", my friendly guide informed me. Around it we went and came upon what looked like the temple at Karnak. It was, in fact, the Odeon Cinema Marble Arch, the whole exterior of which had been transformed to resemble an Egyptian temple for the premiere run of Gabriel Pascal's prestigious film of GBS's 'Caesar And Cleopatra' starring Claude Raines and Vivien Leigh. "That's the first film I'll see", I told myself as we rumbled up the Edgeware Road…

We turned right into the Marylebone Road and stopped a short way along at number 222, a large red brick building that had been a hotel before the war and would be one again many years later when it became the elegant London Landmark Hotel. At that time, however, it was a troop transit hostel.

My two compatriots and I were put in a small room at the very top of the building where the hotel maids would have slept, and lugging our kit up all those hundreds of stairs was quite an exhausting climb. The room had a small attic window through which I peered, but all there was to see was a poster on the wall opposite advertising Guinness.

After a fairly disgusting meal in the canteen downstairs, tired though we were from our long journey we did not yet feel ready to turn in, and, deciding to have one last adventure together, set off in search of a jolly old English pub and some liquid cheer. On leaving the building we made the mistake of turning right instead of left – left would have led us straight to the warm and welcoming pub, The Globe – right landed us back on the dark and dismal Edgeware Road. We wandered down it for a while but there was no sign of a pub anywhere, or even a workers' cafe where by then we would have settled for a warming cup of Camp coffee or stewed tea. An icy wind was blasting us in the face, and then it started to sleet, so we decided to abandon our quest, return to our chilly little maid's room and pile on the blankets and greatcoats. It had not been one of our more successful expeditions, but as I said to my two charges when we finally turned out the light, "After all, chaps, tomorrow is another day."

By morning the wind and rain had gone and there was even a little sunshine about – weak and watery sunshine to be sure, but sunshine nevertheless – and to the busy day we had ahead of us it made a bright and cheerful start. The first thing we had to do was to go to the South African UDF office in Princes Gate and be officially released from the army. We would then receive what monies were due to us, plus a grant to buy a demob suit (in my case a Harris Tweed jacket and a pair of grey flannel trousers from Selfridges. I already had two smart suits).

Our next port of call would be South Africa House in Trafalgar Square to register our presence in London and apply for passports, etc. As we were then still part of the British Empire there would be no need to seek residence or work permits. What I would need though would be a Ration Book – a little brown book of coupons without which it would be almost impossible to survive. In France there was no shortage of food as long as you could afford it, but in Britain it was very different, and I think much fairer: everyone, rich and poor alike, received exactly the same rations, and the black market was very severely frowned upon. Ivor Novello had gone to prison for being in illegal possession of petrol coupons. The fact that he in all his naivety had accepted them as a gift from a fan did not satisfy the law: they were looking for someone important to make an example of and he very neatly filled the bill.

Finally we would need to go to the medical unit at Chelsea Barracks for a physical and dental examination. These being satisfactory we would be free men; and after five years of army life, glamorous though some of mine had been, the thought of being my own master was a thrilling prospect.

Before we set off from the hostel that morning, the sergeant, who I shall call Doug, and I joined a lengthy queue in the lobby to use the public telephone; he to call his fiancée, I to call Mrs. Freeman. I noticed that the smaller the queue got the greater Doug's anxiety grew, and when he entered the booth he looked like a condemned man going to his execution. The call was brief, and stumbling out flushed of face and tremulous of voice he announced that he was meeting Helen for lunch at Simpsons in the Strand, which she said was quite near to South Africa House. It was my turn now, and I too entered the booth like a condemned man. Nervously I dialled the number; as the phone rang I crossed my fingers and held my breath; and then, when I heard the receiver being lifted, I felt my heart leap into my mouth!

Marie Freeman's voice was sweetness and light itself. She said she had been expecting my call and was looking forward to meeting me. I explained that I had various duties to perform that day and she suggested that I came along at teatime. It was only after I had left the booth that it struck me nothing had been said about my coming to stay with her. Now I was in a quandary. What to do? I decided that I had better leave my kit at the hostel until I knew exactly where I stood – or to be more precise, where I slept.

We took a taxi across Hyde Park to Princes Gate, and driving over the Serpentine Bridge with the sun gleaming on the water we all thought how beautiful the park looked. The UDF office was on the second floor of a large terraced house overlooking the park. Another of these houses, a few doors away, would achieve great notoriety as the scene of the 1980 Iranian Embassy Siege, when the whole world watched on their television sets as the SAS dramatically stormed the building, leaving seven dead.

Our business at the UDF Office was over quite soon, and Doug and the corporal, who I shall call Ruud, agreed to walk with me down Queens Gate, which was only one street away, and have a quick look at where I might be sleeping that night. Going along Kensington Gore with Albert's Hall on the left and his Memorial on the right I thought how imposing they both were (I would meet many who did not share my enthusiasm). Alexandra Court was a short way down Queens Gate on the left. It was a large Edwardian block of flats with a spacious drive-in courtyard and three entrances with marble steps leading up to them. We all thought it looked very posh and worked it out that number 5 would probably be on the left hand side and facing the front. I only hoped that Mrs. Freeman was not looking through her lace curtains at that moment and, being psychic as she was, recognise that I was one of the three soldiers giving her flat the once over.

At South Africa House Doug and I suggested that Ruud, who was wanting to get away to Holland as soon as possible, be attended to first, and while we were sitting waiting our turns he asked me if I would do him a very great favour. I said I would if I could. He said I could if I would, so I asked him what the favour was.

"Come to lunch with Helen and me."

"Are you mad," I said, "I couldn't possibly do that."

"You said you would if you could. Why can't you?"

"You and Helen have not seen each other for over six years, what is she going to imagine if you turn up with a casual soldier acquaintance in tow. She'll think it's the brush off."

"No, she won't. She'll understand. She'll be just as nervous and tongue tied as I will. You can talk, Neville, you're an actor. Make her laugh – tell her about our terrible sea voyage – talk about the theatre, she likes plays – talk about anything – you know, break the ice – loosen things up, and when everything's nice and relaxed we'll be able to go on from there. Please, I can't cope with this alone." He looked at me with pleading eyes. He was a frightened man.

"I still don't like the idea," I told him, "but I said I would if I could, and as I can I will, but don't you go making a habit of it."

He laughed, I think mostly out of relief.

She was already waiting in the foyer of Simpsons when we arrived. We had purposely got there early but she had got there even earlier. As I expected it would, my presence surprised her, but she quickly recovered and was charming and polite to me. Helen was a tall, attractive woman in her early thirties with fairish hair and grey-green eyes. Her manner was reticent but not stand-offish and she had a shy, winning smile.

Simpsons in the Strand has been famous throughout its long history for the magnificence of its Carvery, but on that austere February day in 1946 the only meat on the menu was stewed rabbit. I had never eaten rabbit before and as far as I am aware I have not eaten it since. It was not that the taste repelled me or that it wasn't expertly cooked, it was just that I couldn't get the image of fluffy little bunnies out of my mind; which, of course, was ridiculous of me because before long I would be dining in smart restaurants on meats far less palatable, such as whale and horse.

The beginning of the meal was very sticky indeed. They both looked tense and awkward and I had my time cut out filling in the pauses with inane banter that was greeted with nervous laughter. But after a while and with a couple of glasses of wine inside them they began to relax and actually seemed pleased to see one another. I had a feeling that the ice had thawed and was not going to freeze again. During coffee I excused myself and went and stood in the gent's loo washing my hands for as long as I thought it might be considered acceptable. On my return I found the pair in animated conversation and their hands resting on the tablecloth were almost touching. 'Eureka',

I thought, 'now I won't have to do my Dickens monologues after all!'

It was time now for Helen to return to her office and for us to make our way to Chelsea Barracks. They were meeting again that evening and, by the expressions on their faces, were looking forward to it immensely. I said goodbye to Helen, and as Doug and I strode along the Strand I noticed a lightness in his step and a gleam in his eye, and felt that everything was going to be all right between them. Our medical examinations completed satisfactorily and now standing outside Sloane Square Station, our place of parting, Doug thanked me for helping out at lunch; I wished him great happiness with Helen and he wished me luck with my acting. It was quite a touching little farewell.

Marie Freeman opened her front door and smiled with a graciousness that royalty might envy. She was a handsome woman in her sixties with sharp, rather French, features, pale skin and slightly frizzy light red hair peppered with grey.

"Do sit down," she said after showing me into the drawing-room, "I'll just put the kettle on." At the door she turned and asked, "What sign were you born under?"

"Cancer," I said.

"Ah, Cancer!" She gave a knowing smile, "I thought so. Sensitive and artistic. I'll tell the Tarot cards later on."

Left alone I looked around the room. It was comfortably furnished in a mixture of styles that gave it an interesting, slightly Bohemian look. At the window hung heavy curtains of plum coloured brocade that must have served their purpose well during the blackout. In the corner facing the door stood a baby grand piano; on it was a beautiful blue and silver Spanish shawl and some photographs in silver frames. One was of Winston Churchill, another of Charles de Gaulle, both signed; there was also one of Denis in uniform, signed: 'With all my love, Denis.' On the wall above was a large portrait of Marie herself painted by Kenalba, a fashionable artist of the day whose speciality was to make beautiful women of a certain age a little more of the former and a little less of the latter.

Marie returned carrying a large tea tray. "No staff I'm afraid," she said with a wistful sigh. "Maybe you would like to help with the crumpets. There's the toasting fork. You can toast them against the electric fire."

Thus I tasted my first English crumpet and there and then became addicted. I realised it would have been nicer smothered in butter instead of that thin scraping of margarine, but the butter ration then was infinitesimal, and it was enough of a treat anyway. In those days one only got crumpets in the winter time, but now the supermarkets stock them all the year round and teatime seldom passes without my having at least one buttered crumpet.

Marie never touched a morsel of food without first testing it; this she did by holding a pendant over it; if it swung in a circular motion it was all right; if it remained quite stationary it was questionable and would require further consideration; if it swung back and forth in a straight line it wasn't to be touched with a barge pole. It was fortunate that when she was hungry it always swung in a circular motion, as indeed it was doing over the crumpets that afternoon.

During my second cup of tea, and in the middle of her telling me about one of her psychic journeys on the Astral Plane, she suddenly segued into, "About the guest room, I have a lodger in it at the moment, a charming young officer from the French Embassy and I will have to give him ample notice so that he can find other suitable accommodation, which he will not find easy, not these days, what with all the bombing and everything."

My heart began to sink.

"However, my daughter, Irene will be able to put you up. Her son, Richard is away in boarding school at Bryanston and won't be home until the end of term so she says you can stay in his room. She only lives across the way, I'll take you over to meet her later. Why don't you toast yourself another crumpet while I go and fetch the Tarot cards?"

The walk took us about eight minutes – on my own it would have been nearer four, along Elverston Place, across Gloucester Road and straight into Kynance Place, a row of charming little houses backing onto a mews (where my present vet has his clinic). We stopped at one of the houses and rang the bell. The door was opened by a beautiful silver haired woman, smartly dressed and carefully made up and coiffured for an evening out. She said "hello" to Marie and then, turning pitying eyes on me, exclaimed, "It's the little match girl!"

At first I didn't know what this meant, but it later transpired that Denis had been on the phone begging them to be gentle and kind to me, and from the description he had given they were expecting a pathetic, tongue tied little waif, homeless and all alone in a strange land. It was enough to make Fagin weep.

Irene was still extremely attractive. At the age of eighteen her then pale blonde hair had suddenly turned a beautiful shining silver, and with her almost translucent alabaster like skin it was a beauty quite rare (forget your platinum blondes). She had been considered one of the great beauties of her day. I worked it out that by then she must have been about forty one or two. She always claimed to be younger than Denis but he swore it was the other way around.

She had lived a wild life in her youth, being very much one of the bright young things and it had taken its toll: she suffered from recurring bouts of tuberculosis (this was an inherited weakness. Denis would suffer from emphysema, and their father had died young of an asthma and lung related illness).

On one occasion, while Irene was a patient in a sanatorium in Switzerland, on the pretext of going on a picnic, she, the composer Constant Lambert and the cricketer Dulip Singh, their clothes concealed in picnic baskets, ran away to the south of France where they remained for the rest of the season, living it up.

In a moment of madness, that she mistook for love, she married a handsome young rubber planter on home leave from Malaya and went to live with him in Kuala Lumpur where she gave birth to their son, Richard. Realising that it wasn't love after all, and hating the country, the climate, the food and, most of all, the British planters and their wives she decided she had had enough; and with her babe still in arms and a faithful old ayah to take care of it, took the first available boat home; and in time the marriage was dissolved.

Her next memorable affair was with a brilliant theatre director who many, including the eminent critic James Agate considered a genius. His name was Peter Godfrey and he ran the Gate Theatre in Villiers Street, the very first club theatre in England, where he produced exciting and daring productions of the new Expressionist plays from Germany and America that the Lord Chamberlain would not allow to be performed in public theatres. Godfrey designed the theatre himself (it was part of an old ramshackle building that had been turned into a bowling alley) and being of the theatre he gave it a really superb stage, but it was out of all proportion with the auditorium; it took up a third of the space of the whole theatre, which left very little room for the audience, so it could never be commercially viable. Some weeks the actors went home with only a few shillings in their pockets; and there was certainly no money for a cleaner, so before rehearsals each morning they had to set to cleaning up from the night before. If this sounds cheap and tacky let me give you the names of some of the artists who were eager to perform there: Flora Robson, Eric Portman, Beatrix Lehmann, John Mills, Gwen Ffrangcon-Davies, Robert Morley, Margaret Rawlings, John Clements, Elsa Lanchester, Esmond Knight, Jean Forbes Robertson, Esme Percy, Veronica Turleigh, Ernest Thesiger, Nanette de Valois and Constant Lambert, plus many many more; and it was through Irene threatening not to sleep with Peter unless he gave her friend Hermione Gingold a part in the Christmas show that the great comedienne began her brilliant career in revue.

Irene appeared in some of the productions, but only peripherally and mostly as decoration, for she was not a good actress, she didn't like acting, and with the snobbish streak that sometimes took her, found actors rather common. It was really not the life for her and, tiring of the hectic, hurly burly, hand to mouth existence she said goodbye to Peter and made her final exit from the stage.

Peter Godfrey would emigrate to America and continue his remarkable work there. The Gate Theatre was taken over by Norman Marshall who ran it until the spring of 1941 when it was destroyed by a German bomb.

Once again in a sanatorium, this time at Midhurst in Surrey, Irene became attracted to a fellow patient, a tall, extremely handsome Commander in the Royal Navy. Harold Wilkinson was his name. He was well born, well educated, well mannered – in fact, the perfect English gentleman – just what Irene was looking for, and it was not long before wedding bells were ringing once more.

Harold, like many a Royal Naval officer before him, was much more alive standing on the bridge of a battleship than sitting in a drawing-room; and as the years rolled by and his initial masculine magnetism lost some of its allure Irene began to find him a little boring – charming, thoughtful and loving, but never the less boring; and although she would never think of leaving him she might now and then, when the fancy took her, and in the most discreet and circumspect way, take a brief detour from the marital path.

On the evening I arrived at Kynance Place Harold was away on naval duty in Portsmouth, and on the sofa was sitting an American army colonel who had come to take Irene to a cocktail party at his Embassy and then on to dinner at the Savoy. They were eager to leave so Irene quickly showed me my room, gave me a front door key and asked Marie to explain the rest. As they were going out of the door she said, "There's some plum brandy in the cabinet. Help yourselves to a drink."

We helped ourselves to a drink, then another, and at Marie's request yet another. Plum brandy seemed not to require the pendant test; perhaps being psychic she already knew which way it would swing. We really should have used the liqueur size glasses instead of the tumblers because by the time it was put away the bottle that had been half full was practically empty, and as we walked back along Elverston Place I realised we were both a little drunk. I saw Marie to her door and then went to the hostel to collect my kit.

The next morning Irene seemed surprised at how much plum brandy had been consumed. She wasn't being mean about it, she was just astonished that her mother, who always disapproved of her drinking, had managed to put away so much liquor herself. I didn't realise it then but alcohol, like everything else in Britain was heavily rationed, and it was quite an achievement to come out of an off-licence with a bottle of spirits. Regular customers were treated with preference, of course, but casual customers were lucky to come out with a bottle of Merrydown cider.

At the American PX in London there was no shortage of liquor, and the colonel of the evening before had brought Irene a gift of a couple of bottles of gin. I would help her drink some of it as we sat together talking over the next few days. The two of us became very close friends, and, apart from a couple of spells when we stupidly weren't speaking, that friendship lasted for many years – right up until her sad death. In her will she left me a case of Gordons Gin.

Irene hated her mother. Denis hated her too, but with him it had the complication of being a love hate relationship. Marie had robbed them both of their inheritance. Their father had left them each a handsome sum of money which they could not touch until they were twenty-one. This was because he knew how extravagant and untrustworthy his wife could be with money. Then into Marie's life sailed a wily old sea captain who sniffed hidden treasure, and in some clever, crooked way that has never been properly explained he helped her to break the children's trusts; and together over the next few years, living in wild luxury, they managed to get through it all – and when the money was gone so was the wily old sea captain.

Marie had given the children lots of expensive presents during this time: lovely dresses for Irene, and for Denis she built a theatre in an Elizabethan barn at Fairlight in East Sussex where they lived, so she couldn't understand why they should hold such a grudge against her.

Denis arrived back in England on Sunday the 10th of March, exactly thirty three days after me. By then Marie's French lodger had gone and I was in the guest room, which now had two beds in it. My time alone in London had not been spent idly. I had been to see many shows. The very first theatre I visited was the 'New' (later renamed the 'Albery' and in 2006 the 'Coward') where the Old Vic Company (their own theatre across the river having been bombed) were presenting a highly successful season of classic plays in repertory with a large and brilliant cast headed by Laurence Olivier, Ralph Richardson and Sybil Thorndike.

My first play was a matinee performance of 'Henry IV Part 2 (I would catch up with Part 1 later), in which Richardson gave a magnificent performance as Falstaff, and Olivier a very funny one as the withered old Justice Shallow. So clever was his make up, his voice and movement that I didn't realise it was him for some time. I next saw Olivier in the incredible double bill of Sophocles' 'Oedipus Rex' and Sheridan's 'The Critic'. Having wrung one's withers with his dramatic performance as the tragic, doomed king, he then after only a short interval appeared as the ludicrous Mr. Puff and had the audience in hysterical laughter. It was an extremely physical performance. The *coup de theatre* came when Mr. Puff, clutching hold of the curtain as he took a deep bow was suddenly whisked up with it into the flies, and on its decent went tumbling across the stage – an extraordinary end to an extraordinary evening of tragedy and comedy. I thought it was the best theatrical experience I had ever had and Laurence Olivier became my favourite actor. I would see this double bill three more times and each time enjoyed it more (theatre tickets were reasonably priced in those days and one could sit in the gallery for one shilling and nine pence, which was what I often did). I then saw Richardson and Olivier give superb performances in Shaw's 'Arms And The Man'. Also in the cast was the lovely young Margaret Leighton. Unlike Richardson, who was a very natural actor, Olivier loved to put on disguises and was particularly fond of nose putty. In the first four plays I saw him in I did not see his real nose once.

Other shows I saw at that time were: Noel Coward's revue, 'Sigh No More', starring Cyril Richard, Madge Elliot and Joyce Grenfell; Ann Casson as 'Saint Joan'; Hermoine Gingold and Henry Kendal in 'Sweeter And Lower'; Flora Robson in 'Man About The House'; Jack Buchanan in 'Fine Feathers'; Robert Morley and Wendy Hiller in 'The First Gentleman'; Arthur Askey in 'Follow The Girls'; Lilian Braithwaite and Mary Jerrold in 'Arsenic And Old Lace'; John Mills in 'Duet For Two Hands'; 'The Time Of Your Life' (cast already mentioned); Ivor Novello in 'Perchance To Dream'; Isabel Jeans in 'Lady Windemere's Fan'; John Clements and Kay Hammond in 'Private Lives'; Freida Jackson in 'No Room At The Inn'; Donald Wolfit as 'King Lear' and 'Hamlet'; Ruth Draper doing her famous monologues; Ram Gopal, his Indian dances, and the Windmill girls minus their clothes playing at statues. I was also taken to the tiny Chepstow Theatre in Notting Hill Gate to see a really dreadful play called 'Crimson Harvest', however there was one young actor in it who really stood out, and when he later became a star I was not surprised. His name was Kenneth Moore.

On non-matinee days I would visit museums and art galleries. I also spent some time with Maurice, Olga and John who had recently arrived and were staying together in a house in Hall Road, Maida Vale. Also lodging there was Alfred Marks (the comedian I had admired in the RAF concert party at the Globe Theatre in Alexandria) and his clever wife, Paddy O'Neil.

The moment Denis arrived a whole new and exciting social life began for me. All his old friends were eager to see him again, and he wanted me to meet them, so for the first couple of weeks, almost every day, at lunch, drinks and dinner I met someone new. This did not please Marie at all. She would have liked Denis to have spent the entire time with her – preferably alone. And the fact that I was included on most of these jolly jaunts and not her made her even more jealous. Nothing was said but the saccharine sweetness of her smile as we left the flat spoke volumes.

She knew better than to make an outright enemy of me. That way she might lose Denis again. Irene said he had gone to live in Paris partly to escape her octopus tentacles. No, she was going to be much more subtle; I was to be her very best friend; cunningly she would get me to divulge all my deepest inner-most secrets and weaknesses, and then when I was completely in her power she would think of some clever way to dispense with me and have her darling son all to herself. She told me she sensed I had a very old soul, although not as old as hers; and she was sure we had met before in a previous life, but she couldn't quite put her finger on when or where (I was probably one of her servants at Versailles). The Tarot cards were in no doubt as to my great talents and it was only a matter of time before fame and fortune came my way. In these predictions it was somehow implied that she had some influence over the outcome. well, look at Anna Neagle – without Marie's help she would probably have remained in the chorus. Irene warned me not to tell her anything that she could later use as ammunition against me, and I heeded her warning. As time went by and she saw her little scheme was getting nowhere she began to show her true colours, and none of them were in gentle shades of pastel. Joy Murchie had not been exaggerating in Cairo when she told me Marie Freeman was a monster!

It did not take long to realise that number 5 Alexandra Court was not big enough for three people, especially when one of them was as overpoweringly egocentric, possessive and devious as Marie, so when a friend offered us the loan of a flat we leapt at it.

Martin Solomon was an old friend of Denis' from before the war. His father had been one of the backers of the revue, 'Spread It Abroad'. They were a wealthy family, great art collectors and benefactors. Some of the fine Chinese Tang horses in the V&A were donated to the museum by the Solomon family.

Martin had served throughout the war as an officer in the Royal Navy. I had met him once in Cairo, on a brief leave from his ship in Alexandria, and I thought he was very charming. He had taken part in the liberation of Crete, and while on the island had met and fallen in love with a beautiful Greek girl. When they finally had to part, so that he would not forget her, she gave him two Siamese kittens which he smuggled aboard his battleship and brought safely back to London, where they were now ensconced in a flat in Duke Street, St James. Martin had to go to New York for three months on business for his father and offered us the free loan of his flat for that time on condition that we took care of his precious cats. We readily agreed.

It was a charming little flat on the top floor above an art dealer, a few doors down from the Cavendish Hotel where its legendry proprietress, Rosa Lewis was still very much in evidence. One evening, passing the window of the front lounge, we saw her sitting in a large high backed chair.

"This is someone you must meet," said Denis who, there and then, took me in and introduced me to her. It was fascinating meeting the woman on whom Evelyn Wagh had based the character of Lottie Crump, proprietress of Sheapheards Hotel in his novel, 'Vile Bodies'. But Rosa Lewis was famous in her own right, having been cook and mistress to King Edward VII; and in 1976 a television series would be based on her, entitled, 'The Duchess Of Duke Street.'

That brief meeting was not our last encounter with Rosa. A couple of times during the summer she sent staff around to complain that our cats (who sometimes went on the roof at night) were keeping her guests awake. We would then shut them in, but knowing the sort of clientele Rosa had at the Cavendish (Tennessee Williams would always stay there) cats, we felt, were the last reason her guests weren't getting their sleep.

Martin was really turning into our good fairy god-father. Not only had he given us a timely refuge from the storm (so to speak), he also provided me with my first job in England. While having dinner one night with his old friends, Taffy Rodd and his beautiful actress wife, Yvonne Marling, she told him she was about to start rehearsals for a new West End play that Peter Daubeny was presenting. Martin mentioned me and wondered if there was anything still going that I might be able to do. She said she would ask the producer, Esme Percy, and true to her word she did. He said the male juvenile understudies were yet to be cast and if I was interested I should come to see him on the stage of the Saville Theatre after the first morning read through of the play.

Esme Percy I remembered from several British films, but most specifically from 'Pygmalion' where he played Count Aristid Karpathy, a character that Shaw had especially written for him. He had had a long and distinguished stage career, having made his debut in 1904. He was trained at the Brussels Conservatoire and had acted with Sarah Bernhardt. Having lost one eye in a playful mishap with his dog did not affect his career or his love of dogs and for the rest of his life there was always one at his side. A statue of one of these much-loved canines can be found in Kensington Gardens. It sits on top of a dogs' drinking fountain that was placed there by his friends to remember him by.

How well I remember that sunny day walking up Shaftesbury Avenue in my new smart grey flannel suit to my first London audition.

Being early (I always am) I took my time looking at the posters and photographs outside the theatres that I passed and arrived at the Saville exactly two minutes before the appointed time. The stage door keeper sent me down to the stage where from the wings I could see the actors sitting on a row of chairs and in front of them, seated at a table was the producer, who I instantly recognised, and his stage director, Patrick Moran (Pat would take me under his wing, we would become good friends, and work together on other shows).

The read through was over and they were now discussing the rehearsal schedule for the afternoon. Pat saw me hovering in the wings and came to see what I wanted. I told him and he went and spoke to Esme.

"Mr. Phillips", called Esme in his beautiful melodious voice, "please come onto the stage."

As if it wasn't scary enough walking out there in front of all those actors I actually recognised some of them. First of all there was Mary Clare who I had seen recently as a mad woman strangling rabbits in a film with James Mason called, 'The Night Has Eyes'; Nova Pilbeam I remembered from the Alfred Hitchcock thriller, 'Young And Innocent', and also as the tragic young 'Tudor Rose'; Peter Coke I recognised from the same film; and Irene Handl I had seen doing several comic cameos. The others who I didn't recognise were Phyllis Dare, one of the famous Dare sisters who had starred in musical comedy at 'Daleys' and 'The Gaiety' before the First World War; Eric Maturin, a matinee idol of the same period; lovely Yvonne Marling who was responsible for my being there; John Penrose, a South African actor who had played the juvenile lead in 'French For Love' with Alice Delysia in the 1939 West End production (John would give up acting and become a theatrical agent, and thanks to him I would work in several repertory companies around England); Cyril Hardingham played a policeman, understudied Eric Maturin and was stage manager to Pat's stage director (today the Management is called the producer; the producer is called the director; the stage director is called the stage manager; the stage manager is called the ASM; and the ASM is called just another ASM). There were four other actresses in the company playing small parts and understudying.

Esme asked me if I would mind going to sit in the stalls where he would join me when he had finished talking to the actors. This he did, and after I had told him about myself he asked me to go up to the stage and read a couple of scenes with Pat Moran reading the other parts. When I had finished he immediately offered me the double understudy plus the off stage speaking role of a radio news announcer. For this I would have to crouch out of sight in the fireplace behind the gram-radio, and when it was switched on read the nine o'clock news full of gloom and doom in a voice as near to a BBC announcer as I could muster (it was long before tape recording was invented. By the time we got to town I had a microphone in the wings that I spoke into). That afternoon I went to Peter Daubeny's office to sign my contract. I was asked if I would also be the ASM on the show and I said I would be delighted to. My salary was to be £10 a week (this was a lot of money at that time for someone in my position. Actors were slogging their guts out in weekly rep for £7 or £8 a week), and later that afternoon I was made a member of British Actors Equity.

The play was called, 'The Day After Tomorrow', and was billed as 'A Satirical Fantasy'. It was about what life in a Mayfair mansion would be like after two more years under a Labour Government. It had echoes (albeit comedic) of Orwell's 1984, with inspectors arriving unannounced to check the number of electric light bulbs that were on, or to remonstrate with the females of the house for not producing the correct quota of babies. This latter inspector was played by Irene Handl and it was by far the funniest scene in the play, due to the fact that she had completely rewritten it herself. At the first day of rehearsal she had torn the pages that had her part on them out of the script and given it back to Pat Moran, saying, "I won't need this." Next day she turned up with an entirely new and much longer scene of her own creation. It was so infinitely funnier than the original that the authors very reluctantly had to allow it to stay. I was not enamoured with the play but hoped that well acted and with an audience I would be pleasantly surprised. In the theatre even when one secretly knows it's a dud, one always hopes for the best. It's the only way.

There will now be a short interval from the play while I tell you about some of the fascinating people I met with Denis on his return.

The first was Baroness Moura Budberg who had edited his book, 'The Road To Bordeaux'. They had known each other a long time and had many friends in common. Maura was famous for her literary salon; anyone who had written anything of any importance at all had been to drinks in Ennismore Gardens: Bernard Shaw..Virginia Woolf..Somerset Maugham..Graham Greene..Ernest Hemmingway..you name them, they had been there. But her greatest claim to fame was that she had been the long time mistress first of Maxim Gorky and then H.G. Wells.

Born into the Russian aristocracy as Countess Marie Zakrevskaya, she had a fine education, spoke five languages and was an avid reader. This would be her salvation in the revolution when she made a living as a translator. She grew up in St Petersberg society, was presented to the Tsar and knew Rasputin whom she thoroughly disliked. At the age of eighteen she married Count Benkendorff who owned large estates in Estonia and they had two children. He held a diplomatic post at the Russian Embassy in Berlin where Moura's beauty was much admired. As she made an entrance at a grand reception one evening the Kaiser was heard to ask, "Who is that Queen of Sheba?"

When the 1914 war broke out they returned to Russia where life for the aristocracy continued as normal. Then came the 1917 revolution and everything changed dramatically. Count Benkendorf was murdered by his own peasants and all his possessions were confiscated. Moura, now a penniless widow with two children to feed, found work in Moscow translating novels for the publishing house, World Literature, and there she met Maxim Gorky. She became his secretary and shortly afterwards his mistress and the torrid affair lasted for eleven years, during which time she translated all his works into English.

In 1918 an Englishman called Robert Bruce Lockhart was charged with having taken part in the attempted assassination of Lenin, and Moura, having once been associated with him, was arrested too and spent five months in a political prison under intense interrogation. Upon her release she tried to flee the country with false papers but was rearrested and spent another four months in prison. Apart from knowing influential foreigners the mere fact of being an aristocrat at that time was considered treason enough.

Gorky, who had been made a sort of figurehead of the revolution, had much power with the Bolsheviks and managed to get her released. He also arranged for her to visit her children, whom she had not seen for four years. While in Estonia she married Baron Budberg. It was a marriage of convenience. The Baron was a dissolute gambler down on his luck and in return for giving Moura an Estonian passport Gorky bought him a one way ticket to Argentina where he made a living giving bridge lessons to the rich of Buenos Aires.

By now Gorky had lost sympathy with the Bolsheviks, and accompanied by Moura went to live in Berlin. But the climate was not suitable for his health, he suffered from tuberculosis, so they moved down to Sorrento in southern Italy where they remained for eight years, he writing prodigiously, she translating it into English.

When his health began to fail he decided to return to Russia. Moura refused to accompany him and with her two children went to live in England, where she became a successful literary agent; but she went to visit him almost every year until his death. It was not long after her arrival in London that she began her love affair with H.G. Wells, who she had met in Moscow when he had come there to visit Gorky, and this second great liaison lasted for sixteen years, until he died on the 13th of August 1946.

As it so happened we were having drinks with her that evening. She was in a very low state and wanted to talk about him to Denis who had known him slightly through her. I felt my presence was intrusive and made a tactful exit so they could be alone. He arrived home in the early hours the worse for vodka and said that Moura had talked about H.G. the entire night.

Back to March of that year, when I first met Moura she was the head of the script department of Sir Alexander Korda's London Films, and it was at her suggestion that Korda asked Denis to do the English subtitles for six French films he had bought that had not been seen outside of France. He would take the Rialto Cinema in Coventry Street for several months and present them in a grand season of modern French cinema. Korda did nothing by halves and he offered Denis a very respectable fee.

The first film was Marcel Carne's, 'Les Enfants du Paradis', which Denis found a daunting task. It was written by a poet, Jacques Prevert, and the dialogue had a poetic quality; it was also full of Paris argot; the film was extremely long, three and a quarter hours (there was an interval in the middle) and it had a great deal of dialogue. To swamp the screen with subtitles for that length of time would have been unbearable. He had to choose the most salient lines to tell the story, and he also tried to keep their poetic quality. He went over to Paris twice to consult Prevert about it.

The film was a tremendous success in London and for weeks there were queues stretching along Coventry Street and up Wardour Street. And it was most gratifying that two of the leading film critics praised Denis' sensitive work. Subtitles rarely are mentioned except to be damned for their inadequacy, for it is usually a poorly paid job and consequently the work of hacks. But Korda only ever wanted the best, he was prepared to pay for it and the quality showed. I would see the film again some years later with different subtitles and they came nowhere near to Denis' fine work.

The other five films were also of an exceptional quality. They were Clouzot's 'Quai des Orfevres', and 'Le Corbeau'; Duvivier's 'Panique'; Cocteau's 'La Belle et la Bete'; and another Carne/Prevert film, 'Portes des la Nuit', starring the young Yves Montand and introducing that wonderful song, 'Les Feuilles Mortes'.

The first show Denis and I went to see after his return was 'Sweeter And Lower' at the Ambassadors Theatre. Hermione Gingold didn't know he was back and to surprise her we sat in the centre of the front row of the stalls. She spotted him immediately and from then on throughout the evening managed to mention his name in every sketch. This was very funny for us but could not have meant much to the rest of the audience who must have been asking themselves, "Who the hell is Denis Freeman?" We went backstage afterwards to see her, she had a dinner engagement that night but asked us to come and have coffee with her the next morning. When we arrived at her charming little house in Kinnerton Street, Knightsbridge, and knocked on the front door, her bedroom window, which was right above it, opened and a key was thrown out. We let ourselves in, made the coffee and took it up to her in bed.

For a while they chatted about the old days and what friends were doing, then Denis told her that I wrote sketches. She said she would like to read one sometime. As fate would have it I had in my breast pocket that very morning a sketch I had written in Cairo. As it was in my untidy handwriting I had to read it to her. It was called, 'Nefertiti was nefer tati'. The scene is Queen Nefertiti's palace in Cairo where she is sitting in her famous headdress having her portrait painted by Salvador Dali who is depicting her on his canvas as a lobster telephone. It was full of jokes about Surrealism (a popular target for comedy at that time) and in-jokes about Cairo life. It ended with her singing him this rather prophetic little refrain:

"What are we going to do about the Suez Canal?
Shall we sell it? Shall we drink it? Shall we give it to the poor?
What are we going to do about the Suez Canal?
We don't want it anymore,
It's a trouble and a bore.
Let's get rid of it before
There's another bloody war.
Oh, what are we going to do about the Suez Canal,
Sal-va-dor?"

To which he replies: "I know what I'd do with it. I'd dye it pink, put a g-string on it and call it Gypsy Rose Lee. It'd fetch a fortune!"

The sketch may have raised a laugh or two in Cairo but in Kinnerton Street on a bleak March morning it meant nothing at all. However, Hermione liked my sort of humour and asked me to show her anything I wrote that I thought might be suitable for her; and so started a long and fruitful association during which she would perform my lyrics in revue, cabaret, on radio, television and record. We also wrote a couple of songs together but they came to nothing.

One night we had dinner at the Ivy Restaurant with Bumble Dawson. Her real name was Beatrice but almost everyone knew her as Bumble.

She was given the nickname as a child. Beatrice was a very fat little girl, and with the large round framed spectacles that she wore she rather resembled a little bumble-bee. She would grow up to resemble a rather large bumble-bee – it was a glandular condition. Spending a weekend at the country home of her dear friend, Bunny Roger, and while playing French aristocrats going to the guillotine, she fell out of the wheel-barrow that was serving as a tumbril, hit her head on a large stone and was concussed. From that moment on the fat began to disappear and she ended up as shapely and svelte as she could only have hoped for in her wildest dreams. No longer was she a bumble-bee, but the affectionate name of Bumble remained. Her friendship with Denis went back a long way. For a number of years she had made a living making costume jewellery in a little flat in Shepheards Market. Her big breakthrough came when Oliver Messel, the costume designer of Pascal's spectacular 'Caesar And Cleopatra', asked her to provide all the exotic Egyptian jewellery for the film. This she felt was the pinnacle of her career as a jewellery maker, and the night we met her she told us that she was changing tracks and was going to be a costume designer for films. At this she would succeed triumphantly, and among the many film stars she would dress were Vivien Leigh, Ava Gardner, Sophia Loren, Marilyn Monroe and Judy Garland.

I liked Bumble very much, and we became good friends. She was an all-weather friend, good times and bad. And in one of my darkest hours she was there to hold my hand.

The actress Margaret Rawlings, another old friend of Denis', had married a millionaire and given up the stage. She was living in a magnificent suite at the Dorchester Hotel, and there one evening we were invited to drinks. Her two other guests were the surrealist painter and writer, Roland Penrose and his beautiful wife to be, the American photographer, Lee Miller. Lee wore on her wrists two heavy bands of gold that when joined together by a gold pin became a pair of handcuffs. I thought this very kinky and kept trying to imagine the tricks they got up to with them.

At the Ivy another night a tall, strongly built man with a shock of brown hair and pale blue eyes came up to our table and held out his hand to Denis. This was the Irish film director, Brian Desmond Hurst, who at that time was at the peak of his career making films for J. Arthur Rank at Denham Studios (one of his most popular wartime films was 'Dangerous Moonlight', which starred Anton Walbrook and Sally Gray, and introduced Richard Addinsall's world popular 'The Warsaw Concerto'). Brian and Denis had not spoken since their acrimonious parting on a country road in 1940. Denis and his very close friend, Iris Levison-Gore had been spending the weekend at Wardrobes, Brian's country house in Buckinghamshire, and he was driving them back to London on the Monday morning in his Bentley. I was never told exactly what he said to Iris but whatever it was she found it extremely offensive. Denis, enraged that his dear friend should be so insulted, called Brian 'a common bog peasant' and made him stop the car. They got out and Brian drove on. So there they were on a cold drizzly morning in wartime standing with their luggage on a lonely country road. They could have been taken for a couple of German spies who had just been dropped by parachute, but fortunately that didn't occur to the lorry driver who very kindly drove them to the railway station at High Wickham.

Meeting Brian for the first time I don't think anyone would suspect his sexual orientation. As I have said, he was a strongly built man, and he spoke in a deep voice with a beguiling Irish lilt. There was nothing feminine about him (he loathed effeminate men) but he wasn't in the closet either – I doubt if he knew such a place existed. Once, when a woman who rather fancied him asked if he was bisexual, he replied, "No, trisexual: the Army, the Navy and the Air Force." His particular weakness was Guardsmen (Horse and Foot – his taste was catholic) and with army pay being as pitifully low as it was then they were never in short supply. For centuries it had been a tradition (unspoken) in the Brigade of Guards to supplement their earnings in this way, and Knightsbridge (the barracks Brian favoured as it was close his Kinnerton Street home) had always been an expensive place to live. He would quite blatantly drive his Bentley up to the front of the barracks and toot the horn. In no time at all a guardsman would appear, hop in beside him and off they'd go. The going rate then was a fiver, which was a lot of money in those days: you could take a girl out for a whole night on the town for that, or buy your wife a new winter coat, or the kiddy a tricycle; and for a hardy soldier of the Queen, with nerves of steel and trained to endure all the horrors of war, it was not that traumatic an ordeal – all you had to do was close your eyes and not think of England.

Brian's audacious behaviour earned him much notoriety and friends worried about his safety. One who often expressed concern for his welfare was Marc Anthony who played the piano in a drinking club in Denman Street called The White Room (Rodney Ackland wrote a play about its peculiar clientele called 'The Pink Room', and in it was the character of a film director that bore an almost libellous resemblance to Brian. The critics all damned the play as decadent and depraved and it was swiftly withdrawn. Fifty years later with its title changed to 'Absolute Hell' it was revived at the Royal National Theatre to unanimous critical acclaim and was an outstanding success. What does that inform us about critics?). Marc Anthony used to say that every Sunday morning when he opened his 'News Of The World' he was amazed not to read that Brian had been arrested or murdered. The reason for his seemingly charmed existence, apart from the fact that he was physically adept at defending himself in awkward situations, was that he had several friends in the police force (yes, he also had a weakness for policemen and they too were woefully under paid. The government ought to have been grateful to Brian, he seemed to be subsidising all the services single-handed) and every now and then when things hotted up and orders came from on high to round up another batch of queers they would tip him off and he would retire to the country until they sounded the all clear. He was extremely generous with all the men he entertained at Kinnerton Street, and he never talked down to them. They must have liked him because they were always coming back for more. Brian had the charm of the devil; he also had hidden away a streak of his treachery too; and although he always treated me with the greatest respect I never totally trusted him.

That night in The Ivy was the first time they had seen each other since their bitter parting on that country road. Denis took the hand that Brian was proffering and returned his friendly smile; after all, it was a long time ago, Poor Iris had died of cancer a couple of years before, there had been a long and tedious war, it was time to bury the hatchet. And that is how Brian came to play quite an important part in our lives. Denis would write a film that he would direct, and he would find parts for me in some of his pictures. Spending weekends at Wardrobes I met a lot of fascinating people: his country neighbour, Terence Young, who directed a couple of the 'Bond' films, the writer, Robin Maugham, Cecil Beaton, Michael Redgrave and the great Hollywood director, George Cukor, who whenever he came to England always paid Brian a visit; and once he invited us along with Brian to dine with him in his suite at the Savoy Hotel. I remember a particular Sunday lunch at Wardrobes; sitting around the large dining room table were La Gingold (Brian's next door neighbour in Kinnerton Street, who would often drive down on a Saturday night after her show), Bumble Dawson (who designed the costumes on several of his pictures), Siobhan McKenna (a fine actress he had brought over from Ireland for his film, 'Hungry Hill'), Roger Moore (whose father he knew and who he helped to put through RADA) and George Cukor, who had brought with him a couple of his friends, Tennessee Williams and Gore Vidal. More of the last two later.

We were invited one evening to the Garrick Club to have drinks with Beverley Nichols (in 1938 Denis had produced a revue of his called 'Floodlight', that starred Frances Day, John Mills and Hermione Baddeley), and a few days later we were asked to have lunch with him and Cyril Butcher at his lovely house in Hampstead, which had a large garden stretching down the side of the Heath. Beverley was mean about heating the house, causing Denis to remark during lunch, "It's one of those funny days when it seems warmer out than in."

Then one night Denis took me round to meet his wife. Katusha was Russian and had been prima ballerina of the Bolshoi Ballet at the time of the revolution. Finding life under the Bolsheviks intolerable she fled the country and spent some years living in Berlin, Paris and London. Having no papers of national identity she was categorised as stateless, and in 1939, when the war clouds were gathering over Europe, Denis (who had known her for some years, and had employed her as choreographer on a couple of his productions) offered to marry her so she could have a British passport. It was agreed that when the necessary time had elapsed they would get a divorce; but somehow neither of them ever got round to it, and so legally they remained man and wife for the rest of their lives. Irene would worry about this. She warned Denis that he would be responsible for any debts that Katusha might incur, voluntarily or otherwise. Fortunately nothing like that ever happened.

Katusha's name, both real and professional, was Catherine Devillier. Her father had been French, her mother a Russian actress. She was trained at the Bolshoi Ballet School and rose to become *prima ballerina assoluta*. She and the great Russian bass,

Chaliapin were the first two people to be made 'Honoured Artists of the Soviet Republic'. But life under the Bolsheviks was very unpleasant for artists and intellectuals who, through their former association with the aristocracy and influential foreigners, were continually under surveillance. By night they would be applauded and garlanded with flowers and the next morning carted off to prison to be interrogated.

On one occasion she and Chaliapin were sent to Vladivostok to entertain the Russian fleet. It was a long, hot train journey through Siberia, although she said the scenery there in summer was very lush and beautiful. After they had done their performances and made the equally tiring journey back she was met at Moscow station by the secret police who wanted to further interrogate her. This she said was the straw that broke the camel's back and as soon as she could she made her escape.

She came straight to London. She had been there once before with her closest friend, Anna Pavlova, who had accepted an engagement to perform on a variety bill at the Palace Theatre but didn't want to travel to England alone and asked Katusha to accompany her. They stayed in a small flat above the Apollo Theatre in Shaftesbury Avenue (the Palace Theatre was just a three minute run up the street) and there, with a couple of Russian archdukes who had come to London to keep them company, played bridge morning, noon and night. Anna would drop out of the game to run up the street, do her 'Dying Swan' or whatever, then hurry back and continue where she had left off. Katusha said she saw nothing of London that trip. The entire time was spent playing bridge above the Apollo Theatre.

When she arrived in London the second time in 1919 the Ballet Russes were taking the town by storm. Having discovered that Diaghilev was staying at the Savoy she went there hoping to see him, and, as luck would have it, just as she reached the entrance he came sweeping out with his entourage. Seeing her he let out a cry of delight and gave her a big Russian bear hug. There and then at a writing desk in the hotel lobby, on a sheet of Savoy Hotel writing paper, he drew up a contract for her to join the company.

Katusha was not the ethereal Karsarvina type of ballerina, she was a strong character dancer with lots of brio, and the ballets she would be most successful in were 'Rite Of Spring', 'Petrouchka' and 'The Three-Cornered Hat'.

Glamorous as it was to be a ballerina with the Ballet Russes, life in the company was not entirely a bed of roses. Backstage it was total and constant chaos with mishaps, injuries, tantrums, rivalries, fights and intrigues. After a year or so in this overheated atmosphere she felt she needed some space to breath. Also she had somehow become the go-between of Diaghilev and a dancer who had replaced Nijinsky in his affections called Serge Lifar. It all came to a head after a performance one evening in Rome.

Diaghilev insisted that she accompany him to the Coliseum where Lifar had gone to sulk. The Coliseum is a fairly large building, and with Lifar sulking on one side of it, Diaghilev fuming on the other and Katusha taking messages back and forth all night she said she must have walked miles; and having already that evening danced two strenuous ballets, 'Rite Of Spring' and 'The Three-Cornered Hat' she decided enough was enough and bid farewell to the Ballet Russes.

In Berlin she joined 'The Russian Romantic Theatre', no way as prestigious but it gave her the personal space that she needed at that time. She would also dance with other companies and then open a dance academy of her own. And it was in Berlin that she met a wild spirited, wiry young English woman with a deep gravel voice with whom she fell in love and would live with for the rest of her life. Dilkusha was her name. It is a Hindi word meaning 'Heart's Delight', her father had served in the Indian Army.

When Hitler came to power in Germany they left Berlin and went to live in Paris where they had many good friends in the arts. Among them were the Russian artists, Tchelitchew, Larionov and Goncharova, who painted a charming portrait of the two of them that hung in their Bloomsbury flat. They also knew Gertrude Stein and her close friend, Alice. B. Toklas with whom Dilkusha kept in regular correspondence until her death.

Fearing that his tomboy daughter was never going to find herself a husband, Dilkusha's father decided to find one for her (for respectability's sake, no doubt) and while he was about it the husband might as well have a title. And it so happened that at that very moment in Paris the penniless Prince de Rohan was on the marriage market. Like Dilkusha he too was what is euphemistically known as 'not the marrying sort', but for a suitable settlement he was prepared to make her his princess, take the money and run. And that is exactly what happened.

The de Rohans had been one of the grand families of France until the Marie Antionette diamond necklace scandal brought them shame and ruin. It was just before the French revolution began. The Prince de Rohan of the day was approached by a man he was led to believe was an emissary from the Queen, who told him that her majesty wished to purchase a magnificent and extremely expensive diamond necklace from a Paris firm of jewellers, but because of her unpopularity with the Parisians, who were accusing her of wild extravagance, she could not be seen to be buying it herself, and she wondered if the Prince would do her the great favour of secretly collecting it and bringing it to her at Versailles. He readily agreed. After all, such a favour would certainly put him in the Queen's best books and elevate his position at court. He did exactly as requested: he collected the necklace, took it to Versailles that night and at a designated spot in the garden, where the Queen, heavily veiled, was already waiting, handed it over to her. Only, of course, it wasn't the Queen but a female member of a gang of jewel thieves who were out of the country with the necklace before anything could be suspected.

When in due course the jewellers asked to be paid, the Queen, quite naturally, expressed astonishment and claimed ignorance of the whole ludicrous affair. It became a scandal that rocked France; the Parisians refused to believe she was innocent, it merely deepened their hatred of her; and some think it might even have hastened in the revolution.

But it was the Prince de Rohan, who had taken possession of the necklace who was expected to pay for it. This not only brought disgrace on the family name, it ruined them financially, and right up until the middle of the 1930s they were still repaying the debt – and that's how Dilkusha became a French princess!

Her grand title opened many a snobbish door in Paris. For a while she had her own dress shop; she then worked as a vendeuse at a couple of the biggest fashion houses. People loved to be served by a princess! Glamorous jobs came easily to her, and when I first met her in London after the war she was the head of the casting department at Sir Alexander Korda's London Films (Korda too was a sucker for titles). She then returned to Paris to work for Pierre Balmain...then someone else...and someone else...she had no trouble getting jobs, her problem was keeping them. I don't know why, but I have always had a slight suspicion that she might not have been completely reliable where money was concerned. Anyway, the glamorous jobs began to peter out and eventually cease altogether. Whether she had inherited anything from her father is not known; if she had it had long since disappeared.

Katusha ran a ballet company in England during the war of which the standard was said to have been very high, but like all ballet companies without permanent subsidy it fizzled out. She taught ballet at the Royal Academy of Dancing and now and then did the choreography for stage shows and operas; she would also arrange ball sequences for big costume films such as 'Anna Karenena', and 'Anastasia', but the glorious days were over. There had been many highs and lows in their lives, and as the years went by the lows began to outnumber the highs. It was sad to visit their flat in Brunswick Terrace and see the beautiful pictures they had gathered during their Paris years slowly, one by one, vanish from the walls to reappear in the auction rooms of Sotherby's or Christie's; and even their wonderful collection of letters, drawings and photographs of the Russian Ballet would end up in the libraries of rich American universities.

After Katusha had died of cancer and Dilkusha was living on Social Security, when desperately in need of a few pounds she would write to Alice. B. Toklas and ask her, for instance, what it was that Picasso had said to Gertrude on a certain occasion. Alice would wrack her brain and reply to the best of her recollection, and no sooner had the letter arrived than it would go winging across the Atlantic to Yale or Harvard to join the Gertrude Stein collection of memorabilia, and before very long a cheque for a few dollars would pop through the letterbox. She once showed me a very sad and completely unsolicited letter from Alice that told of how the moment Gertrude had died the Stein family swooped down like a flock of vultures and removed all the paintings from the apartment, leaving her sitting there with empty walls. It was ironic that Dilkusa too was sitting in an apartment with empty walls; and even the few little treasured mementos of Katusha's that she refused to part with were stolen by a woman who offered to come and look after her mynah bird while she was in hospital having an operation. She spent her last days sitting in an almost empty unheated flat drinking cheap bottles of Wincarnis and talking to the mynah, whose reply would invariably be, "This is the BBC Home Service, fuck off", followed by a terrifyingly lifelike imitation of Dilkusha's loud raucous laugh.

The tour of 'The Day After Tomorrow' started in Sheffield and we travelled up by train on the Saturday. I was shocked at how ugly and satanic the city looked; all the buildings were coated with soot and grime from the smoke of the steelworks; there was no colour to be seen anywhere; everything was grimly black. As it was the opening week and we needed to be close to the theatre, the stage director, Pat Moran and I stayed at the nearby Grand Hotel (as did most of the principals) and when I got my hotel bill – it is true I had been buying everyone drinks – it was for more than my week's salary. Pat had to bail me out. After that I mostly stayed in digs, usually with Pat. He had done a lot of touring over the years and knew the best landladies in most of the towns. On the Saturday night of our arrival we went to the theatre and saw the play that was on that week. It was the pre London tour of Terence Rattigan's 'The Winslow Boy', starring Emlyn Williams, which I thoroughly enjoyed and was not surprised when it became a big West End hit.

On Sunday we got in, set up and lit the show, and in the evening had our first dress rehearsal. It all seemed to be going quite smoothly until Phyllis Dare, making her first entrance suddenly stopped centre stage and called out into the auditorium, "Esme."

"Yes, Phyllis?" said Esme from the mid stalls, "What is it, dear?"

"Where are the footlights? I can't see any footlights."

Esme made his way down to the front. "Plays are lit differently these days, Phyllis dear," he told her, "They don't use footlights anymore."

"No footlights," she cried. "I can't work without footlights!" and bursting into tears fled back to her dressing room.

We now had a problem on our hands. But it was not insoluble. In a very short time the electrician had fixed some bulbs to a baton and placed it at the front of the stage. Phyllis, on hearing that she now had her footlights, remade her entrance, saw the warm surprise-pink glow at her feet and happily continued with the play.

It was difficult to tell how the first night was going. There were not a lot of laughs, except for Irene Handl's hilarious scene, but the audience didn't seem restless either, and at the end the applause was quite warm. In the second act a rather large actress called Marjorie Gresley, who was playing a snooping government inspector, was so busy putting the final touches to her make up that, although she had been called in ample time, missed her entrance. Mary Clare without a moment's hesitation (she was never one for hanging about) jumped straight in with the line that followed Marjorie's exit and the play continued. The scene was not missed at all. In fact, the play was too long anyway and it was much better without it. So poor Marjorie returned to London on Tuesday morning never having appeared at all.

We next played Bournemouth and were astonished to find our producer, Esme Percy, had been replaced by Max Adrian who saw the play in much more realistic terms and proceeded to reproduce it that way. The result was even less laughs except for Irene Handl's scene where, if possible, they increased (nervous relief, I thought).

Oxford came next, and Denis who was keen to visit old friends there, came along too (an actor friend was looking after the cats). We stayed at the lovely old Mitre Hotel, and also staying there was a handsome young American ex GI called Joe who had been on the scene in Cairo. He was with his new English lover, Lord Henry Audley, who had a flat in Albany, Piccadilly and a house in the country, and at both we would be lavishly entertained.

We rehearsed little changes to the script every morning, but our afternoons, apart from matinee days, were free, and on one of these Denis took me to tea with two of his oldest friends, the painter, Paul Nash and his wife, Margaret, who were charming and most hospitable. Paul was in a poor state of health; he was asthmatic; and surprisingly for a famous artist he was extremely poor. He said it was over a year since he had been able to buy Margaret a new dress. One of the paintings he was working on was a large yellowy sun-like abstract that had just been commissioned by Queen Elizabeth. She had seen a picture in his exhibition at the Tate Gallery that had particularly appealed to her and asked him if he would paint her something in a similar vein. It was interesting to know the Queen collected modern art, and I only hope he was royally remunerated.

Irene Handl never went anywhere without her fluffy little dog (I think it was a Pomeranian), but the New Theatre Oxford had a rule that no pets were allowed backstage; so it was wonderful watching the way she would hurry past the stage door keeper with the dog wrapped around her neck like a fur tippet. It was well acquainted with backstage life and would lie quietly on a chair in the dressing room throughout the performance; then at the first strains of the National Anthem it would stir, open its eyes, yawn, stretch, stand up and wait to be wrapped around Irene's neck once more and whisked past the stage door keeper's booth.

We then played Wimbledon, Brighton, Southsea, Llandudno, Nottingham, Hull and Birmingham, and by this time Max Adrian had been replaced by Vernon Sylvaine, author of the famous farce, 'Madame Louise'. He now saw farcical possibilities in the play and tried to bring them out. The old laughs returned and there were a few new ones, but still it was only Irene Handl's scene that got the really big laughs.

At the end of the tour we had a four week break while waiting for a West End theatre to become available and to do some recasting as certain members of the company had decided to do a bunk. Mary Clare was replaced by Marjorie Fielding, Peter Coke by Andrew Osborn and Yvonne Marling by Antionette Cellier. Vernon Sylvaine remained as the producer.

During the break Henry Audley and Joe invited us to spend a weekend with them in the country. It was a lovely old house with a superb garden, and as it was perfect July weather we spent most of our time in it. On the Saturday night after a delicious meal we visited a fun fair on the local village green and I went on all my favourite rides: the big wheel, the whip and my most favourite of all since early childhood, the ghost train. Joe accompanied me on the ride and so frightened were we that we clung together very tightly throughout. We even stayed on for another ride – that's how scary it was!

To lunch on Sunday they had invited some members of The Ballet Theatre who were paying their first visit to London. I had seen these wonderful American dancers at Covent Garden the week before and couldn't wait to meet them. One of the ballets I had particularly liked was 'Fancy Free', which Jerome Robbins and Leonard Bernstein would later turn into a Broadway musical and then a film called 'On The Town'. There were six of them at lunch: Jerome Robbins, his boyfriend at the time, Donald Saddler, Nora Kaye and Muriel Bentley (two very witty ladies), John Kriza and Michael Kidd. They were all great fun and we had a lovely afternoon lazing in the garden. It was sad though to hear that they had not been having much of a social life in London. In New York visiting artists are bombarded with invitations but the British are much more reserved about that sort of thing, and their reticence can be mistaken for indifference or arrogance.

As it was soon to be my twenty-second birthday, a few days after the play would open, we decided we would give a small after the theatre party on that night at the Duke Street flat. We invited our hosts and the American dancers and they all gladly accepted. From the British dance world we asked Frederic Ashton and William Chappell whom the Americans had already met, and the other guests were Katusha and Dilkusha, Bumble Dawson, Brian Desmond Hurst and a few other theatre people. We were rather cramped for space in that small flat but judging by the volume of the conversation and laughter everyone was having a good time. The sitting room had two windows opening onto a small space with a low parapet overlooking the street, and with agility one could climb out there and precariously take the cool night air, which is what some of the younger and more intrepid guests did.

Quite late in the party when I was in the kitchen opening another bottle of wine Donald Saddler wandered in and asked if he could help. I knew he and Jerome Robbins were an item so when he started to flirt with me I was somewhat surprised, but so physically attractive was he that I couldn't prevent myself from flirting back; and one afternoon the following week in his room at the Cumberland Hotel we spent an exquisite couple of hours in bed together. As neither Denis nor Jerome Robbins ever knew anything about it no harm was done and we had had a thrilling little adventure that I still remember with nostalgia to this day.

Our play opened at the Fortune Theatre, a small house across the street from Drury Lane. Both these theatres had been closed to the public during the war and used as the headquarters of ENSA. (Drury Lane also suffered some bomb damage). Ours was only the second show in since the theatre had reopened; the first was a short-lived transfer of 'Private Lives' from the Apollo. The play got one favourable review from a very right wing newspaper and the others ranged from iffy to dire; but Peter Daubeny refused to admit he had chosen unwisely and nursed the play for several weeks; when he finally realised that business was not going to improve, he reluctantly took it off. So my instincts had been right all along, and if it hadn't been for Irene Handl's hilarious contribution to the script I am sure 'The Day After Tomorrow' would never have made it to the West End.

———

And then I fell in love with Paris. We spent a week there. For Denis it was partly work, for me it was purely pleasure. He wanted to show me the city at its most spectacular and he certainly did. I have visited Paris many times since but never have I done it so thoroughly and in such style.

We took the Golden Arrow train from Victoria Station to the Gare du Nord. A dear friend of ours from Cairo, Graham Eyres Monsell who was a colonel in the British Army, came with us and we all stayed at the smart but not flashy Hotel Pont Royal on the left bank close to the Seine. That night in the hotel bar we had drinks with a beautiful French woman Denis had known from his pre war Paris days. She was an acclaimed poet. She was also, sadly, consumptive and was just recovering from a long bout of the illness. In less than a year the disease would claim her life. While they were catching up on news of old friends a dark and rather handsome man came up to the table and warmly greeted her. She introduced him to us. He was Albert Camus, and he was drinking at a nearby table with Jean-Paul Sartre. Having become a tourist attraction at the Café Flore they had recently abandoned Saint-Germain-des-Pres for the more secluded atmosphere of the Hotel Pont Royal.

I saw all the sights of Paris that week: the Louvre, Notre-Dame, the Champs-Elysees and the superb views of the city from both the steps of the Sacre-Coeur and the top of the Eiffel Tower. And I was taken to some of the finest restaurants: the Tour d'Argent, Grand Verfour, Pruniers, Maxim's. It was at Maxim's that we lunched one day with Graham's lovely sister, Joan Eyres Monsell and her handsome lover who she would eventually marry, Patrick Leigh Fermour – both of whom I had met at Denis' flat in Cairo. After a sumptuous meal and a great deal of wine Paddy insisted that Joan should buy a hat and we would help her choose it. We went to a very opulent looking salon in the Faubourg-Saint-Honore, full of grand Parisian ladies of a certain age seated at gilded rococo mirrors trying on exquisite concoctions of twisted buckram and straw. Joan scarcely had time to look at one of these millinery miracles before Paddy decided to run up and down snatching hats off the heads of startled women and trying them on himself. Not surprisingly we were asked to leave. Graham, Denis and I were highly embarrassed but Joan, who was well acquainted with Paddy's little pranks thought it quite amusing, and it meant she didn't have to buy a hat that she would never have worn anyway.

Lunchtime at the Ritz Bar the next day we had the great surprise and pleasure of running into Joy Murchie with whom we consumed several champagne cocktails. The elegant woman sitting at a table in the corner, Denis informed me, was Coco Chanel. That night with Joy we went to some boites on the left bank where singers in funereal black strummed guitars and sang mournful existential songs. We then crossed over to the right bank to the gaudy, glitzy 'Carousel', just off the Champs-Elysees, which boasted a spectacular transvestite cabaret. Then, much later that night while sitting in the bar at 'Le Boeuf Sur Le Toit' drinking fine a' l'eau, in came Charles Trenet with a matelot on his arm; he sat at the piano and to the matelot standing close by sang his famous song, 'La Mer'.

One evening we went to see Jean Cocteau's 'Les Parents Terrible' which had been running at the same theatre for several years. Denis knew an elderly actress who had been in it throughout and she came to supper with us after the show. She told us about some of the unpleasant things that had occurred during the run. There were those in the Resistance who believed that Cocteau had been too friendly with the Germans during the occupation, and many performances were disrupted by demonstrators barracking the play and chanting "Collaborateur!" But worst of all was when they released live rats in the auditorium causing the audience to panic. Jean Cocteau became a member of the Academie Francaise in 1955. Surely this honour would not have been bestowed upon him if the accusation had been true.

We also did the obligatory 'Follies Bergere' and 'Moulin Rouge', both of which I enjoyed enormously. And then one of those magical experiences one never forgets; we went to the ABC Music Hall to see the fabulous Edith Piaf; the memory of her singing, 'La Vie En Rose' still sends shivers down my spine. Later that night we visited a small nightclub off the Place Pigalle that was actually called La Vie En Rose. Les Sisters B, a drag duo, were the stars of the cabaret. They were a couple of middle-aged, rather plain looking men whose repertoire and costumes (all feathers and sequins) were of the Mistenguette 1930s era. We found their act a little sad but rather endearing. After the show we asked them to join us for a glass of champagne and they told us all about themselves. Life for them during the occupation had been a nightmare; unable to perform in cabaret they were reduced to doing the most menial jobs, just to keep alive; and they lived in constant fear, for like Jews and gypsies, homosexuals were often rounded up and sent to camps. After leaving the club – it was almost dawn – we went to a little bistro high up in Montmartre and sobered up on large bowls of delicious French onion soup.

One day accompanied by Joy we went to lunch at Cecil Robson's lovely house in Montparnasse, full of wonderful paintings and antiques that he had collected over the years. I had met Cecil in Cairo during the war; he worked at the British Library with Elizabeth Glynne (David), and was a regular visitor to Denis' flat. He was a dear, sweet man with a passion for the theatre, and it was through him telling Robin Chancellor and me about the Lyceum Melodramas he had seen in his youth with titles such as 'The Bad Girl Of The Family', and 'The Worst Woman In London', that gave us the idea to write a 1913 Ragtime Musical Melodrama which would eventually make it to the West End, and Cecil would come over from Paris for the first night.

Another guest at lunch that day – also from our Cairo past – was Alice Delysia who I had seen acting in Alexandria and lunching at the Taverne Francaise but had never actually met. I found her enchanting and her stories of the C.B. Cochran revues were fascinating. She was married to an Englishman, The Admiral of the Cinque Ports, and they lived in Southampton.

Cecil had two loyal servants, a Polish husband and wife, who had been with him since before the war and to whom he owed an incalculable debt of gratitude. I shall call them 'The Old Faithfuls'. In 1940, with the Germans speedily advancing on Paris, Cecil fled to England leaving all his precious belongings behind; and in Cairo he would often wonder what had happened to them all.

What had happened was this: the Germans took possession of the house and used it as a home for the Gestapo. But in the brief time between Cecil's departure and their arrival 'The Old Faithfuls' had emptied the house of its contents, paintings, furniture, books, the lot, and concealed them in a disused cellar. Then, when it was the Gestapo's turn to flee Paris and before Cecil returned, everything was retrieved from the cellar and put back in its proper place. When he arrived home he found his loyal staff waiting at the door to greet him. With trepidation he entered the house – looked about – and it was as if he had never been away. After all that, I thought, they must definitely have been due for a pay rise; and however sulky, insolent or infirm they may become he would never be able to dismiss them.

I left Paris very early on Sunday morning. I hated to go, I had fallen in love with the city, but I was due to start rehearsing a new play in London the following morning. Denis and Graham were staying on for a few days. Denis still had work to do that had been neglected because of me. At the Gare du Nord, suffering one of the worst hangovers of my life, I was more or less carried onto the train. My condition was the culmination of all the rich food and drink I had consumed over the week. My whole system was in shock; it was not conditioned to cope with such extravagant feasting and carousing. In England food and spirits were still heavily rationed, and even at our favourite London restaurant, the Ivy, one had to choose between a three course meal or a two course meal with bread; the third course was a choice of dessert or savoury, and as one was often still peckish at that point in the meal one usually opted for the savoury which was either welsh rarebit or mushrooms on toast – anything to fill one up; but there was no cream, no butter, no foie gras, no soufflés, no beef fillet steaks, no rich sauces or runny cheeses such as I had been gourmandising on for a whole week – not to mention the many bottles of champagne, wine and brandy. Yes, I definitely had the mother of all hangovers that morning.

The play we were starting to rehearse the next day was, 'The Anonymous Lover', by Vernon Sylvaine (third and final producer on, 'The Day After Tomorrow'). He had written and produced several successful farces in the West End, 'Madame Louise', being the most recent. His new play however was something quite different. It was a light drawing room comedy with four highly sophisticated characters: a modern playwright, his histrionic actress wife, another couple and a plot about a silly misunderstanding. The cast consisted of Hugh Sinclair, Valerie Taylor, Raymond Huntley and Ambrosine Phillpots, four very distinguished actors. Vernon Sylvaine was producing it himself and Peter Daubeny was presenting it. Pat Moran was the Stage Director and he asked me if I would like to be his Stage Manager. There were no parts I could play or even understudy; both the men were a lot older than me. I suppose I could have had a go at putting lines on my face, streaking my hair with grey, sticking on a false moustache and walking with a stoop but the option never arose. Stage management was not what I wanted to do, I would much rather act, but it was a well paid job in the West End theatre working with highly talented people; I felt I could only gain from the experience. As I have stated already, I never had the burning desire to be a star (as most young actors have), I knew my limitations. I just loved the theatre and if I could spend my life in it one way or another (although, of course, I would rather it was acting and writing) I would not end up twisted and bitter.

Peter Penn was engaged to understudy the two men. I would also learn both parts and at understudy rehearsals play whichever one Peter wasn't doing. During the tour we became good friends and that friendship would last well into the 1960s when he retired to Brighton and we somehow lost touch with one another. It was Peter who introduced me to rowing on the Serpentine, and in summer swimming in it. The water was a rather unpleasant shade of grey but it was very refreshing and I never heard of anyone becoming ill by swimming in it. The Serpentine in summer was a great meeting place for the young and beautiful of London. Olga and John were often there; Lionel Blair and his sister, Joyce; the Rank starlets, Joan Collins and Maxwell Reed; Peter Glenville, John Slessinger (who had started playing around with a small movie camera. He was then still an actor and would perform a number of mine in a revue); dancers from West End musicals; waiters from restaurants and night-clubs; airline stewards and stewardesses on their free days. It was an interesting mix and there was quite a gay element too. Many an assignation began while sunbathing on the grass at the Serpentine.

Hugh Sinclair had been a romantic leading actor in the theatre for over twenty years, half that time in the West End, the other half on Broadway. He was not a versatile actor, he always played variations of himself: handsome, debonair, suave and witty. His forte was brittle, light comedy, which is why Noel Coward, who never appeared for more than twelve weeks in any production, usually asked him to take over for the rest of the run. Hugh and Valerie Taylor had been married for nearly fourteen years. Their acting styles could not have been more different: she was a dramatic actress of tremendous power with a magnificent voice. She had just finished playing Lady Macbeth at Stratford Upon Avon, which was where I first met her. When 'The Day After Tomorrow' was playing in Birmingham, Pat, who knew her well, took me over to have lunch with her there and we got on splendidly. 'The Anonymous Lover' was not really her cup of tea; she was more suited to intense, emotional roles such as in 'The Seagull' and 'A Month In The Country', both of which she had triumphed in. However, the part was of a histrionic actress who had to chew up the scenery every now and then, and Valerie could do that with the greatest of ease, but she was not a natural comedienne.

In 1926 she had scored a great hit in a play called, 'Berkley Square'. In 1929 it was revived successfully in London and transferred to Broadway where it was equally successful. Hugh was also working there at the time. They met and fell in love. Valerie was then asked to repeat her role in the film of the play, and while in Hollywood, during a break she had in filming Hugh appeared, married her and off they went honeymooning on a yacht. When it was time for her to start work again she was still very much at sea, and to the angry and distraught cables she received from the studio demanding to know where she was she replied, "In the arms of my husband where every good wife should be." It will come as no surprise that her Hollywood career was a brief one.

Few actors could play the pompous, priggish, po-faced snob better than Raymond Huntley, the reason being that it didn't require an awful lot of acting on his part. I don't think he ever bothered to speak to me except once, and that was not in friendship. It was early on in the tour when he was still fairly shaky on his lines. Pat warned me not to leave the book for a second and when he dried to come in quickly and clearly with the prompt, and this I proceeded to do. When on one occasion he didn't take up the prompt I repeated it louder and clearer only to discover that he hadn't dried at all but was doing an effective comic pause. He was furious with me, but as he had needed several prompts he couldn't be quite as insulting as I am sure he would like to have been.

Ambrosine Phillpots was a charming woman. Again I thought she had been cast very much to type: posh, elegant and delightfully scatterbrained.

Once again I was not completely sold on the play but I thought that with four such accomplished performers they might very well pull it off. The tour began in Cambridge and several towns later we opened at the Duke of York's Theatre in

London to tepid reviews and ran six weeks. Hugh and Valerie's marriage had been slightly bumpy for some time; I had noticed it in rehearsals; on tour it got even bumpier and in the West End it came to a thumping halt. They had started to behave with childish animosity towards one another, and sometimes in front of a paying audience – albeit not a very large one. At a matinee during the final week, playing to a few old ladies with noisy tea trays, they really went to town. There was a scene where Valerie had to storm on in a rage, snatch a newspaper from Hugh who was reclining on a sofa in a silk dressing gown and read out a damning notice she had received. That afternoon she stormed on as usual and went to snatch the newspaper but it was not there. She looked to Hugh in desperation, he responded with a blank smile, whereupon she hurried across to the prompt corner and yelled at me, "The newspaper! Where's the newspaper?" I went cold. I must have forgotten to set it in the scene change. I ran to the prop table at the back of the stage but it wasn't there. I was almost certain I could remember setting it. I got back to the prompt corner in time to see Hugh pull it out from under the sofa where he had hidden it, hold it out to her and ask, "Would you like to see the paper?" But there was worse to come. In a big slanging-match scene they had together Hugh decided to underplay his performance making Valerie sound over loud and shrewish. She realised what he was doing and deciding that two could play at that game brought her performance down slightly below his. He got softer. She got even softer, and so on... until all I could hear from the prompt corner were whispering mumbles; and those poor old ladies in the audience must have thought they had suddenly gone deaf. After the performance Pat went to their dressing rooms and read the riot act to them both. On the final matinee day Hugh invited me to join him for a welsh rarebit and a pot of tea at the café across the road between the shows. He then had to cancel the invitation because Valerie said she thought it was a bad idea. I can't imagine what was going on in her head. It could not have been more innocent, and it was not as if I hadn't been there to tea with both of them before. I shall never know the answer to that one.

In Bournemouth on our pre London tour Pat and I stayed in the same digs as Hattie Jacques and John Byron who were touring in the Young Vic's production of 'The Stag King', and we all got on swimmingly together. Hattie had a wicked sense of humour that particularly appealed to me and by the end of the week we had become good friends. As we had different matinee days I was able to catch theirs, which I thought was excellent. I never said so but I thought it was a lot funnier than ours. And it seemed incongruous that they with their large cast should be cramped on the small stage of the King's Theatre while we, with just four people, looked rather lost on the vast wide-proscenium stage of the Pavilion Theatre.

John Byron, a very fine classical actor, gave a beautiful performance, but Hattie Jacques was a complete revelation. Although she was a large lady (very large, in fact), her movements were dainty, light and graceful, and she had a way of playing comedy that put me in mind of the great Beatrice Lillie. Those who only remember her from the 'Carry On' films will never know what a subtle, sophisticated actress she could be. After the tour Hattie returned to the Players Theatre where she was a permanent member of the company. It was a long, narrow theatre under the arches in Villiers Street that specialised in old time music hall, and she was by far the most popular performer there. She had a pretty voice and, like Miss Lillie, could take an innocuous old Victorian or Edwardian ballad and with just a few intonations and expressions give it another meaning entirely. She could make a song like 'Riding Down To Bangor On A Train' quite sexy by undulating ever so slightly to the motion of the train. But she was never coarse or vulgar, Hattie was the pass mistress of subtlety. Every year the Players Theatre put on a traditional Victorian pantomime, which was done with tremendous style, and Hattie always played the fairy queen. She did it on her toes wearing pointe shoes and to see that great hulk of a fairy floating across the stage as light as thistledown was an annual sight not to be missed.

She introduced me to Don Gemmel and Reggie Wooley who ran the theatre and thanks to her I got to do a couple of my comic monologues there. The salary at the Players was very poor but Hattie remained there because it was the one place where she could use her talents the way she wanted to. Many lucrative stage and film offers came her way but because the parts always made capital of her size she turned them down. But as the years rolled by and she was getting no younger or richer she allowed her resolve to weaken and started accepting the grotesques on offer such as the 'Carry On' films, etc. They made her well known to the public but not in the way she deserved. Only working with Eric Sykes on television was she ever allowed to be just sweet Hattie with no attention to the fact that she was a big girl.

Hattie was a magnificent cook and I was often asked to dinner at Eardley Crescent in Earls Court, where she and her husband, John Le Mesurer lived. John in those days was a struggling actor more out of work than in and Hattie was the bread winner. The time would come when he, having developed into a fine character actor ('Dad's Army', etc.) would be more successful than her. That would take a few years though. It was sad when their marriage ended; I thought they were an ideal couple; they had the same sense of humour and seemed so at ease together. I suppose one never really knows what goes on in another person's head.

On Christmas Day they had an open house and throughout the day and night friends would drop in and be given food and drink. They were joyous occasions and I always tried to spend a couple of hours there before attending the horrendous feast awaiting me at Alexandra Court, which Denis would be helping his mother to prepare. I dreaded those meals. They always ended in disaster. Marie would eat too much and be ill. On one occasion when she had violent stomach cramps (she suffered from diviticulitus) she accused us of having poisoned her, which did not make for the happiest of yuletides.

During our short run at the Duke of York's I heard that Norman Marshall, who was then running the Arts Theatre, was producing, 'Boys In Brown', a play about a Borstal institute, and in it there were several parts for young men. Denis, who had known Norman from the old Gate days, rang him up and asked if he would see me. He did, I auditioned for him and was offered a part. He had produced the play once before, at the Gate Theatre in 1940. It had barely begun its run when the blitz started and all the London theatres closed. (The Gate would never reopen – a German bomb fell on its roof.) Norman felt the play deserved a second chance, also John Carroll who had played the lead with great success. John by then was really too old for a Borstal boy but in those days they weren't as pedantic about casting people at their right age, and no one could have been as wonderfully creepy in the part as he was. The other leads were Nigel Stock, Andre Morell and Anthony Oliver.

We opened in Cambridge and came straight into the Arts Theatre. The reviews were excellent and we played to full houses. At the end of the run Henry Sherek transferred the play to the Duchess Theatre, and then occurred one of those strange coincidences that happen in the theatre. William Douglas Hume, who had been imprisoned during the war for being a conscientious objector, wrote an excellent play about prison life called, 'Now Barabas'. It had been playing at the little Boltons Theatre in South Kensington and just a couple of days after we opened at the Duchess it transferred to the Vaudeville. There was not room in the West End for two prison plays with a homosexual theme and as 'Now Barabas' had in it a charismatic young actor everyone was talking about called Richard Burton we sadly lost out.

Before leaving the subject of coincidence, here are some others: Denis was asked to produce a comedy about a mermaid and just before rehearsals began 'Miranda', a similar comedy about a mermaid opened. Weirder still, two musicals arrived in London simultaneously, both about girls getting fossy jaw from working in a match factory; one was called, 'The Match Girls', the other, 'Strike A Light'. More recently two quite different plays about Florence Foster Jenkins, the stone tone deaf diva who in 1944 packed Carnegie Hall, opened within a week of each other in London and New York. Spooky, isn't it?

The week after 'Boys In Brown' closed the BBC televised the play in their studio at Alexandra Palace. Television was still very primitive in those days. There was no recording then, plays were done live and performed twice, Sunday night and the following Thursday; and there were no breaks in the performance so actors were constantly running from one set to the next changing clothes as they went. Doing costume dramas could be a nightmare.

A film was made of, 'Boys In Brown', but no one from our production was seen for it. I thought maybe it was because we would have been too old, but the boys in the film were even older. They were Richard Attenborough, Dirk Bogard, Jimmy Hanley, Andrew Crawford and Michael Medwin. I didn't bother to go and see it.

Denis was asked to direct (producers were now being called directors) a play at the New Lindsey Theatre in Notting Hill Gate. It was called, 'Golden Rain', and in it there were parts for five teenage boys. Surprise, surprise, I was cast as one of them, and there were three others from, 'Boys In Brown': Hugh Munroe, Frank Coburn and Dennis Eagan. The grown up parts were played by Noel Howlett (Cairo), Barbara Leake (Foggia) Philip Stainton (his successful career as a character actor in films started from his being seen in this production. Until then he had only ever worked in northern reps. His career was at its zenith (he seemed to be in every British film) when he suddenly had a heart attack and died), Pauline Jameson (her first London play), Andrew Crawford (under contract to Rank), and a brilliant young actor called Patric Doonan (he would take over from Richard Attenborough in 'The Mousetrap', and just over a year later commit suicide). The play was well written, well acted and well received by both critics and public, but it was not the stuff of the West End, it was definitely alternative theatre.

One Saturday night Patric asked me along with a couple of the others to an after show party at his parents' home in Bayswater, where he and his younger brother still lived. The Doonans were a theatrical family, warm hearted and wonderfully hospitable. Lots of people came on after their performances and it was a very lively party. Several of them did party pieces. Today that would be frowned upon, but then it was quite the done thing, and very entertaining it could be too. I can think of a couple of reasons why it went out of fashion. First: few people today have pianos. Second: the advent of the LP record. The old gramophone record only lasted for about three minutes and usually left one wanting more. Today the record player blares out continuously and, sacrilegious though it may sound, I find that even artists of the calibre of Ella Fitzgerald and Frank Sinatra after a while become monotonous and start to pall. As my mother used to say about my tap dancing up and down our stairs, "One can have too much of a good thing."

At the Doonan's party that night Hubert Gregg sat at the piano and sang a couple of his own well known songs: 'Maybe It's Because I'm A Londoner', and 'I'm Going To Get Lit Up When The Lights Go On In London'; and an attractive dark haired northern girl called Gail Kendall, who was appearing in the Billy Milton revue at the St. James's Theatre sang a Betty Hutton style number with great exuberance. I thought she was terrific, and later that night when we got to talking I told her I was writing revue material but had not yet found the right composer (I had already met several would-be composers but found their music tinkly and insipid in the worst sort of genteel English way).

"You must meet Robb," said Gail, "he's playing the piano for our revue. He writes wonderful tunes. I think he's brilliant. Would you like to meet him?" I said I would, we did, and there began a collaboration, both smooth and extremely bumpy, that lasted for nearly forty years.

Robb Stewart was his name. No, actually, it was John Brougham and he came from one of the poorest districts of Manchester. In the great depression, with his father one of the millions of unemployed, John, barely out of short trousers, kept the family from starving by playing the piano in local pubs. He was already a fine musician (self taught) and the pub patrons were only too happy to throw a coin in the clever young fellow's cap.

In the late 1930s he toured the music halls of Great Britain as accompanist to the famous xylophone player, Teddy Brown; and when they were about to play the Glasgow Empire, a notoriously tough house, especially on a Saturday night, Teddy thought it might be wise if his accompanist had a good old Scottish name and changed it for him to Robb Stewart. John quite liked the name and as it was easier to pronounce and spell he remained Robb Stewart for the rest of his life.

Gail first met him in 1945 when she was in the cast of 'Sigh No More' at the Piccadilly Theatre and he was Noel Coward's musical assistant on the show. He would work in that capacity on two more of Coward's West End musicals: 'Pacific 1860' at Drury Lane starring Mary Martin, and 'Ace Of Clubs' at the Cambridge Theatre starring Pat Kirkwood. Gail would appear again in the latter – and so would I.

Robb started working for Coward in 1940 as his accompanist and musical assistant, and toured with him all over the country doing shows in army camps, munitions factories and hospitals. He also accompanied him on several recordings that were made at that time. He must have been considered pretty good at his job because at a gala concert in Paris, attended by Churchill, Eisenhower and De Gaul, he not only played for Coward but was also asked to accompany Marlene Dietrich and Maurice Chevallier.

As a musical assistant this is how he told me he worked. In Coward's house in Gerald Road, Belgravia, there was a large studio with a raised dais at one end and on it were two grand pianos facing each other; Coward would sit at one and Robb at the other; Coward would play a tune he had just composed (he only composed in one key), Robb would pick it up on the other piano, find the most suitable key for it, embellish it with the right chords, etc, and when the composer was entirely satisfied with the result his assistant would write it down. He was also often left to do the musical intros to the songs. On one occasion Coward asked him to play a South American rhythm, Robb came up with one and it was to that rhythm that he then wrote the witty song, 'Nina From Argentina.'

Having such an important and rather personal job you might imagine, as I did, that Robb would be extremely well paid and kept on some sort of a retainer when Coward was in Jamaica or wherever for long periods. Neither was true. His salary was quite meagre and when Coward was away he had to find other means of employment, such as playing the piano in drinking clubs or for singers at auditions or, as when I met him, in the pit for the Billy Milton Revue. Yet he was expected to drop everything and be ready and waiting the moment the composer wished to resume work. As time went by Robb began to grow a little disillusioned, especially when we started writing songs together and, far from giving him any encouragement, Coward actually tried to dissuade him from doing so, saying he would be far better off just working for him.

At parties in the Gerald Road studio Robb was sometimes asked to provide background music on the piano (predominantly melodies by the Master), and later in the evening if the host could be persuaded to sing Robb would fortunately be there to accompany him. At one such do Robb had the audacity to slip in one of his own tunes. It was a song we had just written that he was particularly proud of and he couldn't resist showing it off. Clifton Webb, one of the guests at the party, asked him what the lovely tune was he was playing, and made him repeat it. Coward was furious, and it only took one look from him for Robb to hastily return to the works of the Master. 'The Master' was how Coward was referred to by everyone in his entourage – everyone except Robb, that is, who thought it sounded sycophantic and only ever called him Noelie. This might have rankled slightly for the Master was never known to object to being addressed as such.

Elsie April had held the post of amanuensis for several years before Robb and had retired with a certain amount of rancour,. When she heard he was about to take on the job warned him not to give too much of himself. "He'll take it all and you'll get no thanks," she told him. Elsie always claimed that a great deal of her own creativity had gone into the score of the operette, 'Bitter Sweet'. It triumphed in London and New York and was twice made into a Hollywood film, and all she ever got out of it was that the printed score was dedicated to her. 'Bitter Sweet' left Elsie more bitter than sweet, and Robb was beginning to feel the same way.

The parting of the ways came during 'Ace Of Clubs.' Robb openly began to show defiance and for Coward, who could accept nothing less than complete loyalty, commitment and Messiah like adoration from all who worked for him, such behaviour was untenable. He turned his back on his ex assistant and forbade his name ever to be mentioned in his presence. (This is why you will read nothing of Robb's ten years with him in any of the biographies, except for one where I supplied the information). Norman Hackforth who was in Cairo with ENSA during the war and had been Coward's accompanist on his Middle East and South African tours now took on the role of amanuensis.

Before you jump to the conclusion that I thought Coward was the devil incarnate and Robb a saint with more arrows in him than St Sebastian I had better tell you a few home truths about Robb. He was an eccentric – a true eccentric – the most eccentric person I have ever known, and his eccentricities took many forms, one of them being an innate vagueness. Time meant nothing to him. If I could add up all the hours I spent waiting for him it would surely work out at weeks. What is amazing though is that he somehow always managed to be on time for a performance – although quite often with literally a second or two to spare. Cool as a cucumber he would be, having made everyone else nervous wrecks. In worldly goods Robb seemed to take no interest whatsoever, except for expensive bottles of scent; the shelves of his dank little basement flat in Pimlico was stacked with them, and the damp walls covered with prints and postcards of the French Impressionists. He cared nothing for wealth. If he had ever made real money, which he never did, he would not have known how to spend it, and he wouldn't have risked putting it in a bank either. It would probably have been hidden in his flat, possibly sewn into his mattress, there for a rainy day, and then completely forgotten about.

He was equally vague about his appearance. With his unkempt hair, straggly moustache and beard and wearing a grey cotton raincoat bought in a second hand shop he could quite easily be taken for a tramp. It amuses me to think how Coward, impeccably turned out as he always was, must have felt arriving at some grand venue to give a performance accompanied by Robb in a tea stained dinner jacket, scuffed shoes and clutching a crumpled old plastic carrier bag containing the evening's music. To have put up with his eccentricities for all those years Coward must have appreciated his talent and really been reliant on his musical expertise.

But of all his irritating eccentricities the one I hated the most was his pathological aversion to writing down his music. While he was procrastinating the tunes would alter, he wouldn't be able to remember the original, and that way several good songs were lost (today one would use a tape recorder but they weren't invented then).

I believe it was this eccentricity that was the last straw to break the camel's back in the Coward Stewart working relationship. On the morning that Graham Payne, who co starred with Pat Kirkwood in 'Ace Of Clubs', was about to start rehearsing one of his big numbers for the show, he discovered that the rehearsal pianist had not yet received the music from Robb. Graham tried ringing him but his phone was off the hook. Enraged, he raced round to Robb's Pimlico flat. Robb saw him storming down the area steps and, fully dressed, leapt into bed pulling the covers up around his neck, the unfinished manuscript clutched firmly between his knees. Robb's partner, Jack (now, there was a saint if ever there was one) played for time in going to open the front door.

"Robb has the most awful migraine," he tried to explain as Graham brushed past him and strode into the flat where he found Robb lying in bed moaning. Graham did not get to rehearse his number that day, he knew Robb's migraine was not genuine and never forgave him – and neither did Coward.

I too would suffer similar frustrations. The first full revue we ever had produced was 'Oddly Enough', directed by Norman Marshall at the New Watergate Theatre. Robb turned up with the music for the opening chorus just after the first night performance had finished. Stanley Myers, a brilliant young musician just down from Oxford (he would go on to write great film scores) was playing the piano for the show and late on in rehearsals when the music for the opening had still not arrived he improvised something of his own so the number could be set. Robb had gone to ground. The phone was almost continuously off the hook and when it wasn't I would get Jack lying to me. Once, by sheer luck, I managed to catch him.

"Where's the opening music?" I asked.

"I'm sorry, Neville," he said sadly, "my muse is not with me."

"Fuck your muse," I shrieked at him, "just write down the opening tune the way you have been playing it for the past few months." He did, and handed it to Stanley as he came off stage having just played the finale of the show. Stanley, quite naturally, threw it away and continued to play his own tune.

Robin Chancellor and I wrote the book and lyrics of the musical, 'Chrysanthemum', that would star Pat Kirkwood, and we were delighted with the tuneful, catchy score that Robb produced. When the time came to start playing it to people our delight turned to concern as we discovered that less than half the music had been committed to paper, and with every playing it differed slightly – and not always for the best. Drastic action had to be taken. For tedious hour after hour, day after day, night after night we sat either side of him coaxing, nagging, threatening him. Robb was frightened of Denis (as he must have been of Coward), for he could be very intimidating when he wished, and for one whole night the three of us stood over him with pots of strong black coffee (provided by Jack) getting him to write down the long and fairly complicated Scena that was the first act finale. By dawn it was completed, but I am sure if it was not for his fear of Denis' wrath he somehow would have wriggled out of finishing it.

Denis was furious with me for wanting to work with him on another show; he said Robb was a hopeless liability, that it was a waste of my time and talent; and he never took any real interest in anything that we wrote together after that. But I liked Robb. I liked his music. He liked my lyrics. We liked working together – it was only in the later stages of the procedure that things got out of hand. In retrospect I realise I should have taken Denis' advice and tried much harder to find another equally talented, more ambitious, really reliable, younger composer: one who wouldn't do the vanishing trick on me at the moment he was most needed (mind you, such rare specimens do not grow on trees). I did try working with a few others, and some of what we did was quite successful, but I never felt as at ease with any of them as I did with Robb, and, weak willed and masochistic as clearly I must have been, back to him I went.

Before we forget about Robb for a while I want to tell you something about his long-suffering companion. Jack Beatty was his name, he came from Edinburgh. When Robb met him, just after the war, he was in the chorus of 'The Song Of Norway' at the Palace Theatre. Jack was a keen Francophile and he thought it would be more glamorous and might even get him more work if he adopted a faintly French accent and called himself, Jacques Gautier. Unfortunately there was not a great demand on the London stage at that time for slightly French chorus boys. However, the name, Jacques Gautier can be found in the programme of 'Ace Of Clubs', in which Jack appeared as a nightclub waiter.

Without Jack I don't know how Robb managed to exist (which he somehow did on a few occasions). Jack shopped, cooked, cleaned, washed and ironed – in fact, he did everything in the flat except play the piano, and as playing the piano was the only thing Robb did do it worked out rather well. Jack lived in hope that Robb's music would one day strike it rich and they would be able to leave their dank little basement for somewhere above ground that was light and airy, and to this aim he ceaselessly strived, giving endless support and encouragement; but Robb seemed almost oblivious to his surroundings (this could be something to do with his deprived childhood) and as long as there was a piano handy and a cup of tea in the pot he was more or less content. In despair at his lack of any real effort to change their troglodyte existence Jack left him a couple of times and went to live abroad. The first time it was to his beloved France, where he worked for a summer as a sort of footman at the country home of Lady Diana Cooper. The overheard conversations at her dinner table as recounted by Jack were both scandalous and hilarious. The second time he went to Amsterdam, where he stayed for over a year selling bric-a-brac in the flea market (he had done a bit of this in the London markets). But deep down he still cared for Robb and once again came back to pick up the pieces – and after a year or so of total neglect there were quite a few pieces to be picked up. If there was any justice in the world Jack should have been canonised. I will always think of him as Saint Jacques, martyr of the Pimlico basement.

Elizabeth David was now back in England and had rented a flat in Abingdon Road, just a short way down from Kensington High Street. One night she invited us to dinner and asked us to bring Irene, who she had not seen since before the war when she was still an aspiring young actress and Irene was living with Peter Godfrey who ran the Gate Theatre. There were two other guests at dinner: tall, lean, handsome George Lassalle, Elizabeth's on and off lover of many years. This would probably be their last night together for some time, as her husband Tony was arriving back from India in a day or so. The other guest was a big bear-like Polish sculptor with wild eyes and a shock of steel grey hair. He spoke no English but was fairly fluent in French. Already slightly the worse for drink, he began to flirt outrageously with Irene who was sitting beside him at the table. Not understanding a word he was saying but in a jolly mood, having had a glass or two of wine herself, she responded to his blurred prattle with smiles and nods. The next thing she knew his hand was up her skirt; and the next thing he knew she had grabbed that hand and bitten it. With a yelp of pain he leapt from his chair and went dancing about the room waving his bleeding paw in the air. After it had been held under a cold tap for a while and had a plaster stuck on it dinner continued more or less as normal, and, considering food rationing, delicious it was too.

"That's typical of Irene," said Denis in the taxi after we had dropped her off at Kynance Place, "you can't take her anywhere. The lady of the manor one moment and a wild gypsy the next." An exaggeration, but not without a certain truth, for there was something of a Jeckyl and Hyde dichotomy in Irene's personality, and at the first sign of the tricky Miss Hyde appearing it was wise to lay low and wait for the amiable Miss Jeckyl to re-emerge.

Near the end of the meal that night (the Pole was now asleep, face down on the table) Elizabeth told us she had seen an attractive Georgian terrace house in Chelsea that she thought she and Tony might buy. It was four storied and would be too large for just the two of them, so they would want to let the two top floors, and as she knew we were looking for somewhere to live she asked if perhaps we might be interested. We said we might be, and as soon as the house was theirs we went around to look at the rooms. The third floor had a large bedroom at the front leading into an almost as large bathroom with bath, shower, washbasin, and bidet; and when we had added a thick pile carpet, a couple of large mirrors, sofa, coffee table, telephone and radio, it would be somewhere I could happily spend an entire morning. The top floor had a sitting room at the front and a kitchen come dining room at the back. We thought it would be ideal for us and immediately accepted the offer. Swiftly but tastefully the flat was furnished (Denis had just landed a contract with J. Arthur Rank so we were not strapped for cash). When it was ready we moved in, and for three of our happiest years together in London we lived at number 24 Halsey Street, Chelsea.

As soon as I met Colonel Anthony David I knew he was not the right man for Elizabeth. Who the right man might be I don't think anyone, Elizabeth included, ever really knew. They seemed a most unlikely pair: his was the world of polo, horse racing (he was an amateur jockey), fast cars and country pubs; and try as hard as the poor man did he was never able to fit in to Elizabeth's hot house world of artists and intellectuals (where he was very often ignored). Nor did he share her overriding passion for all things Mediterranean – especially the food! They were as different as chalk and Feta.

That summer Roland Petit brought his Ballet de Paris to London for a season at the Prince's Theatre (now called the Shaftsbury) where, to great acclaim, he premiered his new ballet, 'Carmen', featuring the dazzling and voluptuous young Renee Jeanmaire (she would change her name to Zizi Jeanmaire, become the star of Paris revues and make several films in Hollywood. She would also become Madame Petit. Another pretty young dancer in the company who would turn to acting and be an even bigger name in Hollywood was Leslie Caron).

I took Elizabeth to a mid week matinee, and a friend of ours from the ballet world, who we were sitting with in the stalls told us to look up at one of the boxes. We did, and saw a grey haired, rather shrunken looking man with a vacant expression on his face. We were told he was Vaslav Nijinsky and this was the third time he had come to see 'Carmen'.

That evening Tony, Elizabeth, Denis and I were in a taxi crossing Hyde Park on our way to a new Swiss restaurant somewhere off Baker Street that Elizabeth had discovered, and we were regaling them with the wonderful experience of the afternoon and the extra excitement of having actually seen the great Nijinsky.

"Who's that?" said Tony.

Elizabeth explained that he was considered the greatest dancer of his day, and that he was particularly famous for being able to do magnificent high leaps where, for a moment or two, he seemed to remain suspended in the air.

"I had a horse like that in Calcutta," said Tony.

I watched the expression drain from Elizabeth's face and I thought then and there, "Oh, dear, this is not going to last."

Nor did it. Elizabeth hung on to the house and Tony went off to the country to run a pub. I never saw him again.

Robin Chancellor who had been with the British Council in Cairo during the war (although we never met there) now worked for the publishing firm, 'Museum Press', and lived at his parents' house in Pavilion Road, Chelsea. As we were writing a musical together he was often around at 24 Halsey Street; and one evening Elizabeth, who had recently had some cookery articles published in Harper's Bazaar, while having a drink with us in our upstairs flat, asked Robin if he would give his opinion on some material she was gathering for a book. He happily agreed and she handed him an untidy sheaf of type written pages, some of which had been slightly stained with food as she had been cooking from them. It consisted of a collection of mouth-watering recipes of authentic Mediterranean dishes, plus gloriously sensuous descriptions of the sun-drenched south that she felt so passionate about. It also included short, evocative extracts from the works of famous authors who too had been captivated by those enchanted lands: Henry James, Arnold Bennett, Norman Douglas, Compton Mackenzie, D.H. Lawrence, Osbert Sitwell, Gertrude Stein, Lawrence Durrell...

Robin was fascinated by it, and was especially impressed by Elizabeth's wonderfully descriptive and literate style, and as soon as it had been licked into slightly better shape – though not completely free of food stains – he showed it to the Museum Press, who immediately turned it down. Embarrassed by the speed of their negative response he took it to another publisher he knew. He too turned it down. He tried a third and the reaction was the same. Before admitting defeat he decided to have one more go and showed it to John Lehman. He had never published a cookery book and was less than impressed at the scraps of crumpled food-stained paper he was shown; but Julia Strachey, who worked for him, read it and saw its great potential. In the austere, food rationed, travel restricted Britain of 1949 such a passionate and sensual evocation of the hot Mediterranean could, with the right enticing illustrations, be the perfect escape book. Lehman agreed to publish it and got the artist, John Minton to do the illustrations, also a delightful dust-jacket depicting a colourful array of Mediterranean delicacies: a lobster, a slice of melon, pasta, fruits and wine all attractively arranged on a table at the edge of a terrace overlooking a calm, blue bay with little red and white sailboats on it. It was wonderfully atmospheric and a real eye catcher.

After much haggling over the title with Lehman, he wanted to call it 'The Blue Train Cook Book' – Elizabeth finally got her way and it appeared as 'A Book Of Mediterranean Food'. It was an instant best seller, and over half a century later Penguin copies of it are still being bought all over the world.

I am the only person alive today who witnessed this, when Elizabeth first saw the

Minton illustrations she burst into tears. They were not what she wanted at all. I think she found their Neo-Realism sentimental. She would much have preferred something abstract by Matisse or Mondrain. But it's my opinion that, although the book would have succeeded anyway, without Minton's sensually arresting drawings and that eye catching dust-jacket it would not have taken off in quite the spectacular way it did.

Lehman commissioned a second book, 'French Country Cooking', and again John Minton did the illustrations. By now Elizabeth had grown quite fond of his work (success works wonders!) It too was a best seller.

Her fourth book, 'Summer Food', was published by the Museum Press, who were still kicking themselves for having turned down the first one. By now Elizabeth had complete control over the illustrations and she chose some finely executed, but to my mind, deadly dull drawings of kitchen utensils. In no way could they compete with the warmth and vigour of Minton's work (but sadly by 1957 his Neo-Realistic style of painting had gone out of fashion, and suffering from deep depression and alcoholism he committed suicide).

Elizabeth became the queen of the British cookery world and took to it as to the royal palace born. She was grand, aloof and autocratic. If she had been a queen in another age, with all the powers that a queen then possessed, I have no doubt she would have gone about saying, "Off with their heads!" quite a lot (and this would particularly have applied to all other English cookery writers , for whom she had no time at all).

Elizabeth was not a happy woman. She could laugh and joke and be wickedly witty at times, but deep down there was always a sadness and a dissatisfaction with life. Readers of her ebullient writing about food probably imagine that she was always surrounded by friends enjoying the magnificent meals she constantly cooked; where as, in reality, she was more often than not on her own, sitting at her kitchen table, paper and pen by her side, sipping her umpteenth cup of Nescafé and nibbling at a Marie Biscuit.

Hermoine Gingold rang me up one day to say she and Walter Crisham were going to do a revue at the Comedy Theatre called, 'Slings And Arrows', and had I any ideas? For some time I had been an avid fan of the Charles Adams cartoons in The New Yorker magazine and I thought Hermoine would make a marvellous Adams lady. There have been television series and two major films based on his cartoon characters, and the lady in question has been given the name of Morticia, but back then when I first had the idea, as far as I am aware, I was the only one. Jean Kent had just made a film called, 'Good Time Girl', so I thought a good title would be, 'Good Time Ghoul'. Hermoine liked the idea so I wrote a lyric, Robb set it to music and with a bit of bullying from me he actually wrote it down.

The scene is a churchyard with swirling mist and up from a grave rises this ghoulish apparition, who sings:

"I could a tail unfold,
(This she does with a great flourish)
When I was just an itty bitty pretty little ghoul
I was disapproved of at the most approved of school.
Time and again I was up on the mat
For bringing to cricket the wrong kind of bat.
And what an ear wigging I got from Miss Crocker
When a mummified prefect was found in my locker –
My report at the end of that term was a shocker!
(I don't recall the rest of the verse, but it then went into a jazzy refrain that began):
"I'm a good time ghoul!
Meet me tonight for a good time fright,
I'm a good time ghoul!..."
(That's all I remember of it and the lyric is now lost.)

Both Hermione and the director, Charles Hickman liked it and thought it should be in the show. I was delighted. The first scenery and costume rehearsal was on a Sunday afternoon and I was invited to it. The churchyard setting and the swirling mist were great fun, and in her black dress and wig Hermione made a gloriously glamorous ghoul. I thought the number worked quite well and couldn't wait for an audience's reaction. The first performance was to be a midnight matinee so actors from all the other West End shows could attend, and as most of the jokes were about the profession they would be the ideal audience for it. On the day of the performance I was filming at Denham Studios and got a message in the afternoon to ring Denis. I did and he told me the theatre had just phoned to say that 'Good Time Ghoul' had been dropped from the show. The management, Linnet and Dunfee, found its humour too macabre, and they thought someone rising from a grave might offend certain people. I was devastated and when I got home that evening I cried a great deal and said I couldn't possibly go to the show. Denis said I must and I wasn't to let my hurt show. He gave me a stern lecture and said if I couldn't take disappointment I should get out of the theatre straight away, for if there is one thing in it that you can count upon more than anything else it's disappointment – and after a lifetime spent one way and another in that ridiculous business I can say, quite unequivocally, he was right.

We sat in a box with Bumble, who had designed some of Hermione's more fetching costumes, Brian was there, and I can't remember who else. Hermione Baddeley and Henry Kendal, having come from doing a performance of their revue 'A La Carte' at the Savoy Theatre, were sitting in a box opposite prominently displaying themselves in shining suits of armour. I laughed and applauded but deep down I was feeling miserable. I also found the show less than completely satisfying; and it wasn't just me, the others felt the same.

The critics were much more damning. They all said it was too parochial and parish pump – although that was how intimate revue had mostly been until then – but they decided enough was enough and this was the time to draw the line. 'Slings And Arrows' had a modest run.

'The Green Box' was a play that the South African author, Rayne Kruger wrote for his wife, the actress, Nan Munro with whom he had just arrived in England. Nan and fellow actress, Margaret Inglis had run a very successful theatre company in South Africa during the war. Two outstanding productions of theirs that I saw in Johannesburg were, 'Ladies In Retirement', and 'My Sister Eileen'. Rayne's play was about the famous Scottish surgeon, Dr. James Barry who served with the British army at the Castle in Cape Town in the early 19th century. He was a very colourful character and had the reputation of being a great ladies man. On the steps of Alphen House in Constantia (now the delightful Alphen Hotel) he fought a duel with pistols said to have been over the affections of a young lady. He was world travelled and had led a most remarkable life, but the most remarkable part of it was that when he died it was discovered that he was a woman. Nan, being tall with long slender legs and not too prominent a chest, had the figure that in British military uniform could pass quite easily for that of a man.

The play Rayne had written for her was completely fictitious and pure romance. The secret of the green box (of the title) that the doctor keeps locked in his bedroom is that it contains several stunning dresses that he, or she as it turns out, puts on in the evening to entertain her lover, a fellow officer at the Castle. It was a silly and most unlikely story but he had written it especially for her and she rather fancied herself in military uniform and pretty dresses, and as they were not short of a bob or two they decided to have a go and gave it a modest production at the Chepstow Theatre. It had a large cast and there were five South Africans in it – I was one of them and I played two parts; for the second one, so as not to be recognised, I hid under a lot of crepe hair and a hump.

During rehearsals I had a phone call from Hermione Gingold to say she was putting 'Good Time Ghoul' back in the show. I had to tell her that it was going into the new Benny Hill revue at the Boltons Theatre and that another actress was already rehearsing it. She was furious with me and said she had always planned to put it back. But she had never told me that, and anyway, although I didn't say so, I thought it stood a better chance in a new revue than one on its last legs that would probably be off in a week or two. She slammed the phone down on me and I expected her never to speak to me again.

Some time later, spending a weekend at Brian's, I was aghast to learn that Hermione was coming to Sunday lunch. How would she behave towards me? I dreaded the meeting. Actually it didn't turn out that bad: she was icy to begin with, but during the meal she began to thaw and by the end of the afternoon our former friendship had been more or less restored. And it would not be very long before she was singing some songs of mine in cabaret at the Café de Paris.

Caryl Brahams and S.J.Simon had written a string of highly successful comic novellas and the latest one was called, 'Trottie True'. It was an Edwardian tale of a little girl from Camden Town, the daughter of a toucher-upper of tinsel postcards, who goes on the Halls, becomes a George Edwards 'Gaiety Girl' and ends up a duchess. Denis read it and thought it would make a delightful film comedy with music. He and an aspiring film producer called Hugh Stewart together bought an option on the book. He then went off to a small country hotel run by some old friends of his, shut himself away and wrote the film script. When it was completed Hugh Stewart took it to the Rank Organisation who snapped it up as a vehicle for their contract star, Jean Kent, who had a beautiful clear soprano voice and was a trained dancer (she began her career as a 'Windmill' girl). Hugh Stewart, naturally, was the producer and the director was Brian Desmond Hurst. Whether Denis had any influence on the choice of director I'm not sure, but knowing how cunning and subtly persuasive he could be it wouldn't surprise me if he had. I can see him thinking that with Brian he would have more control over the script than he might have with another unknown, perhaps unsympathetic, director. And that is what happened: seeing how keen he was, and by then being a little jaded himself, Brian made him his dialogue director; so he was able to rehearse all the scenes in advance and in that way ensure that the acting had the style and wit that the dialogue required. Brian also gave him his head over the casting; he had complete faith in Denis' good taste and ability and, light comedy not being his forte, he let him get on with it. So, assisted by Maude Spector, the casting director at Denham Studios with whom he formed a close and lifelong friendship, he practically cast the entire film.

He was also responsible for Benjamin Frankel (a friend and colleague from pre-war revue days) composing the delightful musical score, and Bumble Dawson designing the exquisite Edwardian dresses that gave the film its uniquely stylish look.

He had recently seen James Donald give a superb display of high comedy acting in Shaw's 'You Never Can Tell' at the Wyndham's Theatre and, with him in mind, he wrote the leading male role of Lord Digby. As good fortune would have it he was available to play the part, which he did with tremendous panache and wit. For me he walked away with the film; when he was on the screen I looked at no one else.

The role of Trottie's first boyfriend, the unreliable balloonist, Sid, was taken by Andrew Crawford (who had been in 'Golden Rain' at the New Lindsey Theatre); Hugh Sinclair played a middle aged roué who tries to seduce Trottie; Philip Stainton ('Golden Rain'), a Bradford mill owner who has the same idea; Olga Lowe ('The Boomerangs') was Ruby Rubarto, a Gaiety vamp with designs on Digby; Hattie Jacques, the comedienne of a George Edwards touring show, May Hallatt (ENSA in Cairo), Trottie's faithful old dresser; Daphne Anderson, her plump, cake devouring younger sister; Tony Halfpenny ('Boys In Brown') her young brother; Trottie as a child was played by a sparky little girl called Dilys Laye; Gretchen Franklyn was the True's maid who fancies the postman, Ian Carmichael; and the parts of two young footmen who appear in most of the big house scenes Denis wrote for Hugh Munroe ('Boys In Brown' and 'Golden Rain') and me.

Eleanor Summerfield was in a play he had directed at the New Lindsey Theatre called, 'And So To Wed.', and so impressed had he been by her sly comedic style that it was her he thought of when writing the character of Bouncie, Trottie's flighty dressing room companion and friend. Sadly she never got to do it. The Studio insisted that the part be played by one of its contract artists, so it went to Lana Morris. She was prettier than Eleanor and acted with great charm and vivacity; no one would guess the part had been written for anyone else. Only we knew that Eleanor would have given Bouncie that extra little bounce!

Other friends in it were Helen Goss, John Vere, Fanny Carby, Frank Coburn…and several others…some days on the set one seemed to know everyone. Denis had no qualms about casting his friends if he thought they were right for the part, and judging from the sterling performances they all turned in I can see no reason why he should have had. Oh, yes, and just in case these names mean anything to you, among the Stage Door Johnnies (non speaking roles) were Roger Moore, Patrick Cargill and Christopher Lee with not a hint of the vampire about him.

It was a glorious summer in 1948, the perfect weather for location filming – there was none of that hanging about for hours waiting for the sun to reappear as is usually the case when filming in England. One of the most spectacular location scenes was the

Gaiety Theatre's annual country outing, filmed in the grounds of Stowe House, where over the Palladian bridge came horse drawn drays filled with pretty girls in beautiful white dresses, wearing large flower laden hats and twirling lace parasols. Bumble had really done them proud.

One day Earl St. John, the head of Rank Films at Denham Studios, called Denis to his office and told him that a film of Arnold Bennett's novel, 'Mr. Prohack.' starring Cecil Parker, was about to start shooting and they had just lost their director. He then said how impressed everyone had been with the work he had done on 'Trottie True', and if that production would now let him go they would like him to direct, 'Mr. Prohack'.

This is where that hidden streak of treachery I spoke of shows itself. Brian knew what a tremendous break it would be for Denis but both he and Hugh Stewart (his first production so of great importance to him) refused to release him, saying his presence was vital to the production, so 'Mr. Prohack' went to another director. Earl St. John assured Denis that he would keep him in mind for future projects, and he might have meant it at the time – but then catastrophe struck!

For the role of the Duchess of Wellwater, a formidable dragon of a character who strongly opposes her son's marriage to a Gaiety Girl, yet in the end turns out to have a heart as soft as spreadable butter, Denis chose the bright, brittle, ebullient actress, Irene Browne, who played the English aristocracy better than the real thing, and gave them an extra little satirical edge.

On her first morning at Denham Studios, as several films were being made there at the same time there was a shortage of dressing rooms, she was asked to share one with old May Hallatt and she threw a tantrum. The third assistant, instead of finding someone in the production office to sort things out went straight onto the set and reported it to Brian. For some reason or other he was in a foul mood that morning and, storming into the dressing room, where Irene Browne was now in full costume, without letting her say a single word, sacked her on the spot.

It's my personal belief that there was more to it than just a fit of temper on Brian's part. I think he had a grudge against Denis for some reason known only to him (perhaps the actors liked him too much – who knows?) and as Irene Browne was his particular choice, and a personal friend, by hitting at her it was also a slap in the face for him. This explanation may seem bizarre but I still believe there is some truth to it. Don't forget that hidden streak of treachery.

Brian gave the role to Mary Hinton; that afternoon Irene Browne's costume was altered to fit her and the next morning she was on the set playing the Duchess of Wellwater. Mary Hinton was the real thing, an aristocratic lady, and she played the part with all the fine breeding and aloof grandeur of one. What her performance lacked was the flamboyance and bright, brittle brio that the impostor would have brought to the role.

Denis was appalled at Brian's dreadful treatment of Irene (shades of Iris) and when she went to Equity claiming unfair dismissal and a tribunal was held, to which everyone was summoned, he felt it was his moral duty to appear as a character witness for her. He was the only one from the production who dared to do so. Irene won her case and was awarded substantial compensation. Foolhardy Denis however was considered a traitor to his side and the Rank Organization never employed him again.

The end of the story has an ironic twist to it. Twelve years later in the winter of 1960 Denis was suffering badly from Emphysema and bronchitis and it was with great difficulty that he ventured out in the cold weather. A friend of his, Barbara Back, who weekly wrote a column for the woman's page of a Sunday newspaper, would sometimes come and take him out for a drive in her car, which, having been cooped up in the flat for days on end, he thoroughly enjoyed. One Sunday she took us to Greenwich Park, where we had a picnic lunch sitting in the car looking down at the beautiful view of the river. The fourth member on the outing was Irene Browne. Denis and she were delighted to see one another and she was being very witty in her usual brittle, bright way. Half way through the meal she became rather pensive, then she suddenly said, "You know, Denis, I know it was a long time ago and all that, and one should try to forgive and forget, but I can't help it, it still rankles the way you didn't stand up for me that day at the tribunal."

It took some time for these words to sink in; when they finally did he exploded: "You stupid woman," he yelled, "haven't you realized it was precisely because I did stand up for you at the tribunal that the Rank Organization has never employed me since."

"Oh," she said in a more subdued voice, "I must have got it wrong then."

"That'll larn ya, Sir Galahad," I thought but didn't say.

Benny Goodman, known in America as 'The King of Swing' brought his band over to play the London Palladium and had a triumphant success. One of the singers with the band, his new discovery, was the young and yet unknown Peggy Lee.

Benny and his wife, Alice, were staying at the Savoy Hotel in a beautiful suite overlooking the river; and it was there that Denis and I were invited to have drinks with them before the four of us went to lunch at the Ivy. Benny had a new toy with which he was having a lot of fun. It was a camera that printed its own photographs in a matter of seconds. This was a new innovation then and we were wildly impressed.

Quite a nice photograph was taken of me standing at the window of their suite that I still have in a drawer somewhere today.

Denis had known Alice since before the war. She was an American who had married an Englishman, a conservative member of parliament, and it was a terrible mistake. Not only did they have little in common, he also turned out to have a rather cruel and sadistic nature, and she was very unhappy. From one of her trips to New York she brought back the latest Benny Goodman records, and while playing them to Denis, a great fan of his music, she told him she had met Benny Goodman through her brother, John Hammond (Hammond is now thought to have been the greatest record producer of all time; among his many successful discoveries were Benny Goodman, Bessie Smith, Count Basie, Billie Holiday, Bob Dylan, Aretha Franklin, Pete Seger and Bruce Springsteen). Alice then confided in Denis that she had fallen in love with Benny and that he wanted to marry her. There and then Denis agreed to help her get a divorce. The law on divorce being as it was then the only way she was going to get one was to be charged and found guilty of adultery; so registering as Mr. and Mrs. Smith they took a room at the Grosvenor Hotel above Victoria Station, and there in their best pyjamas and nightdress sat late into the night playing cards. When the detective, whose job it was to burst in and discover them supposedly in flagrante, eventually turned up he found them sitting at the table, slumped over their cards, fast asleep. There were no signs of adultery for him to report so the whole night's endeavour was a complete wash out. Next time Alice employed a professional correspondent who knew all the tricks of the trade and this time she got her divorce.

Alice came from one of New York's wealthiest families, the Hammond-Duckworths, and was related to the Roosevelts, the Vannderbilts and the Witneys. You might imagine they would have looked down their aristocratic noses at her marrying a bandleader, but not so, they were thrilled to have the great Benny Goodman in the family. But serious opposition came from the other side: old Mrs. Goodman in Chicago was appalled at the thought of her nice Jewish son marrying a goy, even if she was in the social register, and it took Alice a long time to win the old lady round; but with the immense charm that she possessed she eventually succeeded.

Not only was Benny a great jazz musician, he was equally at home with the classics, and several classical composers, Stravinsky included, wrote clarinet works for him to perform.

Whenever the Goodmans came to London, together or separately, they always looked us up and either came to tea at the flat or we would meet somewhere for a meal. Benny was so unlike what I imagined a bandleader to be; he was gentle, charming, cultivated and a great collector of modern art. On one of his visits Denis introduced him to Gerald Corcoran (once married to Bumble Dawson, they parted amicably and remained close friends). He owned an art gallery in Mayfair, and when Benny bought a couple of expensive paintings from him, as a thank you present for the introduction, Gerald gave Denis an etching by Cezanne, which, while I now write, hangs on the wall opposite.

We were often invited to go and stay with the Goodmans in their beautiful home on Long Island (their next door neighbour and close friend was the composer, Richard Rodgers) and it would have been lovely to have done so, but somehow we never managed it.

As the years rolled by Alice tired of the hectic life of travelling around with a band and tried to persuade Benny to slow down and spend more time at home; but that was something he couldn't do, performing was his life. She eventually became something of a recluse and hardly ever strayed beyond her garden, while he continued to tour with the band to the very end.

It was wonderful to have had them as friends, and when Denis became very ill, unable to work, and life for him was at its lowest ebb, they proved what true and charitable friends they really were.

My mother came to England in 1949 and spent the summer with me. Denis very generously provided the money for her fare. She sailed on one of the Union Castle Line ships (long since defunct) and when it docked at Southampton I and a lot of other excited people were waiting on the quay. The ship rail was crammed with eager faced passengers trying to identify someone in the crowd below. It took me some time to locate her and when I did I waved; a short while later she spotted me and happily waved back. Having not seen each other for four years it was quite an emotional reunion. Mind you, my mother cried very easily: you only had to say the word 'puppy' or 'wedding' for the tears to well up.

On the train up to London she brought me up to date on all the Cape Town news, and apart from my brothers and their wives having babies, not a lot seemed to have happened there. She no longer helped organise charity concerts, a labour of love she threw herself into when I joined the army and deprived her of being a stage mother. These concerts were mostly a wartime activity to raise funds for various allied causes; also the young talent that she was able to call upon then (my contemporaries) had now grown up and dispersed. A few had come to London. Three of the girls were in the *corps de ballet* at Covent Garden, one was a dancer in 'Brigadoon' at His Majesty's Theatre and another in a summer show at Margate.

My mother's Christian name was Clare, and to save me having to write 'my mother' every time I refer to her I shall call her that; although I never did in real life; I called her 'Mom' which was the South African equivalent of 'Mum'.

At that time she was living with my eldest brother, Gordon (ten years my senior), his wife, Daphne and their two young daughters in a bungalow on 4th Beach, Clifton. My other brother, Clive (seven years older than me), his wife, Nancy and children had a bungalow on 3rd Beach. Before I left home we all lived in a house on the mountainside above 1st Beach.

I knew nothing of this at the time, but Daphne did not feel comfortable living in such close proximity with her mother in law, which I can understand, and when she and Gordon built themselves a house with a garden and swimming pool on the mountainside above 4th Beach she stipulated that Clare would not accompany them there. Clive then asked her to come and live with his family on 3rd Beach, which she did. But for similar reasons this proved equally unsuccessful; so she found herself a small flat in Sea Point, close to where her sister lived. Daphne would come and collect her laundry every Friday and do whatever heavy shopping was needed, and my brothers saw to it that she never felt abandoned. It was quite the best solution all round. She never once told me of the domestic differences she had had with her daughters in law; I discovered them for myself much later on; they must have caused her quite a lot of distress at the time.

When she was still living with Gordon and Daphne she spent most mornings with her sister, Vera, who I always called Auntie V. and shall continue to do so. She was two years younger than Clare, also a widow, and had a son seven months younger than me named Dennis, who we all called Denny, and with whom I played a lot until I got the stage bug and he didn't. They lived in a neat little house in a small residential square off Arthur's Road, Sea Point. It was called Trafalgar Square but bore resemblance to the London original in name only: where London had its Statue and stone lions, Sea Point had peppercorn trees and hibiscus bushes; Denny and I often climbed those trees collecting peppercorns to use as ammunition for our pea shooters.

Unlike her intrepid elder sister, Auntie V. was of a very nervous disposition and seldom ventured out alone. Sometimes it was all Clare could do to get her to attend their Stutterfords mornings. Stutterfords was an old fashioned department store in Adderley Street that had a café on the first floor with a large, covered balcony where in summer it was pleasant to sit in the shade and watch life going on in the street below.

Once every week a group of old friends gathered there, drank cups of tea, munched slices of Anchoviette toast, and for an hour or two engaged in convivial conversation, and, perhaps, occasionally even a spot of gossip. Clare was one of the regulars and did her best to make Auntie V. one too.

Nancy Millard and she were still friends, though I doubt if Denis and I ever came up in the conversation. Maurice had already divorced his first wife. He had married one of the showgirls in 'Hellzapoppin', and on the ship that was taking the show to tour Australia he caught her in bed with a sailor. I don't suppose that got mentioned much either. Nancy was not part of the Stutterfords set. I imagine her wealth put her slightly higher up the social ladder than the ladies who gathered there.

But Clare's favourite day of the week was Saturday. That was the day race meetings were held at either Kennilworth or Milnerton race courses; and something very dramatic would have to have happened to keep her away. She was an ardent race goer and studied form intently, as did my brother, Clive, who thought he was going to be a jockey until he got too big.

They usually went to the races together; she had her friends there, he had his, then at the end of the day they would meet up and he would drive her home. She liked to have a little flutter on every race. Some weeks she would win and some she would lose, and at the end of the season she more or less came out even.

I can remember when I was very small I could tell by the click of the garden gate whether she had won or lost. A slow soft click meant she had lost; a quick loud one meant she had won. Excitedly I would wait for her return, listening intently for that particular click that told me I was going to be given money for sweets and to attend the evening performance at our local cinema that was literally across the road from where we lived then in Sea Point. In those days no one worried about children being out alone at night. Cape Town must have been a very safe place then. A lot of my early childhood was spent in the Marine Cinema and mostly alone. I even managed to see films the censor deemed unsuitable for persons between the ages of six and sixteen by claiming to be under six. In that way I saw all the Mae West movies, Dracula, Frankenstein, King Kong, The Mystery of the Wax Museum, The Old Dark House. These were the seminal films that that helped to shape my character and make me the sort of person I am today.

As the flat in Halsey Street only had one bedroom, I found Clare a comfortable room in a very nice neighbour's house. She used it only to sleep in and make herself a pot of tea in the morning, otherwise she lived at number 24 – not that we were in it very much that summer. When she first arrived Denis was away in Madrid polishing someone else's dull dialogue for an irascible Rex Harrison who was making a film there, so until he returned I gave her the bedroom and I slept on a chaise-longue in the sitting room above. It was a very comfortable chaise-longue; several friends who had slept on it had said so, and now I was finding out for myself.

My relationship with Denis was never discussed. We were two very good friends and that was all she wanted to know. Once in my early teens I had tried to tell her I was gay but she quickly changed the subject. Ignorance was a state that she was more than happy to dwell in where anything to do with that subject was concerned.

On the day of her arrival I knew she would be tired; she had been up since six o'clock, so we stayed in and had an early night. The next evening I took her to the Theatre Royal Haymarket, which I consider to be the most beautiful theatre in London, to see Peggy Ashcroft and Ralph Richardson in 'The Heiress'; also in the cast, playing the cruel adventurer, was the magnetic James Donald. I had seen the play before and knew that she would love it. Afterwards we went to dinner at the Ivy. Denis had an account there. He and one of the owners, Abel, were old friends. The Abel family and Irene had been close neighbours in the country during the war. Before he left for Madrid Denis asked Abel to see we had a good table that night, and Clare was thrilled to find Jack Hulbert and Cicely Courtenedge sitting on one side of us and Evelyn Laye and Frank Lawton on the other.

Among the other plays I took her to see were Edith Evans in 'Daphne Laureola', Gertrude Lawrence in 'September Tide', and Flora Robson in 'Black Chiffon'. And, of course, we did all the musicals: 'Oklahoma!', 'Annie Get Your Gun', 'Bless The Bride', 'Brigadoon', and she was particularly fond of 'The Crazy Gang'. She also liked to go to the Players Theatre and see Hattie perform her witty numbers.

That summer I took her everywhere I thought she would like to go: the Derby, Covent Garden, to see Margot Fonteyn dance in 'The Sleeping Beauty', Kew Gardens, down the river to Greenwich, up to Hampstead Heath for the bank holiday fair. We went to Bournemouth to try to find the house where she was born, but it had long since been demolished and where it once stood was now part of a petrol station. We visited her cousin, David Divine and his wife in their lovely house in Keats Grove, Hampstead, directly opposite the house where Keats once resided. David wrote for *The Times* newspaper and was the author of a best selling novel, 'The Boy On A Dolphin' that was made into a film starring Sophia Lauren. We also visited Bluebell in Tooting, a very sweet cousin on my father's side. Marie Freeman invited her to Alexandra Court a few times and told her fortune with the Tarot cards. She took her to Kensington Gardens to see the Peter Pan statue and to tea at Derry and Tom's roof garden. I was always wary that the ogre in Marie would suddenly emerge, but fortunately it never did. Clare found her slightly weird but most charming.

Apart from a day or two on a couple of films and the odd radio play I did no acting that summer. I couldn't leave Clare sitting alone while I went off on tour or into Rep. This was her holiday and she had come to spend it with me. Even if I had got a part in a West End play it would mean at least three weeks of rehearsals and then a pre London tour. What would Clare have done on her own all that time? However, as no such glamorous offer came my way that problem did not arise. But to keep the coffers from becoming completely empty, I managed to get some part time work writing for BBC radio. Peter Myers, who would go on to write some very successful West End revues, asked me to work with him providing the sketches and linking material for a weekly hour long radio programme called, 'Starlight Hour', featuring Peter Knight and his orchestra. Bernard Braden and his wife, Barbara Kelly, who had just arrived from Canada, would have a spot on the show which they would write themselves. Alfred Marks was the resident comedian, and each week there would be a famous guest star singer who would first be interviewed and later sing with the orchestra. One week it was Gracie Fields (my childhood idol) another it was Yves Montand, one of the greatest singers of French chanson. Piaf was his tutor. He was appearing at that time in a variety bill at the Saville Theatre in London and playing to empty houses. England had not yet heard of Yves Montand.

In 1949 Peter Myers was still extremely poor, and with his wife, Pru, and small son lived in a sparsely furnished house in Cricklewood. One of the rooms, with just a small table and two upright chairs in it he used as his office, and it was there that we worked. On fine days, and that summer there were quite a lot of them, he kindly let me bring Clare along, who was more than happy to sit in the garden watching the birds and squirrels as she puffed away at her cigarettes (she was a chain smoker), and every now and then be given a cup of tea by Pru. She also enjoyed the novelty of travelling on the tube from South Kensington to Cricklewood and back.

The programme went out live on Sunday nights from Broadcasting House in Portland Place, in front of a large studio audience that always included Clare. She liked to hear my name being mentioned among the credits, although I think she would have preferred it if it had been as an actor rather than merely one of the writers.

Here is a little anecdote that might be of interest. During the long Sunday afternoon rehearsal that preceded the broadcast a mysterious young man in a duffle coat could be seen hanging about the corridors of Broadcasting House trying to flog gags to comedians on the show at ten shillings a gag. They were good gags and he usually went away with a few quid in his pocket. He was unknown then, but it would not take long before he became the famous Spike Milligan.

The weather had turned quite autumnal when it was time for Clare to leave. I don't think she would have liked a winter in England. She felt the cold very keenly. Anyway, the holiday was over. She had been away from home for over six months. It had been a wonderful time, but apart from me everyone she cared about was in Cape Town – that's where her real life was. and she was probably looking forward to resuming it: seeing Auntie V., the Stutterfords mornings, the races on Saturday, lunch on Sunday with either Gordon or Clive, and being an affectionate grandmother to their children.

I too had put my life on hold for the entire summer and was ready to kick start it again. Although he never said so I sensed that Denis at times was a little irritated that I devoted so much time to Clare at the expense of everyone else. But it was something I had to do; partly for the pleasure it gave me seeing how positively she reacted to everything I showed her; and partly from a feeling of guilt for having been absent from her life for so long, and for abandoning her at a time when being part of my stage work meant everything to her.

There were two things I knew she would miss about London, one was seeing me and the other was going to the theatre. When I visited her some years later I found she had kept all the programmes of the shows we had seen together and fondly remembered each one. She loved the theatre and I can only think it was through her that I inherited my life long passion for it. Auntie V. told me that when she was a girl, Clare had a beautiful singing voice and had given an impressive performance in an amateur production of 'The Pirates Of Penzance'. Whether she had any real talent we shall never know, but I have a feeling that she would have liked to have gone on the stage. However, at the turn of the century for the respectable daughter of a British Army doctor that was not an acceptable option.

So she lived out her stage fantasies through me; and at the first signs I showed of thespianism (dressing up and showing off), much to the horror of my brothers, she not only allowed it, but actively encouraged me, and by the age of eight I already had my own top hat, white tie and tails. But it had begun a long time before. When I was about five we had some gramophone records of Rudy Vallee and Ruth Etting that I learnt off by heart and would perform for anyone who cared to listen. My stage was a deep wide windowsill in the dining room upon which I would stand wearing a table cloth or tea cosy or whatever else I thought suitable, one hand concealed from view clutching a chord that, when surreptitiously pulled, slowly closed the curtains at the end of my song.

This was all right for a start but I soon craved a wider audience. So, on the tramcar we usually took to go shopping in Cape Town, to the delight of all the passengers, I would dance up and down the aisle singing:

> "She's got eyes of blue,
> I never cared for eyes of blue,
> But she's got eyes of blue,
> And that's my weakness now."

For the return journey I would vary my repertoire and perhaps give them:

"You're the cream in my coffee,
You're the salt in my stew,
You will always be
My necessity,
I'd be lost without you."

My brothers would rather walk several miles than travel on a tram that I was on.

On one of these musical tram rides I heard the conductor saying to some of the passengers, "You know what he is, don't you?" When they shook their heads he told them, and loudly enough for the upper deck to hear, "Stage struck!" he said.

He was right, I was stage struck, and I had just seen in the window of our local shoe shop in Sea Point a pair of pink satin ballet shoes, the sort that enable ballerinas to stand on the tips of their toes and twirl like anything. They were called pointe shoes and I was determined to have a pair.

"Boys don't dance on their toes," said Clare and Auntie V. and everyone else.

"Maybe not in Sea Point yet," I said, "but I'll bet quite a few do up in Montmartre." They had no answer to that. Eventually I wore Clare down and off we trotted to the shoe shop. She tried to persuade me to have the black canvas pair as they would be more serviceable. Pink satin, she said, would show the dirt very quickly, but I was adamant. "Serviceable?" I cried. "Do you think Pavlova wore serviceable shoes? I don't want serviceable, I want pretty."

Pretty I got. When we had all agreed on the perfect pair and the saleswoman was about to untie the ribbons I stopped her.

"Thank you," I said, "I'll wear them home." Clare tried to dissuade me but she was putty in my hands and she knew it. It must have been quite a funny sight, this embarrassed looking woman hurrying along the street pretending she had nothing to do with the little boy in the short trousers and pink satin ballet shoes who was following her on the tips of his toes. I was very proud of the fact that not once all the way home did I get off my toes, and even managed to execute a couple of quite elaborate twirls.

To everyone's relief, especially my brothers, the toe-dancing phase did not last long; and then I discovered Fred Astaire and tap, which they all agreed was noisier but nicer.

Seeing Clare off at Waterloo Station I knew was going to be highly emotional. I had been dreading it for weeks. Luckily cousin Bluebell suddenly appeared on the platform so she had to control herself more than if it had just been the two of us. The last few torturous minutes at the train window, seeing her pale desperate face and trying to think of jolly things to say, seemed endless. Then, when the whistle went and the train began to move the flood-gates opened; and by the time her small waving hand had vanished from sight I too was awash. It must have been catching because even Bluebell blubbed a bit. After we had wiped our eyes and blown our noses we repaired to the station café where, over a cup of British Rail dishwater (laughingly called coffee) we pulled ourselves together and I got ready to face the world again.

〜〜〜

I came across Tennessee Williams and Gore Vidal in the bar of Le Boeuf Sur Le Toit (named after Jean Cocteau's ballet of 1920). I was in Paris with a dear old actor friend of ours called John Vere, whose great passion in life was Marie Antionette; he had read practically everything that had ever been written about her, and his main reason for coming to Paris was to visit the Palace of Versailles. As often happened at that time the French civil service was on strike so the Palace was closed to the public. However, John insisted we take a train to Versailles and get a glimpse of it from the gates. We did manage to visit the Conciergerie on the Quai de l'Horloge and see the cell where the Queen spent her last tragic days. John was very moved by the experience, and it was to lighten the mood that evening that I suggested we go to Le Boeuf Sur Le Toit, and who should we meet there but the aforesaid. They seemed pleased to see me again and invited us to join them for a drink.

The last time I had seen them was at Brian's house in the country when George Cukor brought them down to lunch one Sunday. I remember well, it was a hot sunny day and I was wearing sandals, and, as all my friends have grown weary of hearing, Tennessee remarked that I had beautiful feet! Yes, he did. His very words were: "You have beautiful feet." And since that day whenever his name is mentioned it's all I can do not to blurt out, "Did you know, he once said I had beautiful feet." I know it's not as poignant a line as, "I have always relied on the kindness of strangers", but it's better than nothing.

Gore Vidal, who in later life would achieve eminence as a radical political thinker, was then in his early twenties and had just published his second novel, 'The City And The Pillar'. He was extremely good looking, bright, charming, witty, and as if that wasn't enough, sexy with it. After lunch, and much wine, while he, Hermione Gingold and I lay on the grass soaking in the hot August sunshine, the conversation somehow got round to the merits of the Boy Scout Movement, of which they both seemed to have extensive knowledge and hold strong personal views. Whether their views would have past muster with Lord Baden-Powell is a moot point. Lying there, listening to their somewhat suspect quoting of the 'Boy Scout Code', and their dubious ponderings as to the exact meaning of the motto 'Be Prepared', I was reminded of a funny line in a sketch Hermione and Henry Kendal had done in their last revue 'Sweetest and Lowest'. In it, when she refers to a young man of their acquaintance as 'quite a dish', Henry Kendall says, "But my dear, he's a mere boy", to which she replies with more than a hint on innuendo, "There is nothing MERE about a boy."

As I lay there, a couple of feet away from Gore, now minus his shirt, I longed to lean over and touch his beautiful bronzed skin; but like a good boy scout I controlled myself. What he thought about me I am not quite sure, although a couple of times when he glanced my way I felt it was not entirely without interest.

Now, standing in a bar in Paris, the attraction I had felt on the grass that day was still there. So when he suggested we take a cab up to Montmartre and go to Madame Arthur's I felt a little thrill run through me. But it was soon extinguished, for Tennessee, who probably had more adventurous plans in mind, let it be known, in the subtlest possible way, that it was not a good idea. So we finished our drinks and said *au revoir,* which in Gore's case was actually *adieu.*

About a year later Denis and Tennessee met up in Rome, and while they were having a drink at a street café he said he was working on a novel about a woman who was going through the menopause, and he was going to call it, 'Moon In Pause.' Denis thought the title was a bit dodgy but didn't say so; and he can't have been alone in thinking that for when the book was published it had the new title of, 'The Roman Spring Of Mrs. Stone'. While they were sitting there with their drinks that day they wrote me a postcard and Tennessee's message read, 'Gore arriving in Rome tomorrow. What a pity you can't be here. Love, 10.' Reading that I felt he must have been aware of my attraction for Gore, and possibly, though this could be pure fantasy on my part, his for me. The answer to that, along with who built Stonehenge, what happened on board the Marie Celeste, and who really wrote Shakespeare's plays, will remain an enigma.

I met 10, as I shall now call him, just once more. Denis and I spent an evening with him in London – an unexpected and, as it turned out, a fairly bizarre one. By then he and Gore were no longer the closest of friends so when I asked after him I received a rather negative reply.

Tommy was an old chum of Denis' from the distant past. He worked for the bookmaking firm, Tattersalls, and must have held a high-powered position there for he lived with great style in a luxurious flat in Berkley Square. It was his fortieth birthday and to celebrate it he had invited some gentlemen friends round for champagne and caviar. We were not part of his intimate circle so were pleasantly surprised to be included in the celebration.

We had just been to tea with John and Olga at their Jermyn Street flat and were passing the entrance of the Cavendish Hotel when out strolled 10. He was on his own and at a loose end. He said he thought he might wander up to Covent Garden and see if he could get a seat for the ballet. When we suggested he come along with us, for we knew Tommy would be thrilled to meet him, he happily (if he ever did anything really happily) accepted our invitation. Little did he know what he was letting himself in for.

The party was horrendous. The other guests consisted of a dozen or so immaculately tailored, coiffured and toiletted, snobbish affected old queens. The unfortunates among them who had to toil for a living were either antique dealers, interior decorators or dressmakers. By then the illustrious name of Tennessee Williams would have been known to all of them, but when he was introduced they affected not to know who he was. On being told that he worked in the theatre one of them asked, "And what exactly is your job in the theatre, Mr. Williams?" to which he replied, "Oh, I'm a sort of chief cook and bottle washer." The conversation was almost entirely about people with titles and double barrelled names, grand country houses, horse racing and Maria Callas. The champagne flowed and when the caviar ran out there were lots of other fine comestibles from Fortnum and Mason, but the company was tedious beyond words and we were desperate to escape – but without offending Tommy we knew not how. He must have sensed that the party needed livening up for he suddenly announced, "Dancing time", rolled back the Aubusson and put on a record; and before you could say, "Victor Sylvester" the floor was alive with foxtrotting gentlemen.

"Would you care to dance?" 10 asked me.

"I don't think so, I replied, "I am not very good at dancing backwards."

"That's all right," he said. "I don't mind, you can lead, come on." So onto the parquet we went and shuffled about a bit. I did not feel comfortable pushing one of the world's greatest playwrights around the floor and I felt that he wasn't really enjoying being pushed. Our eyes met and we burst out laughing at the sheer absurdity of it all. One dance we decided had been quite sufficient.

The next thing I knew Denis was whispering to me that he and 10 were leaving. He had told Tommy they had to meet a film producer at Claridges. He then said that when I could get away I should come and join them, not at Claridges, of course, but at the Fitzroy Tavern in Bloomsbury. I was furious with them for leaving me stranded there like that. I had a couple more glasses of champagne, declined an antique dealer's invitation to a waltz and, when I felt that sufficient time had elapsed, made a feeble excuse about an early morning rehearsal and left.

In the 1920s and 30s the Fitzroy Tavern in Charlotte Street was the centre of bohemian London and many of the Bloomsbury painters and writers regularly met there. It had a slightly raffish atmosphere which they found to their liking. After the war it still retained a little of its character and at lunch time you might occasionally see Augustus John or Nina Hamnett drinking at the bar. At night, though, the raffish side took over and it became the haunt of Sailors and guardsmen touting their services.

When I arrived, 10 was busy chatting up a sailor, but after a while he lost interest, and seeing no one else there to his particular taste, decided to move on to the Turkish Baths in the Harrow Road. (of great notoriety then). That was not our cup of tea, but then we had not been invited. 10 was very much a lone nighthawk. It was a bright clear night and feeling in need of some air he said he would walk, but then he wasn't quite sure of the way so we agreed to accompany him as far as the Edgeware Road, after that it would be plain sailing. There, after apologising for subjecting him to Tommy's ghastly party, when he might have been having an enchanted evening at the ballet, we bid him a fond farewell.

And that was the last I saw of 10, that sweet, funny, sad man; poetic genius of the theatre; and lover of all things exotic and beautiful; who once upon a time on a lovely summer's day in a rose scented English country garden summoned up those immortal words: "You have beautiful feet" (size 7 then, but with age they spread and I now take a size 8).

Joy was in town. Mrs. Joyce Murchie was her name but everyone called her Joy because that was what she gave them. I had met her first at Denis' flat in Cairo, then at the Ritz Bar in Paris, and now she was in London for a few days. It seemed that she was only ever anywhere for a few days, so far from 'custom cloying the appetite' (or words to that effect), seeing Joy was always a refreshing surprise. With her ginger hair and freckled nose she was not conventionally beautiful, but her smile was enchanting and she had the most effervescent personality of anyone I have ever known. For many years she had not had a permanent residence, nomad-like she just wandered where her fancy took her, never staying anywhere for long. It was as though she was wearing an invisible pair of red ballet shoes that wouldn't let her keep still.

Born at the turn of the century into a wealthy New Zealand family, her mother having died when she was still an infant, she was brought up very strictly by her Victorian father. Being of a high spirited nature and bored with all that empty scenery about her she longed to travel, but he would not allow it. So on her twenty first birthday, the day she came into a not unsubstantial inheritance, she boarded a ship and set sail for Europe, never to return.

Young and foolish, she made the mistake of a hasty marriage to Mr. Murchie, a dentist from Hampstead, who found her exuberance as unnerving as she found his humourless disapproval reminiscent of her father. They quickly divorced. She then very much became one of the bright young things and gave lavish parties in her luxurious flat in Pall Mall. Among the many friends she entertained there were Nancy Mitford and Evelyn Waugh. But she found English life too staid for her liking (the barbaric licensing laws, for one thing) and for most of the 1920s and 30s she just flitted about Europe from one pleasure spot to another enjoying the sort of night life that was not even dreamed of back in Auckland. Joy was a party girl. She was not highly sexed so that messy side of things seldom got in the way of real fun. Her pleasures were quite simple and innocent really: staying up late and laughing a lot with like spirited souls, and, perhaps, taking a sip or two of the local brew. After all, hangovers were what mornings after were for.

'These delights if thou cans't give,
Mirth with thee I mean to live.'

When John Milton wrote those words he must have had someone exactly like Joy in mind for that was her credo to a T.

She spent the war years in Cairo working for the MOD by day and boosting the allies morale by night. And there she met a soldier called Andy, the one and only true love of her life. He was several years her junior but that didn't matter. They were devoted to one another and spent three or four blissful years together. Then tragedy struck. On a return visit to Cyrenaica, while driving through a desert sandstorm Andy's car met another full on and he was killed outright. He was on his way to meet Joy in Benghazi, where she was being held in quarantine due to a typhoid epidemic in the area (now, there is a plot Shakespeare could have done something with).

After Andy's death Joy never looked at another man. She was forty-nine and that side of her life she decided was over. From then on it would be party time all the way. Parties, though, can be quite expensive and she was dismayed to find how much her inheritance had dwindled. This was partly due to her solicitor cousin, who handled her money, gambling a large sum of it on a dicey speculation and losing it all. He should have gone to prison for his negligence but Joy refused to press charges. Unable to practice law after that he went into exile in Cyprus, and in a very short while drank himself to death. Joy's extravagant life style had also made a large dent in her fortune: she would take villas in France and Italy, fill them with amusing people, entertain lavishly and always insist on grabbing the bill. One day she woke to find her fortune was no more.

Sensibly her father had left some extra money for her in a trust that, try as she may, she was unable to break. This brought her in a quarterly annuity that might have been enough for a careful person to manage on adequately, but for Joy it was a laughable sum. So, as she had no intention of relinquishing her present life style, she began juggling her finances, and quite an expert juggler she became. On the knowledge that her next quarterly payment was soon due she was able to borrow from Peter to pay Paul to pay Andre to pay Pedro to pay Hamid… She was not dishonest, everyone would get their money, it was just a matter of waiting their turn, and it taking slightly longer than expected.

Her present visit to London was more than likely to plead with her trustees to advance her the next quarter's payment, which probably had already been advanced more than once, and owed to goodness knows how many people. Joy's juggling, that would have given most people a severe headache if not a heart attack, she just took in her stride. Well, she was practically half a century old and was not going to change her ways now for the sake of mere money.

That night she was having dinner with us at 24 Halsey Street, and Elizabeth, who was also an old friend of hers, came upstairs and joined us. Denis was due to go to Rome in a day or so to work as English dialogue director on an Anglo Italian film that he had co-scripted with Suso Cecchi d'Amico, one of Italy's most eminent screen writers (the film would turn out to be a disaster and not get a release but that was nothing to do with the excellent script). When Joy said she might also be going to Rome, Denis came up with the idea that we both join him there, and if he gave up the expensive room the company had booked for him in one of those grand hotels overlooking the Spanish Steps the money saved would pay for all three of us to stay in a more modest hotel. This sounded like a sensible idea, and, as I had not yet seen Rome, an exciting one. Joy then remembered that she first had to go to Venice where she had left her old jalopy to be repaired. She suggested I went with her and we drive the car down to Rome. As I had not yet seen Venice either the idea became even more exciting. It then transpired that she first of all would have to go to Paris (there was probably some juggling to be done there), so it was arranged that I meet her at her hotel and we catch the night train for Venice.

She was staying at the Hotel St James in the Rue de Rivoli and when I arrived to pick her up she told me she would need to spend another day in Paris (the juggling had obviously gone awry), so she had booked me a room in the hotel. That night we ate at a lovely new restaurant nearby called 'Paul et Virgine', that specialised in the most superb soufflés (the next time I was in Paris I hurried there but it no longer existed).

In those days the most Sterling the Government allowed one to take out of Britain was £30. Those of one's friends who visited France regularly all seemed to know a little man in Paris who would provide them with francs in exchange for pounds in England (the French too had their money restrictions). I knew no such little man, but then I thought my £30 (quite a lot of money then) should, if I was careful, see me through to Rome.

By lunchtime the next day my £30 had gone – it went towards paying the hotel bill – and Joy's juggling seemed to have encountered an unfortunate hiccough (or whatever the word is in juggler's jargon). Quite frankly we were francless! So what did we do? What would you have done ? That's right, we went to the Ritz Bar and ordered champagne cocktails.

George, the doorkeeper at the Ritz was known as the 'Mr. Fix It' of Paris. Whatever needed fixing George could fix. He had known Joy over many years and had often been the recipient of her generous tips, so he was only too happy to assist her through this temporary little hiccough.

While we sat in the bar drinking our champagne cocktails one of his minions went to the railway station and bought two third class tickets for the night train to Venice. Leaving George with the bar bill, and having extracted from him enough francs to pay for a taxi to the station and to buy a couple of ham bagettes and a bottle of cheap red wine for the journey, we thanked him for his kind assistance and, now staggering ever so slightly, departed the Paris Ritz.

We shared our third class compartment with a thin spinsterish looking American woman who I thought might be a schoolteacher on her way to Italy in search of romance. Out of politeness we tried to draw her into the conversation but she didn't want to know. I think she was actually scared of us. When we started taking swigs of wine from the bottle she looked appalled; and when Joy, out of devilment, offered her a swig she physically recoiled, shook her head violently and turned her face to the window. I got the impression she might be thinking we were a couple of white slavers wanting to drug her and pack her virginal white body off to one of the fleshpots of North Africa.

We got as much sleep that night as one possibly can sitting upright on a hard seat in an unheated third class compartment in mid December. By morning we were in Switzerland, passing through beautiful scenery of mountains and lakes; then on through Italy and a longish stop at Milan Station where we watched enviously as people bought cups of hot coffee that had the most enticing aroma.

It was getting on for dusk when we reached Venice. As we walked out of the station carrying our suitcases I was filled with trepidation. I had not asked Joy what we were going to do in case she said she didn't know. It was one of those occasions when one wished one was a believer and had a saint one could turn to for help.

"We don't have the fare for the Vaporetta," said Joy, "so it will have to be a gondola. Anyway, you've not been to Venice before and one's first journey down the Grand Canal has to be by gondola." So into a gondola we got and Joy called to the gondoliere, "Harry's Bar."

Gliding silkily down the Grand Canal I felt a mixture of cold fear for what was going to happen to us and wonder at the breathtaking beauty of it all. Joy looked pensive, but then I remembered it was here that she and Andy had last spent time together before the fatal accident. When we got to the jetty at Harry's Bar a couple of the staff helped us out of the gondola.

"Uno momento," Joy called to the gondoliere and swept up the steps into the bar, followed very closely by me. "Is Cipriani about?" she asked the barman.

"No, Signora Murchie," he said, "but he is expected soon."

"Ah," she said, "well, we've got no lira so will you please pay off the gondola and bring in our luggage, and we could do with two of your very special dry martinis."

It was to my great relief that when Cipriani arrived he seemed delighted to see Joy. She asked him if he could find us a small hotel nearby, which he could, and to send on our luggage in advance, which he did. After a couple more dry martinis, which we put on the slate, we repaired to our hotel, a three-minute walk from the Piazza San Marco. When we had bathed and changed Joy took me to look at the Cathedral. We approached from the far end of the piazza and as I caught sight of that magnificent Byzantine building with its ornate mosaic and sculptural decorations I gasped with wonder. Then, in a famous, centuries old restaurant in the square, called Florian we dined. I, of course, had to have what has been my favourite dish since that wonderful black market meal in Vasto in December 1943: Spaghetti Napoletano. As I lifted my fork and spoon to start eating Joy grabbed the hand with the spoon in it. "Put that down!" she said, "You don't eat spaghetti with a spoon."

"Then why do they always provide one ?" I asked.

"For people who don't know," she said. "People who know only use a fork." From that night on, now being one of the people who knew, I have forgone the spoon; and once you have mastered the knack of twirling it around the prongs of your fork there is no more satisfying way of eating spaghetti. For dessert we had Zabaione, and finished off with coffee and grappa. When finally the bill arrived (the moment I had been dreading throughout), Joy explained to the waiter that we had no money on us but were staying at a nearby hotel, the name of which she gave, and would they send the bill there. After much wrangling the manager was summoned. He was not at all happy with Joy's request, but apart from calling the police there was not a lot he could do, and probably recognising her as an old regular, he reluctantly acquiesced.

Next morning Joy got up early and went out juggling. I sent Denis an urgent SOS and he immediately telegraphed me some money. At lunchtime in Harry's Bar, where we had agreed to meet, Joy arrived looking radiant and began throwing lira about like confetti. We were in the money!

Denis rang to say he was leaving Rome. The filming schedule had altered and location work was starting sooner than expected. The Unit would be based in Isernia, a small town high up in the Abruzzi mountains (not far from Campobasso where the Troopadours performed in December 1943). He would be staying at the local albergo and suggested that we joined him there and all drive back to Rome together. As there was no desperate hurry now to get to Rome Joy thought we ought to stay in Venice for a few days more, so that I could see all that I should and also sample a little of the city's social life. And that was what we did. I must have been into every church and art gallery that there was; we attended a Vivaldi concert in the Fenice – probably the most beautiful theatre in the whole world; and were invited to several lovely houses. Our first host was Arthur Jeffries who we both knew from London. He owned the prestigious Arthur Jeffries Gallery in Mayfair and lived in a sumptuous house in Pelham Crescent crammed with wonderful pictures. My favourite one was a large oil painting by Henri Rousseau of some men in a field playing football. He also owned a house in Venice, on a canal, and moored at the entrance steps was his own long, sleek, black and gold gondola, and to go with it a handsome gondoleire in matching livery. Arthur was American but had lived in Europe most of his adult life. His great wealth came from Virginian tobacco. In case you haven't guessed he was also a tremendous snob and collected principessas like poorer folk collect beer mats. Arthur was delighted to see Joy. She wasn't exactly a principessa but was a hell of a lot more fun. I was certainly not on his social list but he had impeccable manners and whenever we met he always treated me in a most friendly and hospitable fashion.

While having a drink with him at one of the cafes in the Piazza San Marco he introduced us to a tall, aquiline nosed, very decadent looking middle aged Englishman. I can't remember his name but, as it was not thought to be genuine anyway, that doesn't really matter. I shall call him Mr. Mysterioso because most things about him seemed to be a mystery. He lived on his own with several servants in a magnificent palazza on the Lagoon that had the most beautiful views of the city across the water, and there we were invited to lunch one day along with some other guests. He offered to send his gondola to fetch us, but Arthur, who was also invited, said he would bring us in his (it never rains but it pours, I thought).

Mr. Mysteriosa had lived in Venice for about a year, and before that in a palace in Tangiers. According to one gossip, he had left that city in quite a hurry. According to another, any contemplation of life in England would be behind bars. And a third came up with the rumour that he had been very closely connected to an Austrian Catholic Archbishop who was on the run from Interpol; his crime being that during the chaotic period following the war he had systematically ransacked several beautiful churches of their art treasures and sold them to unscrupulous dealers; and it was thought that Mr. Mysteriso had been the go-between in some of these lucrative transactions.

On entering the palazza I couldn't help wondering if there might be some truth to the last rumour. Its contents were entirely of a religious nature: there were several crucifixes, with and without our lord on them, marble, wooden and plaster statues of the Virgin and the Saints, oil paintings and tapestries depicting holy scenes, a lectern, a finely carved screen, rich velvet and silk hangings, altar cloths and copes embroidered with gold and silver thread. I suppose he could have been a fanatically religious man, only his conversation during lunch tended to be rather on the louche side. There was something very sinister about him and I felt that he would be a dangerous person to know. This was rather born out the following night in Harry's Bar. He and an American woman tourist were sitting at a nearby table having a heated conversation; he had said something derogatory about her country to which she had taken offence and accused him of having no manners; upon which he took up a soda siphon and sprayed its entire contents over her. He was asked to leave the bar, but as soon as the tourist had left town he was warmly invited back.

Crossing the Rialto Bridge we ran into Martin and Bill. Both Joy and Denis had known Martin before the war. They invited us to go and stay for a few days at their lovely house in Asolo, a pretty village in the Veneto hills. I spoke to Denis on the phone; he said Isernia was deadly dull and, as he would be working most of the time, we ought to accept, so we did.

Martin was English and had spent the war years in Hollywood working as a scriptwriter, mostly on films with a British theme. He had also written a stage adaptation of Mrs. Gaskill's 'Cranford' that had been successfully produced in Los Angeles, and he was forever hoping that it might one day get a showing in London or New York. He was a charming man, if a trifle prissy and pedantic. Bill on the other hand was easygoing and always full of fun. He was American and, although only thirty, because of premature baldness, looked a little older. They had met some years before when he was dancing in the chorus of an MGM film musical. He had been in several but 'Rosalie' (with a delightful score by Cole Porter) was the one, he said, where his pretty round face and wavy blonde hair could be spotted to the greatest advantage. As he told me of his childhood I grew green with envy. At the age of six he was already a seasoned Vaudevillian. In a spotlight, wearing top hat, white tie and tails he would sing, "Carolina moon keep shining..." as his mother in a dress of silver bugle beads slowly descended from the flies sitting on a crescent moon. Oh, how I wished my mother and I could have done that! Joy and I wondered if Bill didn't sometimes feel a little stifled living in a small Italian village with nothing much to do while Martin was shut away writing. I know how happy and excited he always was coming to London and going to the theatre.

Their next door neighbour in Asolo was the intrepid traveller Freya Stark, who came to lunch one day and asked us round to tea the next. I found her fascinating. The thought of that lone frail looking woman riding camels across endless scorching deserts filled me with wonder. And I was intrigued by her appearance. She wore flowing robes of Arabic influence that she designed herself and had woven by the local girls she kept busily employed in her village workshop. We were shown some of the beautiful materials they made, for which she had one or two exclusive outlets in Venice. She had been a keen weaver all her life and I suppose it was a sign of her intrepidness that she returned to it after her appalling accident. When still quite young her hair got caught in a loom and part of her scalp and face were ripped away. She wore a bang of false hair over the now bald patch and a false eyebrow that she stuck on, which during lunch I noticed was starting to come unstuck. How weird, I thought, that she didn't pluck the existing eyebrow and draw them both on with an eyebrow pencil as so many women did, Garbo and Dietrich included.

One day we went to look at the beautiful buildings Palladio created in and around Vicenza: the Basilica, the Villa Rotonda, the Villa Barbaro, and a superb little theatre with a permanent stage setting designed in perfect perspective; there were streets leading off that stretched far into the distance, yet the depth of the stage was no more than about twenty feet. Standing at the back of one of these streets the buildings were not even as high as one's knees but from the auditorium the illusion of great distance was simply amazing. It was the most perfect example of perspective design I have ever seen.

Martin had *The Times* newspaper sent to him regularly by a friend in London and one morning he said to me, "I've just seen your name in the paper."

A Peter Myers revue entitled, 'In Tempo' had just opened at the Boltons Theatre and *The Times* critic had reviewed it. I had given Peter permission to use some of my material and told Robb to let him have the music to the numbers he wanted. As might be expected the music never arrived. Peter eventually gave up on him and asked John Pritchitt, who was writing other music for the revue, to do the settings to my lyrics. I had several things in the show: two songs, a monologue, a sketch and the first act finale that I had written with Peter. It was an idea I had of what Russia's musical answer to, 'Oklahoma!' might be like. It was full of topical and political gags that we both thought were quite funny. But it was my monologue that *The Times* critic had particularly enjoyed; he praised Ronnie Stevens for his funny performance and mentioned that the witty piece was written by me. I felt very chuffed and longed to see the show.

It was now time to leave Asolo and head south for Isernia. Joy's car had conked out again so the journey would have to be made by train. Just before leaving she said she needed to spend a couple more days in Venice; so I decided to travel ahead, partly because I was wanting to see Denis and partly because I didn't know how much there still was in the kitty and I had no desire to languish in a dank Venetian debtors' prison.

Talking of Venetian prisons here are a couple of sad little stories. One would imagine that in a city like Venice, with its history steeped in centuries of decadence, that the attitude towards homosexuality would be benign. But that was not the case. The city fathers and the police were fiercely homophobic, and they were especially harsh on foreign residents. As these were usually men of wealth and property one can't help feeling that greed and gain had important parts to play. Harry's Bar was started by an American called Harry who was gay; one of his employees shopped him to the police and he was banished from the city, never to return. Cipriani, who was the barman there at the time, took over Harry's Bar and the Cipriani family have run it ever since.

Arthur Jeffries, in a similar scrape with the London police, by no means his first, and fearing that this time it might lead to a prison sentence, fled to Venice where he waited, hoping that in time his London lawyers would inform him that the case had been dropped and it would be safe for him to return. Then one night in Venice he had the misfortune to fall for the wiles of a sexually attractive police provocateur who, in the middle of an intimate embrace, arrested him. The mayor of Venice at the time was both a communist and a rabid homophobe, and Arthur, like Harry before him, was ordered to leave town immediately and never return. Barred from both his exquisite homes and the two cities he loved the most, and unable to face the humiliation of his smart friends finding out, he caught the first train to Paris, booked himself into the Hotel Creon and committed suicide.

I took the train to Rome and then a bus to Isernia. On the way we passed beneath the ruins of the monastery of Monte Casino, which had been one of the great gems of Renaissance architecture. A woman on the bus who spoke English said how wicked it was of the allies to have destroyed such a sacred building. I didn't want to get into an argument but I remembered the heavy casualties sustained in the long, hard battle for Monte Casino and how little the Germans who occupied it cared what buildings they destroyed.

Denis was right about Isernia, it was a dismal little town; the hotel was primitive and the food monotonous – though for me with my passion for pasta it was not such a hardship; the film crew were a disgruntled bunch; the British members complained constantly about the tea (there was a sulphur spring nearby and the water tasted slightly of sulphur); the actors lacked the light touch that is needed for comedy; and the director, a real little Mussolini, although he spoke not a word of English, resented Denis working with the actors on the English dialogue; the weather was atrocious, it only stopped raining to snow; and to cap it all Denis was confined to bed with a severe attack of bronchitis.

For Isernians the big moment of the day was the arrival of the bus from Rome. Half the town would turn out to see who the new arrivals were. I never expected Joy to make it to Isernia so it was a lovely surprise when one day she hopped off the bus, stayed for a couple of nights of grappa fuelled mirth, then hopped on again saying she had some business to see to in Rome and would wait for us there.

In Rome, as Denis had arranged, the three of us stayed at the Albergo d'Inghilterra, a short way from the foot of the Spanish Steps. It was a friendly hotel with a distinctly bohemian character. 10 Williams often stayed there; so did Brian Howard, Janette Flanner and Sybille Bedford; and in the past, Henry James and even further back, Byron. During the day, while Denis was out at the studio, Joy showed me the sights of the city; I was knocked out by the beauty and grandeur of it all and couldn't decide which I thought was the more beautiful, Rome or Venice.

One evening a friend of Denis' from a previous visit, Count Masimo something or other, took the three of us to the studio of the famous communist painter, Renato Guttuso, a leading exponent of Italy's Social Realism. It is surprising how little his work is known in England, though one of his pictures does hang in the Tate Gallery. In the late 1930s he helped form an anti-Fascist association, then bravely went on to work with the Resistance during the war. Much of his work was inspired by the struggles of the Sicilian peasantry and many of the pictures are large and painted in vigorous Expressionist style. Denis bought a small watercolour of crab fishers among the rocks by the sea. It was quite an expensive purchase but after a few camparis he was unable to resist it. We then took the Count and Guttuso and his lady (wife?) out to dinner at one of Rome's oldest restaurants called, Cannelloni, famous for its delicious pasta dish of that name. It was the best cannelloni I have ever had. After a convivial evening of luscious food and lots of wine we said goodnight to the Guttusos and the Count and the three of us returned to our hotel. On the floor we were on, where we had two rooms next to each other, there was a cubicle at the end of the corridor where the maid kept the various tools of her trade. I can't remember why but Joy went into the cubicle for something and called to us to come and have a look. And there, pinned to a cupboard door, was a large signed drawing by Guttuso of a lean faced young peasant man in a cap shouting at a cringing, half turned away, woman. The anger on his face and the fear on hers created by just a few bold strokes was remarkable. It was probably a sketch for a painting. Whatever, it was a most powerfully alive drawing. The maid, who appeared at that point, was amused at our interest in it. She had found it rolled up on top of a wardrobe some days before. Obviously a guest had forgotten it was there and left it behind. If we liked it, she said, we could have it. We liked it and gave her a generous tip, so everyone was happy (maybe not the careless guest). I still have that drawing hanging in my sitting room and enjoy it and the memory of how we came by it every time I look at it.

The watercolour of the crab fishers I had to sell in one of my lean periods. I was told that in Italy it would have been worth quite a lot but I got very little for it in England.

On Christmas Day we boarded the train for London. At the last minute Joy decided to stay on for a few more days. We hoped she got a refund on the ticket Denis had bought her. It was an ideal way to spend Christmas Day, sitting in a private coupe' drinking champagne as the beautiful Italian countryside rolled by. And what a relief not to be at 5 Alexandra Court with Marie Freeman – but then practically anything would be a relief from that.

Should you be thinking that my life so far seems to have been spent mainly in the pursuit of pleasure you might have a point. The theatre was my greatest love, but every now and then distractions of a frivolous and hedonistic nature somehow managed to get in the way. Instead of cavorting around the Continent with Joy I should have tried to get myself a winter season in rep as most of my contemporaries had done, laying down the ground work for a serious career on the stage. Denis must take his share of the blame for this; he didn't want me vanishing into the provinces for months on end. And by then I had become a little spoilt: I knew the difference between dinner at the Ivy and fish and chips on pay night in Bridlington. The truth is Denis took far more interest in my writing than my acting and tried to steer me in that direction. He really believed I had creative talent and would one day write a good play. Alas, it never happened. That particular knack eluded me. I had several attempts but was never satisfied enough with the results to show them to anyone. Where I did feel at home was with revue and musical comedy (the former genre now sadly extinct), and I look back with a certain amount of pride at my achievements in both those mediums. I was particularly happy writing lyrics. That my work never brought great riches was partly due to luck and partly to not possessing the ruthless drive and burning ambition that I believe is necessary in achieving such rewards. Maybe all that hot South African sun had made me just a little lazy. And then, of course, there was Robb!!

1950 was the year when things began to go wrong. The bronchitis Denis had contracted in Isernia returned with a vengeance, and the first symptoms of Emphysema were diagnosed. And suddenly there was no money. We had been living far too profligate a life, spending everything as soon as it came in, always thinking another job was on the way – and then discovering that it wasn't. Two film projects that Denis expected were going to be offered to him both failed to materialise. He directed a West End play starring Harold Warrender (a popular actor of light comedy in the 30s, he spent the war years in the Royal Navy and had only recently returned to acting) and, in her first West End leading role, a young actress whose comedic style Denis much admired, Eleanor Summerfield. Bumble did the décor and costumes. It was a translation from the French of a Boulevard comedy that had been a big hit in Paris where it was called, 'Ma Vie Avec Caroline'. In the English version by Reginald Beckworth (who wrote, 'Boys In Brown) the title somehow became, 'Gooseberry Fool'. As much as the French critics had praised it the English critics damned it, and its run at the Duchess Theatre lasted barely three weeks. Apart from the initial director's fee no money came from it. The BBC asked him to direct a couple of operas for the Third Programme. One was the delightful frothy 'Die Fledermaus', in which there were a few non-singing parts that were played by Olga Lowe, Roger Moore and me. It was fun to do but as anyone in the business will tell you, the words 'BBC' and 'generous remuneration' do not go together, so financially our situation was as dire as ever. I went to Great Yarmouth and did some weekly rep, but after paying for digs, food and the occasional half pint of cider all I had over each week was about four pounds. And the money that Robb and I earned from our numbers being done in fringe revues and cabaret was equally laughable. One of us needed a lucky break and it didn't happen.

Noel Coward's new musical, 'Ace Of Clubs', with which Robb was still heavily involved had premiered at the Opera House in Manchester and was about to open at the Cambridge Theatre in London. Robb's friend Jack Beatty, using his stage name, Jacques Gautier, had been playing a waiter in the nightclub scenes and for some reason, I know not what, decided not to come in with the show. Knowing how skint I was Robb asked Freddie Carpenter, who was assisting Coward on the production, if I could take Jack's place. He agreed, and I was also given a couple of nice parts to understudy. It was exciting to actually be in a Noel Coward production, although the pay, as I have already stated, was a pittance. However, for the six months of its run it kept us in groceries. They never bothered to alter the programme so my name did not appear in it, but should you have seen the show in London (not Manchester, mind) and remember a waiter called Jacques Gautier that'll be me not Jack.

It was not one of Coward's best shows. The book was very poor and the dialogue lacked the sparkle that one expected from him, but there were a few excellent numbers. One of them was, 'Sail Away', which he would use again in another show called 'Sail Away'; and a sure fire hit every night was a comic trio, 'Three Juvenile Delinquents'. I understudied all three but not one of them was ever off.

The first night was a very glamorous affair. The stalls were packed with celebrities. From the stage I spotted Marlene Dietrich, Beatrice Lillie, Frank Sinatra and Ava Gardner. Someone else spotted Princess Margaret and Abbot and Costello. Through the curtain one could feel the mounting atmosphere of excitement and anticipation, and when the curtain rose on a smoke filled Soho nightclub in full swing the air was electric. The opening number was, 'Top Of The Morning' performed by the cabaret girls headed by Jean Carson (she would go to America, change her name to Jeannie and star in her own television series called 'Hey Jeannie!'). Among the girls supporting her were Gail Kendall, June Whitfield and Vivien Merchant. It was a very ordinary number but the audience gave it a warm welcome. Pat Kirkwood and Graham Payne were equally well received, but as the evening wore on and anticipation turned to disappointment the show began to go steadily downhill and by the end the applause was polite rather than rapturous. Someone called for "Author!" and Coward made the mistake of obliging. As soon as he stepped on the stage the booing started. It came from the cheaper seats in the upper part of the house. A well-bred voice from the stalls told them to, "shut up" which made them boo even more. Then a less than well-bred voice from up there shouted, "Why hasn't Sylvia Cecil got better billing?" This amused everyone except, I imagine, Sylvia Cecil. Coward affected a yawn, took Pat by one hand and Graham by the other, led them forward and as they all three bowed the curtain fell.

The critics were less than kind but because of his famous name we managed to struggle along for six months. As he had backed it almost entirely himself (no one else would touch it), Tom Arnold merely managing it for him, he must have lost a great deal of money. Shortly after the opening he left for Jamaica and the company never saw him again.

Talking of money, Elizabeth was growing restless for her rent. It was now three months overdue and we couldn't do anything about it. We quite understood her irritability, she must have had bills of her own to pay, and the big money she would earn from her books hadn't started to come in yet. Her sister, Felecité, had been looking for a flat in Chelsea, so as to be close to Elizabeth, and it turned out that ours was the very one she had been looking for. In our present predicament we had no option but to relinquish it and promise to settle our debt as soon as we could. Elizabeth said she had a much better idea: she would keep our furniture and fittings in lieu of the rent owed. As crafty as she was, she was no match for Denis, and before she knew what was happening a removal van had been called and our precious possessions gone into store. She was furious and for several years not one word passed between us.

It was she who made the first move of reconciliation. Having heard from a friend (possibly Joy) that Denis was in very poor health she telephoned and asked if she could come to tea. She came, and the warm friendship they had once known began to be rekindled. Later on, when he was more or less housebound, she would sometimes visit with delicacies she had brought from Paris or a wonderful French shop that existed then in Old Compton Street, called Roche. The painful wound to their friendship had finally healed.

On leaving Halsey Street we rented a room in Chelsea. A friend of ours who had a house in Milner Street let one of the rooms to a lodger and it had just become vacant, so we took it. It was somewhere where we could quietly lick our wounds and decide what we were going to do. As luck would have it (luck has always played an important part in my life) a writer Denis had been working with on spec adapting an R.F. Delderfield novel for the screen (it never made it there) was going to live in Cornwall for six months and wanted to let her furnished London flat while she was away. With financial help from an old friend, Graham Eyres Monsell, we were able to put down a quarter's rent in advance. It was a charming little flat just behind New Bond Street on the west side, smaller than Halsey Street but quite comfortable and nicely furnished in a conventional English way; and it was very handy for me, being only a fifteen minute walk from the Cambridge Theatre. Now all we needed was for something nice to happen for one or, better still, both of us. Something did happen, and it was for both of us, but 'nice' is not how I would describe it. And it all started off so well.

Hermoine Baddeley rang me up. She liked my work and had already done a number of Robb's and mine in cabaret. She had been asked to do a revue and wondered if I had any suitable material. I said I thought I might have and we arranged for me to go around to her house one afternoon and read some of it to her. At that time she lived in a beautiful little house in Belgravia, just south of Eaton Square. (In a very few years she would lose it, having been declared bankrupt.) On the day at the appointed time I rang the front door bell. There was no reply. I rang it again. There was still no reply. I knocked loudly and waited. Silence. As I was walking away I heard an upstairs window being opened, I looked up and there leaning out of it was Hermione clutching a dressing gown about her, her hair all tousled. "Come on up, " she called. "Here, catch the key." I caught it and let myself in. This was uncannily like my first meeting with the other Hermione, only then it was mid morning, now it was three o'clock in the afternoon. As I made my way up the stairs I could hear muffled voices and laughter coming from her bedroom. She wasn't alone. When I entered she was already back in bed and lying beside her, naked with the sheet down to his navel, was Laurence Harvey whom I had known in the Entertainment Unit as Larry Skikne. They both had glasses of red wine in their hands, there was a half full bottle on the bedside table and a couple of empties lying on the floor.

"You know Larry, don't you?" she said. I said I did. "Have a drink," she said. "You'll find a glass in the bathroom." I fetched a glass and poured myself some wine. She then told me about the girls. Two women who were great fans of hers were going into theatrical management and their first production was to be a revue starring her. They had pots of money, so that was no problem. It was just the matter of finding the right material. Harry Kendall had also been approached and shown interest; and, film commitments permitting, Larry might be in it.

"Yes, so you must write me something funny," said Larry.

"I'll try," I said, hoping my smile looked more genuine than it felt.

"Now read us something," said Hermione, as she snuggled up to him.

"Yes," he said, putting his arm around her, "read us something."

I was extremely cross. It was bad enough that they were slightly drunk, but to have to audition my material for Larry Skikne, whose knowledge of revue was absolutely nil, was too humiliating; and besotted with him, as I could see she was, I felt she might easily be swayed by his opinion.

I started off with a sketch that I thought would suit her quite well. In it two gypsy fortune-tellers find themselves sharing the same table in a self-service café and start to tell one another's fortune by reading the tea-leaves, palms, cards, crystal balls and bumps on each other's head; the revelations becoming more personal and unpleasant with each reading. It ends with one foreseeing that the other is going to have an accident and on being asked, "When?" she replies, "Right now!" and hits her over the head with a tray (not a very subtle ending but the best I could come up with).

It made Hermione laugh quite a lot. Larry laughed a little. He wasn't going to make it easy for me. After I had read about six items of various sorts I noticed that he was dozing off and she had become more interested in contemplating his navel than listening to my witty words. I said that was all the material I had with me and if she wanted to hear any more I could come back another time. She said she had liked what she had heard and would tell the girls about it. "You won't mind if I don't see you out?" she said as she snuggled closer to Larry.

"Not at all," I said and made my way down the stairs. As I walked away from the house I wondered if she would even remember I had been there.

She did remember and really had liked what she had heard, for one of the girls rang me up to say so, and to ask if I would go to their flat the next day and read the material to them. By strange coincidence they lived in a mews just across Grosvenor Street from Avery Row, less than a two-minute walk. The one who rang me was Joan Rayne, a member of the Rayne Shoes family, so she was obviously not strapped for a bob or two. Her partner was an American woman called Sabina Storm, who was the daughter of the famous Hollywood screenwriter, Leonora Coffee. They called their company, 'Rayne Storm Productions.' In time, borrowing a line from King Louis the 15th, we would re christen it, 'Apres Moi Le Deluge Productions'.

At precisely eleven thirty the following morning, carrying a large folder of material, I crossed over the road to meet the girls. I was given a cup of coffee and before I had time to finish it a large gin and tonic was placed before me. To keep me company, they said, they might have one themselves, and did. I then started to read and they were a most attentive audience. After each item, as they gave me their verdict, mostly positive, I took a sip from my glass. Every now and then they replenished it. Theirs, I noticed, were being replenished all the time. To one lyric they took great offence, especially Sabina. It was a love ballad sung by a southern belle sitting on a swing waiting for her lover. The last part of the lyric went:

> "From Saturday to Thursday my life could not be finer,
> But Friday night is swingin' night in Carolina,
> So I'm swingin' on a magnolia tree
> Waitin' for my sweet
> To take off that sheet
> And come on home to make love to me.
> I'm swingin'…
> Swingin' …
> Swingin' on a magnolia tree."

Sabina said how could I possibly write a love song about the Ku Klux Klan? I tried to explain that it was meant to be ironic, but that word didn't seem to exist in her vocabulary. I wonder what she would have made of, 'Springtime For Hitler'? ('Swing Song' was eventually performed in two shows. In the first, 'The Park Lane Revue', a member of the first night audience, obviously of the same mind as Sabina, rose from his seat, muttering, "Disgusting!" and stomped out of the theatre).

Apart from 'Swing Song' the girls seemed to like most of the stuff, and some of it a great deal, and they couldn't wait to hear Robb's music. I rang him up, he said come over straight away, so we jumped in a taxi and headed for darkest Pimlico; Joan bringing a bottle of gin in case of an emergency. They simply adored Robb's music and made him play some of the tunes over and over again. We had written a bright opening number called 'We're going On The Tiles Tonight'. We thought the show might be called 'On The Tiles'. The setting could be a London rooftop and the cast all dressed as cats. It seemed an original idea then.

"Joanie, we've got a hit!" said Sabina, slightly slurring her words. By then it was five o'clock, we had not had a bite to eat all day and far too many gin and tonics. They then mentioned that Hermione had told them Denis Freeman was a brilliant revue director; she had worked with him before the war on, 'Floodlight', which also starred John Mills and Frances Day, and she thought he would be perfect for our show. So Denis was telephoned and asked to go across for a drink with the girls that evening (Robb and I, by then, would be at the theatre). He went, laid on the charm that he could do better than anyone I have ever known and a couple of gin and tonics later the job was his.

Denis had very strong opinions about revue. He believed they should not be written by one person alone; that made for a sameness and predictability, whereas different attitudes and styles gave a show freshness and surprise. The Beverly Nichols revue had suffered from his refusing to have any interpolations in it: it was strong on charm and sentiment but weak on humour; whereas Herbert Farjeon, a supreme humourist, fought Denis tooth and nail not to have the sentimental song, 'These Foolish Things (remind me of you)' included in 'Spread It Abroad'. He thought it would cheapen the show. Fortunately Denis won the argument, it became the hit number of the revue and soon everyone all over the world was singing it.

Robb and I would be credited as the main contributors and the billing would read:

'On The Tiles'
A new revue
Book and lyrics by Neville Phillips
Music by Robb Stewart
Additional material by:
(list of contributors in alphabetical order)
Devised and directed by C. Denis Freeman.

Denis went ahead immediately looking for material, for no matter how big the star and lavish the costumes and scenery the most important element of a revue is always the words. Noel Langley produced a very funny sketch about Father Christmas. Peter Myers sent some good material. So did Diana Morgan and Robert McDermott, and other writers promised to do so. Richard Lake, a very talented stage designer, came up with a lovely design for the main setting. Orchestraters and costume designers were being considered. And Denis was determined to have some beautiful and talented girls in the show: among the many he interviewed were Natasha Parry and Kay Kendall.

Everything seemed to be falling into place very nicely. There was one subject however that had not yet been broached and that was money (something of which we were in very short supply). Negotiating one's own fee is always very difficult. It is wiser to have someone else do it for one, and a friend of ours, Dennis van Thal who was with London Management, then the most prestigious theatrical agency in London, and who admired my work, agreed to handle the business side for us. All his attempts to draw up a contract with the girls were met with stony silence. He had also asked for Denis to be given an advance on his director's fee in lieu of the work he had already done on the show (he knew how broke we were), but this too went unheeded. The meetings he set up they failed to attend and his phone calls were never returned. He came to the conclusion that something fishy was going on.

We had sensed from the beginning that they were not the most normal couple of women on the planet, but in the theatre one comes across some very strange people and one always hopes for the best; after all, it is the one place where miracles do still happen. Many a doomed show, having played to hostile audiences on a pre-London tour has limped into town expecting to last one night and run for a year (and vice versa); and Agatha Christie in her wildest dreams could never have thought that her little pot boiler thriller (the least interesting of all her plays) 'The Mousetrap' would still be running in the West End almost half a century after her death.

Whatever the fishy thing was that was going on we felt it couldn't be the lack of money, for they entertained in the most lavish style. Most days they would take us to lunch at Scott's, a lovely old restaurant in Piccadilly (no longer in existence), and ply us with champagne, oysters, lobster and the finest wines. Those meals must have cost them a fortune, and as they were always warmly welcomed by the manager and treated with great respect by the staff their account must have been settled quite regularly.

What we didn't know then but would later find out was that Joan was a serial alcoholic who spent much of her life in clinics and had recently come out of one (where, perhaps, she had met Sabina). She had no bank account of her own: her family knew where the money would go. They paid the rent of her mews flat, her grocery bill at Fortnum and Mason (whence came the gin) and the account at Scott's where she was allowed to entertain. But apart from a little pin money each week she was virtually penniless.

And so was Sabina. Having been disowned by her family in America and cut off without a cent she had come to England to try her luck; and as her luck would have it she met Joan, and together, as mad people often do, they decided to go into show business. I suppose on Hermione Baddeley's name they expected to raise backing from elsewhere. Who knows what went on in their blurred minds.

After another week of non negotiation Dennis van Thal, with our consent, issued them with an ultimatum: unless by Friday afternoon at five o'clock they had come up with some sort of contractual agreement, and produced the advance money as requested, all association with them would cease to exist (shades of Neville Chamberlain there). Their answer was to attack. They told us that our agent was not only professionally inept, he was also a dangerous troublemaker and they would have nothing more to do with him, and they advised us to follow suit. He was just complicating matters and we would be far better off without him. We didn't think so, at least Denis and I didn't think so. They had already poisoned Robb's mind with some ludicrous story of how the three of us were plotting to cheat him out of his rightful share of the royalties, and silly, gullible Robb, always a sucker for anyone who flattered him about his music, fell for it. They told him to stick with them, they were the only ones who really appreciated his talent and they were going to make him famous. His attitude towards us suddenly changed and he became quite distant.

Then it was my turn, and this shows how deranged they were. They asked me over to the flat and told me that Denis was not a true friend, he was my secret enemy. He and van Thal were plotting to remove all Robb's and my material from the show and replace it with the work of their other friends. They also told me that behind my back Denis was saying vicious things about me. Like van Thal he was a treacherous man and they were going to sack him and find a better, more sympathetic director who would have Robb's and my best interests at heart. I sat there dumbfounded, I could hardly believe my ears. As they ranted on about Denis' disloyalty I felt a rage simmering up inside me and suddenly I exploded: I told them not only were they a pair of pathetic drunks but certifiably insane to boot, and on those harsh but apt words I stormed out of that crazy little bijou Mayfair madhouse.

At five o'clock on Friday the unanswered ultimatum expired; the whole nightmare experience was over and the feeling of release was immense. At five twenty that afternoon Dennis van Thal arrived at Paddington Station to catch the five thirty train to go to his country home for the weekend, as he usually did, and as he was walking down the platform he heard his name being announced on the loudspeaker. He was requested to go to the Station Master's office immediately where an urgent phone call awaited him. Fearing that something awful had happened to his family, and all the other dreadful things one thinks of at a time like that, he hurried to the phone. The speaker was Joan Rayne, who had discovered from a secretary in his office that he was catching a five thirty train from Paddington. In a voice slurred with gin she informed him that he was the most unpleasant agent Rayne Storm Productions had ever had dealings with, and they wished him to know they wanted nothing more to do with him or his ungrateful and disloyal clients. The show was going ahead without them and would be all the better for it. He didn't bother to reply, he quietly put the phone back on its hook and went to catch his train, but for once it had left on time.

And that was the last anyone ever heard of, 'Apres Moi Le Deluge Productions.' But just to add insult to injury, Hermione Baddeley started going about town saying she was furious with Denis and me for getting her involved with those two mad women.

In case you're still curious about the Hermione/Larry affair, it lasted a very short while. Through her brother in law, Glen Byam Shaw, a director of the Shakespeare Memorial Theatre at Stratford Upon Avon, she got Larry into the company. His first part was Charles the wrestler in 'As You Like It' where his handsome, tanned torso, glistening with oil, caught many an admiring eye, including that of the fair maid Rosalind who was being played by Margaret Leighton, and before you could say "As you like it", they had embarked on a ardent affair (much to the chagrin of Ralph Richardson with whom she had been having a slight dalliance till then). When Hermione found out she went beserk and kept rushing to Stratford and making terrible scenes. Larry had her banned from coming backstage, and on one humiliating occasion she had to be forcibly thrown out of the stage door while screaming abuse at the lovers.

Margaret Leighton would serve her purpose and then Larry would move on again. John Wolf, a film producer whose love for Larry lasted many years, starred him in several pictures. One was 'Room At The Top' where he and Simone Signoret were co starred as lovers. To play the part of the blousy landlady in whose rooming house the pair conduct their illicit affair, Larry suggested Hermione, and to everyone's utter astonishment she accepted the role.

———

1951 would have to be a great deal better than 1950 if we were going to survive, and fortunately it was. Nothing spectacular happened for either of us but we managed to work fairly consistently and Denis' health had much improved. Although this would turn out to be just a temporary reprieve.

It was the year of The Festival Of Britain, exactly one hundred years after The Great Exhibition with its magnificent Crystal Palace that people came from all over the world to see and marvel at. The 1951 Festival was to celebrate the beginning of a bright Socialist Britain after the long war and bleak years of austerity that followed it. In actual fact, the austerity had not completely gone; food rationing continued until 1954. But that didn't stop Festivals from breaking out all over the land. Everyone seemed to have caught Festivalitis. Well, not actually everyone. Noel Coward took a very cynical view of it and wrote a song for The Lyric Revue called, 'Don't Make Fun Of The Festival' in which he proceeded to do just that. He also produced another equally witty song of doom and gloom called, 'There Are Bad Times Just Around The Corner'. One must remember that the enfant terrible was now 51, held staunch conservative views (except where sex was concerned) and although he was prepared to poke fun at the upper classes ('The Stately Homes Of England') he was perfectly happy with the social system the way it was.

Everyone I knew was doing something in a festival somewhere. It was a bit like the Edinburgh Festival is today: in every nook and cranny something festive was occurring. I appeared in the role of 'Friendship' in a production of 'Everyman' at the Festival Church, just across Waterloo Bridge, directly opposite the entrance to the South Bank Festival site. Denis directed a Hadyn masque in the great hall at Hampton Court, for which Katusha did the choreography. He also directed two comic operas for the Bath Festival. The first was Pergolesi's 1733 opera, 'La Serva Padrona', in which I had a very nice mime part as Uberto's mute manservant, Vespone. The second was Wolf-Ferrari's 1911 (Art Nouveu) opera, 'Susanna's Secret', a performance of which was broadcast on the BBC Third Programme live from the Theatre Royal, Bath, with me as the narrator. There was a lot of silent action in it that, without being explained would have left the listeners completely in the dark; so I sat in a box high up in the Theatre Royal and, in subdued tones so as not to disturb the audience below, reported on what was happening. Susanna's secret, in case I have whetted your curiosity, is an addiction to tobacco, and all her sly little subterfuges and manoeuvres to be on her own are not, as her jealous husband suspects, to meet a lover but to have a good, long puff on a cigarette (very non PC these days). My contribution to the performance was of vital importance, for without me the BBC Third Programme audience might have gone to their graves still wondering what Susanna's secret could possibly be. Although I suppose for those with vivid imaginations a drag on a fag might be rather a let down. After the Bath Festival the two operas came in to the Fortune Theatre, London for a few extra performances.

I would appear in three more of The London Opera Club's productions, all at the Scala Theatre, London (now a hideous office block). The LOC was formed by a group of rich opera lovers to present first-rate revivals of worthy operas that, for some reason or other, had not been seen in opera houses for a number of years. They had no trouble attracting singers of distinction and the excellent Kalmar Orchestra was usually conducted by John Pritchard, who would later become the permanent conductor of the Royal Ballet. One of these operas was 'Il Mondo Della Luna' (Life on the Moon) by Joseph Hadyn. It had a mime ballet in it that Katusha choreographed and I took the part of Pantaloon. They also presented the British premier of a modern Italian opera, 'I Due Timidi' (The Two Shy People) by Nino Rota, with a charming and witty libretto by Suso Cecchi d'Amico; and the speaking role of an irate lodger was played by me. The opera was a great success and we later broadcast it for the BBC Third Programme at their orchestral studios in Maida Vale.

That summer I worked on two films. The first was 'Scrooge', directed by Brian with costumes by Bumble and starring Alastair Sim as Scrooge and George Cole as his younger self. I was one of Mr. Fezziwig's apprentices. Another apprentice, whose first film this was, having just left drama school, would go on to become one of our most distinguished actors. His name was Alec McCowan. The interior scenes were all filmed in Walton Studios at Walton-on-Thames. They were small studios and only two films could be made there at the same time. The other production in progress was 'Another Man's Poison' starring Bette Davis, her new husband, Garry Merrill and Emlyn Williams. It was a dreadful film with an abysmal script and why any of them wished to make it I cannot imagine.

My old friend, Hattie Jacques was playing Mrs. Fezziwig in 'Scrooge' and for two days running we lunched together in the studio restaurant. Most of the others used the canteen which was much cheaper, but we were hoping to get a glimpse of the great Miss Davis and to our sheer delight both days we found ourselves at the very next table to her and her husband. There was a telephone by the entrance, close to where we sat, and during lunch she would ring her young daughter who had come to England with her and was in a house they had rented nearby that had a large swimming pool. Never known to mumble, we heard every syllable of what Miss Davis said to her daughter, and on returning to the table and recounting the conversation to her husband every syllable of what her daughter had said to her. We would never have presumed to start a conversation with them: it was she, on the second day, that spoke to us and she was utterly charming. She told us her daughter was having a whale of a time splashing about in the pool. It was a hot summer day and we said how much we envied her, dressed as we were in our heavy Victorian costumes.

That day the Fezziwig Ball sequence was being shot and during the afternoon our new friend from lunch came in to have a look. Before leaving she told us how wonderfully authentic it all looked and that our attention to detail was far superior to anything

Hollywood did. I am not sure how truthful she was being but it made us all feel very grand.

'Where's Charley?', Frank Loesser's first stage musical, based on Brandon Thomas's famous 1892 farce, 'Charley's Aunt'. Was a big hit on Broadway in 1948 starring Ray Bolger (the scarecrow in 'The Wizard Of Oz'). Ten years later Norman Wisdom would have a success with it at the Palace Theatre, London. In 1951 Warner Bros decided to make a film of it with the original Broadway stars, Ray Bolger and lovely young Allyn McLeery; and, bizarre for Hollywood, they chose to film it in the very location where the story is set: an Oxford college. So instead of, as they usually did at that time, building vast sets in Madrid or Rome they used Kings College, Oxford during the summer vacation.

The director was David Butler, an old hand at Warner Musicals, not wildly inspired, but safe, and known in the business as 'one take Butler.' The choreographer was Michael Kidd whom I had known slightly in 1946 when he came to Covent Garden with The Ballet Theatre. He had already carefully picked his team of highly talented dancers for the film, but still needed half a dozen or so young actors who, besides speaking lines could mime to the pre recorded songs and be able to dance a bit. He held an audition one morning at the Rudolph Steiner Hall, a friend told me about it, I went along and was one of the chosen few. It was several weeks work on very good money so I was, as the cliché goes, over the moon! I had several friends on it: John Heawood, Norman Warwick, Larry Drew, Lionel Blair, Malcolm Goddard...and one or two others so rehearsals were a great deal of fun.

One day Michael Kidd said to me, "You know, Neville, you should have seriously trained as a dancer. I think you could have been good." I considered it a great compliment coming from him and over the years I have repeated that remark almost as often as the one 10 made about my feet (page 176).

Another day, it was at the end of the lunch break and we were all just sitting about in the rehearsal room waiting to start again; Lionel Blair, who had brought along his tap shoes that day and was now wearing them, affected not to see Michael Kidd enter the room and, pretending to be deep in concentration on something of his own he was rehearsing, went into his most spectacular tap routine – buck & wings – the lot! We all despised him for it but it showed what a burning ambition he had in him.

The opening sequence of the film had all of us miming to the title song, 'Where's Charley?' as we danced along the walls of Kings College, leapt over balustrades, ran down steps, across lawns, and popped up from behind hedges all wanting to know; 'Where's Charley? How's Charley? When's Charley coming home?'

Another big production number shot in the grounds of the college had a title almost as long as the song itself: 'The New Ashmolean Marching Society And Student's Conservatory Band'.

The interior scenes were all shot at Elstree Studios. They also filled the big studio tank with water and transformed it into the River Isis with flowers along the grassy banks and a beautiful old stone bridge across it; and it was here that Ray Bolger performed his big song and dance number from the show, 'Once In Love With Amy', while we, in straw boaters and blazers, punted pretty girls with frilly frocks and parasols up and down the river. Two whole days we spent in that tank before the star was finally satisfied with his performance. I had two pretty girls in my punt; one was great fun and we got on very well together, the other was a prissy little miss who didn't smile once at anything we said and looked horribly shocked if anyone used a swear word, however mild. I dismissed her then as just a silly little prude who had strayed into the wrong profession, so imagine my surprise when a year or so later I was told that she had married Sid James. Well, you could have knocked me down with another feather from one of Maurice's Red Skelton bird costumes (page 25).

George Minter of Renown Films asked Denis to do some first aid on the script of a film he was making starring the American actress/singer, Julie London and Anthony Steele, the subject being (very daring for those days) artificial insemination. It was in no way prurient, having come from a very serious stage play, and the finished film was not without its qualities, but at the box office a discussion on artificial insemination was no competition for Doris Day or Frank Sinatra singing about the real thing: making love!

An American film producer then commissioned Denis to write a story outline on the life of the famous French dancer, Gaby Deslys, who (I now quote from Denis' introduction) 'in a flutter of silk, feathers, flesh and jewels, flashed across the world's stage with the glitter of a bird of paradise. The herald of a new epoch, this extraordinary woman dazzled, enchanted – and disturbed a little – the last days of the happy, carefree Edwardian era.'

She took Paris, London and New York by storm, and was the first incarnation of Parisian 'chic', the first woman to make the world 'Paris dress-conscious' in the modern sense...the first great international mannequin. Lewis, the famous milliner, placed on her head all the birds of paradise, all the sprays, all the plumes he could lay his hands on; it was she who started the fashion for them; and it was she who was the first to emancipate women from their heavily boned bodices, their linings, their petticoats and voluminous skirts. "Some people," she would say, "think I wear too little, the point is that I don't wear too much."

Harry Pilcer, her American dancing partner of many years, who was then 65, had persuaded the producer that there was a film to be made of their great partnership. I imagine he envisaged another 'The Story Of Vernon And Irene Castle'; and it is true that they were the first to bring Ragtime and jazz bands to Paris; they also triumphed in London and New York. But when Denis met him to find out more he tried to infer that theirs had been one of the great love stories of the age; whereas, in actual fact, he was as gay as a cricket and she the mistress of King Manuel of Portugal, who, it is said, lost his throne for the love of her. She also had liaisons with the Kaiser Wilhelm's son, the Crown Prince of Germany, Sacha Guitry, Max Linder, George Grossmith, an American newspaper magnet millionaire and many other men of wealth. By the time she died, at the young age of 39, she had amassed a fortune of nearly half a million pounds (a great sum in those days). She was buried in the little cemetery of her birth-place, Marseilles. It was only then that people understood what she had meant when she told them, "I dance for the poor." For when her will was read, after bequests to family and friends, she wrote: 'I leave the rest of my fortune to the poor of Marseilles – the place of my birth. For all my life I have danced for the poor.'

It would have been an extremely expensive film to make, also Harry Pilcer and the producer were no longer on speaking terms, so the project was abandoned.

When Marilyn Monroe was in England a few years later making the film 'The Prince And The Show Girl' with Laurence Olivier, Bumble, who designed all the costumes for the picture, had Marilyn's manager and Denis to supper one night and somehow 'Gaby' got mentioned. He thought it might be a possible vehicle for Marilyn and showed her Denis' story outline. For a short while she seemed quite interested in it, and then, a fate that must have befallen so many scripts held briefly in those pretty little hands, it got tossed aside and forgotten.

Joy suddenly turned up in London and bright lights seemed to go on everywhere – that was the effect she had on one. She had just acquired a 'new' old jalopy (the old old jalopy had eventually conked out for good) and she was about to drive it down to the south of France to stay with the French painter, Jean Hugo and his family; and thinking it would do Denis good to have a holiday in the sun she suggested he accompany her. I also thought it would do him good and insisted that he went. Having wished them 'bon voyage' I decided to put my nose to the grindstone and went off to do some weekly rep in Palmers Green and Maidstone.

My last play at Maidstone was Noel Coward's very first comedy, 'I'll Leave It To You', which he wrote in 1921. He also appeared in it playing the young son, Bobbie, a part he had carefully tailored for himself: 'a slim, bright youth of twenty, witty and effusive, all mannered epigrams and gestures.' Needless to say he was a tremendous success in the role. I too would play Bobbie and have great fun with it. 'I'll Leave It To You' was not vintage Coward, it was very much a forerunner to the better plays that followed: 'The Young Idea' and 'Hay Fever', in both of which he would again use some of the same characters. Bobbie and Evangeline, a precocious young brother and sister, sophisticated and mundane beyond their years, were a little too close to Philip and Dolly Clandon in Shaw's 'You Never Can Tell' for comfort, and Coward, fearing he might be accused of plagiarism sent Shaw the manuscript to read. Shaw wrote back saying he showed every indication of becoming a good playwright, providing that he never again in his life read another word that he (Shaw) had written.

I had an elder brother in the play called Oliver, a priggish, humourless character that was played by a handsome young actor, perhaps a year or so older than me, whom I thought extremely sexy; and travelling down to Maidstone by train on the Monday we found ourselves sharing a compartment – we also found ourselves alone in it. On the Maidstone line there were no corridors to the carriages, so once the train was in motion no one could enter, and we had not gone far, just past Clapham Junction to be precise, before I discovered to my delight that the feelings I had for him were equally reciprocated; and as it was warm weather and we were not overburdened with clothes we spent most of the journey, apart from short stops at stations when we hastily adjusted our attire, with our shirts off and our trousers around our knees.

That whole week we could hardly keep our hands off one another; in the dressing room we shared; in the changing cubicles at the Maidstone Municipal Baths, where we went to swim between performances on matinee days; and especially on the train at night. After the show we would go and have a drink in a pub and, forgetting to keep an eye on the clock, miss the train that the others all took. On a later one, with hardly a passenger on it, we would choose a compartment in the last carriage where we knew no one would bother us and, for six nights running, throw off our clothes and revel.

On the Saturday, after our last journey together, which was also the most intensely enjoyable, we said goodbye on Victoria Station and never saw one another again. He had a partner, an actor who had been on tour and was returning the following day and Denis was due back soon from Provence. We had no wish to complicate our lives, it had been a blissful week, an exquisite dalliance, a sublime diversion, but that was all it was.

I have no idea what became of him. I imagine he gave up acting for I have not since seen his name on a theatre programme or the television screen or ever heard other actors mention him. And I have never tried to find out – it is better that way – to just keep it as a perfect memory: six heavenly rides on the 10.59 from Maidstone!!! Who could ask for anything more?

PART THREE

"THE PLOT THICKENS"

And sometimes curdles

But the melody lingers on

THREE

On Tuesday the sixth of January 1952 King George VI died and the nation went into mourning. Royalty then was held in far greater esteem than it is today and the King was much admired for his stoicism and personal bravery. George, or to give him the name he was christened with, Albert, was a shy, meek man, uncomfortable in company, with a bad nervous stammer and no wish to take part in the affairs of state; and suddenly he found himself thrust upon the throne when his elder brother, Edward, abdicated to marry Wallis Simpson. As unsuitable as he felt himself for the daunting role, he took it on and performed it impeccably – even when severe illness dogged him.

During the Blitz, when even Buckingham Palace was a target for bombs, he refused to leave London although many, fearing a German invasion imminent, advised him to take the Queen and Princesses to Canada and continue his reign from there.

On the night after he died not a theatre, cinema, restaurant or bar opened, and in the heavy silent pall that hung over London Hermione Baddeley, due to perform in cabaret that evening at the Café de Paris, said to Robb, who was to accompany her at the piano, "Why does everything have to happen to me?"

For three days the King's body lay in state in Westminster Hall where his subjects could come and pay their final homage to him, and for three days there was a continuous queue of mourners. I joined the end of the line on the north side of Westminster Bridge, it stretched over the river and westward along the south bank, back over Lambeth Bridge, eastward down Millbank, past Victoria Tower Gardens, the House of Lords and in through the west entrance of Westminster Hall. The coffin lay on a bier in the centre of the hall; it was draped in a Union Flag and summounted by the Imperial State Crown. While officers of the Household Cavalry and Foot Guards, resting on reversed arms, and Yeomen with their halberds stood statue like, two lines of mourners, one either side, moved softly yet swiftly through the hall and out by the east door.

It had taken hours to get there but I would not have missed the experience for anything. I myself am not much of a royalist but the feeling of deep loss and veneration that permeated the atmosphere in Westminster Hall that day is something I shall never forget.

A friend from my Cape Town childhood, Victor Glasstone, knew the theatre director and writer, Ann Jellicoe, who was about to direct a production of Vanbrugh's 'The Confederacy' at the Cockpit Theatre and had not yet found a suitable actor to play the very good role of 'Brass'. Victor mentioned my name and she asked me to go and see her; I did, auditioned for the part and got it. It was a very happy production and I found playing 'Brass' a most rewarding experience.

Although he did not review it, the drama critic of The Observer, Kenneth Tynan, came to the first performance and happened to sit beside my old actor friend, John Vere, who he also knew. John told me later that Tynan had enjoyed the production very much; his one quibble being that we took it at too fast a lick. I shared his criticism but it was the pace Ann had set it at and she was adamant that we kept to it.

'The Stage' did review it and this is what its critic said: 'Ann Jellicoe's production, though mounted in modern dress, moved with such smoothness and speed that this incongruity was forgotten about at once. The portrayal of Brass by Neville Phillips had so much grace and vivacity that the fruits of his roguery seemed only too well deserved' – then he went on to mention two or three of the others.

Ann's next production was Shakespeare's 'The Comedy of Errors' in which she asked me to play 'Dromio of Ephesus'. During rehearsals when she tried to hurry me through a piece of business I had become rather attached to, in a fit of irritation I blurted out Tynan's criticism of her speedy direction. There was no reply but the look on her face seemed to say, "With actors of high calibre I might allow a little self indulgence, but with the sort of material I have at my disposal the less hanging about the better."

It actually was a very good cast and the fast moving production was considered a great success. At least two members of the cast would go on to make names for themselves in the profession: Edward Hardwicke and Ronnie Corbett.

Ann would then write a rather obscure play called, 'The Sport Of My Mad Mother', which was produced at the Royal Court Theatre and highly praised by the more serious critics. She then wrote a delightfully wacky, fast-paced comedy called, 'The Knack', which after its run at the Royal Court, transferred to the West End; it then went to Broadway where it was directed by Mike Nichols and ran for two years; Dick Lester then made a film of it starring Rita Tushungham, Ray Brooks and Michael Crawford.

By now we were living in Wyndham Place at the top end of Bryanston Square. The owner of the Avery Row flat was returning to London and needed it for herself. Our new abode was a sparsely furnished basement flat that neither of us liked very much but it had presented itself at the very moment we needed to find somewhere, so we took it as a stop-gap. Our effects: furniture, pictures, books and the many artefacts

Denis had brought back from Egypt were still in store. It was costing money to keep them there but until we had somewhere more permanent to live, there they would have to remain.

In contrast to us, Helen Wissa and her charming daughter, Josephine, were living at the Ritz Hotel. They had a large suite on the corner of the fourth floor overlooking Green Park and Piccadilly, and there we were often invited to dine. Sometimes we would eat in the elegant restaurant on the ground floor but mostly it would be in their magnificently appointed suite where the atmosphere was less formal and Josephine could play her gramophone records. One I was particularly fond of at the time was the show recording of the Broadway revival of, 'Pal Joey'.

The Wissas were one of the grand old Coptic families of Egypt. Some believe the Copts are the direct descendants of the Pharaohs; they were the indigenous people who Saint Mark converted to Christianity, and they clung on to that religion after the Arab conquest in 640 AD. The Copts were great landowners and politicians, and during World War Two, being Christians, they were popular with the British and held high status in Cairo society.

That was when Denis met the Wissas and formed a close friendship with Helen who often visited 16 Midan Abdel Monim. Until Nasser came to power and confiscated it all, the Wissas owned property in both Cairo and Alexandria as well as vast acres of cotton fields in Upper Egypt. Helen was an astute woman and sensing that after the British left things might not go well for the Copts, had transferred as much of her wealth as she could to a bank in Switzerland; and now, while her friends and relations were beginning to feel the pinch, she and her daughter were sitting pretty at the Ritz. On arrival in London she had renewed her friendship with Denis and our visits to the Ritz began. Of course, we could in no way return her lavish hospitality, but she understood this. As many have, she found Denis the most stimulating company, and I'll give him this, he certainly knew how to sing for his supper. Beside him on these occasions I always felt like a dull clod.

As with most women in Cairo society Helen was more attuned to Continental flamboyance than British reserve and I think she felt more at home in Paris and Geneva, where she spent much of her time, than in London. But Josephine had had an English nanny who had instilled in her an indelible love of all things English; and since early childhood she had craved the taste of Mackintosh Toffees, Huntley and Palmers biscuits, Ovaltine, Marmite, Coopers Oxford Marmalade, Enos Fruit Salts, Dr. Colliss's Cough Mixture; visits to Marshall and Snellgrove, Debenham and Freebody, Whiteleys, and that Aladin's cave of wonders, Harrods, where it was said you could get anything you needed from a pin to an elephant. Josephine, a solitary child, having been taken to see, 'Dumbo' couldn't wait to get to Harrods and have a baby elephant for a pet.

England, when she eventually got there, was all that Nanny and Shakespeare had said it would be: a demi-paradise – and the service at the Ritz wasn't bad either. Having seen all the sights that Nanny had told her to, she enlisted as a student at the Byam Shaw School of Art in Notting Hill Gate and attended classes there every day. She had no artistic talent whatsoever, but it was somewhere to go while that terrifying hoard of maids swept through the suite hoovering, dusting and polishing everything until it looked as if no one had ever been there. With her sweet nature she got on well with her fellow students and, to Helen's horror, began to dress like them in both style and quality, while her pretty little Dior frocks hung unloved and unworn in the wardrobe. None of the students ever guessed the terrible secret of where she lived; they were under the impression she had digs somewhere in South Ken. I am almost prepared to believe that if Helen had said to her, "We're leaving the Ritz and going to live in a nice little semi-detached in Fulham", she would have been delighted.

Helen still owned a house in Maadi, a smart green suburb of Cairo, where she usually went for a couple of months in the early spring each year, and seeing how ill Denis had been through the winter she invited him to go with her as her guest. His health had deteriorated badly and our doctor, Patrick Woodcock, advised him to spend as much time out of the fogs and smogs of London (they had been particularly prevalent that year) as possible.

Patrick was a highly successful GP who had a passion for theatrical celebrity, and behind his back was known as Dr. Footlights. Among his patients were such illustrious names as Noel Coward, John Gielgud and Vivien Leigh. Bumble went to him and so did Elizabeth, to whom I introduced him when we lived in Halsey Street. I had known Patrick for some years. His was rather the 'Cinderella of the National Health' story. When I first met him, through a mutual friend, he lived in a small flat at the Worlds End of Chelsea and was the locum to a local doctor. I often saw him peddling down the Kings Road to visit a patient, bicycle clips on his shabby grey trousers. How the transformation was achieved I have no idea, but now he drove a smart car, wore finely tailored suits, owned his own house, and with the rather grand manner he had adopted I could hardly see any resemblance to the scruffy young locum with the bicycle clips on his ankles and the final remnants of acne on his chin. He still saw us on the National Health but his more illustrious patients, I imagine, went to him privately and paid accordingly. Patrick's other great love was the opera and he was often seen at Covent Garden. It was a joke among some of his patients that one dare not be ill during the opera season.

On hearing of Helen's offer Patrick insisted that Denis accept it, and Irene and I backed him up, but he still felt trepidation and anxiety about the trip: he was not at all well, and had very little money to take with him so would be at Helen's mercy the entire time, it would not be the old Cairo he had known, and to go anywhere near number 16 Midan Abdel Monim where he had spent some of the most poignant years of his life would be too painful to bear.

During his last year in Cairo and for a short while afterwards he said he was going to write a book about Cairo society during the war, which would be called, 'A Thousand And One Parties'. He had many fascinating stories to tell and everyone thought it was an excellent idea; but back in England, what with one thing and another, it never got written. I now suggested that while he was sitting quietly in Helen's garden at Maadi he might give it another thought, and he said he might.

But before he left we had to make a very difficult decision: he would be away for some time, I was going off to do some more rep, and neither of us were happy in the Wyndham Place basement for which we would have to continue paying rent during our absence; so, as Marie had shown signs of mellowing and was delighted at the thought of having us back, with dragging footsteps and reluctant hearts we returned to Alexandra Court. The mellowness turned out to be a mirage – the nearer one got the less there was of it, and it would only be a matter of time before she had reverted to her old scheming, spiteful self. Fortunately I had a bolt-hole over at Irene's where I could escape to when the going got really rough.

While Denis and Helen were winging it to the sun I was sitting on a train travelling north to the rainy and windswept town of Bridlington on the Yorkshire coast, to appear twice nightly with the Harry Hanson Court Players in a couple of truly dreadful farces, the titles of which I have mercifully forgotten. Apart from me, the company were all Harry Hanson stalwarts and had been at Bridlington for several seasons; and a more unfriendly, intrigue ridden, reppy, in the worst sense, bunch of actors I had never before and hoped never again to meet. Bridlington, I thought, would be the nadir of my acting career – but I was being over-optimistic.

It rained my entire stay and I lingered not an instant longer than was necessary. The others I could see remaining there, back biting and bickering, season after season, until either they or that tacky old theatre collapsed.

Back in London I auditioned my, 'Head-Shrinking For Beginners' lecture for the Players Theatre and was invited to perform it on one of their fortnightly bills. I had adapted it slightly to give it the Victorian flavour that was the prerequisite of a Players Music Hall bill. It went down very well and the management asked me to come back again when I had another suitable monologue. This I did as a creepy, waxen faced toucher-upper of waxworks at Madame Taussards who, at night, when the place is deserted, boasts familiarity with some of the famous female waxworks; and who also, now and then, seems to be turning into a waxwork himself.

It was a bit bizarre and not to everyone's taste, but I thought it was quite funny and the Players Theatre allowed me to do it.

The 'Head-Shrinking' monologue I would later repeat on a Saturday night variety show on BBC Television called 'It's a Great Life.' Also on the bill was a charming singer called Betty Driver who in later life would enjoy a long, prosperous career in 'Coronation Street' as Betty Turpin, whose hotpots were the staple diet of the Rovers Return.

One night I went to have a drink at the Cross Keys, a charming old pub near the Chelsea Embankment that some of my friends and I frequented then. None of them were there that evening but I happened to meet a sexy young American sailor from Deleware called Bud. He worked at the American Embassy in Grosvenor Square and had a flat in the Chelsea Cloisters, where we instantly embarked on a wild little fling. American sailors then must have earned a lot of money for he was always taking me to restaurants, theatres and even the opera. As flings fling it flung well, and it was a relief to get away from the oppressive atmosphere of Alexandra Court where I am sure Marie was keeping a careful count of the nights I didn't sleep there.

And then a very nice television job came my way. The BBC was to present the most ambitious production ever attempted on British television. It was to last the entire evening and involve dozens of actors, singers, dancers and musicians. It was to be a tribute to the late theatrical impresario, Charles B. Cochran and would tell the story of his life in drama form, including fully staged numbers from some of his most famous revues and musicals. By then it was technically possible to film certain scenes in advance and slot them in at the appropriate spot, otherwise such an audacious under-taking would have been impossible.

The tribute was going to be called, 'Cocky', the name by which he was affection-ately known in the theatre, until his widow, Lady Cochran, objected on the grounds of disrespect, so it was changed to, 'C.B. Cochran Presents.' The evening started with a sort of cocktail party in the BBC lounge where some of the older, glamorous leading ladies from his shows – Evelyn Laye, Anna Neagle, etc., reminisced. There was also a splattering of old Cochran Young Ladies – these were the elevated chorus girls who, under his strict supervision, whenever they appeared in public were always immacu-lately dressed and coiffured, and never without hats and gloves. To be a Cochran Young Lady in those days was quite a feather in your cap.

Then the play began. I had three parts in it; the first was as the teenaged Charles

Cochran touring the provinces as an ASM with a hammy old actor-manager played by Michael Horden. Cochran when older was played by Frank Lawton who, with the help of the makeup department looked as young as possible to begin with and then was slowly allowed to show his age as the years rolled by. My second part was as the young John Mills auditioning for Noel Coward at Drury Lane for a role in 'Cavalcade'. Coward was played by Dennis Price. And thirdly I was Oliver Messel who designed all the scenery and costumes for Cochran's famous 1932 production of Offenbach's 'Helen' starring Evelyn Laye. Messel, having got above himself, demanded more money. Furious at the audacity of this young pup Cochran sends him a telegram cancelling his offer of the job. Pretending he hasn't received the telegram Messel goes to Cochran's office carrying the large intricate model he has made of Helen's bedroom (it was entirely in white with a vast divan bed on a low dias flanked by white swans (Helen's mother was Leda), and from a high baldacchino hung immense lengths of white muslin looped in great swirls up to the flies. This setting made Messel's reputation as a designer). We were actually loaned the original model for our scene and it was indeed magnificent, but it was also quite large and I found it very heavy and cumbersome to carry. On seeing the model, Cochran says, "By the way, I sent you a telegram. Don't bother to open it, just tear it up." At which point I took the open telegram from my pocket and smiling tore it in half. The scene ended with us both laughing as the camera zoomed in on that vast, white bed.

As always in those days the show went out live and it seemed to go without a hitch, which was practically a miracle considering the amount of performers, costumes and scenery involved. A short while afterwards I heard through Arthur Jeffries, who had watched the production with Oliver Messel that he had been delighted with the choice of actor to play his young self. Perhaps he was just relieved that I didn't portray him as a limp wristed queen.

By the time Denis returned my little fling with Bud was flung. It was fun while it lasted but it was just mutual lust and it had run its course. We would still see each other occasionally but by then we had become, as Bud would say, "A cuppla good ol' buddies."

The holiday in Maadi had been a total disaster and Denis returned earlier than originally planned. The warm, dry air of Egypt must have been kinder to his lungs than the cold damp mists of England but Helen, whose hospitality had been so generous in London, the moment they got to Maadi started treating him like a poor relation. Those were his words and he was probably exaggerating slightly: he had always been the perfect host and now the shoe was on the other foot he expected the same amount of courtesy and consideration he would have shown his guests – and Helen had not come up to scratch. Perhaps having paid his fare there and given him a roof over his head she felt she had done enough charitable work.

They had only made two excursions into Cairo and on both occasions it was because she had business to see to there. He had not contacted any of his old acquaintances, Helen had made no offer for him to invite them to the house, so if he wished to see them he would have to, at least, be able to offer them entertainment in Cairo, and what little money he had he was saving for the emergency he could see looming on the horizon.

The one person at Maadi he felt at ease with was Josephine's old nanny, who had been kept on as a retainer. She cosseted him when he was feeling poorly with comforting English nursery food.

Rich people who are generous with their money are not always generous for generous reasons. Some are generous for selfish reasons and so it was with Helen, Denis decided. She had bought herself a court jester and having paid good money for him no longer felt obliged to consider his personal feelings or wants. The person he felt most angry with was himself for allowing her to put him in this humiliating position. As you are probably aware by now he was not the most humble receiver of charity; he was a proud man and sometimes could be a little difficult – sometimes extremely difficult – on occasion, downright impossible! This was partly due to his ill health but it was also a trait he shared with Irene, and I have a pretty good idea from whom they inherited it.

As I have stated before he could be the most wonderful company imaginable and his many friends absolutely adored him. His enemies though remained enemies. I don't know why and I never asked but there was no love lost between him and Hugh Beaumont. Binkie, as he was called in the profession, was the head of H.M. Tennent Ltd, and at that time the most powerful man in the British theatre. Having crossed him an actor might as well stand centre stage at Drury Lane and cut his throat. Noel Coward was another with whom Denis had at some time crossed swords, or perhaps pens, and in public they never acknowledged one another's presence.

As Denis' resentment grew, a frost developed between him and Helen that got colder and heavier by the day; before it could develop into a full blown iceberg he took a taxi into Cairo and booked himself an early return flight to London; and sadly the book I hoped he was going to start writing in Maadi, 'A Thousand And One Parties' was abandoned forever.

We no longer dined at the Ritz but we still saw quite a lot of Josephine. She would come to tea at Alexandra Court and Marie would tell the Tarot cards for her. Again, one of her predictions came true: she told Josephine she would get her secret heart's desire, which I guessed was to be a happily married English suburban housewife. The man she married was not English born but he held an English passport, which she thought would do; and his name wasn't Smith or Brown or anything like that, but why wish for the stars when you own the moon? He was a one-eyed, impoverished young Polish painter she had met at the art school. The black eye-patch he wore gave him a look of mystery that was quite attractive. I thought to begin with that he might be after her fortune, but as time went by I could see he was genuinely fond of her, and when I last saw them in the mid 1960s, at their studio off the Kings Road, Chelsea, they still appeared to be very happily married.

Tommy, at whose flat in Berkley Square I had once danced the fox-trot with 10 Williams, had turned his back on the life of a bachelor gay and married an extremely rich widow with whom he now lived in Gloucestershire in a beautiful Queen Anne house with topiary garden and ha-ha. And it was there that Denis was often asked for weekends. Tommy and, especially, his wife enjoyed his witty, erudite conversation and couldn't get enough of it.

I was never invited. I think Tommy would have felt uncomfortable having the two of us there together, and it might have been too strong a reminder to his wife of his own former bachelor existence. It didn't worry me not being asked (though I would have liked to have seen the house), I was not enamoured with either of them and as their interest in the theatre was minimal, I would have been sorely stumped for conversation.

Denis and I didn't live in each other's pockets; he had friends of his generation, I had friends of mine and we often saw them separately. After eight years together we felt perfectly secure in our relationship. We couldn't imagine life without the other. All the same, on the rare occasions that I did dally in a stranger's bed I did not rush home to confess. A wiser man than me once said: 'What the eye doesn't see the heart doesn't grieve.' And I am sure that ours was not un-similar to a great many long-lasting, happy relationships.

The film producer, George Minter, with whom Denis had worked the previous year, had a couple of scripts in his drawer that he felt needed polishing and he asked Denis to do it. George had heard through their mutual friend, Maude Spector, that he had been ill and could possibly do with some money. This he felt was a genuine way he might help. It was in no way a hand out – he would expect Denis to deliver the goods, and he had never been known to be lavish with his cheque book.

Denis found it absolutely impossible to work in the flat. Marie tried her best to cooperate, but she couldn't go for very long without making her presence felt: a deep heavy sigh, the rattling of teacups, the slam of a door. But worst of all were the long silences: "What on earth," Denis would sit there wondering, "is she up to now?"

So when Tommy's wife insisted that he come to Gloucestershire and do his work in their library, where there would be no disturbances whatsoever, he gratefully accepted. This, of course, left me alone with the monster mother from outer space; but as it was a lovely hot summer that year; the Serpentine just a ten minute walk from the flat; and Irene only one street away; I was hardly ever there except to wash, change my clothes and sleep.

On Whit Monday bank holiday my dear friend, Hanns Ebensten, invited me to lunch. He would not divulge their names but he assured me that with two of the guests I was in for a pleasant surprise. I couldn't possibly imagine who they might be.

On my last army leave in Cape Town John Cranko had told me about his childhood friend, Hanns, who was then in the army and stationed in Pretoria. He thought we might get on well and suggested we met. We did, instantly hit it off and became good friends. Like Konni Hirsch, Hanns and his mother had escaped from Germany in the mid 30s, emigrated to South Africa and settled in Johannesburg where he and John met and, both being artistic children, formed a close friendship. They designed and made their own puppet theatre where they gave performances for family and friends of the sophisticated plays and ballets they wrote: hugely influenced by the Russian Ballet and German Expressionism.

Hanns grew up to be a talented painter and writer. After a year or so in London he abandoned painting to concentrate on his writing. He would have several books published, although after writing the first two there would be a hiatus of many years.

When his first book was finished I introduced him to our old friend, Graham Eyres Monsell, who had just started up in the publishing business. He liked the quirkiness of the book and agreed to publish it. It was a History of the Art of Tattooing with many colourful illustrations by Hanns, plus photographs of an intriguing and, in some cases, lurid nature. Today practically everyone one sees has a tattoo of some sort, but in the 1950's it was still considered a subversive form of body adornment and mainly adopted by sailors, prostitutes and the lower stratus of society. The book was very informative and also gave an inside glimpse of Hanns's own fascination with the underworld and sadomasochism. Jean Genet, seeing a copy of it on a Paris bookstall, I am sure would have knicked it.

His next book was a novel set in 1950s London that Graham liked and and agreed to publish. It was actually printed and the copies were waiting to be distributed when he was suddenly forced to withdraw and destroy them all. Someone who had got hold of an advance copy recognised in two of the characters a far from coincidental resemblance to a well known South African actress and her husband, both close friends of his, who were being portrayed in a most unflattering light. He showed them the book and they threatened to sue the publisher if all copies were not instantly destroyed. Graham lost a great deal of money over that, and he severed all connections with Hanns.

Dejected by this humiliating setback, Hanns decided to give up writing altogether, and joined Swan Hellenic, an elite travel firm in Mayfair that took small groups on exclusive tours of Greece, Turkey, Jordan and Egypt, accompanied always by a famous archeologist or classical historian. Hanns travelled as the tour manager, and with his immense charm, wit and intelligence became very popular with the regular clients. He could have remained there forever and would probably have been promoted quite soon, but when he felt he knew all he needed to about the business he gave in his notice and shortly afterwards emigrated to America.

With headquarters in Greenwich Village (and later Key West when he moved to Florida) he started his own unique, probably the first ever, travel agency catering exclusively for gay men seeking adventure. It was an instant success. With his vivid imagination and slightly weird inclinations he was able to offer his clients an exciting choice of original male bonding experiences: canoeing down the rapids of Colorado, as in the film, 'Deliverance'; sailing up the Nile on a primitive Arab felucca (and all the discomfort and hardship that entails); camping in the Andes. For the less intrepid adventurer there were his tours of the gay night life capitals of Europe.

Business flourished and today,'Hanns Ebensten Travel Ltd' is still going strong, although he sold out some years ago to return to his writing. He had several more books published, largely based on his own travels to exotic places and heavily imbued with homoerotic overtones.

When we first arrived in London in 1946, John Cranko, Hanns and I saw a lot of each other. We would spend evenings doing the pubs of Chelsea, Soho or Limehouse and it was always great fun. We once spent a week in Paris together and each had an amorous adventure. Mine was an Egyptian called Aziz Izzet who was studying to be a concert pianist; Hanns went for something a little rougher; and John's I don't think I saw. Near the end of the week when we had seriously run out of money and were sitting in the hotel counting our francs and wondering how we were going to manage, a telegram arrived for me. It was from Denis and simply read: 'Look in inside pocket of spongebag.' I did and discovered a French franc note with several noughts on it: the equivalent of about twenty pounds – a lot of money then. Our worries were over and that night the bars of the Rive Gauche were delighted to see us back.

Sadly, when big fame came John's way with his successful ballets and a wonderfully surrealist revue called, 'Cranks', he dropped us. I felt hurt for I thought we were real friends, but mostly I was sad for Hanns who had been his closest companion since childhood.

Hanns lived in Soho. He had a top floor flat on the corner of Old Compton St. and Dean St. There was an Italian café on the ground floor and a couple of ladies of the night on the floors between. It was an enchanting flat. One could stand at the window for hours watching the exciting and occasionally violent nightlife in the street below. Almost diagonally across was the York Minster, better known as the French Pub. The landlord was French and during the war it was a popular meeting place for the Free French in London. Its walls were plastered with signed photographs of famous Frenchmen who had been there: artists, actors, sportsmen, there was even a signed wartime photograph of General de Gaul. In the late 40s and into the 50s it became the haunt of Soho Bohemia: Dylan Thomas drank there, so did Francis Bacon, Lucien Freud, Quentin Crisp, Nina Hamnet, John Minton, George Melly, Daniel Farson, the Vogue photographer, John Deacon, whom I knew slightly, and many more famous and infamous Soho characters. On warm evenings they would spill out onto the pavement with their drinks, and sometimes even I could be spied there sipping Pernod and puffing a Gauloise.

On the Whit Monday Hanns invited me to lunch I was indeed in for a couple of pleasant surprises. The first was Frank Rogaly who I had not seen since I left Pretoria. He now worked for African Consolidated Theatres in Johannesburg as production manager, not that they produced much live theatre. Apart from the annual pantomime, which he directed himself, and the odd foreign tour, ACT were almost entirely concerned with the exhibiting of motion pictures. He said he was in London on the lookout for new shows and talent – I don't know how truthful that was.

Frank hadn't changed at all, he was still his funny, outrageous self and it was lovely seeing him again. I was sad that Denis couldn't meet him but he was going to be in Gloucestershire for some time.

My second big surprise was Freida Locke in whose bed I had frolicked for a few nights in 1945. We were delighted and rather amused to see one another again. She had left South Africa and was now living in Portugal. Her present visit to London – we didn't know it then – was to see a specialist. Freida had cancer and a couple of years later would be dead.

There were two others at lunch, Victor Glasstone and a young friend of his from Cape Town who had only shortly arrived in the country. I shall call him, H. He had just turned twenty-three, and was of slim, lithe build with fine chiselled features. I thought he was terribly attractive and during lunch, try as I might, I could not prevent my eyes from stealing glances at him. To begin with I thought he and Victor were an item but conversation soon revealed that was not the case.

Frank was in great form that afternoon and we all laughed a lot. About four o'clock, when no one was showing any sign of wanting to leave, Hanns offered us tea, but he had nothing to go with it. I had noticed on my way there that a patisserie in Old Compton St. was open so I offered to go and get us some cakes. To my surprise the young South African volunteered to accompany me. By the time we returned with our purchase his telephone number was in my pocket, and the very next morning I rang him up.

We arranged to meet that afternoon. He had a room on the north side of the park by Lancaster Gate, I lived on the south side in Queens Gate, so we agreed to meet in the middle and go rowing on the Serpentine.

It was a beautiful afternoon and the setting could not have been more idyllic. We took turns to row and each time it was his turn I noticed the way the muscles moved beneath his shirt. I longed to lean across and touch them. As the afternoon wore on I grew more and more consumed with desire. I had not had this sort of feeling for a long time and it was most disturbing. I dreaded the thought that when the boat ride was over he might say he had to go. It was early evening when we left the boathouse and started walking aimlessly through the park, neither of us talking. Then suddenly he said, "Would you like to come back to my room?" A feeling of relief and joy swept through me as I hoarsely mumbled, "Yes".

In no time at all we were naked and feverishly exploring each other's eager bodies. I was in ecstasy! (the Chambers Dictionary describes ecstasy as a state of rapture, temporary mental alienation, diminished consciousness, exalted feeling, excessive joy, and that was precisely how I felt).

A couple of hours later, lying quietly side by side, we began to talk and he told me something of himself. In Cape Town he had worked as a sub-editor and feature writer for the magazine section of the Cape Argus. He was probably the youngest sub-editor they had ever had, having started writing book reviews for the newspaper while still at boarding school. He had come to London with excellent references to get a journalistic job but was unable to work here because of the Fleet Street journalist union's rule that one had to be over twenty-four. He was offered work in York or Cardiff but wished to stay in London, so was surviving by doing temporary secretarial work. What his plans for the future were he didn't get round to say, for suddenly we began to feel gnawing pangs that we recognised as hunger, and I suggested we went out soon and found something to eat. He had a better idea and produced from a small food cupboard an apple, banana, carrot, stick of celery, some dates, raisins, nuts and a bottle of milk (I was to discover he was a bit of a health freak), and there, sitting cross legged on the bed, we had a delicious naked picnic. After a pause of about half an hour or so in respect for the digestive system, the love making recommenced.

It was quite late when he walked with me across to my side of the park. Not wanting to part just yet I crossed back with him to his side of the park. He then crossed back with me halfway, and there in the middle where we had met that afternoon we finally said goodnight. "Parting is such sweet sorrow," I murmured as I turned to go. It was so Verona 1590s.

My feelings for H were far stronger than I wanted them to be. After all, nothing could come of it. My life was with Denis, and for H I imagined it was just a bit of summer holiday fun. We never once expressed our inner feelings. There was no point, it was just a transitory thing; one day he would go, and when he went it would all be over. But until he went I needed to be with him every moment I possibly could. I thought I had grown out of that sort of thing but it was Sea Point and Lionel all over again. So day after day we lay sunning ourselves beside the Serpentine, our bodies only a few tantalising inches apart, till it was time to go to his room and make love again. And so passed that glorious happy-sad, guilt-ridden, lovesick summer of 1952.

On the 16th of July the Royal Academy of Dancing was to hold a summer fete in a beautiful old garden in Holland Park, and Katusha was asked to provide a short divertissement using some of the ballet students. The performing space was a raised grassy bank surrounded on three sides by shrubbery and flowers, and to go with this Arcadian setting she devised a Dance Champetre with music by Couperin and costumes after the paintings of Fragonard; and it would include a spoken poem (one of her favourites), Waller's. 'Go lovely rose...' Katusha asked me if I would recite the poem and then join in with the girls for a final bit of dancing and the tableau, and naturally I said yes. It meant I would have less time to spend with H, which was a wrench, but work had to come first. I have never turned down a job for the sake of pleasure, however attractive the prospect, which I think may allow me to call myself 'a real pro'.

The fete was a great success. The weather was perfect and it was a record turn out. The ballet world was very much in evidence, and in the crowd I recognised Nanette de Valoise, Margot Fonteyn and Frederic Ashton.

We performed our piece quite early in the afternoon and it was very well received. An hour or so later, when some of the original crowd had dispersed and others were arriving, we were asked to repeat our performance; then near the end of the day with still new arrivals we were persuaded to do it yet again – it was what I imagine doing non-stop variety at the Windmill must have been like.

Denis came to see it. So did H. Separately. They had met a couple of times and

Denis thought him charming and well mannered. One day I invited him to tea at the flat and Marie, of course, told his cards. I wonder what dark secrets the Tarot revealed to her. I don't know if Denis suspected anything, I think he might have, he was very sensitive to atmosphere, but he said nothing. He probably thought it was a mild flirtation and not worth mentioning. He can't have known, and I doubt if H even did, the strength of my infatuation.

That summer Denis and I had spent quite a lot of time apart. If the sun shone and I wasn't working I made straight for the Serpentine. It wasn't just to be with H, I would have done so anyway, so there was nothing suspicious about it. Used to the hot African sun I needed to soak in every little watery English sunbeam that was going; and Denis seemed to understand this. Even if he had been in perfect health he would never have come to the Serpentine. Apart from the age thing – it was mainly a showcase for the young, beautiful and tanned – he would have loathed the discomfort of lying on the hard rush matting by the water's edge where my friends and I gathered, and he would never have put a toe in that grey, murky looking water where we so merrily swam every day, but he knew how much I enjoyed it and was happy for me to do so.

For the summer regulars it was a sort of social club. I recognised most of the people there and knew quite a few of them. Many were in show business and there was plenty of shop-talk. One even sometimes heard about jobs that were going. I actually found myself a literary agent through an introduction from a writer at the Serpentine. The agent had only just started up in business and, as yet, did not have a great many clients, but the time would come when she would be the most important play agent in London. Her name was Margaret Ramsay. Peggy, as she was called, liked my writing and would manage to get some of it placed in West End shows.

In the warm weather Denis's breathing much improved and, with care, he was able to resume quite a social life. He and Maude Spector had become close friends. She had been the casting director on, 'Trottie True', and was now the doyen of her profession. Most of the big Hollywood companies used her to cast the films they made in Europe. She greatly enjoyed Denis' company and often asked him to escort her to theatre first nights and film premieres, and in that way he met and dined with some of the big men of Hollywood: Walt Disney, Sam Spiegel, Mike Todd, King Vidor, Joseph Mankiewicz... Maude also managed to get him little rewrite jobs on some of the pictures and, being Hollywood productions, they were extremely well paid. I always had the feeling that Maude was a little in love with Denis, also that she was slightly jealous of me – though she did often get me a day or two on a picture.

One night H and I went to have a late drink at the Players Theatre where the bar stayed open until midnight. All public bars in London then closed at eleven o'clock, so after their work at other theatres actors would come along for the final hour. As alcohol was not supposed to be served without food at that hour there were always a lot of tired looking sandwiches lying around on the tables. In the bar that night, Johnny Heawood, one of the regular performers at the Players (he was also a regular at the Serpentine), introduced us to a couple of American visitors: the poet and film maker, James Broughton, and his leading man and lover, Kermit Sheets. The films they made were poetic, slightly surreal fantasies; never seen on large commercial screens but often shown at film festivals and art houses. Their next picture was to be made in London and they were in the process of casting it. James asked us if we would like to be in it and we said we certainly would.

Featured in the picture were Hattie Jacques, John Le Mesurer, Jill Bennett, Lindsay Anderson (in a rare acting appearance. He was also production manager on the film), Maxine Audley, Derek Hart, Jean Anderson, Diana Maddox, John Heawood and several others. The setting James chose to film it in (to my knowledge never used before or since in a film) was the ruins of the ornamental garden of the Crystal Palace, which was destroyed by fire in 1936. Abandoned and left to the wild caprice of nature the garden had become a most romantic and eerie sight: flights of stone steps now had trees growing out of them; wild flowers and grass had sprung up between the paving stones; balustrades with large Grecian urns on them were being possessed by creepers, as were stone sphinxes and arched colonnades; of the many statues in the garden some had fallen from their high plinths and lay like nude sunbathers in the long grass; and down by a pond lurked large stone dinosaurs. The whole place had a strange other world feel about it, which was exactly what James wanted for his film, where, as he described it, 'curious strangers meet in an afternoon's daydream'.

Two of those curious strangers, who have already met that afternoon, are H and me. We are discovered in the garden in brief bathing costumes, oblivious of all that is going on around us as we manfully arm wrestle and give to that combatant sport a slight hint of homoeroticism.

The message or plot or whatever you want to call it was, I suppose, the struggle of the free spirit against authority and repression.

Hattie, eccentrically dressed with coiled plats over her ears, a ribbon tied around her forehead and wearing long strings of beads (a dead ringer for Madame Arcati), dances gaily through the garden dispensing mirth and joy, and with the aid of a magic stole brings shy couples together.

John Le Mesurer, looking like an undertaker in black frock coat and top hat, is the man from the Ministry of Dignity or Death. He can't abide seeing anyone enjoying themselves and spends his time separating couples, nailing fig leaves on the male statues and putting up posters prohibiting any form of pleasure. Hattie follows close behind removing them all. The Ministry has decided to turn the garden into a cemetery and soon men in black suits arrive in a large black hearse, carrying picks and shovels to dig graves. Then all the couples in the garden are rounded up and brought before John who, having stamped their hands with a rubber stamp, sends the females up a flight of steps to the left and males up a flight of steps to the right. All is going like clockwork until the couple he finds standing before him are H and me. Lost as what to do he has to consult a large book of rules that is brought to him. Around this point, without going into too much detail, Hattie, who we have recently witnessed executing a delightful little ballet solo on an dilapidated bandstand, comes to the rescue, and with her magic stole (which she has only just repossessed – John having stolen it) turns all the men from the Ministry into statues: minus their black suits they grace stone niches artistically posed in their underpants. The lovers are all reunited and return to the garden to pursue their pleasures as Hattie sings her jolly little anthem:

'Tis a pleasure
To come together
One by one...
And two by two...'

Making the film was great fun and it was wonderful spending those hot summer days in what, for me, really was the Pleasure Garden.

In October the film was given a screening at the Academy Cinema in Oxford Street, supporting a foreign feature film, and Denis and I went to see it. I thought it had great charm and it brought back fond memories of the summer. Denis found it nauseatingly whimsical. I suppose we were both a little biased – for our own personal reasons.

Hermione Gingold, who had gone to live in New York a few years before and become famous there as the queen of camp, came over to London for a few weeks to appear in cabaret at the Café de Paris where she sang four of Robb's and my songs, and quite superbly. That most acerbic of critics, Milton Shulman wrote in the Evening Standard: "When it comes to mixing a cocktail of vinegar, acid and wit there is no bartender with the skill of Miss Hermione Gingold. At the Café de Paris she makes every drop sizzle and count. Gingold's world is the one where the normal, the irreverent and the ludicrous tread hard on each other's heels and poke each other in the ribs for good measure. A song begins romantically enough about Venice. "Come share my gondola with me," she trills. But soon we find ourselves travelling along the dirtiest canal in Venice taking an inventory of such delectable floating objects as "a scantie that says 'much love to Beatrice' from Dante". And I liked her idea of "The Vortex" done as a musical, with the theme song "Cocaine" " (both these numbers were by us). While in London she did some radio broadcasts for the BBC and used some of our stuff in those. That year we also had material performed in repertory theatres outside London: Bromley, Leatherhead and Hayes; and in London in two revues at the New Lindsay. The first was 'Ring In The New' in which our old chum, Gail Kendall sang a song of ours called, 'Please, Mr. Degas'. The second was 'In The Lap Of The Gods', which I thought was a brilliant little show and should have made it to the West End. It had some excellent talent in it. There were two dancers in the show, Malcolm Goddard who would become a choreographer and work a lot in television, and Gillian Lynn who, after choreographing several musicals, would do Andrew Lloyd Webber's 'Cats', which, having triumphed all over the world, would make her rich enough never to need to work again. Also in the revue was a dark haired, very funny little girl who sang one of our songs and appeared in a sketch of mine. I thought she had something very special and I made a note of her name: it was Fenella Fielding.

Later in the year I made a return visit to Great Yarmouth to do six plays. On one of the Saturdays (we were doing Somerset Maugham's 'Rain'). H travelled up, saw the show and spent the night with me. Seeing him off on the 6pm train on the Sunday I felt utterly miserable. My infatuation for him had not abated.

He then went off to live in Cornwall for six months, working as a labourer on a farm near Truro for a rich South African man he had met through Hanns. During the week he milked cows and cleaned pigsties, but in the evening, having the foreman's unused drawing room to himself, he played Lizst on an old upright piano and read books by Jung drawn from the St Austell library. The weekends, however, were spent in great luxury at the owner's home in Mevagissy; he also accompanied him as his secretary on one of his business trips down Africa.

When the demands on his services became too excessive he gave up farming and went to sea as a ship's writer (pursers clerk) on one of the P&O liners that sailed to and from Australia. He was down to his last pound in the bank when the job was suggested to him by one of our Serpentine companions, James Clark, an ex actor who was working as a laundry steward on one of the liners.

Each time his ship docked in Tilbury, H would come up to London and we often met. It was always a joy to see him, but to my great relief that hungry need I had felt for so long had faded away. I was in control of my feelings once more. My life was back to normal – if that's the right word – and Denis and I had become closer again. The feeling of relief was immense.

In 1954 H returned to South Africa and resumed his journalistic career. I still see him whenever I visit Cape Town; he has a partner, so do I, and we are now two dear old friends who once, over half a century ago, spent a blissful summer together by the Serpentine.

—*∿*—

1953 saw the crowning of Queen Elizabeth the Second in Westminster Abbey; Denis directed a new German play called 'Trapeze In The Vatican' at the Arts Theatre; and I spent the entire summer at the Spa Theatre in Whitby, a holiday resort and fishing port on the north Yorkshire coast; and to this day, apart from London, it's the place in England about which I feel most nostalgic.

It is a picturesque little town built on the sides of two hills, its old red brick buildings sloping down to a small port at the mouth of the River Esk. A bridge crosses the river, joining the two sides of the town together. On the south hill a long flight of steps climbs up the steep face of a cliff to the ruins of an old abbey. It was here that in 657AD St. Hilda built a large monastery that has long since disappeared. On the north hill, high up and facing the sea, stands an elegant terrace of Georgian houses; below it is a beautiful sandy beach, and in between, near the top, the Spa Theatre and Floral Pavilion Ballroom where after our performance on Saturday nights we often waltzed to 'Goodnight Sweetheart'.

Whitby is steeped in history. Captain Cook lived here, and it was from this little port that he set sail on some of his great voyages of discovery. Another famous name linked to the town is Count Dracula, for it is in Whitby that a great deal of Bram Stoker's novel took place. It was on the steps leading up to the abbey where in the early light of morning sailors' and fishermen's bodies were discovered drained of their blood. And it was in one of the terraced houses on the north hill where Miss Mina was staying when a bat flew in through the window and bit her lovely neck. All the owners of the terraced houses (now hotels) emphatically claim that theirs is the one where the incident was supposed to take place, and say they can produce written evidence to prove it.

It was the Dracula connection that first appealed to me about Whitby. As a small child it was one of my favourite films and I saw it many times. I was sexually advanced for my age and I wonder if subconsciously it was the sexual symbolism of it that so attracted me. Playing at vampires was very much one of my childhood pastimes and my poor cousin Dennis got several nasty bites on his neck. That was one of the reasons Auntie V. didn't like us playing together; another was the time she caught him with a little girl called Bobbie and me under the bed with our knickers off. He wasn't allowed to visit our house for a long time after that.

Forgive me if I delay the narrative still further but having just mentioned Bobbie, my very best friend and close Sea Point neighbour; it has suddenly reminded me of another incident that took place around that time that involved Bobbie, me and Dracula again. In the early 1930s, when we were both about eight or nine, there were, at the bottom of Adderley Street, a couple of scruffy old flea pits called, Tearoom Bioscopes. Their programmes started at midday and continued without a break until the final evening showing. People came and went as they pleased. In front of each seat was a small shelf with space for a cup or glass and refreshments could be ordered and consumed while watching the film. Tea, coffee or a cool drink was included in the price of admission. Anything else, a knickerbocker glory or banana split, say, was paid for separately, and what with having to call a waitress, place your order, be served, pay for it and receive your change (no tip necessary) everyone's attention was constantly being distracted from the film. The cheaper and scruffier of the two still screened silent movies; the other, scratched and cut about prints of talking pictures that had seen better days in better cinemas; and it was here that I saw Dracula was being shown again, so one afternoon I persuaded Bobbie to come into town with me and see one of my favourite films. Beside the box office was the familiar sign saying persons between the ages of 6 and 16 would not be admitted and I was getting ready to do my 'under six' act, but the dozy old doe selling the tickets either didn't know the sign was there or had forgotten about it and let us in. We sat through the film once, then twice, and were nearing the end of the third time when a slide appeared on the screen that read: 'If Bobbie Kelly and Navel Philips are in the audience will they please come to the foyer now' (or something to that effect). This we did and were amazed to find it was dark outside and well past 8 o'clock. Our mothers were on the telephone and quite distraught. They insisted we came home immediately. The manager, after telling us we were far too young to have seen such a film and reprimanding the dozy old doe for letting us in, ordered a waitress to remove her lace cap, put on a coat and take us to the nearest bus stop, where she was to make sure we got on the Sea Point bus. I think he was worried about the possible repercussions of us being allowed to witness an X-rated film. Our mothers were waiting for us at the other end and were extremely cross. But it really wasn't our fault. If anyone was to blame it was that dozy old doe for letting us in, and Bella Lugossi for keeping us so enthralled.

Today it is quite amazing to think how freely young children were allowed to roam about then. Oh, how the world has changed! I don't know whatever became of Bobbie. I only hope that being subjected to Dracula at that tender age did not have any long lasting ill effect on her psyche, as I fear it may have done on mine.

Now back to the plot. Whitby was a quiet resort. It mainly attracted middle class, middle aged to elderly visitors wanting a relaxed holiday by the sea. There was a small fun fair down by the harbour where the young and raffish gathered but otherwise it was a very sedate town, and luckily for us the locals as well as the visitors enjoyed going to the theatre. Throughout the season we played to excellent and very receptive audiences; and the programme was changed on a Thursday so that visitors who were only there for a week could see two plays, and many of them did.

Clare Foden who ran the theatre had excellent taste and chose the plays very carefully. We performed none of the cheap farces being done down the coast at Bridlington. We performed no farces at all, and the comedies we did were by Shaw, Priestley, Rattigan and Thurber.

The company on the whole were charming and talented: James Roose Evans, a fine actor, would also become a distinguished writer and director and found the Hampstead Theatre Club that still flourishes today; Ronald Frazer, an Australian, on returning to Sydney would make a name for himself in revue and become a household name on television; Lynn Reid Banks, who we all thought rather prim and prissy then, would one day write a very adult novel, 'The L Shaped Room'; Ann Way, as sweet as she was clever, would soon be in films playing a dreadful St. Trinnian's school girl; and our ASM, a very tall, lanky lad with acne who brought us cups of tea and biscuits and was very quiet and shy, and who I never really got to know till later, would become the famous television director, John Davies, responsible for such magnificent BBC costume dramas as, 'War And Peace' starring Anthony Hopkins.

The Spa Theatre had a small group of local fans that loyally came to every production, and in the theatre bar afterwards would give us their blunt Yorkshire no nonsense opinion of the play. One such was a middle-aged woman called Dorothy who owned the fish and chip shop down by the harbour. She had a hopeless crush on Ronald Frazer and when the theatre bar closed on Thursday nights we would all be invited down to the shop for free fish and chips. Ron was once asked to her flat and given a Dover sole. We begged him not to do anything foolish that might jeopardize our free meal on a Thursday.

Two other stalwarts were Fred and Eric. Fred was the engine driver of the little train that shuttled between York and Whitby every day. Eric was his partner who worked from home making fairly lurid lampshades. They lived right beside the railway line and each time the train got near to their house Fred would blow the engine whistle, Eric would run to the window and they would wave. Knowing this, whenever we heard a train whistle blowing in the distance we would think of Fred and Eric waving to each other, which conjured up a touching picture.

One morning while we were rehearsing on the stage, John, the ASM, came to me

THE STAGE STRUCK ME

in the wings and said there was someone asking for me at the stage door. I knew I still had several minutes before my next entrance so I went to see who it was. To my great delight it was Mathew Dixon, the British army major that I had met in the bar opposite Springbok House in Cairo, who introduced me to Denis. He was in Whitby with his aged parents, had seen my name on a playbill in the town and wondered if it could possibly be me (actually, there are not a lot of Neville Phillipses about). We met for tea and he came to see one of the plays. I felt a great affection for Mathew, after all, if it hadn't been for him I would never have met Denis, and how very different my whole life would have been. It's really too scary to think about.

The season at Whitby lasted until the end of September and during that time I made some good friends. I also slipped into an easy-going sexual relationship with two of the company: one male, one female. The male I shared digs with over a pub in the town; the female was a young girl who couldn't act for toffee but was extremely beautiful; she was also a bit of a nympho and had been through most of the available talent (there was not a lot), and now it was my turn. Having two admirers sometimes called for a little juggling, but neither of them made any really serious demands on me, and the season sailed along quite smoothly.

At the last performance of the last play one felt both relief and sadness. It had been exhausting learning all those lines every week (and with Shaw there were quite a few to learn), but it was gratifying doing such interesting plays, and I had fallen in love with Whitby. I have often thought I would like to go back there sometime, just wander around and recapture those happy days. I don't suppose I shall.

―❧―

Returning to London, I was shocked to see how gaunt Denis was looking. When I asked him how he was he became evasive and quickly changed the subject. That night we went out for a meal in a quiet little restaurant in the Brompton Road that we both liked. To start with he was very subdued and I did most of the talking, telling him about Whitby. Then having had a couple of glasses of wine he suddenly came out with it: Patrick had sent him to St. George's Hospital to have his chest x-rayed and it had been discovered that he had Tuberculosis in both lungs and would need to be hospitalised for some time. I was stunned. "Oh, God!" was all I was able to say. I could now see in his eyes how utterly miserable he was and I found it hard not to cry. Marie had not yet been informed in case she had started playing the tragedy queen and blurted it out the moment I came in the door. He then told me Patrick was arranging for me to go to St. George's for an x-ray to make sure I hadn't contracted the disease. This in due course I did and to my great relief was given the all clear. But for Denis I felt terribly concerned. He was such a proud and very private person and the prospect of spending months in a public ward of a NHS hospital surrounded by the sick and dying I knew he was dreading. I could see him thinking it was the equivalent of going to the poor house in a Dickens novel.

The day of his admission to hospital I accompanied him in a hired chauffeur driven car. The Chest Unit of St. George's was not, as one had expected, in its Hyde Park Corner building but in an obscure part of Tooting in South London. To get there by public transport meant two busses and a walk down an ill lit road, and as the visiting time coincided with the evening rush hour the journey could take anything from one to two hours. The Tooting hospital was an ugly red brick post war utility building, and the ward he was in was long and narrow and full of beds occupied by men in various stages of the illness, from recovering to dying. They were predominantly working-class and there was a small, rough element that found amusement in Denis' monocle and posh voice. Normally he would have won them over in a trice but the way he was feeling he was in no mood to lay on the famous charm. The window opposite his bed looked out on a hideous modern cemetery, all gleaming white tombstones and vividly coloured plastic flowers; some of the graves looked quite new which he did not take to be a good omen; it certainly was not the ideal view upon which to gaze while trying to think positively about the future. The nurses were very able and polite but, run off their feet as they were, had no time to linger over pleasantries, not that he would have wanted them to at that stage.

To begin with I visited him almost every day; Irene, twice a week; Marie, Sunday afternoons that became alternate Sunday afternoons. Her legs were troubling her and she found the waiting about in the cold, changing busses and the long walk a great strain, and she would spend the entire visit telling him so. The medication he was being given was making him feel nauseous and distrait, and with the lowering effect it had on his already low spirits he felt in no way up to seeing the many friends who wanted to visit him. I think he also didn't want them to see him in such unfortunate circumstances. It was my job to keep them away until he was more able to cope. Some came anyway, unannounced, and as patients were only allowed two visitors at a time there were some awkward clashes that in his distrait and nervous condition he found distressing.

For the first week or two flowers and gifts flooded in and the nurses had their time cut out looking for extra vases and space in the fridge for the perishable luxury edibles. Maude sent a beautiful orchid plant (she knew how much he loved them) which had pride of place on his bedside table; Bumble, books she thought he would like; Graham, a warm winter dressing gown from Turnbull & Asser; Elizabeth Welch, Stephanotis toilet water from Floris; Tommy and his wife, caviar from Fortnum's, for which Denis had no appetite and gave to Irene and me to share.

After a while he suggested that I didn't come every day. He knew what a pain it was to get there, and as his news from one day to the next was practically non-existent and mine minimal there were long pauses in our conversations; we had no need for aimless chat. I then visited every second day, and when he was feeling a little better and I knew for certain that friends were coming I would keep away.

Hanns paid him a visit one evening and brought a bag of grapes. He put them on the bedside table and then proceeded to eat them all himself. This incident got funnier on reading an account of it in his novel (the one that had to be withdrawn). In it a character, poor and hungry, spends his last penny on a bunch of grapes to take to a friend in hospital. As the friend languidly toys with one or two, he, now wracked with hunger, stares at the grapes longing to be offered some, but never is. On reading this we had a really good laugh. I wonder if Hanns saw the funny side of it?

These weeks were the lowest period of my life so far, and without Irene's support I don't know what I would have done. She was as firm as a rock for me. Marie was away in her own little selfish psychic world where everyone but she was to blame for the rotten hand she had been dealt. I kept as clear of her as I possibly could. Being Denis' sister, Irene was able to deal with the official and medical business that had to be seen to. As I was neither kith nor kin they would not discuss any of it with me.

Nearing the end of November I received a phone call and it was the first good news I had had since arriving back in London. Before going to Whitby I had left some of my revue material at the New Watergate Theatre in Buckingham Street, where I heard they were going to do a revue. I heard nothing back from them, and I don't think the revue ever materialised; anyway, I went to Whitby and forgot all about it. While I was away the management of the theatre changed and Norman Marshall took over. I read in 'The Stage' that he was doing a Christmas revue to be written by Diana Morgan and Robert McDermot, two writers who had served him well in the past. Norman had directed several successful revues at the old Gate Theatre and in the West End; among the latter were 'Swinging The Gate' with Hermione Gingold and Michael Wilding, 'Better Late' with Beatrice Lillie and Walter Chrisham, and 'A La Carte' with Hermione Baddeley and Henry Kendal. The material Diana and Robert had so far produced for the new show was, Norman felt, not up to their usual high standard and there was not much of it, so he had begun to worry. Clearing out a cupboard in his office, that he had not had time to do since taking over, a large brown envelope fell out, he opened it and there was my material. He, of course, remembered me from 'Boys In

Brown', and out of curiosity started reading it, and liked what he read.

It was Norman on the telephone. He had decided to postpone Diana and Robert's show till a later date and, if I agreed, he wanted mine to be the Christmas show. I took him to hear Robb's music, which he liked enormously, and I asked Robb if it had all been written down and, lying to me, he said it had. I couldn't wait to tell Denis the good news and for the first time in all those horrible weeks I saw a look of pleasure in his eyes.

My idea, and it was a very original one for a revue at that time, was for the contents to be of an odd and macabre nature (the Charles Adams influence again) and to call the show, 'A Little Sinister', which was the title of the opening number.

Three witches dance around a cauldron and sing:

"A little sinister, a little quaint,
A little tough but not enough to make you faint.
A bit peculiar, we must confess,
And if it wasn't for the censor we'd undress"... etc

Suddenly from out of the cauldron rises a lovely Christmas tree fairy with a tinsel wand who assures us that while she's around everything's going to be "nice... nice... nice...", but unfortunately for us and her she is gagged, bound and thrown back into the cauldron. At this point a St. John's Ambulance nurse makes her way down from the back of the house and tells us she has sal volatile on hand should things get really disgusting. And so the show goes on. One of the songs, 'In The Red' is sung by a suburban bank clerk who turns into a vampire and leaves his customers severely overdrawn. As 'Good Time Ghoul' had only had a brief outing in The Boltons Revue I thought it should be included. There was also our song about the Ku Klux Klan ('Swing Song' had not yet been publicly performed), there was a sketch about funeral catering, and the 1st act finale explored life on the planet Mars. It was called, 'The Thing And I', and was a parody on 'The King And I', that had recently opened at Drury Lane.

Norman and I spent a few days sorting through the material and putting it into some kind of shape. Then he started to get cold feet. People were telling him that, 'A Little Sinister', was not a good title for a Christmas show, so I was asked to think of another and came up with, 'Oddly Enough', which was jollier but still had a certain quirkiness to it.

Then, having been attracted by it in the first place, he began to worry about the darkness of the humour, and in some cases the poor taste, which he thought might offend certain members of the audience. So, one by one, the suspect numbers were replaced by lighter, more cheerful ones. The opening chorus remained, so did, 'The Thing And I', but the show now became just another charming little conventional revue with a few quirky touches. 'Oddly Enough' was well received and enjoyed a successful Christmas run, but to my mind it was rather bland and lacked the strong impact that I thought 'A Little Sinister' would have had.

Norman had cast it very well: Noel Dyson was a very elegant and witty lady; Edwin Richfield, a good leading man; Beverley Wright and Allan Gabriel, fine singers; Roland Curram, a versatile young actor; Jane Downs had just won a gold medal at RADA and this was her first professional engagement; then there was a young actor whose strong physical magnetism put me in mind of the sensuous faun in, 'Apres-midi d'un Faune', and for that reason he will be known as, F. He was an outrageous flirt and when it was my turn he tried his faunish charms on me. I was amused to begin with, then slightly attracted, then rather intrigued, then totally hooked. I was eager to bed him and discovered that he was not adverse to the idea.

He shared a flat with a couple of friends just south of Sloane Square, and there in his bed that night all the pain, fear, anguish and misery that had been building up inside me for weeks was released in a frenzy of love making. I don't know what this says about me, probably something not very nice, but in all the darkest moments of my life I have sought escape through liquor and sex. The escape may have been brief but it always served its purpose and gave me a little respite. When I walk through a storm I do not hold my head up high. What's the point of getting your face wet? I keep my head held low and look for a warm little refuge where I can shelter until the worst of the storm has passed. Call that weak, but it has got me through some really bad times.

Of course, I was wracked with guilt. Seeing Denis lying there in that awful hospital and knowing I would soon be in someone else's bed made me feel quite dreadful, but there was nothing I could do about it, I needed F's body close to mine – I craved his warmth.

Irene rang to warn me that Denis had received a telegram from Marie to say I had not slept at the flat for over a week and she was worried about me. I hadn't slept at the flat but she had seen me there every morning when I came to wash and change my clothes. Visiting him that night he made no mention of the telegram and behaved as if everything was normal, although he did seem a little quieter than usual. How I longed to tell him he was the only really important thing in my life, that I would never leave him, and what I was going through at the moment was a mad aberration that had nothing to do with my feelings for him. But, of course, I couldn't say that.

Nightmare Abbey had nothing on Alexandra Court. Marie's loathing of me had finally surfaced and the sneering smile that greeted me on arrival was now accompanied by mumbled vituperation. I dreaded going to the flat, and when I told Irene what was going on she suggested I moved in with Harold and her for a while; Richard was working abroad so I could have his room. I grabbed at the offer like a thirsty man at a straw. Together we hatched a plot and on the following Sunday morning, while Marie was at the Brompton Oratory bending the ear of her Lord, Harold arrived with his car, bundled my belongings into it and off we fled to Kynance Place. And there I sat nervously waiting for the explosion to happen, and I didn't have to wait long. The phone rang, Irene answered it and it was her. Being psychic she had known the moment she entered the flat that the bird had flown; the empty shelves and cupboards might also have given her a slight clue. She asked Irene if she knew where I had gone, and was told, with barely concealed pleasure, that her dreadful behaviour had driven me away and I was now residing with Harold and her. Quicker than you would think it possible for someone with bad legs she was banging on the front door. Irene let her in, and straight away she started calling me all the names she could think of, and when stumped for one, 'fancy boy' became a popular reiteration. Having run out of steam and realizing there was nothing else she could do, except send more telegrams, she stormed out; and to celebrate my freedom we all had a large gin and tonic.

I continued to spend as many of my nights with F as I could. I don't know what Harold made of all my comings and goings, but Irene understood, she had been there once or twice herself, and she also knew I would never abandon Denis. Spending as much time as I was doing with F, in a flat he shared with two others was not an ideal arrangement, so we decided to look for a little den of iniquity that was all our own; and we found one in Harrington Road, close to South Kensington Station. I told Denis that for the time being I was sharing a flat with someone but as soon as he was well enough we would find somewhere for the two of us. He nodded and smiled, but for him that time still seemed very far away. F was never in doubt that Denis and I would one day be reunited, but for him also it seemed far away, he lived very much in the present and he probably expected to have several more lovers before then.

A few nice things came out of 'Oddly Enough'. A couple of television producers asked me to write material for them. For one of the programmes, which was all about shoes, I wrote a song for a woman who had two left feet. Noel Dyson performed it and I played a startled shoe salesman. I also worked on three films: 'A Yank In Ermine', a pathetic comedy starring Harold Lloyd Jnr. who had none of the talent or charisma of his famous father; and two films cast by Maude, Disney's 'The Sword And The Rose', and 'Svengali'. Robert Newton was playing Svengali, and superbly I thought, but he was an alcoholic and after being unable to work for several days was sacked. He was replaced by Sir Donald Wolfit who gave an excellent performance, but it was nowhere as fine as Newton's, which had a quality of danger about it that was quite frightening. All his scenes were then re-shot, and as I was in some of them my contract had to be renewed and I was paid my full fee again, which made it quite a lucrative job. The New Watergate Theatre would do several more revues and Robb and I had material in most of them. In, 'First Edition', Beryl Reid sang a song of ours, 'At The Wedding', with great success, and afterwards, as variety performers did in those days, she bought an option on it for a year and, I believe, performed it quite a lot.

On one of my visits to the hospital with Irene, a doctor said he would like to speak to her privately. He told her that Denis' consumption was being slowly but effectively eradicated, and if there was somewhere he could go where he would be carefully taken care of, and be sure his medication was regularly administered they might be able to release him. Knowing how much Denis hated being in that crowded ward, Irene, without a moment's hesitation, said she would look after him at Kynance Place. He could have her light, airy room at the front, and she would move into Richard's empty room. Harold already slept in one of his own. And that is what happened.

Harrington Road being only a few minutes away I was able to help Irene look after him and do some of the many chores she had taken on: shopping, preparing his meals, going to the library, etc; and later on when visitors started arriving, making tea and pouring drinks. Marie popped over whenever she felt like it and we treated each other with cool civility. She was playing her cards carefully in case we might wish to return to the flat some day. Denis by now had become the main focus of the house. Everything revolved around him, and the stronger he got the more demanding he became. I don't wish to be disparaging but there were times when he reminded me of the character, Sheridan Whiteside in the play, 'The Man Who Came To Dinner'. Some days he felt low and demanded to be left alone, others he was bright and cheerful and wanted company, and we had to somehow fit in with these difficult moods. Irene, of course, took the brunt of it, and sometimes being worn out by it all she would have a little too much gin and become maudlin, which made him cross, which made her cry, which made him even crosser. Harold would hide himself away with a book somewhere. It was a very difficult period for all of us. One day Denis said to me he would like to meet the young man I shared the flat with, and so F was invited to tea. I knew it was a bad idea but I couldn't think of any way to get out of it. F sat cross legged on a rug and laid on his faunish charm which, with Denis' loathing of whimsy, was the worst thing he could have done. Denis remained polite, if a little remote, throughout and after F had departed no comment was made on him whatsoever. They never met again.

Humphrey Bourne came from a wealthy family who owned half of the famous West End store, Bourne & Hollingsworth. He went to Cambridge and while there appeared in a 'Footlights Revue' that was directed by Denis. They became good friends and remained so. When I met him in 1946 he owned a beautiful house in Hill Street, Mayfair, where he gave lavish parties. To please his family he studied Law and several times failed the exams – his heart wasn't in it – and being rich enough not to need to work he didn't see why he should and embarked upon a life of hedonism and dissipation. Finding Atlee's austere, Socialist Britain (not to mention his family's disapproval) restricting he set off for the warm and freer south. He finally settled in Cyprus where he bought a house in Kyrenia and happily entertained anyone who happened to drop in on their way through the Mediterranean. One such guest was Joy Murchie, and on hearing how ill Denis had been he immediately invited him to come and recuperate in the warm Cyprus sunshine.

Denis was now back on his feet, though still rather weak. Feeling he had strained Irene's hospitality far enough and that it was now time to move on, he accepted Humphrey's kind invitation. Being away from the cold and damp was just what he needed, and he was looking forward to seeing his dear old friend again. It's awful to say this, but having seen him off at Heathrow we all sighed with relief, hoping that on his return, when the weather was warmer, he would be nearer his old self again.

The director I had worked with at Great Yarmouth now had a play out on tour that was being performed twice nightly (it was very short) and he asked me if I would take over one of the parts for the final three weeks of the tour. As the two last dates would be in London I agreed to do it for the paltry fee he offered. The venue for the last week was what really did the trick: it was Collins Music Hall on Islington Green, where all the greatest music hall artistes had performed in their day: Dan Leno, Marie Lloyd, George Robey, Vesta Tilley, Charlie Chaplin…etc…I would now be able to say that I too had played Collins Music Hall – in fact, I do, whenever the famous name crops up – and on occasion even when it doesn't.

The play was called, 'Vice In The Streets', and I was to play a vicious teddy boy (don't smirk). It was supposedly a serious exposé of prostitution and crime in London's Soho. The poster for it was in lurid colours with large Xs all over it and read: 'BANNED – the play London was not allowed to see!' As our last two dates were actually in London this didn't make a lot of sense – but then neither did anything in the play.

I joined the company on the train call at Paddington Station early on Sunday morning and rehearsed my scenes as we travelled across to South Wales. We changed at Cardiff and took a funny little train to Tonypandy, a small, forgotten mining town in the valleys that had a crumbling old theatre where the seats had been replaced by wooden benches. It was dark by the time we arrived and there was not a bar or café open anywhere. Those of us who had not already booked digs had to go from door to door up dark steep narrow streets asking if they had rooms to let. Eventually we were all accommodated but most of us went to bed hungry that night.

I already knew the play was rubbish, but it was only on Monday morning when I saw the set being put up that I fully realized the horrible tackiness of the production. The scene was supposed to be a Soho prostitute's bedroom but the flats were obviously from different sets and they had not gone to the bother of painting them the same colour; even when the door didn't stick the frame for it wobbled; and for the Soho street scenes, of which there were a few, a cut out lamp post was plonked centre stage in the middle of the bedroom. I thought I had reached the nadir of my acting career in Bridlington, but compared to this they were like H.M. Tennent Productions. It is the only time in my life when I have felt ashamed to be standing on a stage knowing that people have paid good money to see the insulting trash we were spewing at them. Strangely enough, during the week we were told by some of the locals how much they had enjoyed it, which made me wonder what sort of shows toured Tonypandy. Most of the cast agreed how dreadful it all was, but one bright young hopeful excitedly announced that some casting directors had promised to come and see the play the following week in Wimbledon. We cringed with embarrassment.

One night between shows I rang F and discovered that H was there with him. His ship was in Tilbury and he had come to Harrington Road in search of me. I found out later, as I suspected at the time, that they spent the night together. I was doubly jealous.

Apart from a few silly ones, the good theatregoers of Wimbledon were wise enough to stay away, and in that great barn of a theatre we played twice nightly to a couple of rows of silent, dumbfounded people.

Then came the reason I had taken the dreadful job: Collins Music Hall! The audiences there were not used to plays and, as they would if it had been a variety bill, they wandered back and forth from the bar at the rear of the stalls and talked a lot. I doubt if any of them sat through the entire play, which, all considered, was just as well. The conditions backstage were really Dickensian: water dripped down from the damp fungus growing walls; the dressing rooms had no running water in them; there was a sink with a cold tap at the end of the corridor; the lavatories I shall leave to your vivid imagination; and because of a broken pipe somewhere the floor of the corridor was flooded and we had to walk on planks not to get our shoes wet. But with all its horror and discomfort the theatre still retained a distinct atmosphere that made me tingle. I was glad I had been there.

Another good thing came out of it. I got to know Betty Hare. She was playing an OAP who gets mugged for the one and sixpence she has in her handbag by an evil teddy boy wot was me. Betty was one of the famous (only in the profession, alas) Hare family that had been on the stage for generations. Its present members were old Mrs. Hare (long since retired), her middle aged son and three daughters: Doris (the posh one who made it to the West End stage appearing in Noel Coward revues), Betty and Molly, whose name sometimes got her mistaken for the French dramatist, Moliere. Apart from Doris, who lived in a posh house with a posh husband in posh Hampstead they all lived together in a shabby old flat in Shaftesbury Avenue where they had been as long as they could remember. I loved going there. It was filled with theatrical memorabilia: old posters, programmes, bits of costume, props. They reminded me of the Crummles in 'Nicholas Nickleby'.

Betty remembered Tonypandy from her early childhood, when she and her siblings toured the Welsh valleys with their parents' fit up company doing one-night stands in small towns and villages. They were carried on stage as babies and put to bed at night in skips. It was the only life they had ever known. Her stories of touring in the early part of the century were fascinating and I could have listened to her for hours. The Hares really did have make up in their veins and I admired their indomitable spirit. I also got to know posh Doris very well, she was a great admirer of Robb's and my work and once sang one of our songs on the radio.

Bill Greene was a six foot two, handsome American actor who trained at RADA and then stayed on in England for several years. He rented a house at the top of Sydney Street in Chelsea where he turned the second and third floors into a self contained flat that he let to a friend. The friend was vacating it and he offered it to F and me. It consisted of a large sitting room, kitchen and bathroom on the second floor and two large bedrooms on the floor above, and he was charging no more than we were paying for our pokey Harrington Road flat so we quickly said, 'Yes, thank you.' He could have asked a lot more for it but he probably wanted to make sure he had the right sort of people living above him and we fitted that category. Bill must have had private means, for he had a fairly lavish life-style that I don't think could have been supported by his earnings as an actor, and the well furnished Sydney Street house must have been quite expensive to rent.

I had first met him through Gingold. When she was appearing at the Café de Paris he was the gorgeous hunk who escorted her down the stairs each night, kissed her hand and departed; only to reappear at the end of the act when the applause was at its height and proffer his arm, which she took with alacrity and, with a wicked gleam in her eye, galloped with him up the stairs. It was a very clever and stylish idea of Hermione's.

Not only was everyone asking, "Who is that gorgeous young man she's got?", it was also the way to help a poor old lady in high heels get up a difficult flight of stairs.

Around this time I was offered a nice part in the comedy, 'Dear Charles' at Leatherhead for two weeks and then a week at Canterbury; and while in it I made two very good friends: Joyce Grant (a fellow South African), an extremely funny comedienne, and James Bree, a fine actor and sweet man. I then went to York to appear in, 'The Trial Of Mary Dugan', and shared digs with two very funny young ladies, Sheila Hancock and Cherry Morris. It was a fairly dismal production and we spent a lot of the time laughing; occasionally, I am ashamed to say, on stage. Also in the company was Pamela Lane, John Osborne's first wife, who would feature very prominently in his play, 'Look Back In Anger'. The director had a very eccentric method of giving notes. For some reason that I still haven't fathomed he didn't like us all being on the stage together when he gave them, so we would wait in the wings until our name was called (the name of the character, that is; I don't think he knew our real names), we would then go on stage, be given our notes and allowed to leave. As none of us knew what notes the others had been given it was quite a surprise when during the performance they started doing different things. But he really must have known what he was about for we never actually all bumped into each other centre stage.

F was beginning to play away from home. It wasn't his fault, he was born promiscuous, but when strange men started ringing up and asking for him I got cross and a little jealous. I had no right to be. After all, it was I who would be leaving when Denis returned. It was then that I began to think that Sydney Street might not be an unsuitable place for Denis to live: it was comfortable, well furnished and I knew he and Bill would get on splendidly. Then a stroke of good luck came my way. F was offered a season at Carlisle Repertory Theatre in Cumbria, which would last from the beginning of May till the end of September. Obviously if he planned to return to Sydney Street he would have to continue paying his half share of the rent while away, which I knew would irk him, so I put my cards on the table: I told him that when Denis returned either I left and he kept the flat on or, preferably for me, he left and Denis moved in. I knew I had a very strong hand; no way was he going to pay the full rent for the five months he was gone, so he agreed to leave.

I was sad to see him go, but the affair was definitely on the wane, and would certainly not have survived the long period he would be away. Although sad it was also a relief, it had caused a lot of pain, and especially for Denis, for which I still feel guilty. All the same, I shall always be grateful to F, he came along at a time when I was at my most vulnerable and lonely and gave me the refuge I so badly needed. I was also lucky with the timing of his departure; he left for Carlisle on the Sunday morning and that very day Irene received a phone call from Denis to say he was returning on the Wednesday. This gave us just enough time to tidy the place up and make the front bedroom look fresh and inviting with a new bright bed quilt, cushions and a large vase of tulips. On Wednesday as we followed him up the stairs carrying his luggage we crossed our fingers and held our breath.

If Maadi with Helen had been a disaster Kyrenia with Humphrey was a catastrophe. At least Helen wasn't drunk all the time. Humphrey when sober was sweetness and light itself, but you had to catch him fairly early in the day. He had two old friends living permanently with him, and on him; one was Joy's disgraced New Zealand cousin who lost most of her inheritance on a dicey speculation. All three got up quite late in the morning and started drinking straight away. By late afternoon none were capable of a coherent conversation, which Denis found boring to say the least. The butler (to use a euphemism) was a large, aggressive Turk who also provided sexual favours when required. He was arrogant and extremely manipulative, and when he saw that Denis was on to his cunning and thieving ways he became quite hostile and insolent. All this, of course, went way above Humphrey's befuddled head. The house was in a terrible state of disrepair. The roof needed mending but it was far less trouble to put basins down when it rained. Denis said it reminded him of the House of Usher. One day at lunch he remarked that the beautiful Georgian silver they were using could do with a polish. At this the butler, also eating at the table, roared with laughter and said, "He doesn't know we don't polish the silver any more.", and to Denis's dismay, Humphrey laughed too.

It was a god-send for Denis that the writer, Lawrence Durrell, whom he had known in Egypt during the war, lived nearby and often invited him to his house or to go for drives and visit Greek ruins, as did some artists who were also close neighbours. Without them there would have been no one with whom he could have had an articulate conversation.

He stood it for as long as he could, and then thinking that even the cold fogs of London would be preferable, he decided to return earlier than expected. And luckily for us his timing was superb.

I don't suppose I need tell you what happened to Humphrey and the two old sponging sponges. In a very short while they were all dead of cirrhosis of the liver; and the butler, I imagine, retired a very wealthy man.

Denis thought Sydney Street would do quite nicely until we could find somewhere more permanent to live with our own furniture, pictures and books. It was quite simple, really; we just needed to make some money. As I thought they would, he and Bill hit it off really well and became good friends. Bill's young lover who lived with him, had been suffering from a persistent cough and, when it was found that he had a shadow on one of his lungs and would need to go into hospital for a short while, Denis was a wonderful comfort to him. He gave him moral support and practical help, and would visit him regularly at Hampstead Hospital. Fortunately, the infection was slight, and being strong and healthy in all other respects he was soon cured.

It took us some time to become really close again. We both had our own personal readjustments to make, and to begin with he was very much on the defensive. He didn't trust me. He thought I was with him out of duty, not because I wanted to be. But as the year wore on and he realized that my feelings were genuine the defences started to come down and we were more or less back to where we left off.

As Bill was appearing in Peter Ustinov's comedy, 'Romanoff and Juliet' at the Piccadilly Theatre six nights a week his main form of entertaining at home was Sunday brunch; and we were sometimes invited down to meet his New York theatre friends. One Sunday we met Leonard Silman, producer of the famous 'New Faces' revues. In his 1952 edition Eartha Kitt made her Broadway debut singing, 'Monotonous', 'Santa Baby' and 'Ces't Ce Bon'. In another edition Maggie Smith made her first Broadway appearance. Leonard liked my material and said he hoped he would be able to use some of it, but it never happened, and soon after that 'New Faces' petered out.

On one of her visits to London Gingold brought the clever actor, singer, dancer, Carlton Carpenter to brunch. They had just been appearing together in the Broadway revue, 'John Murray Anderson's Almanac.' He had spent some time in Hollywood and had worked with Judy Garland on 'Summer Stock', about which he had some fascinating gossip. But what he was most remembered for, much to his annoyance, was singing, 'Aba Daba Honeymoon' with Debbie Reynolds.

Carlton wrote music, he liked my lyrics and suggested we worked together. We managed to write a couple of songs, but with him in New York or LA and me in London and it being the days before cassette recording it all proved too difficult and we gave up. During his brief stay in London he invited me to a matinee of 'The Mousetrap', which I had managed to avoid until then. He was curious to see for himself why it had been running for over two years. We lunched at Bianchi's in Soho, saw the play and then had tea at the Ritz. While nibbling at delicious thinly sliced cucumber sandwiches we puzzled as to how such an un-thrilling little thriller could have lasted for so long. That was fifty-three years ago, 'The Mousetrap' is still running, and I remain as puzzled as ever.

Peter Myers had a successful show on at the New Lindsey called, 'Intimacy At Eight', and I had a lyric in it. Knowing Robb of old, Peter did not wait for him to deliver the music but gave it to Norman Dannatt to set. It was called, 'Signs Of The Times', and was sung by Leslie Crowther, Ron Moody, Dilys Laye and Vilma Ann Leslie. It consisted of several worrying news items that appeared in *The Times* newspaper in the 1850s that bore an uncanny resemblance to the worrying news items that were appearing in *The Times* newspaper of the 1950s – the main scare being the Russian bear! It was a gentle satirical number without big laughs, far subtler than the rest of the material, which was really quite broad, so when 'Intimacy At 8.30' (by now the title had gained half an hour) opened at the Criterion Theatre 'Signs Of The Times' was no longer in the show. I was sad to see it go, the small weekly cheque would have been welcome, but I fully understood Peter's reason for dropping it, and by then theatrical rejection no longer broke my heart. I had become a convert to the Doris Day school of philosophy: *che sera sera*. And that was the last professional truck I had with Peter.

'Intimacy At 8.30' ran for two years, and he followed it with other hit shows. Apart from his great success, what I envied most was Peter's prolificacy. He could write a sketch almost as quickly as it took him to type it, whereas I would labour over one for days. I often thought his work could do with a little polishing, but it was always spontaneous and fresh and the audiences lapped it up.

It was a terrible blow when in early middle age he suffered a severe stroke and was confined to a wheelchair. This didn't stop him from writing more shows and going to the theatre; until, sadly, a more serious illness brought the curtain down on these activities. Peter retired to the country, where he spent his final days longing for the smell of a London theatre and dreaming fondly of his one true love: intimate revue.

Two streets away from Sydney Street in Church Street, Chelsea, there stand side-by-side, a couple of very distinctive detached houses that, when built in the 1930s by the German architect, Walter Gropius, were the cause of much controversy. From the street they look fairly formidable and fortress like with their lack of formal windows, but from the garden side where the walls consist almost entirely of glass they have a most delightful open airy aspect.

In one of the houses lived the playwright, Ben Levy and his beautiful American wife, the actress, Constance Cummings. Their close neighbours and equally close friends were the publisher, Dennis Cohen and his beautiful American wife, the ex-actress, Kathryn Hammil. Denis knew the Cohens well: Dennis was Martin Solomon's uncle (his mother's brother), he owned the Cresset Press and had published Denis' book 'The Road To Bordeaux'; and Kathryn had been in Herbert Fargeon's revue, 'Nine Sharp', at the Little Theatre (destroyed by a bomb in the blitz).

Kathryn was a remarkable woman. At the age of forty she decided to give up her stage career and become a doctor. Considering her background this was a most formidable task: born in the Bronx into a poor immigrant Jewish family, her education was practically nil; however, blessed with beauty and brains, she made it onto the Broadway stage. She was not particularly gifted as an actress, singer or dancer, but with her lovely face, beautiful dark hair, tall, slim figure and a natural elegance, sophistication and wit, friends and admirers she lacked not. George and Ira Gershwin adored her and always tried to find something for her in their productions; and the Marx Brothers took her to Hollywood to be in one of their films. In the 1930s she came to London with a show, met Dennis Cohen, married him and made England her home.

When the war came she said goodbye to the stage and started studying medicine – in her case this meant first having to catch up on the schooling she had missed. After slogging away at it for several grinding years (fortunately money was no problem), she finally achieved her goal and became a consultant psychiatrist at St George's Hospital, specialising in hypnosis.

Discovering that Denis was a patient at the hospital she kept a watchful eye on him, and made sure he was receiving the best attention available. Afterwards, as we were fairly close neighbours, despite a gruelling schedule she would find time to pop in to Sydney Street for a cup of tea or a drink and see how Denis was getting along; and occasionally we were invited round to dinner at Church Street. One particular evening I remember very clearly. The other guests were Ernestine Carter, the editor of *Harpers* (and subsequently *The Sunday Times*, women's section), who lived just a few doors away; George Devine, founder of The English Stage Company at the Royal Court Theatre; and visiting from New York, Arthur Schwartz, composer of many Broadway musicals and revues. I suppose the most famous being 'The Band Wagon', which starred Adele and Fred Astaire (their last show together before she became Lady Cavendish and went to live in Ireland leaving her poor little brother to dance all on his own – then tap, tap, tap, along came Ginger!). A haunting song from that show was 'Dancing In The Dark'. After dinner, as seems to be *de rigueur* with Broadway composers, Arthur made straight for the grand piano and for the next hour or so entertained us with his enchanting music. Constance Cummings came in from next door to join us for coffee and I can still see her and Kathryn looking gorgeous together, one fair, one dark, standing at the piano and singing along with Arthur. For me it was a most memorable evening.

Kathryn did very important work at the hospital but it was both mentally and physically exhausting, and she found it frustrating that she was unable to see her patients as often as she felt she needed to. When I told her about a dancer friend of mine, Derek Rosen, who was suffering from a plague of boils that the doctors seemed unable to cure (a particularly horrible affliction for a dancer); she thought the cause might be psychological and suggested he came to see her. He did and in no time at all the boils ceased, never to return.

But Kathryn's end was very sad. Her taxing work had put a terrible strain on her mentally, and I believe an emotional involvement with a colleague had gone horribly awry. No one knows why for sure but one morning she was found dead in her bed having taken an overdose of sleeping tablets.

Poor Kathryn, the courageous life she chose – probably too late – proved to be too difficult in the end.

———

The little Irving Theatre in Irving Street off Leicester Square was in its heyday presenting intimate revue and seldom seen plays of an esoteric and effete nature, such as 'Salome' by Oscar Wilde, and 'The Princess Zoubaroff' by Ronald Firbank. In the latter the role of the Princess was played by the always newsworthy, once ravishing now ravaged, oft arrested, society blonde, lesbian, drug addict, Brenda Dean Paul, who, owing to her addiction, was not able to do all the performances, giving the ones she could manage the extra frisson of wondering if the police might burst in at any moment and make an on-stage arrest. Her mother, Polish born Irena Lady Dean Paul, who had composed music under the male pseudonym of Poldowski, had also been a notorious gay morphine addict, so it seemed only natural that her son and daughter should follow in her glamorous footsteps. I met Brenda once, at the Cross Keys pub in Chelsea. Denis introduced us; he had known her slightly in the late 1920s when as a young man he hung around with those two wild women, Gwen Farrar and Tallulah Bankhead. At our Cross Keys meeting I found her charming and witty, though she looked rather gaunt and raddled. Having just mentioned those two wild women of Denis' acquaintance reminds me of a funny incident involving the three of them that he once told me about (Gwen Farrar was half of the vaudeville act, 'Farrar and Blaney'. Norah Blaney was the charm of the act; she wore frilly frocks, played the piano with roguish charm and sang like a demented nightingale. Gwen Farrar on the other hand was Eaton-cropped, wore dinner jacket and monocle, performed on the cello with masculine virtuosity and had a mordant line of humour. Their repartee and witty back chat was considered hilarious. Gwen was in the fortunate position that if the act ever laid an egg her family owned a diamond mine in South Africa.)

Tallulah Bankhead was the darling of the London stage, and her off stage shenanigans were equally newsworthy. She resided in a lovely Georgian house overlooking

Regents Park that had in its main bathroom a large sunken bath of rose pink marble, in which she liked to lie, Cleopatra like, to receive morning callers. For non-acquainted visitors such as journalists and tradesmen the experience could be a little unsettling.

Late one morning, bathed and fully clothed for a change, Tallulah was in the drawing room with Gwen and Denis having a quick glass of champagne before they sped off in Gwen's new sports car to go and create mayhem somewhere, when the maid announced that Miss Gladys Cooper was downstairs waiting to see her. Gladys Cooper then owned the lease of the Playhouse Theatre and Tallulah wanted to rent it for a play.

"Oh, my God, I'd forgotten she was coming," moaned Tallulah. "Sorry about this, darlings – it won't take long – amuse yourselves."

"I know what," said Gwen who was famous for her practical jokes. "Let's hide." Hiding was one of her favourite wheezes just then. "Nowhere subtle, somewhere simple." So under the grand piano she and Denis crawled and there, crouched on hands and knees, remained as still and in control of their giggles as they could. Gladys Cooper came, briskly did what business she had to with Tallulah and left, but not without pausing at the door to remark in an un-amused voice, "I must tell you, Tallulah, I know there are people under your piano." At this the giggles under the piano became hoots of raucous laughter. That was the 1920s for you – the age of the bright young things. Today I can't imagine anyone deriving pleasure from such silly innocent fun – more's the pity!

Returning to 1955, Leicester Square, and the little Irving Theatre. Although they did the occasional play their main fare was intimate revue and Robb and I had material in several of their shows. In one of them a talented young Welshman gave a very funny rendition of a number of ours about a masochist. It came as no surprise when, shortly afterwards, he became a member of Joan Littlewood's famous Theatre Workshop at Stratford East. His name was Victor Spinetti.

When the novelty of the 'Irving Revues' began to wear off, as all novelty must, the owner of the theatre, a charming Asian gentleman called Mr. Chaudri, decided to follow in the footsteps of the Windmill Theatre and make it a home of 'Non-Stop-Nude-Revue', five shows a day, commencing at noon, and changing its programme every six weeks. These shows still required a certain amount of original material (openings, finales, etc.) and Robb and I were often asked to provide it, and at times this could be fun.

At the afternoon dress rehearsal of a New Edition (a posh way of saying, change of programme) there were usually a few stage mothers sitting out front, and it was amusing to watch them proudly preen as their teenage progeny swivelled their hips suggestively in the near buff. Rivalry amongst them was rife, and once, when a girl came on to do an exotic dance with a live python, I heard one jealous mother say to another, "There's that little show off, Sonia, doing rude things with her snake again."

That summer I worked on a couple of films, 'The March Hare', and 'Privates Progress'. I also did a few radio plays. And then, as the year was drawing to a close, good luck came my way again. As I have already stated, all the good things that have happened to me in my life have been by chance; none were ever planned; what was planned, and most carefully planned, never came to anything.

After seeing a show at the New Lindsey Theatre one night I went for a drink in the bar upstairs and ran into John Reagan who had directed some of Peter Myers' fringe revues, including 'In Tempo' in which I had several items. John Reagan was a real maverick of the theatre. There was no job in it he had not done. He was a child performer, then a dancer and during the war ran his own small ballet company that toured the Middle East with ENSA. He had done his stint of revue, variety, concert-party; he had directed, choreographed, stage-managed, painted scenery, and now ran a small variety agency in the West End. I don't suppose I need to tell you he was also slightly mad – but mad people do sometimes get things done. John told me he was looking for a musical he could direct at the New Lindsey; he had a rich friend who loved musicals and would put up the money if the right one could be found, and he asked if I had anything up my sleeve. I mentioned that Robb, Robin and I had written a musical called, 'Chrysanthemum' that we believed in but had not as yet been able to get off the ground, but I said I thought it would be far too big to stage at the New Lindsey: it was a period piece set in 1913, had twenty characters and several changes of scenery; the finale even included a burning building. The nice thing about John Reagan was that nothing fazed him. If asked to stage Wagner's Ring at the New Lindsey I think he would have had a go, so the mere thought of a musical comedy with twenty actors and a burning building in no way intimidated him and he asked if he could read the script. I dropped a copy in at his office in Goodwins Court the following morning, thinking that would be the last I saw of it or him; but late that afternoon he rang to say how much he liked the book (as a child he remembered his parents touring in melodramas of the sort) and how soon could he hear the music. I spoke to Robb and that night I took John down to his flat and he played him the score. He was equally enthusiastic about the music and wanted Mr. Moneybags to hear it. So a day or two later we went to Leonard Urry's office in Old Compton Street, Soho, and auditioned the show for him. I never discovered what Leonard Urry did in that office but there was a piano in it so I imagine it was something nearer to music than real estate. As it so happened, Denis had also known Leonard Urry back in the 1930s, when Len was employed by the Café de Paris to dance with female patrons who wished to shake a limb but had no partner to do it with. Under the Trades Description Act the job would probably be classified as gigolo. While working there he met and married the popular American cabaret singer and recording artiste, Marion Harris: famous for the song, 'My Canary's Got Circles Under Its Eyes', which Len claimed to have partly written. The marriage ended tragically when she fell asleep in bed with a lighted cigarette in her hand and burned to death.

When we met Len he was married again. This time to a very beautiful young woman who, sadly as it turned out for him, fancied ladies more than gentlemen; however they did somehow manage to produce a pretty little daughter called Sheba.

Len adored the score and made Robb play some of the songs over and over again, singing along with him. He said that if John thought he could stage it at the New Lindsey he would produce it. John could see no problems whatsoever. We realised that Len was really serious when he insisted that we sign a contract right away. We had no literary agent at the time, Dennis van Thal had vanished from our lives and I was not yet with Margaret Ramsay, so a friend of mine, Laurence Harbottle (Harbottle & Lewis were yet to become the most important firm of solicitors in the British film and theatre world) agreed to draw up the contract for us. Frederick Piffard who was running the New Lindsey had read the script, liked it, and agreed on a production date with Len. Jefferson Strong would design the décor and two clever young designers John had discovered, Hilary Virgo and Rosemary Carvill, would do the costumes. We told them we thought it was time Art Nouveau made a serious comeback in the theatre; they all agreed and came up with some stunning designs. It was almost time to start auditioning.

But first I must tell you something about the show itself. When Robin Chancellor and I decided to write a musical with Robb and we were looking for a subject our Paris friend Cecil Robson suggested we might adapt one of the Lyceum Melodramas by Frederick Melville that he had seen in his youth. Robin and I went to the Lord Chamberlain's office in St James's Palace where, for a fee, one could read any play that had ever been publicly performed in England and we staggered through several of Melville's many plays. Two of the titles that appealed to us were, 'The Bad Girl Of The Family', and 'The Worst Woman In London'. The plays themselves were pretty awful and apart from a few bits of plot, of no interest to us; but we thought that a ragtime musical based on a famous Lyceum melodrama called, 'The Bad Girl Of The Family' might be of interest to the theatre going public. We discovered that a descendant of Melville's who owned the copyright to the plays was living in London. At her suggestion we met in a pub at the bottom of the Edgeware Road. On arrival she was already slightly sloshed, she then proceeded to knock back the gins as fast as we put them in front of her, and then to Robin's horror she groped him under the table. We tried to explain what we had in mind but she was not interested in details, we could do anything we liked with those dreadful old plays as long as she got fifty percent of all the royalties. We told her that this was out of the question, all we wanted to use was the title and perhaps a couple of plot twists. She remained adamant, fifty percent or nothing. We decided it would be nothing and sat down to write our very own melodrama using certain aspects of the genre that we had now grown familiar with.

In Cairo I had come across a yellowing-paged, short paperback from the early part of the century that was a warning to young English girls against white slave traffickers. The style was hysterical and the content jingoistic to an extreme. It suggested that all foreigners were suspect and not to be trusted. I don't recall the title but on the cover was a colourful illustration of a sinister Latin type with a curly moustache (described in the book as a greasy dago) molesting a frightened young golden haired English virgin. I found the book hilarious and thought I would like to use the idea someday. We decided the day had come.

'The action takes place in London at the beginning of the Neo-Georgian period, just before the first world war. Ragtime, the Bunny Hug, and the Turkey Trot are all the rage. Melodramas such as 'The Lights Of London', are enjoying great success at the popular theatres. Women are wearing fabulous dresses designed by Poiret. Novels like 'The Road To Buenos Aires' are tucked away behind cushions. Suffragettes are chaining themselves to railings. Limehouse teems with opium dens. And Chrysanthemum Brown is a name one does not mention!' (this blurb appeared on the programmes and posters of the New Lindsey production).

The following synopsis (more succinct than I could manage) is mostly borrowed from the remarkable 'Ganzl's Book of the Musical Theatre' (published by The Bodley Head Ltd) which summarises some three hundred of the best musical shows of the contemporary and bygone repertoires of the English, French, German, Hungarian and Spanish language stages. It is the most knowledgeable and definitive book on the subject that I have read, and I am more than a little chuffed that 'Chrysanthemum' should be included in such illustrious company.

ACT ONE

It is a summer's afternoon in 1913 and we are in the garden of Captain Brown's house at Greenwich, a homely place with characteristics hovering undecidedly between late Victorian Gothic and blushing Art Nouveau, where the daughters of the good sea Captain, Lily, Rose, Daisy and

Lavender, are entertaining their beaux to a *thé dansant* to the strains of an up-to-date gramophone ('Alexander'). Their Uncle Fred, a sanctimonious Victorian gentleman, strongly disapproves of these 'songs of Satan', but their father sees no harm in the music. He is a happy Captain, for today his sailor son, Bob, returns to the bosom of the family from a trip to South America. All his little brood will be together. All, that is, except Chrysanthemum. Three long years ago his darling eldest daughter went out to fetch the milk and never returned, and from that day to this no one has seen or heard from Chrysanthemum Brown.

Bob heaves to with a sailor song ('Ships At Sea'), a heart full of love for Mary Ann Blessington-Briggs, and some strange news: down Argentina way he could swear he saw Chrysanthemum. The good Captain is horror struck. Argentina! Better to be dead than amongst those immoral foreigners! It cannot be true. Imagine, therefore, his surprise when, no sooner has Bob gone off to rendezvous with his Mary Ann, than Chrysanthemum appears at the garden gate, glittering in the latest Paul Poiret gown, weighed down with jewels and furs and gifts, and carrying the milk. "Here I am Father!" she announces, "And here's the milk. Please don't ask me why I've been so long." Plying presents on her papa she refuses the answer to only one question…where has she been? ('Don't Ask Me That'). The Captain, exasperated by her refusal to answer, comes to the only possible conclusion: she has, indeed, been in Buenos Aires. She is a fallen woman, a weed in his garden of flowers. She must go hence from his house.

Alone, with only a spotlight for company, Chrysanthemum, in defiant mood, sings of her fall from grace: "Though the prospect could be finer I've a heart the size of China/ and I live to give wholeheartedly./ If my life should wind up sadly I can say I've lived 'not badly',/ Sinner me! Sinner me! Sinner me! ('Sinner Me'). As she wends her way to the seamy side of the river and the degrading depths of Chinatown she suddenly stops in her tracks. A wheelchair inhabited by an old woman with a mop of curly red hair skitters across the stage. "Ma Carroty!" gasps our heroine and without pause sets scaldingly off in pursuit.

In Greenwich Park Bob is waiting starrily for Mary Ann while, in another part of that self same park, that self same young lady is getting a lecture from her very upright brother, John. He suspects her of making an assignation with a gentleman behind his back and he warns her expressively of the dire consequences of flirtation: "every single night in London/ nice young girls are being undone" ('Watch Your Step'). Mary Ann, alas, is heedless. Sending her maid to post a conveniently forgotten letter to Aunt Mildred, she hurries to the arms of her Bob ('Mary Ann'). All is decided. The following morning he will come and officially ask brother John for her hand in marriage.

They part and, as Mary Ann waits for Emily to return, an old redheaded lady in a wheelchair rolls up and offers her a toffee. Mary Ann is well enough brought up to refuse it and the other delicacies the old lady proffers, but she cannot resist a look at her collection of picture postcards. After all, what harm can there be in a picture postcard? But as Mary Ann bends her golden head over the photos, the old lady whisks out a syringe: "Aha! That completes another batch for South America." The drugged Mary Ann is bundled into the wheelchair and trundled off as Chrysanthemum arrives at a brisk trot: brisk but alas too late!

Down in Limehouse our heroine, disguised as a Chinee with coolie hat and pigtail, penetrates the notorious Skull and Chopsticks dance hall where Ma Carroty has her headquarters. There, in a secret back room, Mary Ann is coming out of her stupor when Chrysanthemum appears ('A Fate Far Worse Than Death') to set her free. She tells Mary Ann what her fate was to be: bundled off to Buenos Aires just as she, Chrysanthemum, had been three years earlier. Contrary, however, to her father's fears she had not fallen there to a fate worse than death but had used her youthful dance training to become Carmencita, the famous tango dancer. But enough of exposition, Ma Carroty is approaching! With the aid of the old one two and a handy vase the girls are soon free and on their way to Park Lane.

In his Mayfair abode John Blessington-Briggs is in a frenzy. Trying to telephone the police, he only succeeds in getting wrong numbers ('Sorry You've Been Troubled') and, just as he gets connected to Scotland Yard, blow me if Mary Ann doesn't walk in. And Bob. And Chrysanthemum. When, with a little fabrication, all the misunderstandings about who has been where and doing what have been cleared up, Bob thinks Chrysanthemum has been in Paris at a finishing school, and John thinks Chrysanthemum is wonderful ('Is This Love?').

Back at Captain Brown's house, despite the disbelieving carping of Uncle Fred, Chrysanthemum is accepted back into the posy ('Understanding') and the multiple wedding plans are made as John and Chrysanthemum celebrate in waltz time the fact that 'Love Is A Game'. So, there is to be a 'Double

Wedding'. Outside the church the wedding guests are gathering 'At The Wedding'. However, fate intervenes in the form of Uncle Fred. Before vows can be vowed, he pushes forward the castanet-clicking Pepe who gaily identifies Chrysanthemum as Carmencita, the Flame of Buenos Aires. She cannot deny it. "A scarlet woman!" proclaims Uncle Fred, and as she slowly walks away, her head bowed low, the congregation point an accusing finger at her and chant: "Sinner you! Sinner you! Sinner you!"

ACT TWO

Down by the river at the Rose and Crown the Saturday night revellers are enjoying themselves ('Saturday Night'). Bob and Mary Ann have been looking in the park for Chrysanthemum. A sudden cloud burst reminds them of their first meeting ('Thanks To The Weather'). Wandering forlornly by the river, Chrysanthemum sings "As the mist starts to rise on the river/ here I hide from the eyes of the night./ As a distant tug cries on the river/ all my hopes disappear out of sight" ('No More Love Songs'). A chance meeting with the inscrutable Chinese laundryman, Ching Loo, gives our intrepid heroine a bright idea, and sets the plot running again. Excited at the daring task ahead of her that night she joins the revellers in a high-spirited reprise of 'Saturday Night'.

Meanwhile, the Brown family have chiselled from the dancing Argentinian the real story of Carmencita. Pepe, needing a saucy dance partner to brighten his act, whisked Chrysanthemum away from a newly landed batch of potential poules, saving her from professionalism and creating a star in the process. She is not and never was a ...! How could they have thought so ill of the Flame of Buenos Aires? But what now? She must be found! With a little prodding Mary Ann recalls the name of the Skull and Chopsticks and the love struck John sets off in pursuit. As he makes his way through the dark, sinister foggy streets of Chinatown he asks: 'Which way?' – where do I go? – how can I find my love?'

His love is currently inside the Carroty den, disguised as the striptease dancer, 'Shanghai Lil', but Ma Carroty is wise to her disguise and tricks her into a secret room behind a moving panel. As the horrid harridan gloats over her victory, John appears and, recognising his beloved's screams, he hurries back to the Brown house to tell them that Chrysanthemum is locked in Ma Carroty's secret room and everyone must come to the Skull and Chopsticks, "and someone call the police!"

In the secret den, Chrysanthemum is tied to a bed as Ma Carroty sprinkles paraffin about. She will send the Skull and Chopsticks up in smoke. It has served its purpose. She is rich now, "I've made my pile and can retire to my cottage in the Cotswolds."

As John and Bob and Mary Ann burst in, the building is going up in flames. They are trapped! It is the end! But no…here come the Fire Brigade (Mack Sennett style) with a hose and a song ('The Fire Brigade'). Everyone is saved, Chrysanthemum making a valiant leap into the firemen's sheet below. John shrugs off Captain Brown's praise. "Any decent Englishman that loved a girl who had been maligned, and who, disguised as a Chinese singer was lying tied up in a den in Limehouse which was about to be burnt down by a fiendish white slaver, would have done the same."

But the evening's action is not over yet. As Ma Carroty attempts to trundle her wheelchair off into the sunset, she is apprehended. Chrysanthemum steps forward with a revelation. Whisking off the red wig, she reveals that Ma Carroty is none other than – Uncle Fred! After a musical warning never to believe things to be what they seem, Chrysanthemum leads the entire company in a rousing reprise of 'Understanding'.

Finding a Chrysanthemum who could sing, dance and possess the necessary comedic style was going to be a major task. The rest of the casting was, luckily, not too difficult. The New Lindsey had a fine reputation and many distinguished actors performed there. Our auditions were held in a sleazy Soho nightclub in Greek Street, Soho, that Len had acquired the use of for a few mornings; and there, in the daytime squalor of that tawdry venue, reeking of stale liquor fumes and tobacco smoke, we saw a lot of fresh young talent and were almost spoilt for choice. To play the youngest sister, Lavender – the cheeky, irrepressible one, and quite a showy part – I suggested a clever little girl I had seen recently in a New Watergate revue who I thought would be just perfect. I found out that she was available and got her to come and audition. Neither John nor Len could see anything in her and the part was given to someone else. That little girl in whom they could see nothing would soon be making a big name for herself and the name would be Barbara Windsor. Colin Croft, well known in Sydney, Australia, for his work in musicals and revues, had arrived in England to try his luck and it was our good fortune that he accepted the role of John Blessington-Briggs. Donald Scott, good looking with a fine baritone voice, had been in several West End shows: he would play Bob. Patricia Moore had recently arrived down from the north, she had a sweet face and an equally sweet soprano voice and she would be Mary Ann.

Richard Curnock, a talented character actor who had been in all the 'Sweet And Low' revues, was our Uncle Fred.

As if having five Brown sisters on a stage the size of a postage stamp would not be enough – if not too many – John now asked us to write in an extra little sister called, Petal. I fought against it but he was adamant. He must have owed the child's father a favour or received a backhander to put his darling little daughter on the stage. Whatever the reason the Brown sisters now had a baby sibling called, Petal.

Finding younger sisters was no problem but finding the eldest one still was. Several well known actresses were approached and all declined the kind offer: some found the part daunting, some thought the New Lindsey beneath them, others were put off by the knowledge that John Reagan was not well known as a musical comedy director. Unfazed by it all, John now offered the role to Diana Dors who he found out was free at the time. She liked the part and toyed with the idea for several days before reluctantly saying no. She probably felt that appearing at a small fringe theatre with an unestablished director might give the impression that her film career was slipping. In actual fact it was slipping, and I do believe that had she been brave enough to take the role, in which I am sure she would have been a knock out, it would have given that career the boost it badly needed right then. Zoe Gail also flirted with the part for a while, unable to make up her mind, but eventually chickened out. Ditto Kay Kendall and one or two other up and coming names.

I suggested a revue actress whose work I greatly admired and who also was a friend of mine, Fenella Fielding. I knew she had the sparkle and wit that the part required; but John had worked with her on a fringe revue at the Edinburgh Festival and they had not hit it off together, so he refused to even consider her.

Now Len came up with a cabaret singer for whom he obviously had the hots. Her name was Tonia Bern. Not for her an audition in a sleazy Soho nightclub, he hired a suite at the Ritz Hotel with a grand piano and even laid on champagne. Tonia, whom I knew slightly through friends and liked as a person, was tall and slim with a lovely face and a good singing voice. The minuses were that she had a strong Swiss accent, no acting experience and failed to find the humour in what we thought were our wittiest lyrics. After she had left, Len, besotted as he obviously was with her, tried to force us to have her. John, knowing on which side his bread was buttered, sat quietly on the fence. But the authors and composer put their combined foot down. A good cabaret singer she might be, we agreed, but in no way could Captain Brown's eldest daughter be a Swiss miss with no sense of humour. Len was furious with us, he had spent a lot of money on that audition. We needn't have felt guilty about turning Tonia down, for it was not too long afterwards that she became Lady Campbell, having married the famous racing driver, Sir Donald Campbell.

Of my next and final casting suggestion I knew even before I mentioned her name that everyone would disagree with me, but I really thought she would make something very special of the part: she sang, she danced, she was a consummate comedienne, she had a pretty face, she could put numbers over in a sly, sexy way, so what did it matter if Chrysanthemum Brown happened to be a big girl? When I said, Hattie Jacques everyone looked at me with horror. "You can't have a romantic lead that size," they all said, "the audience wouldn't accept it." I didn't know if that was true or not, but it made me feel very sad. After all, weren't people always saying, 'Size isn't everything'? And so the gruelling search continued.

On a snowy Monday morning in mid February rehearsals began at the New Lindsey and we still had no leading lady. This didn't seem to perturb John unduly and he spent the first two days choreographing the ragtime opening number, 'Alexander.' One whole morning was wasted trying to teach the boys to roll a straw boater down an arm, catch it and throw it back on their heads. Not all managed to master it and the time consuming hat trick had to be abandoned. I was beginning to feel a little worried.

On Tuesday Len arrived with some hopeful news. Valerie Tandy might be interested. She had been in 'Kiss Me Kate' at the Coliseum, having taken over from Julie Wilson in the role of Lois Lane and sung 'Always True To You, (darling, in my fashion') which was a good sign. She had also been a stooge with The Crazy Gang at the Victoria Palace: this meant her comedy timing would be good. At present she was in the last week of a panto season in Portsmouth playing principal boy. John took the train down to Portsmouth that evening and gave her the script to read. On Wednesday she rang Len to say she had read it and liked it, and would come up to London on Thursday morning to look us over and give her answer. When she arrived the boys and girls were in the middle of 'Alexander', a number with which they were now fairly familiar (one of very few). She liked what she saw and also liked Colin Croft with whom she would have her main scenes and duets. If we still wanted her, she said, she would be free to start rehearsing first thing on Monday morning. If we still wanted her – that was a laugh! We were about to drag in the first woman we saw on the street.

Physically, Valerie Tandy was not the ideal Chrysanthemum; she was tall and thin with a long angular face and a plethora of teeth. In no way was she a beauty, but in performance that face lit up and she became lithe and vivacious, her timing was immaculate and she attacked the songs 'like a tigress' (to quote Kenneth Tynan). She also had a very strong sense of camp, which would be her way of approaching the part, and it served her well:

(Vamping John as she reclines languidly on a chaise-longue she says: "Now, that's enough about me, let's talk about you. Do you find me attractive?" and lies back with a string of pearls between her teeth.)

Now I will let you into a little secret that very few knew, including Robin to begin with. When I first thought of our heroine and named her after a large gaudy multi petalled over blown bloom I had someone very definite in mind. I saw her as a young, English, comely, blonde, less overtly sexual Mae West (Diana Dors came near the mark). As a child Mae West was my favourite film star. I even impersonated her on the stage and have a glowing write up to prove it (see page 11). Our Chrissie would be a very knowing young woman, worldly wise beyond her years (travel broadens the mind), unrestrained by the moral attitudes of the day, always ready with the wry aside, the *double entendre*. She would have the ability (as Mae had in her pictures) to keep cool in the most awkward situation. Irony would be one of her main attributes: to be able to stand on the outside and observe with silent mirth the absurdity of it all. And above all she would be sexy.

In the various productions I have seen she has never been played this way (Valerie Tandy came the nearest with her camp vamp). They have all gone for the safe jolly hockey sticks, good scout, what a lark, I'm a good girl really, no sex, please, we're British approach: the sort of character Gracie Fields played in her 1930s films. Whereas I would like the audience to be left wondering if Chrysanthemum was really quite as pure as the story makes out. Censorship was still very much in existence then and the Lord Chamberlain would never have allowed a woman of easy virtue to come to less than a sticky end, and with 'Chrysanthemum' being a musical comedy we had to have a happy end – so we lied a little.

On the following Monday morning, with just two weeks of rehearsal left, John started setting one of Valerie and Colin's duets, which included thirty two bars of the Turkey Trot over which he was taking an inordinate amount of time. Only four numbers had already been set, no dialogue rehearsed and the second act was virgin territory. I was now very worried and coming to the conclusion that John was not simply eccentric but actually slightly mad. That night at home I expressed my concerns to Denis who said that if he could help in any way he would. I asked John if he might come and watch a rehearsal and he said he would be delighted: he had admired Denis' theatre productions from before the war and would be most grateful for his knowledgeable opinion. Denis came and was as appalled by what he saw as I was. Robb who was playing the piano for rehearsals, being the eccentric soul he was, failed to notice the chaos we were in, and Robin, who worked for the Museum Press, and could only attend the occasional rehearsal, not being of the theatre, wasn't sure what to expect.

Len rolled up looking pale and anxious, and after watching John spend ten minutes fiddling around with a dance step grew visibly agitated. Denis spoke to him. He said he wanted no remuneration or director's credit, it was purely to help the authors, if Len wished he would try to pull the show together. Len wished. John, now realizing he had bitten off more than he could chew, wished too. He could concentrate on setting the rest of the numbers and leave Denis to get on with everything else. And that is what happened.

We asked if we could delay the opening by a week but Frederick Piffard said it was impossible, we had to open on Wednesday March the 14th as the critics had already been invited. So there we were with just fourteen days to produce a full scale musical on a pint sized stage with a cast of twenty, forty costumes and fourteen changes of scenery, including a burning building. Only a miracle could save us. But as I have stated somewhere earlier, the theatre is still the one place where miracles can happen; and it is that thought in mind that allows one to carry on in the crazy business.

I was concerned about Denis' health. February was a bad month for him with the cold and damp. His emphysema was getting worse and he was using his inhaler puffer more and more. The heavy task he had taken on was daunting; and having to take the bus up to Notting Hill Gate and back every day (at that time we couldn't afford taxis) with the waiting in the cold at bus stops and then having everyone cough and sneeze all over him really frightened me, for when Denis caught a cold it usually turned into bronchitis and sometimes worse, which meant confinement to his bed and visits from the doctor. This was what I dreaded most of all. Luckily the Gods were smiling on us for once and it didn't happen. Amazingly in the little time we had left he managed to lick the show into shape and instil in the actors the style required for the period. John, chivvied along, set the rest of the numbers, and very well too. He had a definite flair for ragtime. Uncomplaining, the company worked their socks off, long hours, weekends included, and although we still could have done with a few more days, somehow by the time we opened the show had acquired the semblance – give or take a little – of a proper professional production. It angered me that someone as talented and skilled at his job as Denis was so little appreciated in the business.

The last few days we were unable to use the stage as scenery kept on arriving and had to be dealt with; so we rehearsed at the Dineley Studios in the Marylebone Road, once the home of Charles Dickens and today a large office building. We had a technical run on the Monday that lasted for several hours and was fraught with difficulties; two of the actors were hit by falling scenery but neither was seriously hurt. On the Tuesday we had two dress rehearsals, one late morning, one in the evening, both fairly catastrophic, but as one knows from experience something very strange can happen between a dress run and an opening. Some superstitious actors believe that a smooth dress rehearsal spells disaster and vice versa. If this was the case we were probably going to be all right.

On the opening night the theatre was packed. I recognised a few of the critics as they arrived. When the show was about to start we sneaked in like naughty schoolboys and stood at the back; and as the curtain rose on 'Alexander' I crossed my fingers and took a deep breath. This was one of those times when one really needed a rabbit's foot. 'Alexander' went without a hitch, the opening scene played well, Valerie got big laughs with 'Sinner Me!', the first scene change went smoothly, we were now in Greenwich Park and the audience seemed to be enjoying themselves. I began to relax a little.

As the first act ended and the applause started we slipped out and ran down the road to a nearby pub where we ordered large whiskies. Very little had gone wrong and I doubt if anyone had actually noticed the mistakes. So far we had been very lucky.

The second act sped happily through and got a lot of laughs. There were two or three slight hiccoughs, but I think known only to us. Ma Carroty setting her secret den alight was a great success, and 'The Fire Brigade' an absolute riot, then all of a sudden the show was over and the audience were wildly applauding. What, we wondered, would the critics make of it?

Kenneth Tynan, who I considered the best theatre critic of the day, and certainly the most knowledgeable about musicals, found it, 'A buoyant evening', and added, 'The lyrics have a beguiling edge', which thrilled me no end. 'A blithe mishmash of a musical', was how he described it. He thought it was unable to make up its mind whether to be a pastiche melodrama or a satire of 1913. A blithe mishmash was exactly what we intended it to be. Had we simply gone for a pastiche melodrama I doubt if Mr. Tynan would have had such 'a buoyant evening'. The buoyancy came from the bright tuneful songs, Chrysanthemum's sly, modern humour, the marching suffragettes and allusions to Eleanor Glynne, Ouida and Dr. Crippen. Two or three others shared Tynan's criticism: 'Whereas 'The Boy Friend' was a perfect pastiche, other elements have crept in here', said one. Well, of course they had, we never set out to write a pastiche musical comedy of 1913. Why do critics have to be such pedants and literalists, always having to analyse everything they see? Why, if they are having 'a buoyant evening' can they not accept a jolly romp for what it is? With Edward Goring of *The Daily Mail* there were no quibbles: 'A bright and breezy new British musical play flowerers in the Kensington Gardens suburb – and should be transplanted to the roomier West End as soon as possible. This well dressed, polished production has all the gaiety and melody that any musical could want.' The *Evening News* was equally favourable. There were a few who thought the show was witless rubbish and the waste of an evening; on the other hand the very literary, erudite Philip Hope-Wallace said,

"'Chrysanthemum' is rather a charming musical and has a nice, dry Cowardly wit. I was a little reminded of 'Evergreen' and 'Nymph Errant' too', and he concluded, 'the lyrics and score are above average witty. A lot of people are going to enjoy it.' Coming from such a highbrow critic we took this as a great compliment. The reviews on the whole were favourable and the word of mouth was excellent so we played to full houses throughout the run. Robin's cleaning lady said she would like to see the show so he bought her a couple of tickets. She came with a friend and afterwards, wishing to pay us a compliment, said, "I've seen worse in the West End."

At the very final performance Pat Kirkwood and her husband Hubert Gregg were in the audience. They had been looking for a suitable vehicle in which to star together in the West End and came to the decision that 'Chrysanthemum' would do very nicely. And so it did; but not without a great deal of frustration; owing to a series of unfortunate circumstances, including a sudden demise, it would be another two and a half years before our flower finally bloomed in the West End.

Carried away by the euphoria of having full houses and some good notices Len announced to the company that as soon as the New Lindsey run was over he was taking the show into the West End exactly as it was. We thought this would be a great mistake and told him so. What looked good at the New Lindsey, on a larger stage would look lost. 'Chrysanthemum', by its very nature a big show, had been squeezed into a tiny space. In the West End the opposite would be necessary: it would have to be opened out and made bigger. The paying audience there would expect more elaborate scenery and costumes (though excellent at the New Lindsey they were on a minimum and miniature scale), more dancers would be expected, and certainly a pit orchestra for the ragtime music; also, sad but I am afraid true, a well known name to play the starring role.

Len kept throwing 'Salad Days' and 'The Boy Friend' at us as examples of small shows that had made it to the West End. 'Salad Days' had come from the Bristol Old Vic where it had been hastily written to fill in a three-week gap and was an instant success. It was an intimate show with a small cast, simple scenery and costumes and performed to the accompaniment of two pianos (Robb for a time played one of them and, to the company's annoyance, would change the tempos according to his whims). Its simplicity was its charm and to have made it bigger would have ruined it. 'The Boy Friend' on the other hand started life as an hour-long pastiche of a 1920s musical comedy that was the second half of a bill at the Players Theatre. Sandy Wilson then turned it into a full lengh three act musical (as was the fashion in the 1920s). A lot of thought, time and energy went into it before it was exposed to the West End.

Len ignored our warnings and went ahead looking for a theatre and a co producer.

There was nothing we could do about it. Our contract with him gave him sole rights on the show for a year after the present production. Only if he failed to produce it again within that time would the rights revert to us. So for the next year he could do what he liked with the show.

When the New Lindsey run ended and he was no nearer to finding a theatre or co producer he finally had to concede that a transfer was not going to happen, and we gave a great sigh of relief. I felt rather guilty and sorry for the actors who had worked so hard and had set their hearts on going into town, but I knew that if they did they would all too soon regret it.

I wish I had heeded this advice myself when more than twenty years later Robb and I had a revue on at the Kings Head Theatre in Islington. It was called, 'Small and Brassy', and was a great success. Harold Hobson in *The Sunday Times*, said of it, 'Small as a diamond, brassy as boldness itself... the most enjoyable musical in London.' A slight exaggeration, perhaps, but I was not complaining.

A mad woman (why do I attract these mad people so?) decided to take the show into the West End as a late night entertainment commencing at 10.40 pm (London needed this sort of thing like a hole in the head). Our venue was Wyndhams Theatre where, earlier in the evening John Guilgud and Ralph Richardson were appearing in Harold Pinter's 'Old Times'. No money, thought or even publicity went into the transfer, and the 'Old Times' management would not allow us to put posters up in front of the theatre until their performance had finished each night. So our little diamond that had glittered so brightly in Islington, on Wyndham's bare stage, lit with Pinteresque gloom looked lustreless and lost; and meant nothing to the half dozen or so Japanese tourists that made up the audience each night. It was a bitter end to what had been such a joyous experience. And that, all those years earlier, was the fate I feared might befall 'Chrysanthemum' at the hands of Len and John.

Harry Foster of Foster's Agency, who represented Pat Kirkwood and Hubert Gregg, contacted us to say his clients were interested in 'Chrysanthemum' as a vehicle for themselves, and were the rights available? Sadly, we had to explain the situation. Pat and Hubert had no wish to join forces with Len and John, and Len had no wish to relinquish his rights. If he couldn't produce 'Chrysanthemum' in the West End he would see to it, for a year at any rate, no one else did. After that Foster's Agency went quiet, and remained so – until a full year had elapsed.

The head of the opera department at the BBC, for whom Denis had directed several operas over the previous few years, had become a personal friend. He owned a small cottage in Brighton that he was not going to be using for a while and, thinking that the fresh sea air would be kinder to Denis' lungs than the thick acrid smog that was menacing London at that time, offered the loan of it to him for a couple of months (it was not until the 1960s when the Clean Air Act came into force that the city was finally freed from the killer fogs and smogs that had plagued it until then).

Denis was unwell again, his bronchitis had returned, and I think the long hard hours he had spent getting 'Chrysanthemum' into shape, for which he received no credit or recompense, had exhausted him; so gratefully he accepted the kind offer. Irene borrowed Harold's car and drove us with our luggage down to the cottage and saw us comfortably installed.

Dr. Brighton's famous ozone, renowned for its health restoring qualities, began to work and slowly but surely Denis's condition improved. I to'ed and fro'ed to London as work dictated: Rediffsion Television was producing a series of potted Victorian Melodramas and I was given a very nice part in 'The Silver King'. I was also asked by the BBC to contribute comedy sketches for 'The Dick Emery Show'. Denis, too, travelled up to London a few days running to direct the radio premiere of a Carl Orff opera for the BBC Third Programme.

Brighton then was a strange dichotomy of a town. It liked to think of itself as London by the sea, but beneath all its trappings of grandeur – the Royal Pavilion, the Nash terraces and squares, the majestic promenade and piers – it was really quite provincial. It had two or three passable restaurants, but during the winter months they closed at a ridiculously early hour, and the almost empty bars had a melancholy out of season feel about them. I found it all rather depressing. At weekends, however, with spring in the air, Brighton took on a less conservative, rather raffish character, ashoards of East Enders roared down for the famous Brighton Races and dubious married couples packed the hotels and boarding houses for what was known as, 'a breath of sea air'. But by Monday morning the town had reverted to, and for the rest of the week remained, its dull oppressive self.

Theatre producers, taken in by the 'London by the sea' boast, often premiered their London bound productions at the beautiful, historic Theatre Royal (one of the oldest theatres in England) and were usually in for a surprise. Plays that Brighton went wild about, on arrival in London often hit the dust, and the ones they stormed out of in droves, banging seats and muttering, "Rubbish!" and "Disgusting!" were the most likely to become West End successes.

Many Brightonians commuted daily to London – it was less than an hour on a fast train – and a lot of distinguished West End actors resided in the town (on the last train from Victoria most nights one could, from among the passengers, have cast quite a stylish H.M. Tennent production), but although Brighton and its environs was home to a host of illustrious people in the arts: painters, writers, musicians, the town somehow managed to remain in attitude and lifestyle both smug and provincial.

Of course, that was a long time ago and things must have changed a lot. Brighton today has a large gay community and I am told that night life there is hectic the whole year round. But in the austere 1950s, apart from the raffish race goers and dirty weekenders, London by the sea was as lively as a doornail – and the only thing I missed on leaving it was the invigorating sea air.

─────

Marie Freeman had been in poor health for some time. Her legs caused her ceaseless pain, and the diviticulitus that had dogged her for years was recurring with greater frequency. Suffering a particularly severe attack she had to be rushed to hospital and instantly operated upon. After that she never fully regained her strength, and in the weakened state she was in her memory began to fail. It was clear that she would never again be able to cope on her own. Constant care would be needed. As she had expressed a longing to return to East Sussex – probably recalling younger happier days when the children were small and her late husband's money had not yet been squandered – they managed to find her a nursing home in Hastings where she had a comfortable room and day and night attention; and as far as they could determine from their weekly visits she was being looked after satisfactorily.

It was a great relief to them when a first cousin of Marie's, an elderly, retired banker who had not been on speaking terms with her for many years (the begging bowl had probably been held out once too often), on hearing of her condition and present circumstances, and feeling it his duty to come to a close relative's assistance, agreed to take on the nursing home expenses, which he, of course, could well afford, and Denis and Irene could not.

As the weeks went by Marie's mind continued to deteriorate and the time came when she could no longer recognise her children. This upset Denis a lot, Irene less so. Marie had done some terrible things to her. Once, while sneaking around over at Kynance Place she had come across some intimate love letters of Irene's and showed them to Richard, hoping to turn him against his mother. Irene never forgave her for that.

She had been at Hastings for about three months when Denis received a phone call early one morning. It was from the nursing home to say Marie had passed away peacefully in her sleep during the night. We were all greatly relieved. Denis felt a certain sadness – theirs had been a life long love-hate relationship – but Irene felt nothing at all. And, I have to admit it, neither did I.

Being Marie's next of kin, Denis inherited the lease of number 5 Alexandra Court, which still had five years to run, and, although it had many unhappy memories for both of us, we decided it would be foolish and weak of us not to return there. The flat was cleared of Marie's effects, redecorated in colours more to our taste and our stuff came out of store, where it had been waiting patiently for far too long. Surrounded by our own furniture, pictures, books, Persian hangings, Egyptian, Greek and Coptic antiquities the flat took on a new and very agreeable aspect, and once more we felt we had a home.

Maude Spector and her mother lived nearby in a large, Victorian block of flats opposite South Kensington Station. Mrs. Spector was a formidable old lady – cross her at your peril – and although her daughter was already in her forties and the doyen of her profession she still remained very much under her matriarchal thumb. Alcohol was forbidden in the home. This was hard on Maude who, like so many of us, at the end of a long hard day wanted to sit down and relax with a soothing little tipple at her side. Once on finding a bottle of gin concealed in Maude's wardrobe all hell had broken loose, and from then on thorough searches of her room were regularly carried out. The heinous offence was never repeated. Sympathising with Maude, Denis came up with a solution: Why didn't she come to our flat around six o'clock each evening, just a five minute walk, and have her soothing little tipple with us? She jumped at the idea, but on one condition, that she provided the tipple. Not being over flush at the time, we happily agreed. And so it was that a Harrods van paid regular visits to Alexandra Court, delivering the gin and vermouth that went into our nightly dry martinis. On the nights that Maude was going out to the theatre or dinner or whatever – which were most nights, really – she would have whoever she was going out with come to pick her up at the flat and partake of a dry martini or two with us before they departed. In this way we got to meet some new and fascinating people. When she was casting 'Laurence of Arabia', she brought along Omar Shariff. On another occasion the yet to be famous Yul Brynner.

Now that we had somewhere again that felt like ours we started to entertain once more. Not lavishly, of course, we couldn't afford it right then, but Denis was an excellent and fastidious cook and once or twice a week we gave a simple lunch or dinner party for two or three guests, and all the old friends were invited in turn: Graham, Moura, Katuscha and Dilkusha, Brian, Bumble, Robin, Elizabeth, Joy hotfoot from Marrakech or Istanbul, Benny and Alice Goodman on their now rare visits to Europe;

also from America, Greta Keller, an internationally famous Viennese cabaret singer and recording artist of the 1930s, who was still performing in smart Manhattan supper clubs. Denis had first met her in Berlin in the late 1920s when she was captivating the town with her new and quite unique style of singing. Marlene Dietrich was just starting out then and it was Greta's low, husky, seductive voice that she copied when she started making records.

And talking of the legendry Miss Dietrich it was about this time, early in 1957, that I met the famous lady. She was appearing in cabaret at the Café de Paris and Johnny Heawood, a friend of mine from the Players Theatre, took Denis and me to see her. Johnny's career was riding high: his choreography for, 'The Boy Friend' in London and New York had earned him great praise, and his reputation in both cities would grow with his brilliant work on, 'Irma La Douce' (sadly, an addiction to alcohol would soon afterwards put paid to his promising career. Sober he was charming and witty, but one drink too many and he became argumentative and belligerent; and as the addiction increased so did the unpleasantness. Eventually nobody wanted to work with him, and he spent his last lonely days drunk and railing against those who had been his closest friends. It was a tragic end for someone as likeable and gifted as Johnny had been. It almost seemed a wilful act of self-destruction). At the Café that evening, over a glass of wine before the performance, Johnny told us how he had met Marlene during her present London engagement and that they had become quite chummy. More than that, he had suggested to her a few clever little touches to enhance the act and she had gratefully accepted them.

Knowing Denis had been in Berlin at the time she was starting her meteoric rise to fame with, 'The Blue Angel', he asked us if we would like to meet her, and naturally we said we would. He scribbled a note on a piece of paper and gave it to a waiter to take to her dressing room. The reply came in the form of Major Donald Neville-Willing, the impresario at the Café de Paris, responsible for booking the many famous performers who appeared there. We all knew the Major well. We knew him as Donald but most others, and he must have preferred it that way, called him 'Major.' Donald had been in ENSA during the war and it was while serving in that capacity that he rose to the giddy rank of Major. As he thought it gave his already distinctive double-barrelled name an extra touch of grandeur he decided on returning to civilian life to keep it, which he did. So in the theatre worlds of London and New York (where he had spent some years after the war) he was affectionately known as 'the Major.' Donald told us that Miss Dietrich would be delighted for us to come to her dressing room for a glass of champagne after the performance. He would come and tell us when she was ready. I was thrilled at the thought of meeting her. Since early childhood she had been one of my favourite film stars along with Mae West, Greta Garbo, Fay Wray and Gracie Fields: an odd mix, but then I was an odd child.

How to describe the act? I thought it the most perfect piece of artifice I had ever seen. It was like watching a mirage – nothing was real. Where Doctor Frankenstein had created a monster she had created a 'Blonde Venus' using her own, subtly enhanced, body parts. Mary Shelley would have been proud of her. Her voice was nowhere as tuneful as Greta Keller's but there was an alchemy in the way she put over a number that kept the audience spellbound. The lighting too had magic in it. It revealed what she wanted revealed and concealed what she wanted concealed, and she did the lighting herself (I read somewhere that in films she always lit her own 'close ups'). She was wearing a long, flowing, rose pink dress of the finest chiffon that rippled and floated slightly in a soft breeze, being made by an out of sight fan in the floor. Beneath the dress her beautiful lithe body, with its long slender legs appeared to be completely naked. But as Johnny revealed to us later this was not the case. Her entire body was encased in a tight flesh coloured body stocking that stretched from her toes up to her neck and down to her wrists, the endings concealed by a necklace and bracelets. As close as the Café de Paris audience was to her the illusion remained intact.

After what appeared to be her final song, although we still craved more, she gracefully ascended the stairs, turned, gave a single bow and was gone. A full two minutes later – it can't have been less for she needed at least that amount of time – with the spotlight still on, the band still playing and the audience still applauding, she suddenly reappeared wearing top hat, white tie and tails. Sauntering down the stairs in a provocatively masculine manner she proceeded to sing, 'Falling In Love Again', seducing with her eyes both the men and women in the audience. The performance was a cool, calculated triumph – a hymn to charisma, contrivance and courage – and the world of cabaret will never see its like again. Amen.

Meeting the Devine La Dietrich I thought might be an overwhelming experience but it was not so. There was not a jewel, feather or sequin in sight. She was wearing a simple cashmere sweater and slacks; and apart from that fabulous face (although not quite as fabulous without the special effects) she could have been any well heeled, well persevered foreign visitor to London that one saw shopping in Fortnums or taking tea at Browns. This may be difficult to believe but she was really quite ordinary – less mythical Greek goddess than middle class German housefrau – and I found it hard to associate the charming, unassuming woman now sitting on the carpet chatting to us with that scintillating siren I had seen bewitching an audience less than an hour before.

To begin with she and Denis reminisced about the old days in Berlin and mutual acquaintances there. Then the conversation moved on and Johnny asked her why she hadn't done the hat trick that night. This was a bit of business they had cooked up together where at the end of the act she whisked off the top hat and shook her hair free. She said she hadn't done it because her head felt hot and she thought her hair might be sticking to her scalp in an unattractive way. Johnny asked her to show us the business, she demurred, but he could be very persuasive; so, to please him, she got up, fetched the top hat, put it on, whisked it off and shook her head (this was slightly reminiscent of the opening scene in, 'Blonde Venus' where she removes the gorilla head she is wearing). We all agreed it was a lovely effect and the perfect way to finish the act, so she promised to keep it in.

Just then Donald came in to say the telephone call she was expecting from Madrid had come through to his office and was she free to take it. She asked to be excused, begged us to stay for another drink and hurried out. She returned about five minutes later roaring with laughter. They wanted her to appear in Madrid in July. As it would be midsummer and scorching hot there she had said no. But each time she said no they upped the fee until they had made her an offer so astronomical she couldn't refuse it. "So," she said laughing gleefully, "think of poor greedy me sweating away in Madrid in July." Then turning to Johnny she added, "And you can forget about the hat trick."

In the post one morning came a letter from Fosters Agency enquiring as to who now owned the stage rights of 'Chrysanthemum'. Just to make sure, I rang Laurence Harbottle who had drawn up the contract between us and Len. (not necessarily to our advantage I often thought) and he assured me that as in the previous twelve months there had been no further productions of 'Chrysanthemum', all rights had reverted to us. I sighed with relief and reported the good news. A few days later Harry Foster's secretary, Miss Abel, rang up to say he would like to see Robb, Robin and me in his office, and an appointment was made.

Fosters was a large variety agency headed by its founder, Harry Foster, which represented many of the famous entertainers of the day. They also had close ties in New York and L.A., and when big American performers came over to appear at the Palladium or do a major British tour, it was usually Fosters that looked after them during their stay. In the 1950s, Variety, if not exactly galloping apace, was still trotting along quite nicely. Television was yet to bury it in the knacker's yard of entertainment.

Fosters occupied the fourth floor of Piccadilly House, a large block of offices on the corner of Piccadilly Circus and Lower Regent Street, and Harry's office took pride of place on the very corner with two large windows overlooking the Circus: there was

Eros in the centre, balancing on one leg as usual; Swan and Edgars to the left; the Guinness and Bovril electric signs just beyond; and, between it and the London Pavilion, Shaftsbury Avenue with its many glittering theatres. I could have gazed out of those windows for hours but that was not why we had been summoned there.

Legitimate theatre hardly figured in Harry's world, and a musical comedy like 'Chrysanthemum' would have meant less than nothing to him were not two of his prized clients eager to appear in it in the West End. He told us that if we agreed he would try to get a West End production set up. There was just one matter to settle. It would be a lot simpler, he thought, if besides the two stars Fosters also represented the authors and composer of the show. In other words, give him ten percent of our earnings or no show. It was blackmail, but that was how Harry did business. For Robb and Robin this was no problem, they would have needed an agent to look after their interests anyway, but I had just joined Margaret Ramsay Ltd. I was thrilled that she had accepted me as a client and had no wish to change agents. Peggy, as she liked to be called, would in time become London's, if not the world's, most eminent play agent, but these were still early days and I was one of her first clients.

I went around to her office in Goodwins Court, just off St. Martin's Lane, and explained the situation to her. She couldn't have been kinder or more understanding. "If he can get it on good luck to him," she said. Peggy considered 'Chrysanthemum' to be part of my past and she was only interested in what I might write in the future. I can think of no other agent who would so readily give up ten percent of an author's earnings from a West End musical that, if it succeeded, could bring them in a lot of money. But that was typical of Peggy. Money meant little to her. She was far more interested in discovering new talent, nurturing and moulding it in the hope of creating something extraordinary, and sometimes she did just that. Peggy loved writers but she could be ruthless with them. She would rather they starve and create a work of originality and artistic integrity than compromise just a little to feed a family and pay the rent. To her the work was all.

I don't know why she was fond of me (I was not going to be another Ibsen) but she must have been, considering the amount of time she so generously gave to me. Many an afternoon I sat in her little office listening intrigued to her stimulating and inspiring words. Her knowledge of plays was phenomenal. And several times we went to the theatre together. On one occasion we were travelling back from Sadler's Wells in a taxi, having just seen the Brecht Weil 'Seven Deadly Sins', when she suddenly realized she had left her briefcase under her seat in the theatre and in it was the manuscript of Robert Bolt's new play. We turned the taxi around and hurried back to retrieve it. I also had drinks and dined at her Pimlico flat a few times, and she came to Alexandra

Court and met Denis. This was a great mistake, for she got it into her head that he was the enemy of my talent. She thought his powerful personality overwhelmed me, and in a way that was quite perceptive of her, I was always a little in awe of Denis, but we had been together for fourteen years and I wasn't thinking of changing things now. Peggy implied, if not in such words, that my writing reflected the comfortable, smug, bourgeois existence I was leading; it lacked fire, danger, pain. She thought it would do me good to suffer a little; to get my hands dirty; to roll in the mire. I was given 'Death In Venice' to read and told that only after one had descended to the very depths of degradation and despair could one have the soul of a true artist. That was all very well, I thought, but what if I took her advice, threw my life away and grovelled in the gutter only to find I was not the next Maxim Gorki or even the next Daisy Ashford?

There was something of Miss Jean Brodie about Peggy. Where the former wanted her chicks to be the crème de la crème, Peggy wanted hers to be great dramatists, and if in the process some of them fell by the wayside that was part of the course. It was no coincidence that one of her favourite clients would be Joe Orton. It was Peggy who persuaded him to keep a diary of his louche sojourn in Tangiers. And it was probably with her approval that he took his final headlong dive into depravity and disease, thinking that something astonishing might come from it. Something astonishing did, but not what she had in mind. He got murdered by his jealous boyfriend, Kenneth Helliwell.

I lasted with Peggy for about five years, until she eventually had to concede that mine was merely a talent to amuse and gave up on me. I was upset at the time for I had grown fond of her. After her death I read in an obituary that she came from South Africa, which surprised me for she knew I was South African, and yet never once in all the time we spent together did she mention the land where we both grew up. I found that strange. But then Peggy was strange – strange and unpredictable, and at times, I thought, even a little dangerous and mad, but always the most fascinating company. Her hunger for new writing was both obsessive and insatiable, and for close on forty years she helped inspire, shape, edit, even rewrite a little, some of the most important plays of the British contemporary theatre. The following are some of the names I have chosen at random from her formidable list of clients during those years: John Arden, Alan Ayckbourn, Marcel Ayme, Enid Bagnold, Edward Bond, Guy Bolton, Howard Brenton, Brigid Brophy, Caryl Churchill, Christopher Hampton, David Hare, Vaclav Havel, Aldious Huxley, Eugene Ionesco, Ann Jellicoe, John Lennon, Christopher Logue, David Mercer, John Mortimer, Iris Murdoch, Peter Nichols, Dorothy Parker, J.B. Priestley, Yasmina Reza, Jean Rhys, Robert Sherwood, Muriel Spark, Stephen Spender, Fay Weldon, Tennessee Williams' Estate, P.G.Woodhouse...and I could go on like this with many more famous names. I think of myself as one of the lucky ones to have been associated with Peggy, and I feel particularly privileged that, for a while at least, I believe we were actually friends.

Back to Harry and the contract. As he handed the signed document to Miss Abel to take away and file I was reminded of an amusing incident Maude Spector had told me about. When she was in her teens her very first job was working at Fosters as a junior secretary, licking stamps, making tea, running errands, etc. One day she happened to be in the outer office alone, it had gone one o'clock and the receptionist and other secretaries had already left for lunch, when in through the door waltzed a famous comedy double-act of the day that Fosters represented. When they felt they had spent sufficient time buttering her up with humorous banter and flattery, one of them casually suggested that while they were there they might as well take a look at their contract – there was a minor detail they wanted to check – it would only take a minute, so would she be a little darling and run and fetch it. Eager to please these two charming and funny men, and keen to show initiative in her newly acquired job, Maude hurried off to the filing room, found the contract and brought it back. As she entered the room it was snatched from her hand and before she knew what had happened the comedy duo had fled the building. Harry was furious and poor little Maude very nearly got the sack.

Watching Miss Abel leave the office, the contract in her able hands, I doubted if, even when she was young, those two funny men would have had tried it on with her.

About a fortnight later Harry rang up to say he thought he might possibly have found a producer for the show. Jack Waller had read the script and wanted to hear the score. Jack Waller – now, there was a name to conjure with. He was producing hit shows before I was born. Two of his biggest successes in the 1920s were, 'No, No, Nanette' and 'Hit The Deck'. He continued to flourish through the 30s and 40s when he produced Cole Porter's 'Let's Face It' with Pat Kirkwood in the cast, and even into the 1950s when he had a successful show on at the Palace Theatre. He must be ancient, I thought, and it's amazing he should have the appetite, let alone the stamina, to want to go through the birth pangs of producing yet another big show. The man must be a musical comedy masochist!

Robb and I were asked to go to his London home one evening and play him the score. He and his wife lived in a large ground floor flat near the top of Queens Gate, a full three minutes walk from Alexandra Court. We were summoned for eight thirty, after the Wallers had dined, and Harry would be there too, to introduce us and to hear the score for himself. I lied to Robb about the time so that he wouldn't be late, and as an extra precaution I invited him for a meal first. At exactly eight twenty seven we set off on our momentous journey north.

Mrs. Waller opened the door to us. She was an attractive, elegantly dressed woman in her mid seventies who chatted charmingly as she hung up our coats and led us into the drawing room. Harry was already there sitting comfortably on a sofa with a glass of brandy in his hand. I realized he must have dined with them. Across from him on a large gold brocade chair sat a frail looking white haired gentleman in a burgundy smoking jacket. This was the Methuselah of musical comedy, Jack Waller. Harry introduced us and when we were seated Mrs. Waller asked what we would like to drink. She offered brandy, whisky, gin, wine? I said I would like a glass of red wine. Robb asked if by any chance she had some dandelion tea (he was hooked on it at the time). She didn't have any so he settled for a small pot of Earl Grey.

The conversation was polite but it did not flow easily, and Harry was making no effort to help it along. I felt extremely nervous – we had a lot at stake here – but Robb blithely sipping his tea seemed to be taking it all in his stride.

The drawing room could almost have come out of one of Jack's 1920s productions. It was decorated in rich warm colours, the furniture was ornate and gilded, the lampshades beaded and fringed, and in pride of place in front of the large bay window, its heavy damask curtains now drawn, stood a Bechstein Grand. Draped across it was a beautiful black Spanish shawl with red roses embroided upon it. Also on the piano and other flat surfaces, all velveted and fringed, stood silver framed photographs of the glamorous stars who had appeared in Jack's shows – most of them now dead. Had Norma Desmond been real she really would have liked this room.

When I had finished my wine and Robb was onto his second cup of Earl Grey Jack suggested we might begin. I stood beside Robb at the piano; he performed the numbers, I filled in the plot and explained which character was singing which song. From our audience's reaction it was difficult to tell exactly how we were doing. Mrs. Waller smiled charmingly throughout but said nothing. Harry seemed to be taking his cue from Jack who at the end of each number nodded and smiled and now and then mumbled things like, "Very nice", "Jolly", "I liked that", but there was no sign of any real enthusiasm there and my heart began to sink. Half way through we were offered more refreshment. I had another glass of wine, wishing it was a very large brandy. Robb had a glass of iced water with a slice of lemon in it. Jack, I thought, was beginning to look tired so as we began again I whispered to Robb to hurry it along. This he did and briskly we ploughed through the second half.

When it was all over Jack gently clapped his hands together a few times and the rest of the audience followed suit. "Great fun…great fun," he said stifling a yawn, then rising to his feet he thanked us for coming. While Mrs. Waller was fetching our coats we shook hands and said goodnight to him, and then to Harry, who was obviously staying on to hear the verdict. On the journey south my spirits were low. I wondered if perhaps we could have given it more sparkle. Robb was a very erratic performer, he seldom played his music the same way twice, there was always a great deal of luck involved. But then I told myself that for a man of Jack Waller's experience a little more or less sparkle was not going to make any difference. Either he liked it or he didn't. We were now in the lap of the Gods. As old Doris used to sing, "*Che sera sera* – what will be will be." And as Mae West once thoughtfully added, "And vice versa." Back at the flat I made Robb a pot of tea (I didn't have any dandelion either – tea wise this was not one of his lucky nights) and gave myself a couple of stiff whiskies, then I walked him down to South Kensington station where he caught the tube back to Victoria. That night I slept uneasily. Like a film I ran every moment of the audition over and over in my mind looking for some little clue as to what Jack might have been thinking, but to no avail, it remained a mystery.

About eleven o'clock the following morning the phone rang and I raced to answer it. It was Harry to say it was almost certainly in the bag. Jack had agreed to produce the show but there were certain financial matters to be gone into before a contract could be drawn up, which might take a little time, but the prospect looked very promising. I was thrilled and immediately rang Robb and Robin to give them the good news.

Later that day Hubert Gregg telephoned to say how delighted he and Pat Kirkwood were with the news. He then suggested that sometime in the near future Robb and I should have lunch with them at their country home, there were one or two things in the show that they felt could do with a little tweak. So a week or so later Robb and I took a train from Marylebone Station to Gerrards Cross where Hubert met us in his car and drove us to their lovely house with a large garden, which had a swing in it and upon which I insisted on having a go before lunch. During the meal Hubert explained the little tweaks they had in mind. I say 'they' but all the tweaks seemed to apply to his part. In the New Lindsey production John had three numbers: 'Is This Love?' and 'Love Is A Game' were duets and 'Double Wedding' was a quartet. Hubert felt that John should have at least three solo numbers as well. This would mean that the show was no longer all about Chrysanthemum but about Chrysanthemum and John, and perhaps if he had his way, about John and Chrysanthemum. I was surprised that Pat was so willing to go along with this, she must have known it would lessen the impact of her starring role, but I could see she was in love with him and I realized there were only two options open to us: either we accommodated Hubert's demands or called the whole thing off. Without Pat there would be no Harry Foster to sell the show and certainly no Jack Waller to produce it. We were completely in their hands and they knew it, so I decided we would just have to sit down and try to write some very strong, funny material for him. He was a good light comedian and performed his own songs with great style, 'Maybe It's Because I'm A Londoner' being the most famous one.

The first one we wrote was, 'Watch Your Step', in which John warns his young sister about talking to strange men. It was mainly spoken, rather in the Rex Harrison fashion, and had a lot of words to it that got faster with each refrain, ending at a break neck speed, which, with Hubert's careful diction and delivery, could be very effective. Our next song for him was, 'Sorry You've Been Troubled'. In it John is trying to ring Scotland Yard to report that his sister has been kidnapped and the telephone operator keeps connecting him to wrong numbers. The third song was a dramatic tango: in the foggy streets of Limehouse with murky figures moving in and out of the shadows John, frantically searching for Chrysanthemum, sings, 'Which Way?'

A week or two went by, and then one morning, just as I was thinking that perhaps I should give Fosters a ring to see if any progress had been made, I glanced out of the window and saw two figures, a man and a woman, going up the steps of the building opposite that had recently become a private nursing home, and although I only saw their backs I was sure they were Harry Foster and Mrs. Waller. I yelled to Denis who was in another room to say what I thought I had seen, and then, glued to the window, I stood and waited. About twenty minutes later out the pair came and I was right, it was Harry Foster and Mrs. Waller, and they were looking most concerned. They stood on the pavement talking for a minute or two, then she walked up Queens Gate towards her home and he hailed a taxi. I knew then that something dreadful had happened, and after a couple of nerve wracked days I heard on the wireless that the famous impresario Jack Waller had died in a London nursing home. He had suffered a massive heart attack. After a few thoughts of sorrow for Jack and sympathy for Mrs. Waller I selfishly remembered what Hermione Baddeley had said to Robb when King George VI passed away on the eve of her opening at the Café de Paris, "Why does everything have to happen to me?" So now we were back to square one, and I only hoped that lovely Pat and tricky Hubert wouldn't be getting cold feet or maybe other offers. Our greatest asset was that they wanted to star in a show together and with the adjustments we were making to accommodate Hubert ours was probably the most suitable vehicle for this.

The film director Ken Annakin and Denis had become friends, Denis having written additional dialogue for a couple of his pictures. He was now about to direct Rod Steiger in a film based on the Graham Greene story 'Across the Bridge'. It had a very strong plot but in the present script several of the characters had not been realized to their full potential, especially the Mexican chief of police who plays a cat and mouse game with the Steiger character. These were some of the most important scenes in the film and Ken asked Denis if he would rewrite them. He did and made a magnificent job of it, enabling Noel Willman to give a performance of great subtlety and dramatic intensity that quite equalled that of the great Rod Steiger, who considered it to be his favourite film. Quite rightly Denis was given co-writer's credit on the screen. The music for the film was written by an old friend of ours, James Bernard. It had a haunting theme tune that Denis thought might make a good song using the title, 'Across the Bridge.' He suggested that James and I got together and wrote it, and this we did. I took it to the music publisher, Kassner, who had recently bought a couple of songs that Robb and I had written. He liked it and 'Across the Bridge' was published as sheet music with the film's poster on its cover, and shortly afterwards Vera Lynn recorded it.

That Christmas Pat Kirkwood did a pantomime season at Brighton and from all accounts her 'principal boy' was a knock out! Then early on in 1958 I heard a familiar voice on the telephone. It was Harry Foster to say that he thought he might have found another producer for 'Chrysanthemum' (I wanted to say I hoped this one would be younger and fitter than the last). Sandor Gorlinsky had for some years been a very successful entrepreneur, bringing to London internationally famous singers and musicians to perform in concert at venues such as the Albert and Festival Halls. He had also been Maria Callas' manager. Of recent times he had broadened his professional interests to include the musical theatre and already had two former Broadway hits running in the West End: 'Plain And Fancy' at Drury Lane and 'Bells Are Ringing' at the Coliseum. Keen to add the glamorous Miss Kirkwood to his list of leading ladies he had read the script Harry Foster had sent him, probably found it a bit bewildering but all the same wished to hear the score and meet the beautiful and talented lady who would be the star of the show.

So Hubert and Pat would attend the audition, and if she felt it appropriate at the time Pat might even sing a couple of the songs from the show. The question was where was this to take place? Hubert thought that Robb's dank Pimlico basement was not the ideal setting for his lovely wife to be seen by the impresario, although he didn't say so in exactly those words. I suggested we hired one of the Dineley Studios, where the final rehearsals of the New Lindsey production had taken place, and the idea was generally accepted. However, a couple of days before the afternoon of the audition Hubert rang to say he thought that the Dineley Studios were too cold and impersonal and he had a better idea. A close friend of his was the theatre producer Peter Saunders, who had made his pile producing Agatha Christie's plays, including the long running, 'The Mouse Trap', of which, incidentally, Hubert was the original director. Saunders and his beautiful wife, Katie Boyle, had a house in the country, also a charming flat in Bayswater that they would not be using for a few days and he suggested that we might borrow it for the afternoon. I agreed with Hubert that a comfortable armchair in a warm drawing room would be preferable to a hard bentwood chair in a draughty studio. Another advantage was that one could offer him tea and cake or whatever (I doubted he would be asking for dandelion tea). Yes, Hubert was right, it was certainly a more agreeable setting for the job in hand. Then, just my luck, fate chose that very time to lay me low with flu: I had a fever, my lungs were congested, my nose ran, my eyes watered and I hardly had any voice. I really should have been in bed but I couldn't possibly trust Robb with his vagueness to handle it all on his own. And anyway, I definitely wanted to be there, so, full of the drugs Patrick had given me to contain the worst of the symptoms for a short while, I took a taxi across the park to Bayswater. Pat and Hubert were already there, he busily arranging the seating. Harry Foster was the next to appear, and just a minute before Gorlinsky arrived Robb strolled in casually carrying an old crumpled plastic carrier bag with the score in it. I was only grateful that he hadn't left it on a bus.

I tried hard to conceal my sickly condition and, considering how terminally ill I was feeling, I think I managed it rather well. Gorlinsky was an easier audience than Jack Waller had been, not that he gave much away, but I sensed he was quite enjoying what he heard, and when Pat rose to the occasion and sang three of the songs, 'Love Is A Game', 'No More Love Songs' and 'Saturday Night', giving them all she had, I saw his eyes light up with delight and I thought, 'with luck we're in.' When we had finished he said almost immediately, "Yes, let's do it!" All things considered he thought rehearsals could possibly start at the beginning of July. The feeling of relief that swept through me was immense. And just then, as if by magic, Peter Saunders appeared from the kitchen with a bottle of champagne. The atmosphere became euphoric and I completely forgot that earlier in the day I actually thought I was dying.

A few weeks later, it seemed much longer, when the costing of the production had been completed and I imagine the stars' salaries satisfactorily negotiated, Robb, Robin and I were summoned to Gorlinsky's office to sign our contract with him. Not long afterwards he invited us back for a meeting with his production manager Billy Jay and Pat and Hubert to decide upon a director for the show. The choice of choreographer, designers, orchestraters, etc, could come later. Gorlinsky said very little during the meeting. I had a feeling that his knowledge of the theatre world was not as acute as that of the concert world; he seemed to rely very much on what his production manager said. Billy Jay had been in the theatre business, one way and another, all of his life, which probably explained his permanent expression of weary cynicism. He came up with the names of three directors he knew who were available and he thought were eminently suitable. Our reaction was less than enthusiastic. The work of theirs that I had seen had not impressed me at all. I found it pedestrian and lacking in the imagination, style and wit that our show needed. I thought I saw a slight snigger hover over Billy's lips. "Oh, Christ," I saw him thinking, "we've got another bunch of precious ones here." A few more names were suggested, then someone said, "What about Vida Hope?" and we all perked up. Vida had done a magnificent job on Sandy Wilson's 'The Boy Friend'. It had been a phenomenal success with both critics and audiences and if she could do something similar for us we would be more than satisfied. Gorlinsky told Billy to check her availability. A couple more names were mentioned but none of them, I thought, would do it as well as Vida.

Robb and I knew her slightly. She had been down to his flat to hear some of our numbers when she was directing 'The Punch Revue' and was looking for some special additional material. She liked our stuff very much but it was not what she needed right then. As soon as I got home I rang her. I told her about Gorlinsky and asked if she was free, and if so would she be at all interested in hearing the show? She said she was and would, so the very next day Robb and I went up to her beautiful new house in Hampstead and played it to her. She loved it. It was very much her sort of humour and she found Robb's tunes both clever and catchy. She said there were things to consider but all in all she definitely was interested. As Robb and I rode back from Hampstead on the tube that day our spirits were high and our hearts full of Hope.

A couple of days later Vida had a meeting with Gorlinsky and, according to Billy Jay, it went extremely well. The next day she met Pat and Hubert and that did not go well at all. That evening she rang me to say that it was nothing to do with the show, she thought it was great, and otherwise she would have loved to do it but she could not possibly work with the Greggs. At the meeting Hubert had disagreed with practically all her suggestions. Being a director himself he had very definite ideas about everything. She felt that they knew exactly what they were going to do with their parts and would brook no outside interference. What they really wanted was a tame director who would look after the rest of the show and leave them to their own devices, and that Vida would not do. The final nail in the coffin came when, having told her that in the pantomime Pat had done in Brighton she had stopped the show every night with her Dixieland Medley, he asked her to find somewhere late in the second half where she could do something similar. Vida was absolutely appalled and at that point completely gave up. She said how sorry she was that we wouldn't be working together and wished us "all the luck in the world." I had a feeling that she would like to have added, "and working with Hubert you are going to need it."

Putting the phone down I felt terribly depressed. I had set my heart on Vida doing the show. There was one consolation however, we hadn't lost, 'The Fire Brigade'. She had found this number extraneous and was keen for it to go. She thought coming so close to the end it held up the plot and destroyed the tension created by the fire. It was strange she couldn't see that this was the joke of it. We leave our two pairs of lovers locked in an upstairs room full of smoke, with flames licking at their feet, and immediately go to the fire station where, with the fire bell ringing, Keystone type firemen in long johns come sliding down the pole and slowly dress as they sing in a proud and happy way about their work. As one boasts, "I cannot count the ladies who have leapt into my sheets." At the end of each chorus, and there are five of them, they leap onto the fire engine as if to depart, then leap off again and tell us, "But just before we go we'd like to say..." When, after the final chorus, the fire engine, its bell clanging, did actually speed away there was often a cheer from the audience. At every performance this was the number that got the most laughter and applause, and it gave a lift to the comic rescue scene that followed that I am sure would not have been there without it. Yes, Vida was definitely wrong there, and as I said to Robb when I rang him with the news, it was sad to lose her but at least we still had 'The Fire Brigade'.

There was something else happening at this very time that we knew nothing about until later. Theatre producer, Michael Codron asked Vida to direct Sandy Wilson's new show which was a musical adaptation of Ronald Firbank's high camp novel, 'Valmouth'. It was far more audacious than 'Chrysanthemum' and I could see why it would appeal to Vida with her sense of adventure and daring. Daring it certainly was with its motley of outrageous grotesques: a self flagellating religiosa who wears holy leaves under her nether garments and pursues young girls, an ancient nymphomaniac who delights in deflowering virgin shepherd boys in the garden chapel, a negress masseuse of dubious practices, a gay sailor, an hysterical nun and even a camp Roman Catholic cardinal who has christened a dog in a cathedral. I could understand why Vida was fascinated by it. It would be a very difficult show to pull off but what a challenge. And Vida certainly rose to it, extracting great performances from everyone, especially Fenella Fielding as the ancient nymphomaniac. As deserved, both she and the show received great critical acclaim. Unfortunately, apart from the cognoscenti who packed the theatre for the first few weeks it was not a commercial success and Michael Codron lost a great deal of money on it, forcing him to relinquish his tenancy of the Lyric Theatre Hammersmith. After that he swore never to produce another musical and kept to his word.

It is not sour grapes my reporting this. I loved 'Valmouth', saw it several times, admired Sandy's witty songs and wished for it to succeed, but by its very nature it would only appeal to a specialised audience. Back in 1958 musical comedy goers were not prepared for anything quite so queer. Like Ronald Firbank's novel, Sandy Wilson's musical was way ahead of its time.

I have often wondered if 'Valmouth' hadn't come along at that precise moment whether Vida might have been a little more prepared to cope with Hubert's vagaries. We shall never know. We cannot ask her now for just a few years later she was killed in a terrible car accident.

Eleanor Fazan was to be our director and we were lucky to get her, she was very much the directorial flavour of the year, having two successful shows running in the West End: 'Grab Me A Gondola', a musical starring Joan Heal, and 'Share My Lettuce', a revue starring Kenneth Williams and Maggie Smith. Eleanor – no one ever called her that – was affectionately known as Fiz, a name that somehow suited her although it really shouldn't have for there was nothing remotely fizzy about her, personality. Laid back would be a more apt description. Her movements were graceful and unhurried, her speech soft and slow, and one never knew what she was thinking because of the dark sunglasses she always wore. Even in a dark theatre lit by a single working light she kept them on. I sometimes wondered if it was less affectation than to hide a vulnerability that her eyes might betray. Also they allowed her time, free from scrutiny, to decide how to answer a difficult question. Dealing with Hubert she was going to be glad of those dark glasses.

At that time she was married to Stanley Myers, a struggling revue pianist and composer whom I had worked with several times on fringe shows. He was yet to become one of the country's most famous composers of film scores – I suppose his most memorable score being 'The Deer Hunter' with its wonderfully haunting, 'Cavatina'. He and Fiz then lived in a flat just off Eaton Square and had a small son.

I don't think Fiz ever really understood the humour of 'Chrysanthemum'. There were things in it that made no sense to her very logical mind. She once said to me, "Why, after being gone for three years, does she bring home the can of milk? She can't possibly imagine that her father will think she has just been down to the dairy and back?" I had to agree with her that it was preposterous for her to expect to get away with it, but it was the very preposterousness of it and the sheer nerve on her part that made it funny, and audiences did find it funny – only Fiz remained fazed. However, I was delighted that she liked 'The Fire Brigade' and understood how vital the number was to the end of the show. So that was a blessed relief.

Disley Jones had designed the imaginative décor for, 'Share My Lettuce'. Working together he and Fiz had become good friends and he was able to help her in various ways with the production, so it was at her request that Gorlinsky asked him to do the sets and lighting for the show. She knew he was right for the job, she also felt the need of a close ally on this, only her third production and by far the biggest and most difficult one. It was good to know that when technical problems arose, as they invariably do, Disley would be there to hold her hand. 'Grab Me A Gondola' was the first show she ever directed, which began at the Theatre Royal, Windsor. It was a small musical and she was engaged merely to choreograph the numbers. John Council, who ran the theatre and was going to direct the show, was so impressed with her work that he handed over the entire production to her. It was a great success and transferred to the Lyric Theatre, Shaftsbury Avenue, where it enjoyed a long run. Fiz's name as a director was made. Michael Codron then asked her to direct, 'Share My Lettuce' at the Lyric Theatre, Hammersmith, and there she was lucky to meet Disley, extra lucky that Bamber Gascoyne had written such a brilliant, quirky revue, and extra extra lucky to have it performed by Maggie Smith and Kenneth Williams.

Another Brighton anecdote: on its two week try out there before opening in London the audience some nights booed the show and walked out in their droves. In a panic Michael Codron rang me up, as he must have done several others, to ask if I had any material he might be able to use to salvage the show. He drove around to the flat (his home was nearby in Chelsea) and took away some sketches and lyrics. Very wisely, and no doubt at Bamber Gascoyne's firm insistence, they kept their heads and the show opened without any changes being made. It was a critical triumph and after playing to full houses in Hammersmith transferred to the Comedy Theatre, which once again explodes the myth that Brighton is London by the sea.

Eleanor Fazan was now a name to be reckoned with. Everyone wanted her for their show and it was our good fortune that she chose us. But despite her fame she was still quite a novice at the job and therefore extremely vulnerable (hence the dark glasses?) so it must have been comforting to know that Disley would be close at hand.

Fiz's good fortune had come about through a stroke of luck, as mine had done, and so many others. I believe that, apart from the great and the nearly great, there are as many talented people who don't get the breaks as the lucky ones who do. Dame Edith Evans once said to an ASM who wished her luck on a first night, "With some of us it isn't luck." But she still had her flops. When on the first night of Robert Bolt's, 'Gentle Jack' at the Queens Theatre the audience started booing she asked Kenneth Williams, who was standing beside her in the line up, "What is that sound?" and he is said to have replied, "The bird, you silly cow." The good Dame may not have needed luck nearly as much as the rest of us, but then that in a way was her good luck.

To choreograph the 'Limehouse Ballet' and stage the musical numbers Gorlinsky engaged Alfred Roderigues – known to his friends and colleagues as Rod. I don't know who suggested him, it was probably Fiz, coming from the ballet world as they both did; but I had known him longer than anyone in London, since childhood, in fact, when we both appeared in children's charity concerts in Cape Town: I reciting or tap dancing or doing my Mae West, he dancing with the Dulcie Howes school of ballet of which he was a star pupil. He was a few years older than me so we were not well acquainted then. Maurice was in some of the shows and I can remember his mother (the Welsh witch) saying to some of the other stage mothers how disgusting it was to see the boy ballet dancers wearing tights. That her son was got up as Betty Boop and I as Mae West she found perfectly acceptable.

Like me Rod joined the Entertainment Unit in Pretoria and like me, he toured the Middle East. The show he was in was called, 'The Amuseliers'. Back in Pretoria he became a production assistant to Frank Rogaly, and with Sid James put together some stylish little shows. He did all our musical numbers for 'The Boomerangs'. He also arrived in London in 1946, a few months after me, and was accepted into the Sadler's Wells Ballet that had recently taken up residence at the Royal Opera House, Covent Garden (in 1956 the company would change its name to The Royal Ballet). Nanette de Valois thought Rod showed creative talent and let him choreograph some ballets for the company, the most popular being, 'Blood Wedding' with music by Dennis Apivor. He married Julia Faron, one of the leading dancers of the company, and they had a son. Rod left the Royal Ballet to go freelance and choreographed and directed operas and revues, mostly on the continent. A London revue he directed that I particularly admired was 'Airs on a Shoestring' at the Royal Court Theatre. After 'Chrysanthemum' we would work together a couple more times on West End revues. Then we lost contact and a few years later I read that he had died. It is sad but true that nowadays I have very few friends and colleagues from my salad days who are not on that great long Equity List in the sky.

Bumble Dawson would have designed the costumes for 'Chrysanthemum' better than anyone I could think of. She had style and wit and a remarkable flair for period costume as witnessed in the films: 'Trottie True', 'The Importance Of Being Ernest', and more recently, 'The Prince and the Showgirl' (set in 1911, two years before Chrysanthemum'). For the stage scenes in this film she had designed costumes of great originality and wit, and if she could do something similar for us I felt we would be half way there. I asked her if she would consider doing a stage musical and she said she would, so I took Fiz and Rod around to her flat in Eccleston Square to see her work and they were duly impressed. A meeting with Gorlinsky took place. What transpired at it I wasn't told but Bumble's name was not mentioned again. I felt too embarrassed to ask her what had happened. I imagine that her fee and the budget she would require to do the job to her satisfaction far exceeded what Gorlinsky was prepared to pay; and as she was always in demand for films there was no reason why she should do a stage show on the cheap and perhaps tarnish her high reputation.

Meanwhile Pat was busy pushing a designer of her own personal preference. Doris Zinkeisen had been an established artist and stage designer since the 1920s. She was most famous for her portraits, paintings of horses and murals of Regency scenes. Her stage work that I had seen (mostly in illustration) was tasteful, gentle and lyrical, her colours soft and muted – not at all right for 'Chrysanthemum', I thought, but Pat asked Gorlinsky to check her availability. Whether she wasn't free, didn't want to do it or was too expensive we were never told but like Bumble her name was never again mentioned.

From the very start I would have been happy to have Hilary Virgo and Rosemary Carvill, who designed the costumes for the New Lindsey production. What they did on a shoestring was remarkable and with a bit of money to spend they could have done wonders. But Pat and Hubert didn't like their costumes, or, to be precise, they didn't like their costumes for Chrysanthemum. Valerie Tandy made her first entrance in a Poiret inspired hobble skirt of vivid fuchsia with orange hat and shoes, a sable stole and muff (fake), strings of pearls and masses of diamonds (ditto). Pat had no intention of coming on looking like an outré Paris dressed vamp. Her legion of loyal fans would not expect it of 'our Pat' with her warm, blunt, down to earth naturalness. She might wear a jewel or two and sport a slightly flirtatious hat but that was as far as she was prepared to go. As for any sultry, sexual innuendo, forget it, she wasn't known as the patron saint of principal boys for nothing. I didn't realize then – perhaps I should have – there had been enough clues – that it was going to be 'The Pat & Hubert Show' and what it was about could be decided later.

I was beginning to wonder if ours might be the first musical to open without costumes (this would have predated 'Oh! Calcutta!' by twenty two years), when Rod came up with the name of a young designer who had done some clever work for the Royal Ballet. His name was Michael Baldwin, he happened to be available, wanted the job and his fee was not going to give Gorlinsky a heart attack. He did some sketches for us that we liked and after several goes at Pat's costumes she seemed to be satisfied, so Michael Baldwin became our costume designer.

Two or three different people orchestrated the score. I have no idea who they were. I never met them and their names didn't appear on any programme. Roy Lowe was our musical director. He was a charming man, talented and most conscientious. He himself did some extra work on the score to make it sound how he wanted it to, and it was most effective.

And then it was time to start auditioning.

———w———

Fiz and Rod refused to see any of the cast from the New Lindsey production. They said they wanted to start completely fresh and didn't want anyone with preconceived ideas. In a way I understood but felt it was unfair on the actors who had excelled in their parts. Three or four of them I thought could not be bettered but it gave me no pleasure to be proved right. Two of the original cast did make it but only because Pat and Hubert insisted on having them. They were Richard Curnoch (a superb Uncle Fred. Until he was dewigged no one ever realized he was also Ma Carroty) and Patricia Moore (a petite, fey little Mary Anne who was going to be no competition for our dazzling Pat).

Open auditions and the recalls that followed took place on the stage of the Coliseum where Gorlinsky's production of, 'Bells Are Ringing' was still playing. On their matinee days we used the Piccadilly or Duke of York's theatres and a great many people were seen. Having spent most of my life as an auditionee I knew exactly how nervous they were feeling, and for some how desperately they needed the job; so sitting in the stalls, part of a team able to nod or shake their heads Nero-like, was a power that, unlike some I have worked with, I didn't relish at all. I wish there was an easier, less cruel way to cast a show but in all fairness there isn't. As long as there is theatre there will always be nerve wracking auditions.

Roger Gage was cast as Bob. He sang nowhere as well as Donald Scott who had played the part at the New Lindsey, but whereas Donald was a fine singer who could act, Roger was a fine actor who could sing. There is a difference. You pays your money and takes your choice, as the saying goes, and Roger looked every inch the handsome young salty sea captain. He was married to the actress Joan Plowright who had been a big hit at the Royal Court in Arnold Wesker's, 'Roots'. What we didn't know then was that their marriage was on the rocks due to the affair she had started with Laurence Olivier, which would culminate in two divorces and her becoming the next Lady Olivier. Roger never gave us an inkling that anything was amiss, but thinking back I can remember being slightly puzzled by the evasive way he answered when asked when Joan was coming to see the show. Only when Vivien Leigh's name hit the newspapers did the cat leap out of the bag. To have the great grandee of British Theatre walk off with your wife must have been a most painful and humiliating experience for a young actor at the start of his career, but stoically he never let it show.

With the casting complete and the scenery and costumes in hand we now had a brief breathing spell during which Pat and Hubert flew off to their house in the Algave to rest up and prepare themselves for the heavy grind ahead. Hubert loved Portugal and he seemed to have rather a soft spot for Salazar. I think he would have quite liked to have been a dictator himself – I suppose in his own humble way he was.

As planned rehearsals began at the beginning of July and took place at the Coliseum where 'Bells Are Ringing' was struggling through its final weeks. On the first day we had a read through with the entire company on stage. The principals sat on a row of chairs in the centre, flanked either side by the supporting cast and chorus, and downstage at a table facing them sat Fiz, Rod and Gerry Phillips, our stage manager, scripts open, pencils and paper at the ready. Robin had taken the morning off work to be there and he, Robb and I sat in the third row waiting nervously to hear what this new lot were going to do to our baby.

The first scene read well and Chrysanthemum's entrance got a good laugh from the chorus, who hadn't seen a script and probably until then didn't know what the show was about. In the first Greenwich Park scene John was starting his warning to Mary Anne when Hubert suddenly stopped reading, got up, went down to the table and whispered something to Fiz. After he had returned to his seat but had not resumed reading, Fiz turned to us and although her expression was concealed by the dark glasses her voice sounded a little strained. "I wonder," she said, "if you'd mind going and sitting a bit further back. Your closeness is making certain members of the cast feel nervous." We didn't need Miss Marple to tell us who the certain members of the cast were. Feeling like three contagious lepers, with everyone staring at us, we slunk out of Row C. and went and sat about twelve rows back. Hubert would have liked us not to be there at all, but we had it in our contract that we could attend all rehearsals and I decided then and there that's what I would do. Over the years I had had enough of my material messed about by smart Alecs who thought they knew better than I did what I was trying to say, and I had a feeling that we might have another smart Alec here.

On the second day of rehearsal, while Rod was working with the dancers in a studio somewhere, Fiz was suddenly faced with a very difficult decision. She was setting the first Greenwich Park scene and had explained to all concerned that the entrance to the park was OP (stage right). Ma Carroty had scuttled across in her wheel-chair, Chrysanthemum had followed her, Bob had entered with a nautical gait and it was now time for John, Mary Anne, her maid, Emily and the chauffeur to come on (Gorlinsky had promised them a vintage motor car for their entrance but like much that Golinsky promised it never materialised, so they would just have to walk on like everyone else). On the four came from the Prompt Side (stage left) and John was about to speak when Fiz, from the front of the stalls, interrupted him. "Excuse me, Hubert," she said, "but the park entrance is OP." There was a longish pause and then in a fairly firm voice he replied, "I'd rather come on this side." Now there was an even longer pause while she had to decide what to do. Having decided she said in a slightly flat tone, "All right." Then clapping her hands she called, "Listen, everyone, the entrance to the park is now Prompt Side." I knew then that she had given up on Hubert and in future whatever he wished to do with his part would be all right with her.

Compared to Hubert, Pat was Saint Theresa of the roses. Though equally strong willed she never threw her weight around. She knew what she wanted, was determined to get it and went about achieving her aim in the most charming way possible. Everyone loved Pat and she was sweet to everyone. Her idea of Chrysanthemum was not mine and I knew it never would be, but she had that thing called star appeal and everything she did was eminently watchable. Hearing her belt out our numbers made me tingle all over. She is the only British performer I can think of who possessed that vibrant, gutsy quality one associates with American singers such as Ethel Merman or Mary Martin.

Hubert's interpretation of John would also differ slightly from our original conception. He had played Professor Higgins on the Classics Club's LP recording of 'My Fair Lady' and it had left an indelible mark on his psyche. John would now take on many of the professor's characteristics and mannerisms and naturally some of the lines had to be changed to suit this new persona. In the verse to, 'Love is a Game' the original John sang:

"I am seldom out of debt,
My horse loses when I bet,
I must be the most unlucky kind of gambler you have met,
And yet,
They say love is a game..." etc.

For the new John we changed these lines to:

"I have never known regret
Through a squalid gambling debt,
I must be the most unsportive sort of man you can have met,
And yet,
They say love is a game..." etc.

A couple of weeks into rehearsals the hair saga began: Hubert and Pat thought that as both Chrysanthemum and Mary Anne were brunettes Mary Anne ought to be blonde, so little Patricia Moore was taken off to the hairdressers and had her hair lightened. A week or so later Pat suddenly turned up with bright golden hair (she now saw Chrysanthemum as blonde). We were back to where we started, only now instead of two brunettes we had two blondes, so little Patricia was taken back to the hairdressers to have her hair restored to its natural colour. Then blow me if Pat didn't turn up two days later a brunette once more (she didn't feel being blonde suited her), and poor little Patricia, now almost screaming and kicking, was dragged back to the hairdressers and re-blonded. Why no one thought of wigs I cannot imagine.

Rod was getting on well with the musical numbers. He had chosen his dancers very carefully. Some of them he had worked with before so he knew their individual talents. One of these was Burda Cann, a tall, slender girl with incredibly long legs who would take the leading role in the 'Limehouse Ballet' (we had to forgo this item at the New Lindsey owing to lack of space and shortage of dancers). The ballet had a slight feel of 'Slaughter On 10th Avenue' about it. It was raunchy, sinister and funny:

'It's just a typical evening in old Chinatown: opium smoking Chinamen, sailors, tarts, pimps, thugs; a sinister looking toff in top hat and cloak and a prim social worker are going about their usual activities. Burda Cann was the social worker who, foolishly having accepted a puff of Ching Loo's opium pipe, becomes wildly abandoned, throws away her bonnet and skirt and starts high kicking like a can-can dancer. This frenetic mood catches on and we are very nearly into a full blown orgy when a brawl breaks out. Joining in, our now not so prim social worker with flailing fists and kicking high buttoned boots succeeds in knocking out the entire assembly. Utterly exhausted, she then collapses on top of the heap. Chrysanthemum, disguised as a Chinese coolie, scurrying across to rescue Mary Anne, stops for a second to take in this scene of human debris, then stepping lightly over the bodies she says with a shrug, "That's Limehouse all over!"'

The first time I heard Pat rehearse the song I knew she was not at ease with it, and was it not an integral part of the show I am sure she would have asked for it to be cut. This was Chrysanthemum's first solo, her big brazen song of defiance, 'Sinner Me!' It was the first song that we wrote for the show. Robb already had the melody, a jazzy, slightly raunchy tune in which the last three notes of the eight bar phrases seemed to cry out for the words, 'Sinner Me!' The lyric was heavily influenced by my childhood heroine Mae West's guilt free attitude to sex – an attitude I had adopted as my own. Hubert and Pat were worried that her loyal fans would not appreciate hearing 'our Pat' sing such an open paean to sexual emancipation, so if the number could not be cut they could at least do the next best thing and dilute its content. Some of the more audacious lines (well, lines that implied that she had had a good time) we agreed to change. For instance in the original lyric the middle eight section went as follows:

'I have kissed one or two –
Maybe three – well, a few.
Thanks to Eleanor Glynne
You can count me in
On your tiger skin.'

To appease Hubert and Pat we altered it to:

'I have danced with a few
But believe me it's true
Reading Eleanor Glynne
On a tiger skin
Was my biggest sin.'

What slightly provocative lines remained and could not be altered without totally destroying the song and most of the plot Pat decided to guy and send up with sly little looks and the raising of her eyebrows to let the audience know she wasn't really the sinner she was claiming to be but just that loveable Northern lass, Pat, larking about a bit. I found this most depressing, because I knew she had what it took to put the number over better than anyone I could think of if only she had the nerve, and hubby, Hubert wasn't insisting that she remained the perfect lady throughout. So what should have been a bold, brassy ballad became an anaemic point number, and where Valerie Tandy, camping it up for all it was worth, got big gusty laughs, Pat got amused little giggles. It was very sad.

A critic in one of the towns we played on our pre-London tour thought that Pat Kirkwood was quite wonderful. In technique and know how she was a complete professional, but one of her songs, all about sin, was sadly out of character and might be more suitable for Eartha Kitt. Yes, I thought, Eartha Kitt would be my ideal Chrysanthemum. Captain Brown could have spent some time in the West Indies, married a local girl who died giving birth to a beautiful baby daughter who he brought home to England and christened, Chrysanthemum. And why not? The show was a spoof after all, not a musical adaptation of, 'Pride & Prejudice'.

Hubert's prudishness concerning his wife would surface again later. During the dress rehearsal a wonderful action photograph was taken of Pat doing her cod striptease number, 'Shanghai Lil.' In it she appeared to be wearing just sequins and feathers and her luscious long 'principal boy' legs were very much in evidence. Gorlinsky seeing the box office value of this eye catching photograph, had it blown up to life size and displayed in a prominent position outside the theatre until Hubert demanded that it be removed. He wasn't going to have just anyone in the street ogling his lady wife's legs.

Another example of his primness would cause much merriment in the company. At one of the theatres in which we played there happened to be a street market with stalls and barrows right outside the windows of the ground floor dressing rooms and this was where the star dressing room was situated. Come matinee day and the market in full swing one of the windows opened and a man with a painted face poked his head out and addressed the stall holders thus: "Excuse me, but would you mind watching your language, there is a lady in one of these dressing rooms." You can imagine the sort of replies he got. Enraged, he rang for the police. Two coppers arrived and upon investigation discovered it was all they could do to keep a straight face. They informed Hubert that it was not in their jurisdiction to monitor the common jargon of street vendors and suggested that the lady changed dressing rooms. The lady had no intention of quitting the star dressing room. The lady may also have been wearing a slight Giaconda smile for she had been on the stage since childhood and would certainly have encountered her full share of coarse mouthed Variety comics. She can't have heard any words that afternoon that she had not heard many times before. A few of them she may even have used herself – but not in front of Hubert it seems. That little incident with the police kept the company in a state of hilarity all through the matinee.

If I am giving the impression that I didn't like Hubert very much all I can say is, where I was concerned he didn't make himself very likeable, and the situation would worsen.

Six hectic weeks of rehearsal went by in a flash, and it was now time for our toddler to try its legs, go out on an eight week tour of the provinces and then, sure of its step, come Turkey Trotting into town to great acclaim and glory – well, that was the general idea, anyway. We would open at The Opera House, Manchester, Pat's home town. This was no mere coincidence, it had been carefully calculated. Mancunians were very proud of their illustrious daughter, star of British stage and screen – she had even starred with Van Johnson in an MGM film in Hollywood! But despite her fame she had never forgotten her roots and on returning home with a new show was always assured of a warm welcome. So the advance booking at the box office was good.

The company would travel up to Manchester on the Saturday, the 'get in' would take place during the night, there would be a lighting rehearsal on Sunday morning, a band call in the afternoon, a full dress rehearsal in the evening (maybe lasting all night), and the show would open to the public and critics on Monday, 8th September, at 7 pm.

On the Friday morning prior to leaving London we had a run through with some of the costumes and full orchestra at The Duke of York's Theatre and I asked Fiz if Denis could attend. I desperately needed his opinion. I was too close to it now to be able to tell what it was like. Fiz had met Denis, liked him and, perhaps thinking his opinion might be of some value, she agreed. This was in spite of Hubert's edict that no one who was not connected with the show should come to a rehearsal. As could be predicted the moment he saw Denis sitting beside me he hurried over to Fiz who was discussing something with Jerry Phillips and demanded to know what that stranger was doing in the stalls. Standing her ground and looking him straight in the eye (as much as one could tell with those dark glasses) she told him quietly but firmly that she, the director, had invited him, and without further explanation continued her discussion with Jerry. Hubert gave a little 'humph' and strode away looking very cross. He would have looked even crosser had he known that the stranger in the stalls was the very person who had rewritten a lot of the dialogue for his (Hubert's) film adaptation of 'Three Men in a Boat' that Ken Annakin had directed the year before, starring Laurence Harvey, Jimmy Edwards and David Tomlinson.

The run through began and Rod's excellent Ragtime opening routine with the full chorus as guests at the *thé dansant* got the show off to a good start. Raymond Newell, a famous leading man in musical comedy of his day, made a fine old Captain Brown and his four aptly named daughters were suitably impressive. Denis sat still and relaxed and I sensed that he was quite enjoying it, as I was; until, 'Sinner Me!', when I felt him tensing up and heard a sharp little intake of breath. Then whispering to me he asked, "What is she doing? Why is she playing it like a principal boy?"

"That's how they see it," I whispered back. "She won't play sexy."

"Can't Fiz do something?" he asked.

"No," I said, "they are a law unto themselves. It's the Pat & Hubert Show, take it or leave it."

He said nothing more and as the show ended he slipped quietly out. We had arranged to meet at the Salisbury, a pub a few hundred yards up the street from the theatre, where in those days at lunch time the clientele was almost entirely theatrical. When I got there he was sitting at a table and there was a large gin and tonic waiting for me. He said nothing. After taking a couple of sips I asked, "Well?"

"It's a bit like Aladin meets Professor Higgins," he said.

I knew what he meant, the piece had taken on quite a Christmas Pantomime feel (an essence of it was probably always there and could have been what attracted Pat to it in the first place). 'Chrysanthemum' had become a big brash show with a Ragtime orchestra and exciting dancing; so much grander than the little New Lindsey production; what I found lacking was the sly humour and subtle charm of the original – but then I suppose with a show of its size the loss was inevitable.

I was not just being facetious when I called it the Pat & Hubert Show. With the building up of his part all the others, apart from her's, had definitely dwindled, and when neither of them was on stage not a lot seemed to happen. Lavender and her boyfriend, Willie, had a comedy duet that at the New Lindsey always went down a treat; the day before our Friday run through it was cut on the grounds that it held up the plot, which upset the young couple terribly – it was their one chance to shine in the show; it also came too close to Hubert's dramatic solo, 'Which Way?' of which, having such a light tenor singing voice, he was very nervous and tried to speak as much of it as he could. The youngsters with their snappy little number would certainly have got more applause.

Not since Cyril Richard and Madge Elliot had there been a famous husband and wife team on the London musical stage (I saw them doing, 'The Merry Widow' in Bari, Italy in early 1944. See page 71). Hubert and Pat, I had a feeling, were now ready to take on the mantle. She was less anxious than he, being already a bone fide star of the genre; but this was his first starring role in a musical and he was determined that both he and their stage partnership should succeed – over everyone else's dead body if necessary. So there was nothing that any of us could do now except wait to see what the critics and public made of this brand new British husband and wife team being so lavishly displayed before them. Would the Greggs be the Lunts of the musical stage? In his mind I imagine Hubert already thought they were.

On Saturday morning Robb, Robin and I joined the company train call at Euston Station. It was in our contract that we would always have first class travel and hotel accommodation so we were somewhat surprised when our train tickets had '3rd Class' printed on them. Travelling third class was nothing new to me and I wouldn't have given it a second thought had it applied to everyone; but no, Fiz and Rod were up in first class with Pat and Hubert. I was cross. This was our first experience of Gorlinsky not keeping to his word – it would not be our last. Sitting in third with the young and eager members of the company was far more fun than sitting in first with the higher echelon would have been, especially now that they had all grown wary of me with my ever watchful eye, but it was the principal that mattered, and it rankled.

Robb went to stay with his elderly mother in Salford, a suburb of Manchester, where he grew up; Robin and I were accommodated in a perfectly adequate hotel not far from the theatre that catered mainly for the better class of travelling salesman; Fiz and Rod along with Pat and Hubert and the Gorlinsky enterage were at the Midland Hotel, the city's largest and grandest hostelry where the food was not up to much but nevertheless one had to wear a tie to enter the dining room. On one occasion the headwaiter loaned me one: it was a striped, slightly food stained regimental tie that had seen jollier days, and very silly I looked with it tied around my smart cashmere polo-neck sweater, still the dining room's reputation for proper attire, if not for proper food, had remained unbesmirched.

On Sunday morning after we had breakfasted together at the hotel, Robin and I strolled along to the Opera House, a large and very impressive building, where we were happy to see our names on the posters out front. They were even spelt correctly. Gorlinsky wasn't all bad. Going inside we found the stage a hive of activity: carpenters and stage hands were busy with scenery; electricians arranging lights; the wardrobe mistress and her assistants unpacking and ironing costumes. It looked like utter chaos but actually everything was running quite smoothly, and although the lighting rehearsal was going to be delayed a little it would, sooner than one might think, take place.

Then someone broke the dreadful news that Pat Kirkwood was ill in bed and a doctor had been summoned. She was thought to be suffering from laryngitis and possibly would not be able to appear at Monday's performance. This was catastrophic. Without Pat there was no show. She was its whole *raison d'etre*, and even if there had been an understudy rehearsed in the part, which at that stage there had not, she could not possibly have taken Pat's place on that particular opening night in Manchester, the house packed with devoted fans. The idea was unthinkable. All performances would have to be cancelled until the star was well enough to resume work. The lighting rehearsal went ahead as scheduled with an ASM standing in for Chrysanthemum. It was followed by the band call with them playing the music to her unsung songs. All day a heavy gloom hung over the company…until…late in the afternoon…there came the news that Pat's condition had improved and she was going to do the dress rehearsal that night. The feeling of relief was immense.

Everyone's eyes were on her when she arrived back stage, anxious to gauge what state of health she was in, and apart from looking a trifle wan – she was wearing no make up – I thought she seemed very much her normal self. During the dress rehearsal she held back a little, saving her voice and energy understandably for the first night, but otherwise she gave her usual high spirited performance. Dr. Footlights had performed another miracle and it was comforting to know we had a Chrysanthemum for our opening night. Even the grumpy, cynical old stage door keeper looked happy.

On Monday evening just after seven o'clock with the house packed to the rafters the orchestra struck up the overture. Robb, Robin and I stood at the back of the stalls our hearts in our mouths as the music finished and the curtain rose on Disley's beautiful garden setting to which the audience responded warmly. When Pat came on with the milk there was loud and prolonged applause and she had to wait for what seemed like ages before she was able to say her first line. She was in perfect voice that night and everything she did they absolutely adored – even 'Sinner Me'. Hubert too was very well received, as was the whole show; 'The Fire Brigade' was an absolute riot. But it was Pat's evening and at the end, holding hubby by the hand, she took curtain call after curtain call. Manchester's favourite daughter had made a triumphal return. And who would have thought that only the day before some were wondering if she would ever sing again.

Gorlinsky gave a first night party for the company at the Midland Hotel and everyone was in a great state of elation. Robb couldn't stay for it as he didn't want to miss his last bus back to Salford. No one was in any doubt that the audience had enjoyed the show; our concern now was what the critics had made of it.

I slept badly that night in restless anticipation and early the next morning Robin and I went out and bought all the papers; we took them back to the hotel and over cups of coffee read the reviews. There wasn't one dud amongst them. Even the most carping, 'The Manchester Guardian', that took Kenneth Tynan's line that it was a blithe mishmash of a musical headed the review: DAZZLING – AND CONFUSING It said: "'Chrysanthemum' is a dazzling and confusing mixture of satire, parody, humour, and sentimentality." And ended with: "In the end the plays inconsistencies were forgotten because it had more in it than ten ordinary musicals." Not bad for our worst review. But most of the notices were just out and out raves for Pat. The following are extracts from some of them:

FRESH, GAY, VITAL – PAT'S BACK

'Five Foot four of Manchester-bred vitality Pat Kirkwood made a rollicking return to Manchester theatre last night. She kept a world premiered musical aglow with a stylish exuberance which nearly produced an unplanned striptease (I don't know what the critic meant by this ???). Pat's stylish attack was splendidly right for this gay, mickey-taking frolic and she plays it up to the hilt, whether she's leaping from a blazing house, saucily losing her tail feathers in a Limehouse den, or going into a song and dance routine with bowler hat and cane… Pat gets solid support from husband Hubert Gregg in his first crack at a musical.'
Evening Chronicle.

PAT TRIUMPHS IN MERRY ROMP

'What a part for the vivacious, talented Pat Kirkwood. Those rounds of applause were not merely a welcome for an actress who had returned to her home town – they were an appreciation for an electrifying performance. And that applause included her husband, Hubert Gregg, making his first stage appearance with Pat and singing and dancing for the first time.'
News Chronicle.

'OUR PAT' DOES A STRIPTEASE

'I never expected to see Manchester born stage and TV star Pat Kirkwood do a striptease. But in this amusing show – world premiered last night – she sheds feather after feather until little more than the bare essentials are left. Pat has come back with her tongue firmly embedded in both cheeks.
And what a homecoming!
She has brought her husband Hubert Gregg with her. It is the first time they have co-starred in a stage show, and his first musical. He tackles it in the manner of Rex Harrison in 'My Fair Lady, saying rather than singing the numbers.
The show is part pantomime, part old-fashioned melodrama, entirely preposterous and the biggest leg pull since 'The Boy Friend.' Nothing is left to the imagination including her final leap from the upper story of a blazing opium den into the firemen's out-stretched sheet.'
Daily Express.

'KEYSTONE' COMEDY AND A STRIPTEASE

'Hardly ever subtle about anything she does, but always bubbling with good spirits and bursting with vitality – that's our Pat Kirkwood. Her personality could probably save a show half as good as this one – and this one happens to be very good indeed.
It is a delightful musical burlesque; in which the ingredients include crime in opium smoking Limehouse; suffragettes who chain themselves to railings; a gloriously funny fire brigade on 'Keystone Cop' lines; and fantastic white-slave traffic kidnappings.
Pat, one of the girls shipped to Buenos Aires who managed to get back, prances her gawky way through to her biggest hit of the night when she does a 'Shangghai Lil' strip act. ("I was born more or less on the Shanghai Express and I've moved at a pace ever since!").'
Daily Mail.

PAT AND HUSBAND STAR IN MUSICAL

'You don't often find a husband and wife starring in the same musical so it's nice to be able to say that Pat Kirkwood and Hubert Gregg have made a flying start with Chrysanthemum.

If it is true what Manchester thinks today London thinks tomorrow then Pat and Hubert have a West End hit. They deserve it.'
The Star.

CHRYSANTHEMUM

'It will be no surprise if Miss Kirkwood earns a considerable run. Few recent musicals have achieved as much laughter on the first night.'
Manchester Evening News.

PAT REVELS IN HER RIDICULOUS ROLE

'Preposterous? Of course – but the whole thing is most amusingly impossible. If you refuse to take it seriously you will enjoy it as much as I did. Behind me two women laughed until they cried.'
Melody Maker.

The whole week was a sell out and the audiences most appreciative. Despite my misgivings it seemed that Pat and Hubert had really pulled it off. Robin stayed for the Tuesday performance then returned to London and his work. Robb and I remained all week in case any changes were needed (not that I saw much of him. He only came in from Salford in time to see the show and then hurried off so as not to miss his bus). We then accompanied the show to Newcastle and stayed for three performances. As there seemed to be no problems and Fiz thought it was safe for us to go, we did. We would visit the show again after a couple of weeks when it had moved further south. I am sure Hubert was glad to see the back of me and perhaps even Fiz was a little relieved. I had been very protective of our precious baby.

Business at the Theatre Royal, Newcastle was excellent as so were the notices: paeans to Pat and praise for the show similar to that of the Manchester critics.

The *Newcastle Journal* wrote:
'If it is true that there is a little of Peter Pan in all of us, then "Chrysanthemum" will be a huge success. It is gay, colourful and not a little sentimental... Yes, there are many things to recommend in 'Chrysanthemum'."

The *Evening Chronicle* thought:

'The pace never slackens, with a musical score matching perfectly the colourful mood of the piece... Blending satire and sentiment 'Chrysanthemum' is a delightful romp.'

And *The Northern Echo* echoed:

'The star is undoubtedly the attractive Miss Kirkwood and, as she has done so often, she steals the show with her singing, gaiety and great sense of fun...Miss Kirkwood is well supported by her real-life husband Hubert Gregg and by Roger Gage, Patricia Moore, Raymond Newell, Richard Curnock and Nicholas Amer. All in all it is a good entertainment.'

Next stop Liverpool and again wonderful houses and wonderful notices. They even found space to say nice things about us.

The *Liverpool Evening Express* wrote:

'The rhythm and tempo of this really delightful production, with its tuneful numbers, comic ensembles and hilarious dancing, are something to marvel at as well as enjoy. A bouquet must certainly be handed to Neville Phillips and Robin Chancellor for the book and lyrics and Robb Stewart for the music.'

The *Liverpool Daily Post* said:

'The solos, duets and choruses composed by Robb Stewart are put over with that sprightly tunefulness they deserve. Whether satirical or romantic, they abound in lyrical merit and felicity of phrase. Authors Neville Phillips and Robin Chancellor have got right off the hackneyed track of rhyme. Apt illusion for once replaces the shop-soiled cliché of revue and musical comedy. It is a jolly, enjoyable show, full of unexpected touches and whimsies.'

We would catch up with the show again in Coventry where it again opened to marvellous notices.

The *Birmingham Post* wrote:

''Chrysanthemum' is a wonderful entertainment – gay, colourful, tuneful... Robb Stewart's music sets feet tapping in a variety of rhythms from ragtime to rumba... it swings along gaily, carrying plot with it and some quite outrageously witty lyrics by Neville Phillips and Robin Chancellor.'

The *Coventry Evening Telegraph* said:

> '...gay and exciting – a creation of many moods with happiness predominant. Neville Phillips and Robin Chancellor, who wrote the book and lyrics, have found room for some broad farce, gentle comedy and witty songs. There is variety too in Robb Stewart's music... Finally there is "The Fire Brigade" a burlesque with comic firemen which had us rocking in our seats.'

Odd man out was the critic of *The Birmingham Weekly Post*. We were indeed fortunate that his was not the only newspaper covering the show that week, for in his opinion:

> 'Its music by Robb Stewart has a lively lilting quality, but this does not compensate for the weakness of its lyrics, and the too, too naïve quality of its dialogue – by Neville Phillips and Robin Chancellor.
> Hubert Gregg is a delight in the role of John Blessington-Briggs and he is ably supported by Pat Kirkwood.' (I wonder what Miss Kirkwood thought of that!).

The day before our visit to Coventry I received in the post an article from a newspaper-cutting firm to which I subscribed. It was an interview that Hubert had given to a journalist while sitting in the stalls of the theatre, where he had been busy with pencil and paper rewriting the lyric of one of his wife's songs in the show. It was probably, 'Sinner Me!' Infuriated, I grabbed the telephone and sent him a telegram at the theatre (ah, what a wonderful thing the telegram was. I suppose an e-mail gets there quicker but I had far more faith in the telegraph service than I do today in my wayward computer). The telegram read: 'Do not change one word of the lyrics. If changes need to be made we will do them.' Next day, arriving backstage at the Coventry Theatre, the very first person I bumped into was Hubert who cut me dead and never spoke to me again for the rest of his life. Pat would continue to be charming and polite but being Mrs. Hubert Gregg she was not at liberty to be more than that. Although I had made an enemy for life, in the 1990s when Hubert had his own BBC radio programme, where he played his favourite gramophone records, he would occasionally include something from 'Chrysanthemum', mostly his own numbers, but he also, more than once, said flattering things about me as a lyric writer, which considering his dislike of me I thought was jolly decent of him.

The next port of call was Bristol and, just to prove it was also a hit there, here is what *The Bristol Evening World* had to say:

'What a pleasure it is to welcome Pat Kirkwood and Hubert Gregg to Bristol Hippodrome in that tuneful – BRITISH – note that word musical "Chrysanthemum". Pat Kirkwood herself is a delight. Gregg has a part that suits him splendidly and these two polished stars, backed by an enthusiastic company willing to sing and dance their hearts out, make this a refreshing entertainment...Bristolians who miss this show may feel like kicking themselves afterwards.'

And on to Cardiff, where the three of us caught up with the show again. It was depressing that Vivienne Grant, who was excellent as Lavender, the irrepressible youngest sister, was off that night with a bad throat and there was no understudy to take her place. Her lines were divided between her three sisters, but three girls instead of four slightly unbalanced their musical numbers. Still, that was not what depressed us the most. Five weeks on the road had taken its toll: the show looked tired. Spontaneity had given way to familiarity. I was reminded of one of those intricate mechanical toys that one winds up and sets in motion – it looks lovely but has no actual life of its own. I made some mental notes that I would give to Fiz and Rod when we dined together afterwards at the hotel (the only place serving food past ten o'clock), but they obviously had no desire to hear them, because when we got to the dining room they were already seated at a table for two in a corner where no one could join them. We were incensed. Having spent the entire day travelling down to South Wales to see if we could be of any practical help nobody even wanted to know what we thought. When we had finished our rather disgusting meal and were leaving the dining room I made a detour past their table. "By the way," I said, "whatever happened to that show called 'Chrysanthemum'?" and walked on without waiting for a reply. I now seemed to have antagonised everyone connected with the production. 'It may be just another job to them,' I thought, 'but it has taken a large chunk out of my life getting it as far as this.' More than Robin with his regular employment and Robb, fairly content in his eccentric existence, I desperately needed the show to succeed.

It was fortunate for all concerned that the critic of the *South Wales Argus* had not also caught the show at an earlier date or he might not have written about it quite so effusively:

'It vibrates with vitality...snappy book and lyrics... 'Chrysanthemum' whizzes, bangs and crackerjacks along...It is another nail in the coffin of that rumour that Britain cannot produce a good musical.'

Ditto the other notices, and again it played to excellent houses. Was I just being over sensitive? I don't believe I was. I returned to London worried about the future of 'Chrysanthemum', and there were other good reasons to be worried, which concerned Mr. Gorlinsky, and which I shall shortly reveal.

We didn't see it again for the rest of its tour. It next played Leeds, and the *Yorkshire Evening Post* said:

'"Chrysanthemum", a new musical play at Leeds Grand Theatre this week... scores heavily with tunes that are far from commonplace, and clever lyrics that would have been good enough for the shows that these new writers parody.' And again it did wonderful business.

Its last date was the Grand Theatre, Blackpool – a sell out week, and the *West Lancashire Evening Gazette* reported:

'"Chrysanthemum", by Neville Phillips and Robin Chancellor, with music by Robb Stewart, is a mirthful musical melodrama which should take root and flourish in the West End.'

The last performance in Blackpool was on Saturday November the 1st, and a week and a half later, on Thursday November the 13th, the show opened in London – but a great deal of drama, heartbreak and even financial ruin had taken place before that opening. I shall now endeavour to explain.

No sooner had we started rehearsals back in July than Gorlinsky began production on another, much larger musical. This was to be the big money maker, and all his resources went into it. It had a modern setting with really up to the minute music; the book and lyrics were by the celebrated comedy and revue writer, Alan Melville; the score by popular pianist and composer, Russ Conway; and the star would be wonderful Frankie Howard. It was called, 'Mr. Venus', and from all accounts it had everything going for it. There was no need to tour (let poor old Cinderella, 'Chrysanthemum' do that), it already had a home and would open mid October at the eminently suitable Prince of Wales Theatre; and there was no shortage of publicity in the press for it. The feeling of expectation in the West End was high.

Although we were playing to packed houses everywhere we went we were completely ignored by Mr. Gorlinsky, and any extras we asked for, another drop cloth that we felt was needed, or a few new costumes, were denied. Every penny he had was going into 'Mr. Venus'. So as 'Chrysanthemum' slogged its way around the provinces with no sign of a West End theatre in view I began to wonder if he intended to close the show at the end of the tour and concentrate his mind and means wholly on the really big one. My fears grew when I read an article in 'The Stage' that was headed: 'PRODUCTIONS IN DANGER: The queue of plays on the road which are waiting to come into the West End grows weekly. There is the danger that at least one production, which has been doing extremely good business, may have to fold-up, if a home cannot soon be found in town. On the road at present, major productions include: "Chrysanthemum", the musical with Pat Kirkwood and Hubert Gregg.' Can you imagine how depressed I felt reading that?

And then a theatre was offered to us, and when I heard its name a cold shiver ran down my spine. The Winter Garden Theatre had been dark for months; it was shabby and dilapidated and right off the beaten track; no show of any quality had played there for years; tacky touring companies would bravely try their luck, come in, and be off in a week. When Harry Foster told me of the offer I accused him and Mr. Gorlinsky of madness and said I would rather the show closed in Blackpool playing to an appreciative audience than creep surreptitiously into the Winter Garden and within days die a sad, lonely, ignominious death. I had now also insulted both Harry and Mr. Gorlinsky, but I felt my objection to the Winter Garden was right.

Luck! Luck! Luck! With me it has always been a case of luck: sometimes good, sometimes bad, and this time it was a wonderful stroke of the good – good for us but not so good for 'Mr. V.' and Mr. G., for seldom have I seen worse notices for a musical. They hated everything about it: the book; the music; the lyrics; the scenery; they even hated poor old Frankie Howard. It was a total disaster and the show lasted for seventeen performances. Mr. Gorlinsky now had an empty theatre on his hands and we had just finished our final week at Blackpool, so as 'Mr.Venus' moved out we moved in and opened in just over a week. As there had been no publicity for the show and no advance booking its success or failure was going to depend entirely upon the opening night reaction of the audience and critics; and after the disaster of 'Mr. Venus' a lot of people would now be wary of another completely unknown Gorlinsky musical opening so soon at the very same theatre. The knockers were already loudly knocking.

Denis was working in Madrid. His health was not good, the emphysema was worsening, but it was film work, and American film work, and that sort of money could not be sniffed at. The film was, 'Solomon and Sheba' and the director, King Vidor, had asked him to come over to Spain and rewrite some of the love scenes between Tyrone Power and Gina Lolabrigida. This he did and got on very well with both the stars. He would fly back to London for the opening of 'Chrysanthemum' and return to Madrid the following morning. Even with the reservations he had about the show and as ill as he was, he wanted to be with me on its first night.

Not being particularly disposed to us – well, to me, anyway – Gorlinsky had not offered us first night seats (he had also not yet paid us our royalties for the last weeks of the tour, having presumably pumped it all into 'Mr. Venus'), but Maude Spector, for whom getting first night tickets was never any problem, secured us eight seats in Row H. These would be taken by herself; Cecil Robson, whose idea it was that Robin and I should write a musical melodrama, and had come over from Paris especially for the opening; Robin and his friend, Andy; Robb and Jackie; Denis and me. I felt uncomfortable sitting in the stalls where I recognised quite a few faces around me, I would much rather have been standing anonymously at the back, but one couldn't look a gift horse in the mouth. This was no aspersion on Maude.

I truly didn't know what to expect. I had not seen the show since that lacklustre performance in Cardiff. Had Fiz and Rod pulled it together or had it completely disintegrated? Also I knew what had pleased provincial audiences but what would the sophisticated London ones think?

The house was full – fuller than Gorlinsky had seen it since his last first night – and there was the usual first night buzz of excitement in the air, albeit a little subdued, but Pat had many London fans and a good sprinkling of them were present. So, as I have said before, we were in the lap of the Gods!

The curtain rose and what a relief: the company were back on form. It was a very different performance to the one we had seen in Cardiff. Whether this was due to Fiz and Rod or just first night adrenalin I don't know but once more it looked fresh and alive, and the eight gruelling weeks of slogging around the provinces didn't show at all. Nevertheless, it took the audience a while to warm up. They were understandably on their guard – for all they knew it could be another 'Mr. Venus' or, as it was only Gorlinsky's second choice, even worse. But from the moment Pat came on with the milk, said her first line and got a huge laugh, the show was away, and everything from then on was greeted with laughter and applause. 'Sinner Me!' went well considering what they had done to it, but if only she had been brave enough she could have wowed them with that number. They took a great liking to Hubert; his two humorous solos got laughs in all the right places and a gratifying response at the end; and their two song and dance duets, 'Is This Love?' and 'Love Is A Game' were big hits; the latter, which included a waltz around the stage, stopped the show and they had to perform it again. Roger Gage and Patricia Moore were also warmly received, and Rod's 'Limehouse Ballet' was a winner.

Pat performed 'Saturday Night' with a bowler hat and cane that she borrowed from a passer by (if she couldn't do her 'Dixieland Medley' this would be the next best thing). At one point in the number she broke off singing for eight bars and drained a full pint sized mug of beer in a single gulp, which pleased the audience no end. On the tour she had used a trick glass that held less than a quarter of a pint – she was probably watching her figure then, but at the opening it was a full pint of bitter and down it went in one swallow (this was one of Pat's famous party tricks. I don't know how much Hubert approved of it).

'Shanghai Lil' with its brief costume of feathers and sequins, gave the gentlemen in the audience an ample opportunity to study the remarkable shape her fine, lithe figure was still in. But, oh, what she did to the lyric. Some of our best lines were sacrificed to funny business with feathers or getting her hand caught in a sailor's string vest, which amused the audience but annoyed me. At one point she departed altogether from the song and in a Bea Lillie like fashion began to trill, "Follow, follow, follow, the merry, merry pipes of Pan." At another she held a feather up behind her head and yelled, "I gotta horse!" This was a take off of the most famous black man in Britain between the wars, a racing tipster called Prince Monolulu who always wore a headdress of ostrich feathers and whose famous catch phrase it was. It didn't worry Pat that 'Chrysanthemum' was circa 1913 and Prince Monolulu's heydays were much later and went on until 1965. This was Pat in pantomime mode and the audience lapped it up. When Noel Coward came to the show and went backstage to congratulate her, Robb, who happened to be nearby at the time, saw him wag a pretence finger of admonishment at her and say in a mock scolding voice, "You're a naughty girl. If they had been my lyrics I'd be very, very cross." 'The Fire Brigade' went as well as usual and there was an extra round of applause when the engine arrived at the scene of the fire. Pat's leap from the blazing building into the firemen's sheet below got a great cheer, and at the end of the show the ovation was long and loud. Pat and Hubert took several curtain calls and were left in no doubt that the audience had thoroughly enjoyed itself.

After the show the eight of us, plus a few other friends who had been present, went back to Alexandra Court for champagne and a cold buffet supper that we had prepared during the day. No one could argue that Pat's fans had not had a whale of a time, but neither could they possibly guess what the papers were going to say. The provincial notices had been phenomenal but it was a known fact that the London critics were a far more cynical, spoilt and jaded bunch.

Denis had to leave for Madrid early the next morning; but before he went we just had time to scan the papers the newsboy had delivered, and we were more than pleasantly surprised. One critic, I thought, summed up the situation rather nicely. He wrote: 'As the publicity boys raved about America's "West Side Story", due to open tonight, a new British musical crept quietly into the Prince of Wales and set the place alight."

I do not wish to show off with paeans of self glorification, but to understand fully what happened to 'Chrysanthemum' it is important that you realise how highly it was thought of by critics and the public alike. Of course, Pat got her usual quota of rave reviews, but the show itself was also highly thought of. Here are a few brief extracts from the notices:

'Witty, stylish – and welcome. A subtle musical. A satirical musical. A musical with style and wit. This is no pipe dream. It actually happened at the Prince of Wales last night.'
Felix Barker, *Evening News.*

'At last! A rival for Boy Friend. It is long overdue. Here it is at last...the whole show has an infectious bounce, bite and buoyancy.'
Alan Dent, *The News Chronicle.*

'This was a happy idea for a musical by Neville Phillips and Robin Chancellor, and they have given it a good book and witty lyrics.'
T.C. Worsley, *The Financial Times.*

'A bright and breezy new British play...has all the gaiety and melody that any musical could wish.'
Edward Goring, *The Daily Mail.*

'Robb Stewart's music is catchy. A firemen's quintet in long underpants, Mack-Sennett-style, is a climax even Broadway hadn't thought up.'
Harold Conway, *Daily Sketch.*

'It is a show that always seems to fetch an amusing little trick out of its sleeve.'
The Times.

Anybody looking for a show for a festive occasion will be well advised to go and see 'Chrysanthemum'.'
Daily Worker.

'In 'Chrysanthemum' there is something to delight everybody and an early visit is strongly advised.'
Geoffrey Tarrant, *Morning Advertiser.*

'My favourite bloom from now on. This musical – a melodrama of the ragtime age – is happy and glorious. It gallops along with the gayest abandon.'
News of the World.

'This musical has pace, humour and high spirits. This is a cross between Christmas pantomime and the Follies Bergère. Definitely not for the kiddies but great fun for everyone else.'
Doris Lessing (standing in for Kenneth Tynan), *The Observer.*

'Those on the look out for striking new developments in the world of the musical need not hurry off to see "Chrysanthemum." Those who fancy an enjoyable evening, during which agreeable and talented people are provided with many good jokes and humable music, will find themselves very well suited.'
Harold Hobson, *The Sunday Times.*

'The show itself is highly original. A clever burlesque of old-time melodrama of the ragtime period, the scenes change and swirl with the speed of a film.'
Ross Shepherd, *The People.*

'Something of a surprise, a musical comedy which has got hold of an amusing idea and exploits it with an exhilarating sense of fun.'
Anthony Cookman, *The Tatler.*

'It's a bright, bouncy, beaming entertainment… I just can't see this cheerful chunk of entertainment failing to please its viewers from start to finish in this beguiling non-stop sequence of song, dance, burlesque and mickey-taking.'
The Record Mirror.

We didn't escape without a few dud notices but they were overwhelmingly in the minority. I was genuinely surprised at how wonderful most of them were.

Later that morning I took the tube to Piccadilly Circus and went and stood outside Swan and Edgars. Looking down Coventry Street I could see our title on the marquee above the theatre and felt quite emotional. This was what I had wished for most of my life, to have a show on in the West End, and at long last that wish had come true. I thought 'whatever happens now' – and began to hum the Gershwin standard –

'They can't take that away from me.' I walked down Coventry Street and stood on the pavement opposite the theatre watching the people going in to the box office. It was a wonderful feeling. I then became aware that someone was standing beside me. It was Mr. Gorlinsky. "Good morning, Mr. Phillips," he said. "Have you ordered your Rolls Royce yet?" I laughed and said something asinine. What I really wanted to say was, "When are we getting the money you still owe us for the tour?" but sense and sensibility prevented me from being so crass.

That night, November the 14th, 'West Side Story' opened at Her Majesty's Theatre and became theatrical history. All the same in the Sunday papers and weekly magazines 'Chrysanthemum' held its own. On our second night the company were told that every seat for the Boxing Day performance had been sold. Everything seemed to be going our way. Good luck was still with us.

On the following day, November the 15th, Tyrone Power collapsed on the set of 'Solomon and Sheba' with a heart attack and died in the ambulance taking him to hospital. Seventy-five per cent of his filming had already been completed. Yul Brynner would take over the role and a great deal of re-shooting would have to be done. Denis returned home immediately. His condition, I thought, had slightly worsened, and as usual the winter was not his best friend.

Two or three weeks later I answered the telephone and an agitated foreign woman's voice asked for him. "Who shall I say it is?" I asked. "Madame Lolobrigida," she said. "Oh, Madame," I gasped, thrilled to be talking to the famous film star, "I shall call him." She was in a miserable state and said to Denis, "I play Sheba as bitch. Yul, he play Solomon as bitch. We now have two bitches and that's no good. I need new scenes." So Denis was summoned back to Madrid. I feared for his health with all that travel and hanging about in freezing film studios, but he was determined to go. He stayed for a couple of weeks, until Gina was satisfied with her new love scenes, and then he returned home, fortunately none the worse for it.

'Chrysanthemum' was sailing along nicely, which was most gratifying considering the stiff competition we were up against: at Her Majesty's Theatre there was Chita Revira and the full Broadway cast of 'West Side Story' that had opened the night after we did; and at Drury Lane Rex Harrison and Julie Andrews were starring in 'My Fair Lady', that had opened in April, so we had every reason to be pleased with ourselves.

One evening a film producer we knew called Kenneth Harper invited us to his flat in Mayfair to meet the famous French comedian and film maker, Jacques Tati. His latest film, 'Mon Oncle', had been a big hit in France and he hoped it might get a general release in Britain; but the British film distributors were adamant that before this could happen it would need to be re-dubbed in English. It otherwise would only be shown, as 'Monsieur Hulot's Holiday' had been, in the smaller art houses.

As he felt his command of English wasn't proficient enough to tackle it on his own he had come to London to seek help and Kenneth had suggested that Denis and I (now I was a famous writer of musical comedy with a successful show running in the West End) might be the right collaborators. Denis had worked a lot on French films, translating and sub-titling them, but this we were to discover was something very different.

Tati did not make talking pictures as we know them; he had a style all his own where the sound design bore no resemblance to naturalism, but consisted of a collage of sounds: the human voice, various other noises and music. What was actually said was of no consequence. He was not interested in dialogue as such. Because people spoke in real life and he was making a sound movie with people in it he felt obliged to let them say something, but what it was mattered not a jot; it was the action alone that carried the plot forward. He himself in the role of Monsieur Hulot never uttered a single syllable. To complicate things further for us he had used non-professional actors and allowed them to improvise their dialogue, sometimes quite indistinctly, and no record had been kept of what they had said.

We were taken to the De Lane Lea Sound Studios in Wardour Street, Soho (famous for post production and re-recording), and there we were shown 'Mon Oncle' a couple of times. De Lane Lea prided themselves on their expertise in the synchronisation of word to lip movement. Often a word would have to be changed and a substitute found that fitted more accurately the movement of an actor's lips, sometimes at the expense of the quality of the dialogue, but to De Lane Lea synchronisation was what mattered the most. Tati, who cared nothing about words or synchronisation, found the whole procedure a crashing bore. Nevertheless he thought it might be a good idea if we came over to Paris for two or three days and see if we could work something out, and this we agreed to do.

But before we move the scene to Paris I want to recall an amusing incident that occurred at our first meeting. Tati, an extremely tall man, was leaning back on a noel-sofa (one of those elaborate seating arrangements with loose sides that tie to the centre with tasselled chords) when a chord broke and his huge bulk tumbled backwards onto the floor. When we saw he wasn't hurt we all laughed. But he, whose film persona, Monsieur Hulot, was always being subjected to humiliations of this sort, didn't find it funny at all and resented our laughter. What strange and unfathomable creatures comedians are.

The day before we were due to fly to Paris, Denis was suddenly stricken with a severe chest infection and confined to bed. I wanted to cancel the meeting, for it was he who had the film writing experience, not me, but he insisted that I went and nervously I did so.

I spent three days with Tati, working – if what we did can be described as that – at his office in a street close to the Arc de Triomphe, and I found him a most charming and hospitable man. Each day he took me to lunch: twice to a favourite small restaurant near the office where the food was quite superb, and once to 'The American Store', a new brassiere that had just opened on the Champs-Elysees that he wanted to try. Everywhere he went he was instantly recognised and he was always being asked for his autograph. Only once did he show annoyance, when in The American Store he was asked to autograph a less than pristine paper table napkin. At lunch one day he said that if I was going to be on my own that evening I should come and have dinner with him and his wife at their home. I pretended I was seeing a friend, I felt I had presumed enough on his hospitality.

Our days were spent playing around with English dialogue that I thought might suit the characters. I tried to inject a little humour into them but I had to be careful for that was not what it was about, and any attempt at wit would have been completely out of place. From the start I felt his heart was not in it, and after three days of not being able to make up his mind he suddenly decided to hell with a British general release, he would leave it as it was and settle for showings in art houses. He was wise to do so, 'Mon Oncle' is a little masterpiece as it is; and had De Lane Lea got their expert hands on it, adding perfectly synchronised English voices, they might well have upset the delicate balance of his intricate and very individual sound design.

Although my stay in Paris bore no artistic fruit I took away with me the memory of three most pleasurable days spent in the company of a unique and humble genius.

'Chrysanthemum''s luck had been going too well for too long, it was time for a change. Gorlinsky foolishly agreed to have an extract from the show performed as the main item in, 'Sunday Night At The London Palladium', a live weekly television show with a viewing audience of ten thousand – almost everyone who owned a television set then. To proceed us on the bill would be Pinkie and Perky, a popular puppetry act; the American comedian, Henry Youngman; ballerina, Beryl Grey and partner in a *pas de deux*; Cyril Ornadel and the London Palladium Orchestra; and the ever popular audience participation game, 'Beat The Clock', with a jackpot prize standing at £500 – no mean sum in those days. Bruce Forsythe was the compere, and the show as always started with 'The Tiller Girls', a famous troupe of dancers whose terpsichorean style could best be described as 'seen one, seen the lot.'

It was well known in the profession that excerpts from musicals seldom fared well on television and more often than not did more harm than good. Out of context of the play, on a small black and white screen, without its own scenery and lighting, accompanied by an unfamiliar orchestra and with one brief run through on the day of transmission the essence and atmosphere of a show could be completely lost. But Gorlinsky, ever the gambler, was ready to take the risk.

Neither Fiz nor Rod were available to oversee the presentation so it was left to Hubert to decide the who, what and how (I was no longer consulted about anything. Since the telegram incident at Coventry he had not spoken to me). As could be predicted, he chose to do one of his fast talking numbers, which out of context of the play went for very little; and 'Love Is A Game', always a hit in the show, looked rather lost on that vast, brightly lit stage. Then a quick costume change of Pat's went disastrously wrong and ten thousand television viewers were left staring at the Palladium stage with nothing happening on it for a full sixteen bars of, 'Saturday Night,' before she scrambled on to retrieve what was left of the number. The whole thing was a stupid, bungled disaster and I knew then and there that any viewer who had been planning to go and see 'Chrysanthemum' in the theatre would now most certainly have second thoughts. Sadly I was right: the box office telephone on Monday morning was dead, and the only people who came to the theatre were those wishing to cancel their bookings. The advance that had stood at £9000 now shrank to £6,700, and the takings for that week dropped by nearly £1,700. It was extremely depressing.

But as the Christmas season approached and the horror of the television excerpt began to fade from people's memories business improved. By January it started to look quite healthy again and we were beginning to feel that the danger was over.

Then one night in late January a dense, freezing fog enveloped London. It was a real pea-souper, thick, yellow and deadening all the sounds of the streets. I remember that night well. Denis was having some trouble breathing and it had me very worried. At the theatre, the show just over, Pat and Hubert were preparing to set off on their eighteen mile drive home to Gerrards Cross. On seeing how bad the fog was she suggested they stay the night at a London hotel, but he wanted to get home. Knowing how important it was after a strenuous performance to keep oneself warm she protested, but no, he was adamant, and she was too tired to argue. The further they got out of town the denser and colder the fog became and she spent the entire journey with her head out of the window keeping an eye on the kerb. It was three o'clock when they reached home, frozen through, and when she woke that morning she could neither breathe nor talk. "Get a doctor," she croaked, "I'm dying!" An hour later the doctor arrived, took one look at her and turned as white as a sheet. With trembling hands he hurriedly opened his bag and prepared a hypodermic syringe.

She was out of the show for ten days. Her understudy was Josephine Blake, who played 'Rose' – we were down to three sisters again. Jo was an extremely talented young performer but she wasn't Pat, and Pat was what the show was about, and it was only Pat the audiences wanted to see. And to make Jo's job even harder Hubert locked Pat's dressing room door so she couldn't wear any of her costumes, and hurried substitutes, by no means as glamorous, had to be found. Business tumbled. According to Pat, Ingrid Bergman was coming to the show with some friends, also the American producer, David Merrick with a view perhaps to taking the show to Broadway, but on discovering she was off they all cancelled their bookings.

Pat had been off for five days when Hubert suddenly went down with flu and also retired to bed in Gerrards Cross, where he remained for four days. So now we had two understudies doing 'The Pat & Hubert Show', and however talented they might have been it was an impossible task: audiences felt cheated not seeing the announced stars and business dropped even further.

Hubert was the first to return. Pat was not yet feeling strong enough to perform but she came and watched a performance from one of the boxes. Bernard Delfont, who owned the theatre saw her there, and was furious; the show was not meeting its break figure by a large margin and he gave them an ultimatum; unless they were both back in it by the very next performance he would give them notice to quit.

Pat returned immediately and the houses began to fill up again. Each week the advance grew and the audiences that came were as enthusiastic as ever, but we were still not meeting our break figure and Delfont had a new twice-nightly revue starring Shirley Bassey up his sleeve – the sort of fare the Prince of Wales was mostly famous for – so when he was ready to bring it in we were given our notice.

As luck would have it the Apollo Theatre in Shaftsbury Avenue became vacant at the very same time and we were able to transfer there. Gorlinsky slim-lined the production: he reduced the size of the orchestra and dispersed with the 'swings' (chorus understudies). Other back stage economies were made – including not paying us our weekly royalties – but at such a delicate moment it was not an issue we wished to pursue. Then, foolhardy as ever, he invited the critics to re-review the show. Considering how nice they had already been I thought this might be straining their good natures rather.

We gave our last performance at the Prince of Wales on Saturday the 15th of February and opened at the Apollo on Monday the 17th. The Sunday was spent shifting our gear the few hundred yards from one theatre to the other. This may sound like a simple little move, compared with all the touring the show had done, but it turned out to be a nightmare. The Apollo stage was much smaller than the Prince of Wales and we couldn't get our scenery onto it. All Sunday and Monday carpenters sawed and hacked away at the sets to try to make them fit. Another problem that hadn't been bargained for was that the Apollo stage hands were used to plays with one or two sets and our large and complicated scenery completely overwhelmed them. There was no time on Monday for a dress rehearsal and poor Gerry Phillips spent the whole of the opening night in the prompt corner telephoning the lighting cues to the electricians.

When the curtain rose that night I thought how much nicer the show looked on that well proportioned proscenium arched stage than the rather ugly, wide, letter-box expanse of the Prince of Wales. The audience appeared warm and appreciative and it seemed as if things were going well until a few scenes in there was a long pause on a darkened stage while the stage hands struggled to get the scenery into place. It felt like forever. I don't think this one hiccough in itself would have had any serious affect but a couple of scenes later it occurred again, and then again. Also the thumping and banging from backstage during some of the scenes almost drowned out the actors' voices and I could feel those around me losing patience with the show. Some didn't return after the interval which in itself was the grizzliest fifteen minutes I have ever spent in a bar, looking at all those grim and bewildered faces. Others walked out when further things went wrong and I just sat there, horror-struck, watching the show disintegrate before my eyes.

Strangely enough the few notices we got were quite complementary, saying it was well worth a second visit and should continue to draw good audiences for some time to come. I had my suspicions that those critics hadn't attended the performance and were just repeating what they had written before. News of our catastrophic first night spread like wildfire around the West End and a lot of punters were frightened off. After a night or two with extra stage staff brought in the show began to run smoothly but the damage had been done, and although the houses got a little bigger each night it wasn't fast enough for Gorlinsky, who hadn't the money to nurse it through, and on March the 21st we closed.

'WHAT HAPPENED TO CHRYSANTHEMUM?' ran the heading of a full page article in 'The Stage' the following week; and other papers asked the same question: how was it a show that had so pleased critics and audiences alike, and was expected to have a really long run, had come to such an untimely end?

The answer was simple: five blows of bad luck, one right after the other. The first, an ill judged and badly botched television extract that scared would-be customers away; the second, Pat being out of the show for ten whole days; the third, Hubert being out at the same time for four days; the fourth, a disastrous first night at the Apollo where everything that could go wrong went wrong; and fifth, Gorlinsky not having sufficient funds to nurse the show through the few weeks it needed to recover from its wounds, which it had started to do. That's what happened to 'Chrysanthemum'. Samuel French bought the amateur rights and over the years there have been various productions by operatic societies in Britain, Canada, Australia and South Africa. Although Chrysanthemum's moment of glory on the London stage was over there was still America to come – but all in good time.

London at last!

'The Day After Tomorrow', 1946. From left: Peter Coke, Yvonne Marling, Nova Pilbeam, Eric Maturin, John Penrose, Mary Clare and Phyllis Dare.

All dressed up to go on for Peter Coke but, curse him, he was never off!

'The Anonymous Lover', 1947. From left: Raymond Huntley, Valerie Taylor, Abrosine Phillpots and Hugh Sinclair,

On the set of 'Trottie True'.

Cooler than the Cape

(Shivering as they come away from rehearsals, these South African visitors find it hard to get used to the climate here.

They are all in the South African play, "The Green Box," starting next week at the New Chepstow Theatre," Notting Hill, and they are from left to right, Margaret Inglis, who produces the play, Nan Munro and Neville Phillips, of the cast.

'The Green Box' with Nan Munro and Margaret Inglis.

Denis with Earl St. John and Brian Desmond Hurst on location with 'Trottie True'.

A 1930s photograph of Denis, the joyous Joyce Murchie, Lord Killanan, Queenie Leonard and a friend.

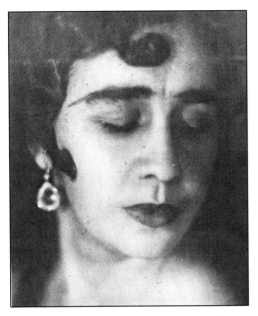

*Catherine Devillier (Katusha) prima ballerina
of the Bolshoi Ballet.*

Portrait of Katusha by Tchelitchew.

*Katusha teaching Yul Brynner a dance
step for the film 'Anastasia'.*

Robb Stewart.

Noel Coward and company on the first night of 'Ace of Clubs'.

NEW WATERGATE THEATRE CLUB

29 BUCKINGHAM STREET, STRAND, W.C.2.

EVENINGS (including Sundays) at 9 p.m.   NO PERFORMANCE MONDAYS.

Continuing for 3 more weeks only.
LAST PERFORMANCE, SUNDAY, 7th FEBRUARY

ODDLY ENOUGH

A Revue by **NEVILLE PHILLIPS**, with music by **ROBB STEWART**
Directed by NORMAN MARSHALL.

Lively and witty.   Should enjoy considerable success.—*Daily Telegraph.*
It bubbles merrily.   Mr. Norman Marshall's production is fast and finished.—*The Times.*
Swift, smart, witty.—*Manchester Guardian.*
Witty and improper.—*Harold Hobson in The Sunday Times.*
A sharp little entertainment.—*Financial Times.*
Saucy wit.— *The Queen.*

'Oddly Enough'.

As Brass in 'The Confederacy' by Vanbrugh.

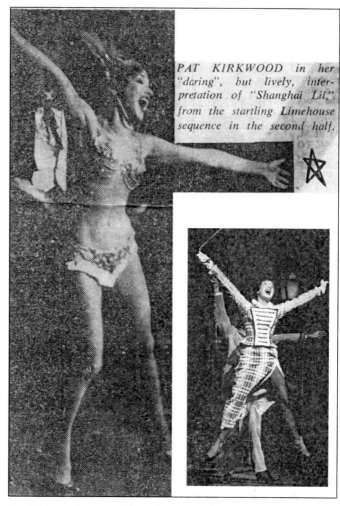

PAT KIRKWOOD in her "daring", but lively, interpretation of "Shanghai Lil," from the startling Limehouse sequence in the second half.

Pat Kirkwood singing 'Shanghai Lil' and (inset) 'Saturday Night' in 'Chrysanthemum' at the Prince of Wales Theatre, 1958.

Valerie Tandy in 'Chrysanthemum' at the New Lindsey Theatre, 1956.

Pat Kirkwood and Hubert Gregg in 'Chrysanthemum' at the Prince of Wales Theatre, 1958.

Chrysanthemum, who went out for the milk, three years ago, is back home at last — with the milk.

ROBERT SCHULER   HOWARD BARKER   FRANK J. HALE
(in association with John M. Johnson)

present

PATRICE MUNSEL

in the American Premiere of

"CHRYSANTHEMUM"

Music by   *Book and lyrics by*

Robb Stewart   **Neville Phillips**   **Robin Chancellor**

Patrice Munsel in the American production of 'Chrysanthemum'.

I'M IN LOVE

Lyric by NEVILLE PHILLIPS

Music by ROBB STEWART

Peter Bridge and John Gale present

STANLEY BAXTER

and

BETTY MARSDEN

On the Brighter Side

A NEW REVUE

with

PIP HINTON

Devised and Directed by JAMES GILBERT
Musical numbers staged by ALFRED RODRIQUES
At the PHOENIX THEATRE

SONGS FROM THE SHOW

I'm in Love
Late Last Evening   2 6
Song of a Wood Nymph   2 6
A Plea for the Throne   2 6
Piano Selection   2 6
                            3 6

KEITH PROWSE MUSIC PUBLISHING CO. LTD. LONDON. W 1

2/6

I WAS PASSING BY
Words by NEVILLE PHILLIPS
Music by ROBB STEWART
By arrangement with Jack Hylton
PETER BRIDGE presents
DORA BRYAN
In her new musical
Six of One
WITH
RICHARD WATTIS
DENNIS LOTIS
AMANDA BARRIE
JOHN HEWER
SHEILA O'NEILL
ENTIRE SHOW DEVISED BY FRANCIS ESSEX
PRICE 2/6 NET
MADE IN ENGLAND
MUSICAL NUMBERS STAGED BY IRVING DAVIES
46565
CHAPPELL & CO LTD 50 NEW BOND STREET, LONDON, W.1

On the roof at Brompton Square.

Jeremy Conway on the roof at Brompton Square.

Jeremy and me in Wiltshire, 2006.

PART FOUR

"THE DENOUMENT"

And a surprise ending

FOUR

This part of the story goes as far as July 1963 when I turned thirty nine (plus a few forward leaps in time where certain facts need to be concluded); and it began in January 1941 when I was sixteen and madly in love with someone I think was called Lionel – whatever he was called, one thing is certain, February that year we joined the South African Army together and became gunners in the Coastal Artillery. Had that not happened, everything in this scenario would be entirely different – I am as sure as anyone can be, that I would have had a life in the theatre, but in no way would it have been the same life. It's spooky when you think about it.

Back to the 21st of March 1959 when, through no fault of its own, poor unlucky 'Chrysanthemum' closed at the Apollo Theatre leaving me feeling wretched and exhausted. So much of my life had gone into that show – far more than I should have allowed. In the ephemeral world of the stage, making close attachments is not advisable, but that is how I am – single mindedness has been both my strength and my weakness. Which brings to mind something I heard a young Hungarian girl say in an early 1930s Laurel & Hardy film: her exuberant high spirits being remarked upon, she explains, "I can't help it, I'm from Budapest!" When I first saw the film I had no idea there was such a place as Budapest, but I loved the line anyway, and have used it as an excuse for my own behaviour ever since. So, you see, I couldn't help feeling the way I did about 'Chrysanthemum', I was from Budapest! Had the show enjoyed the long successful run everyone was expecting it to have, life for Denis and me would have been very different: there would be money in the bank; we would have had our own home; and Denis could have escaped the worst of the English winter. But as it was, we had not received our royalties for the final weeks of the run, so once again we were as poor as a couple of church mice.

Another reason I was anxious for the show to succeed was that it would make it so much easier to get the next one on. A commercial success draws producers and backers like bees to clover, but if your last show has not made money – whatever the reason may be – those careful bees remain incommunicatively in their hives. I had already completed the book and lyrics of one and a half new musicals. The completed one was a fantasy set in the African jungle and entitled, 'The Girl On The Ostrich'. It was inspired by the African stories of Ryder Haggard and the jungle paintings of the

Douanier Henri Rousseau. As far as I knew, nothing of the sort had been done before. Some fifty years later 'The Lion King' would open at the Lyceum Theatre with all the superb production values that would have been so right for 'The Ostrich'. The half completed show was called, 'Twas Brillig', and was a spoof of an 'Old Dark House' horror movie that I had originally written as a play but decided would be better as a musical. When it was almost completed, with a bright, witty score by Dennis King, 'The Rocky Horror Show' opened at the Royal Court Theatre and overnight 'Twas Brillig', with its many similarities but not nearly as much daring, was consigned to the scrap heap of obsolete musicals.

At the time I had the book and lyrics of one and a half musicals, I was looking desperately for a new composer. I didn't feel I could go through the ordeal of dragging another full score out of Robb. The first time had been a nightmare for all concerned and he wasn't getting any less eccentric. Also I dreaded what Denis would say had I even suggested it. But finding the right composer was not easy. My agent, Peggy Ramsay, thought 'The Ostrich' had great possibilities and introduced me to a new young composer she had just taken on, who had written the score for a musical adaptation of a Pinero farce that had had a brief West End run. He was charming and no doubt very talented but his music was not right for the show. It was heavily influenced by Benjamin Britten and Leonard Bernstein (in his less tuneful mode), and melody to him I imagine was just a dirty word. What 'The Ostrich' needed was a composer who had been influenced by someone like Harold Arlen whose score for 'House Of Flowers' was much nearer to what I wanted; but such composers don't come two a penny, and less so in Britain than America.

Our collaboration was brief and a cause of much embarrassment. He did not want my opinion of how the songs should be set, and would not let me hear any of the settings until he had almost completed the score, which worried me a great deal: Robb and I had worked so closely together and he was always open to my opinion and suggestions – I did, in fact, have a great deal of influence over his music. Eventually the day came when I was summoned to hear the score and I was horrified – there was not a noticeable tune anywhere. Cowardice prevented me from telling the truth, but with as few lies as possible I made a hasty exit and rang Peggy. That evening after her office had closed we sat in a pub in New Row and over several glasses of wine I poured out my tale of woe. She couldn't have been more understanding; she told me to forget about it, not to worry, she would handle the whole thing. And this she did. He returned the script to her and I never saw or heard of him again. For all I know he might have made it big in the musical world, but of one thing I am certain, it was not in the field of musical comedy.

Full of frustration and desperation, plus a fair amount of self deception, I did something that you may find utterly despicable considering all the moaning and groaning you have been subjected to and, as Denis did, you may not wish to hear another word concerning 'The Ostrich': I rang Robb and asked him to write the score. He read the script and accepted the offer. He was probably surprised that I had written a whole new show without ever mentioning it to him; he was probably also aware of the reason, but he made no comment.

And so began another long hard struggle with Robb and his capricious muse. I suppose the reason I went back to him after my unhappy experience with composer number one was that I knew I could have control over the music. I wanted it to be melodic with a distinct African flavour. Robb I knew could do melodic; drums, flutes and traditional African rhythms would provide the flavour I hoped.

As we have gone thus far on 'The Ostrich' we might as well take the story through to its final conclusion. On and off, several people showed interest in it. One management even bought a six month option on it, but it was going to be a difficult and expensive show to stage – although I don't suppose John Reagan would have flinched. Both Greenwich and Guildford theatres wanted to stage it but they couldn't afford to do so unless we brought in some extra backing, and that was something that neither Robb nor I were particularly adept at. And then, sadly, the events of the times took over: first, as I recall, came trouble in the Congo, followed rapidly by Angola, Mozambique, Uganda, Nigeria, Kenya, Somalia, Rhodesia … soon it seemed the entire continent was in a state of turmoil and a light hearted musical comedy suggesting it was a Garden of Eden where beautiful carefree people and exotic wild animals all frolicked together under the an aphrodisiacal African moon would not have gone down very well with the critics of the day. And as the years went by other aspects of the show became blatantly non PC. So, alas, 'The Ostrich' too found its way onto the scrap heap of unperformed musicals. I still think that had it been done at the time it was written, 'The Girl On The Ostrich' could have been a most charming and original show; and, like 'The Lion King', a wonderfully fantasized evocation of the African jungle. Once again it was a matter of timing and luck. Oh, and just in case you have been wondering: no, not a lot of Robb's tuneful score was ever committed to paper.

—⁓—

Exactly ten years after her visit in 1949 Clare came to spend another summer in England. Great Aunt Mabel had died and left her and Auntie V. a few thousand pounds each. That is not exactly true. What actually happened was this: on the demise of Great

Uncle Colonel Frank Devine (Boer War veteran) his entire fortune went to his wife Mabel. This was no meagre sum, he having been the senior partner of Devine Gates, the biggest shipping agents in southern Africa. The Devines were notoriously mean. At Christmas my brothers, our cousin Dennis and I each received a five shilling postal order, even after we had grown up. They lived in Kennelworth at 'The Lothians', an imposing Victorian Gothic villa with enormous grounds and a long winding drive from the great iron gates up to the gloomy, stained-glass front door (flats now cover the entire area). Great Aunt Mabel hated being alone in the great empty house with only the servants for company, so dangling her money bags before her two nieces (both widows and her only close relatives) she asked them if they would take it in turns to come and live with her. Knowing their dragon aunt of old it was not a prospect either of them relished, but it was also not an offer they were able to refuse, so biting the bullet they agreed to take their turn at 'The Lothians', a month on, a month off. Never an easy woman to please, they noticed with each stay that she grew more demanding; and then as her health began to fail and she required their constant attention they found they really needed their month off to recuperate from their month on. It was always with a heavy heart that they returned to 'The Lothians'. But, as stressful as they found it, they knew better than to look the goose with the golden eggs in the mouth. When the old bat eventually shuffled off this mortal coil and went to join the Colonel on their specially-reserved Church of England cloud, the sisters breathed a sigh of relief. They felt like a couple of caged birds that had suddenly been set free. But, as sometimes happens to such birds, freedom brought an unexpected shock, for they were to discover that the fortune the Colonel had left his wife was for her lifetime only; upon her death every penny of it went to the Church of England. Whether she had been aware of this one will never know – she was always extremely vague so perhaps she should be given the benefit of the doubt. Fortunately the solicitor handling the estate, who was also a family friend of long standing, agreed that the sisters had been given a raw deal and somehow wangled it that they each received a few thousand pounds (don't tell the Church of England).

The first thing Clare did with her money was to buy Clive, the less well off of my two elder brothers, who had a wife and five children, a brand new family car. She gave presents to all her grandchildren and then booked herself a passage on a Union Castle liner to come and spend the summer in England with me.

Not having seen each other for so long it was a very happy reunion. I was only sad that she had arrived just too late to see 'Chrysanthemum'; I knew she would have loved it and been terribly proud of me. As Clare was a chain smoker and Alexandra Court a smoke free zone on account of Denis' lung condition I found her, with the help of

Irene, a very nice bed-sit in Gloucester Road, a few houses down from Kynance Place. The landlady, a charming woman, was also a smoker so the two of them got on very well puffing away together. As a birthday treat Clare took me to Paris for a week. It was her first time there so I showed her all the sights, Versailles, the lot. We stayed in a small hotel I knew just off the Champs-Elysees and spent our evenings having lovely meals and going to the theatre. On my birthday we went to The Lido and saw a marvellous cabaret that included the Bluebell Girls, amazing waterfalls and spectacular fireworks. How they managed it all in that limited space was incredible. We also went to the Follies Bergere, the Casino de Paris, and best of all a dazzling new revue starring the fabulous Josephine Baker. The weather was perfect and we really had a wonderful week together. Denis, who was not feeling at his best just then, seemed rather irritated that I was spending so much time with Clare. I thought this was unfair of him; after all, she was my mother, I had not seen her for ten years and she would only be staying for a limited length of time. She, I felt, must be my priority. It would have been a lot easier if we could have spent more time at the flat, but as she was unable to smoke there, and being as addicted to her cigarettes as she unfortunately was, she found it hard to stay comfortably in a room for any length of time without one; so her visits to Alexandra Court were mostly of a short duration; not that she and Denis would have had a lot in common to talk about but that way I would have been around more. If you are now picturing a lonely man sitting day after day in an empty flat, that was not the way it was: Maude still came around in the evenings for her dry martinis and other friends would drop in, Bumble – Brian – Graham – Elizabeth – Joy suddenly appearing from out of the blue and then disappearing into it again just as suddenly. Denis was not lonely for company, he was just not feeling very well and a little jealous of Clare occupying so much of my time.

A few days after our return from Paris I received a letter in the post from an American called John Johnson who had got my address from Fosters Agency. He had seen 'Chrysanthemum' at the Prince of Wales Theatre, thought it terrific and wanted to know if the American rights were available. They were: as Gorlinsky had not paid us our royalties for the final weeks of the run he had forfeited all rights of the show. I telephoned Johnson, who was living in Onslow Square, just a few minutes walk down Queens Gate, and that afternoon I went to meet him. He was a charming, cultured, good looking man in his early thirties, and if his flat was anything to go by I'd say not short of a bob or two; although what he did for a living, if anything, I never did discover. Mind you, I didn't ask.

Over tea, John, as he asked me to call him, told me that one of his very best friends in New York was the Metropolitan Opera star, Patrice Munsel, whose recent successes at the Met had been, 'Lucia', 'Lakme', 'Romeo and Juliet' and 'Die Fledermaus'. And if that wasn't starry enough they had gone and stuck her face on the cover of 'Time' magazine. Already she had made several excursions away from the opera house: in the theatre she had appeared in, 'South Pacific', 'The King and I' and 'Kiss Me Kate'. She had also made some films, and in 1953 came to England to star in the Sam Speigal production of, 'Melba'. Patrice, John said, had a great flair for comedy that had not yet been fully realized and she was on the lookout for a stage vehicle that would allow her to explore that other side of her talent. 'Chrysanthemum', he thought, might be just the thing.

I gave him, to send her, a copy of the script and the LP of the show (when I first heard this LP, standing in a booth in a record shop in Coventry Street, I almost cried. It had been roughly put together during one hurried session at a recording studio on a Sunday, when most of the cast seemed to be in poor voice. Hubert must have been in charge, for his numbers were featured the most prominently and in their entirety while everyone else's were either shortened or completely cut. Pat's voice was not heard until the sixth track and then it was in a duet with Hubert, who had already done his two big solos. Needless to say, 'Sinner Me!' was not recorded) .Unhappy as I was with the LP I thought at least it would give Patrice Munsel a chance to hear the music.

It was not long before John heard back from Patrice and her theatre producer husband, Robert Schuler, who had produced most of her stage work, that they loved the show and were seriously considering it for production. They were coming to London later in the year – Patrice to do some programmes for the BBC – would like to meet us then, and we could take it from there. In due course they arrived and, just as John had said I would, I found them easy going and friendly. As they were keen to hear the full score as soon as possible but were not yet in possession of a piano I took them down to Robb's Pimlico abode, which struck them as quaintly Dickensian with its kitchen under the pavement; and they were particularly fascinated by the old Victorian closet type loo at the end of a dark, subterranean passage. I caught them exchanging a private laugh over that. But they loved the music and the way Robb played it. He was on top form that night.

By the next morning they had already made up their minds that they wanted to do the show and offered to buy a year's option on it. John Johnson would be joining them as one of the producers. Fosters handled our side of the business and when the Schulers returned to New York the contract was already signed and sealed. You can imagine how excited we were at the thought of 'Chrysanthemum' being done in America. Then, as happens with musicals, there was the long silence while the heavy lumbersome vehicle is slowly assembled, oiled and set in motion. This can take quite a while, so we will leave it now and return at a more appropriate time.

Clare's departure from Waterloo Station was almost a rerun of the first time: the torturing wait for the whistle to blow; then the flood gates opening as the train began to move. There was one difference though; I can't say how but we both seemed to know that this was not really goodbye. Denis gave a great sigh of relief at her leaving, and I must admit that I too gave a little sigh; juggling my attention between the two of them had been an enormous strain.

Maude offered me a couple of days work with nice pay on a film she was casting. It was 10 Williams' 'Suddenly Last Summer', scripted by Gore Vidal and starring Katherine Hepburn, Elizabeth Taylor and Montgomery Clift. The director was Joseph. L. Mankowitz. There is a scene in the film set in a lunatic asylum where Elizabeth Taylor, trying to escape from the clutches of her evil aunt, who has brought her there to have her brain lobotomised so that she won't remember what happened last summer, runs by mistake into a snake-pit of a room occupied by a group of seriously disturbed male mental patients. This was quite a short scene but very important in its sudden eruption of violence and fear, and Mankowitz insisted that although they were non speaking parts as such the male patients had to be played by good actors whom he could direct, so Maude presented him with a talented selection of would be lunatics – myself included. On the first morning he spent quite a while working with us, giving each a definite character and suggesting how we might react to seeing a beautiful young girl in our midst. I, who was sitting at a table weaving a basket, flung it aside and with a cry hid my face in my hands; someone else shouted obscenities; two others tried to grab hold of her; another began to masturbate; and so on... Although it was a scene of short duration it took two whole days to complete, and so unrelenting was it in its intensity that by the end of the second day some of us began to wonder if we really had gone a little mad. Now and again between takes Elizabeth Taylor would come over and chat with some of us. Her manner was charming and natural, and she was just as beautiful off the screen as she was on. The only thing about her I did not find attractive was the way she chewed gum throughout, even keeping it in her mouth, stuck behind her teeth, when she had to scream in terror. I was disappointed that neither Katherine Hepburn nor Montgomery Clift were at the studio either day as I would love to have caught a glimpse of two of my favourite actors. But I did get a peek inside the sinister looking conservatory set Oliver Messel had designed, full of the poisonous blooms and carnivorous plants that the sadistically decadent Sabastian of the story had lovingly cultivated.

When the film came out I went to see it and managed to catch the quick close up of my face registering shock and distress. It was not a completely satisfactory film despite its stella cast, and neither 10 Williams nor the majority of the critics liked it.

C.A. Lejeune wrote: 'I loathe this film. To my mind it is a decadent piece of work, sensational, barbarous and ridiculous.' On the other hand, Arthur Knight wrote: 'A wholly admirable rendering into film of a work at once fascinating and nauseating, brilliant and immoral.' My own opinion was somewhere in between. I have seen the stage play three or four times and have never felt altogether at ease with it.

—⁓—

In the spring of 1960 Robb and I had a revue on at the Bellevue Theatre in Amsterdam. Some of the material was new, some old. The cast were all English and most of the rehearsals took place at the Players Theatre in London. Robb decided he would go to Amsterdam with the show; Jack was living there then and he could stay with him. Another reason for going could have been that he didn't have all the music written down. The revue was called, 'Going Madly Dutch!' (not my title I hasten to add) and was geared to the English speaking tourist, but the Dutch seemed to enjoy it just as much and it ran successfully until the end of September when the season finished. The Dutch critics had been most generous, and to our surprise we even got a favourable mention in the continental edition of The New York Times. So pleased with the show were the management, an American couple called, Jack and Jill Lardis, that they asked us if we would do something similar the following spring.

Peter Croft, who directed a couple of the revues at the little Irving Theatre for which Robb and I had written material, liked our stuff; and he was now a producer of light entertainment at Associated-Rediffusion Television, which had newly relocated to a tall, new building on the South Bank east of Waterloo Bridge with magnificent views of the river and City. It would later become London Weekend Television; and then in the 1970s, between it and the bridge, architect Sir Denys Lasdun would erect a vast concrete bunker-like edifice that would be the home of The Royal National Theatre.

Peter Croft asked me if I would like to write the linking material for a summer spectacular he was doing. It was called 'Summer Fair' and would all take place in a fairground. The links, he suggested, might be in song form and sung by various people at the fair; each link as well as being informative, could be an amusing little interlude set at one of the fairground's many attractions. I thought it was a nice idea and said I would like to do it.

Robb was in Amsterdam and hiding from me. Getting through to him on the telephone was about as easy as getting through to someone on the other side with a wonky Planchette; and any chance of him writing down all the fiddly little tunes and delivering them on time I knew was less than nil. I told Peter he was working abroad and couldn't be contacted, which was almost true, so he found someone in the music department who, without any fuss or bother, quickly and adequately did the job.

The show went out on the evening of July the 16th, and Peter rang afterwards to say that the viewing figures had been excellent. I was then asked if I would like to write the sketches and some original lyrics for one of their main Christmas shows. I kept mum about my affinity with Scrooge on the subject of Christmas and replied with the merriest of affirmatives. It was to be called, 'Merry With Medwin' and be hosted by Michael Medwin, then starring in the company's number one sitcom. His guests were to be Shirley Bassey, Sidney James, Betty Marsden, Ron Moody, Vince Eager and several other well known names of the day; plus The George Mitchell Singers, The Denny Bettis Dancers and Billy Tennant and his Orchestra. Although it was to be a lavish show going out at prime time on Christmas Eve, because I was not famous as a television writer, I was offered a very meagre fee. My agent, Peggy Ramsay, who as a rule didn't give a damn about money, was incensed at their mean spiritedness towards me and went into fierce battle to get what she considered was the appropriate fee for the job; her attitude being, 'if they really want you they'll pay it, and if they don't, why bother?' Having the fearless Miss Ramsay as an opponent and, luckily, really wanting me, they gave in and paid what she asked – quite a respectable sum.

Robb and I wrote some original songs for the show. One was for a trio of disreputable store Father Christmases who loathed children and spend their time making the little ones' visits to Santa's Grotto as unpleasant as possible by breathing beer fumes in their faces and sticking chewing gum in their hair. Another was, though I say it myself, a very pretty lullaby sung charmingly by Nicolette Roeg (Peter Croft's beautiful and talented wife) as a mother singing her child to sleep. The scene then segued into the child's dream of Toy Land (a ballet). Most of the musical items though were traditional Christmas fare: 'Silent Night, Jingle Bells, White Christmas, etc, plus a new fangled rhythm that I thought would be just another passing fancy and was called, 'rock and roll'. Robb decided he would handle his own contract and not have to pay 10 per cent commission to an agent. This was being a penny wise, a pound foolish I thought, for knowing how hopeless he was at bargaining and forgetful at signing and returning contracts he was certainly not going to be 10 per cent better off; not that he probably would have noticed anyway.

At the first day of rehearsal I met some of the cast, a few of whom I already knew; Sid James, of course, from way back. Although we had seen each other a few times over the years we were never close friends. It was because of his second wife, Meg, of whom I was really fond, that we usually met. Now, meeting again, and in such special circumstances, I expected he would at least pretend to be pleased to see me. But not Sid: by the warmth of his greeting I could have been any old fan stopping him in the street for his autograph. Perhaps he was unhappy with the sketches I had written. I didn't talk to him long enough to find out. It was the last time our paths crossed and I was as sad about that as I am sure he was.

On Christmas Eve, Peggy Ramsay came to Alexandra Court to have dinner with us and watch 'Merry With Medwin' on television. I can't remember if she had a set of her own; I do remember that she wasn't very enamoured with the medium and thought her writers ought to be doing better things. I was extremely nervous as to what her reaction would be. It was, after all, very much the usual asinine Christmas fodder. Luckily nothing of mine was too cringe-making, and we all seemed to agree that for what it was it had worked perfectly well. And then I went and committed the unforgivable sin: the nervous tension over, sitting in a comfortable chair, full of good food and probably too much wine, I fell asleep and Denis had to wake me. I'll take a bet on it that I am the only client Peggy Ramsay ever had who fell asleep in her presence. I'm not sure that a little black mark didn't go against my name for that.

But it wasn't black enough to stop her endeavouring to find me work, sometimes far in excess of the normal call of duty, as in the following instance: Peter Bridge and John Gale had gone into theatrical management together, and on hearing that their first venture was to be a revue, Peggy invited them along with their director, James Gilbert and choreographer, Alfred Rodrrigues to a buffet supper at her flat to meet me and my musical collaborator. After we had all wined and dined and the guests were seated comfortably facing the piano, Robb and I performed our latest material. They were a very appreciative audience and straight away said they wanted two of the songs. I then read them a sketch I had just written and they wanted that too, saying it would be the perfect item to introduce the two stars following the opening chorus. Peggy had stage managed the evening brilliantly, and I can't believe any other agent would have gone to such trouble for a client who was not going to earn them big money. But as I have said before, Peggy was unique.

The revue was called, 'On The Brighter Side' and starred Stanley Baxter and Betty Marsden. Among the supporting cast were Ronnie Barker, Pip Hinton, David Kernan, Amanda Barry, Una Stubbs and Judy Carne (Daisy in 'Chrysanthemum'). After a short tour it opened at the Phoenix Theatre on April the 12th 1961. The reviews on the whole were good (our contributions getting favourable mentions) and the show had quite a respectable run. The one obstacle to it being the hit revue of the season occurred on the 2nd of May when four young Cambridge graduates arrived at the Fortune Theatre with a revue they had written themselves called, 'Beyond The Fringe' that ran for 2,200 performances. At the Edinburgh Festival the year before, the very same show had met with tepid reviews, but the London critics were ecstatic about it, hailing it as a great new form of satirical revue; and in time it would be considered seminal to the rise of satire in Britain. I thought this was an exaggeration, there had been some good satirists before them, but the material was brilliantly written and performed with consummate skill by four remarkably talented young men with perhaps even a spark of genius in there somewhere (genius is not a word I bandy about lightly. I have seen many great performances in my life, but only five or so I thought touched by genius). Kenneth Tynan, at the vanguard of modern theatre, in his unstinting praise of the golden boys dismissed all other revues that were running then as old hat and obsolete. As a critic he had much sway at the time and it took a lot of the shine off our show and probably shortened its run. I often felt that in his infatuation with the new he sometimes threw the baby out with the bath water. He was mainly responsible for Terrence Rattigan, one of the finest playwrights of the 20th century, not writing plays for several years: a sad loss to the theatre. Surely there was enough room at the same time for both John Osborne and Terrence Rattigan. I suppose, though, by being fair minded and considerate as well as being daring and avant-garde you don't land the job of theatre critic on 'The New Yorker'.

Some of the songs from, 'On The Brighter Side' were published by KPM Music, and two of ours, 'I'm In Love' and 'Little Nell' were among them. The head of KPM Music (Keith Prowse/Peter Maurice) was a charming man called Jimmy Phillips who himself was a lyricist and over the years had penned several well known songs. He liked my work and one day invited me to lunch at the L'Escargots Restaurant. Jimmy was good company and told many amusing anecdotes about the business. One that particularly appealed to me was how the lyric of the Charlie Chaplin song, 'Smile' (published by KPM) came about. Jimmy was driving his young son back to boarding school after the summer holidays; the boy was reluctant to go and on the edge of tears – Jimmy said he was pretty near the edge himself, and to lighten things up on the long journey he suggested they put words to the Chaplin tune he had been humming. "Smile though your heart is aching...", Jimmy began. Half way through the journey they were up to, "Although a tear may be ever so near...", and by the time they reached the school gates father and son were singing, "You'll find that life is still worthwhile if you just smile." I found it a touching story and think of it every time I hear the song.

Jimmy had put me on a retainer to write English lyrics to some of the foreign songs he bought from France, Italy and Greece. Some were published and a few recorded but none, sad to say, ever made the hit parade. My favourite was by the French composer, Marguerite Monot, who had written that superb musical, 'Irma La

Douce' and several of Edith Piaf's hits. The song's French title was, 'L' P'tit Francais'; in English it became, 'The Bad Young Man Of St. Tropez'. Both French and English versions were recorded by Colette Renard, who had created the role of Irma La Douce in Paris. It had a catchy tune and I was hoping it would take off but I only heard it once on the radio.

One afternoon Jimmy rang me up and told me to hurry over to his office in Denmark Street (London's Tin Pan Alley), he had someone coming who he wanted me to meet. It was Leslie A. Macdonnell, the managing director of the London Palladium. Over a cup of tea and a biscuit I was asked if I would like to write the lyrics for the next Palladium Pantomime, opening in December and running through till March. The music would be written by Laurie Johnson, who had recently had a success with his score for the musical, 'Lock Up Your Daughters.' The pantomime was, 'Little Old King Cole', created and produced by Robert Nesbitt, and starring little old Charlie Drake in the little old title role. The romantic interest would be provided by Janette Scott (Thora Hurd's pretty daughter, recently divorced from Mel Torme) as the Shepherdess, and Garry Miller as the Prince (there was a weird trend in the 60s for the principal boy to be played by a boy – it was most confusing).

Working with Laurie Johnson was not easy, you couldn't even really call it working with him. He wrote the tunes and I then put words to them. That didn't worry me; it was, after all, what I had been doing with Jimmy's foreign songs. What did worry me was the infinitesimal amount of time we had together to discuss the work. He was living in the country, busily writing film music, and only came up to London one afternoon a week, during which he would manage to squeeze me in half an hour or so of his precious time. We always went to a steamy little café in Charing Cross Road, just around the corner from Denmark Street, and over an unappetising cup of urn-brewed tea he would hand me some sheets of manuscript with a top line of music on them, hum me the tunes a few times, and then with a relieved, "Next Friday then," beat it back to the country. How much easier my life would have been had the tape recorder and audio cassette existed then. Still, somehow I managed and I think, everything considered, the songs turned out quite well.

When I say, everything considered, I am actually referring to my relationship with Robert Nesbitt. Since the early 1930s he had been known for his staging of spectacular revues with French sounding titles and masses of girls in sequins and feathers; he had also staged the annual Palladium Pantomime for some time. At our first meeting I could see that he had already made up his mind not to like me. He was probably furious having someone thrust upon him whose work he didn't know; he might even have had another lyric writer in mind and been overruled by Macdonnell. Whatever the reason he was determined to make the job untenable for me. His reaction to every lyric I showed him was the same: he would look at it for a full five seconds, sigh heavily and hand it back to me saying it wasn't good enough. I knew the lyrics were far better than he was making them out to be but what could I do? I became so intimidated by him that I was on the point of asking Peggy to get me released from my contract – which was exactly what he wanted – when someone I knew who had worked with him a few times gave me some advice. Nesbitt always had to have a whipping boy and in the early stages of a production when he didn't have a great deal of choice it was usually a new writer or designer. The secret was to keep one's nerve and just hang on. When the cast was assembled and the costumes and scenery began to arrive the persecution would cease, one would be completely ignored and someone else would be the whipping boy. Difficult as it was I took the advice and sure enough it happened exactly as said. Nesbitt was suddenly off my back and bothering me no more – in fact I don't think he even spoke to me again – and then, to my astonishment, he decided to use some of the very first lyrics I had shown him – the ones he had so scornfully rejected – and they worked very well. I felt rather smug when Milton Schulman of the *Evening Standard* said the lyrics had a wit unusual in pantomime. No matter how much money I was offered, I told myself, I would never work with Robert Nesbitt again. I needn't have worried, he didn't ask me to. I saw the pantomime twice: on the opening night and one of the last matinees in March. The production was slick and the songs did what was expected of them, but I got no pleasure watching it, I had too many bitter memories. However, this unpleasant episode does have a satisfying conclusion of sorts, for after the first run through with full orchestra and my presence no longer required, I saw neither Robert Nesbitt nor Laurie Johnson ever again.

I was taking Denis to the first night, not that he ever wanted to see another pantomime, he was just curious as to how my contribution had worked out. Then a couple of days before the opening he developed a bad chest infection and was confined to bed. Patrick came, was very concerned and straight away put him on a powerful antibiotic. I had noticed during the summer that his health was slowly deteriorating and with the onset of winter the condition had accelerated. He sometimes found it difficult to breath and the puffer he used to relieve this symptom was now always close at hand. I was extremely worried, and no longer did I have Irene to call upon in need; she and Harold had sold their Kynance Place house and gone to live in Norfolk. I knew she would hurry down in an emergency but it wasn't the same as when she was just one street away and could pop over to see how he was and if there was anything she could do. I was now very much on my own and watching him as he sometimes fought for breath, and not being able to assist in any way was horrible. Fortunately the antibiotic did its trick and the chest infection cleared up, but the emphysema was never going get better, it could only worsen. Denis was able once more to resume normal life as best he could and he put on a cheerful front but inwardly I knew how wretched he must be feeling.

Christmas 1961 was one of the four most miserable Christmases of my life. I am not going to put them in any order of misery or even describe them in any way, just take my word for it, they were all miserable – and I am not including those dreadful Christmas dinners I had to endure with Marie Freeman. Denis was ill in bed and had absolutely no appetite, so turkey with chestnut stuffing, mince pies or even a glass of champagne were the last thoughts on his mind. Under the circumstances I felt equally disinterested so we gave the whole yuletide thing a miss. I did cheat a little by slipping over to Eardley Crescent and spending a couple of cheerful hours with Hattie and John and some of the regulars who were old chums: among them, Beryl Reid, Johnny Heawood, Stella Marais, Bruce Copp and a few others. As usual it was great fun and I hated having to drag myself away, but I had to get back to see if there was anything Denis needed. As I have said, his appetite was nil and it was all I could do to get him to swallow a few teaspoonfuls of Brands Essence. For my own Christmas dinner I made myself a delicious omelette the way Elizabeth David showed me back in the Halsey Street days.

At the start of 1962 feelings of excitement and expectation began to rise inside me once more; for on the 22nd of January 'Chrysanthemum' starring Patrice Munsel opened the season at the Royal Poinciana Playhouse, Palm Beach, Florida, to an audience packed with gold coast society that included Senator Joseph Patrick Kennedy and his wife; and from New York, Hermione Gingold and some other theatre folk had flown in for the show. How I longed to be there, but neither Bob nor John had invited me and I couldn't afford it myself.

Florida is five hours behind us in time, so when the curtain rose there at 8 pm it was 1 am in London. I was in bed but by no means asleep and when the hands of my watch showed one o'clock exactly I crossed my fingers, took a deep breath and wished like anything. I had to wait until late in the afternoon to hear the result: John Johnson rang me to say it had been a tremendous success. Patrice had triumphed in the role, and everyone was saying the show was surely Broadway bound. He then read me some of the reviews:

'An absurdly wonderful piece of stylised nonsense starring the peerless

Patrice Munsel is the musical "Chrysanthemum". If Miss Munsel had not already won her laurels at the Metropolitan Opera, in musical comedy and on TV, she could start a new cycle by becoming the toast of Broadway in this refreshing satire. This is one of the few "American premiers" worthy of the name. The gay music is by Robb Stewart and the book and lyrics by Neville Phillips and Robin Chancellor. Some of the lines are excruciatingly funny.'
Miami News.

'An explosive outburst of melody and merriment. "Chrysanthemum", circa 1913, emerges as mirthful, attractively mounted, filled with tuneful songs. The "Fate Worse than Death" scene in Act 1 is a high point of comedy acting in a musical comedy for all times.'
Palm Beach Daily News.

'An exaggerated romantic, exciting and improbable world if you will, is being staged at the Royal Poinciana Playhouse, where on Monday night the curtain went up on another season with Patrice Munsel bringing a bubbly and memorable evening to a first night audience of huge capacity. "Chrysanthemum" is the thing to see… scene follows funny scene with Miss Munsel in baggy pants imitating her abductors from Limehouse, Miss Munsel in toreador pants, romping through the swift beats of a Spanish dancer; and Miss Munsel singing songs to be remembered – "Saturday Night", "Shanghai Lil" and "Love is a Game".'
Palm Beach Post.

'A bloomin good show.'
Miami Herald.

'Gold coast society showed up en masse last night for Frank Hale's Royal Poinciana Playhouse and first hand reports say former Met star Pat Munsel as the heroine of the British made musical "Chrysanthemum" has everyone talking about the show's sure Broadway potential.'
New York Telegraph.

A week or so later I received a letter from the Schulers saying how delighted everyone had been with the show and that they were now keen to mount a Broadway production. Enclosed were copies of the reviews and the theatre programme. It was the programme that informed me that Howard Barker, producer of the hit Off Broadway musical, 'Little Mary Sunshine' (1,143 performances), was now the co-producer of the show and that John Johnson's name had been relegated to a small bracketed credit below theirs which read (in association with John M. Johnson). I wasn't sure what this meant but I had a suspicion that he had been edged out by the two more experienced producers. I did sense during our telephone conversation that his warm relationship with Bob and Patrice had cooled rather but he gave no reason why. It was never explained to me what had happened, all I know is that after the Palm Beach production John Johnson faded out of the picture completely.

The next letter I got was signed by Barker and Schuler and contained a piece of startling information. Their belief in 'Chrysanthemum' was as strong as ever and they were going ahead trying to get a Broadway production set up but with a different leading lady; Patrice did not wish to go in with it. It can't have been that she was dissatisfied with the part or her performance in it, and the opinion of public and critics alike had been unanimously good. All I could think was that she had proved to herself and everyone else what a fine comedienne she could be, and it was now time to return to the opera house and do some serious, less frivolous work.

In subsequent letters various leading ladies names were mentioned. Carol Channing, they said, had shown great interest, but by a few letters later her name ceased to appear. Weeks of silence turned into months and then one day a telegram arrived saying: 'Gower Champion to direct Tammy Grimes as 'Chrysanthemum'.' I was overjoyed for they were both at the peak of their careers on Broadway and there was now the chance of us having a big popular success. There followed some weeks of ominous silence and then came the letter to say Gower Champion had been offered a four picture deal in Hollywood that he couldn't refuse and had reluctantly bowed out. Without Champion, Tammy Grimes began to get cold feet and unless they could come up with a director of equal brilliance she was bowing out too. Several directors were approached and to my utter dismay I learnt they had even sent the script to Sir John Guilgud, who was working in New York at the time. I thought this was madness; he had never directed a musical before, and anyway I couldn't see the subject being remotely his cup of tea – and of course it wasn't. The next name to come up was Christopher Hewett. I had known Chris since the late 40s; he was one of Gingold's closest friends and had appeared in all her London revues since, 'Sweet and Low' during the war. When she went to live in New York he quickly followed and there continued a successful career as actor and later director. His biggest directorial success was the revival of Rodgers and Hart's 'The Boys From Syracuse'. When he came to London to restage it at Drury Lane we met up and discussed, 'Chrysanthemum': with the right leading lady, he said, he would very much like to do it – and that was the last I heard of Chris. A few names later came Donald Saddler who had just had an enormous hit with the revival of, 'No, No, Nanette' starring Ruby Keeler. I had not seen Donald since 1946 when he was dancing with The New York Ballet at Covent Garden and we spent a heavenly afternoon in bed together at the Cumberland Hotel. A letter or two later Donald's name had gone the way of all the others. Then followed a period when they either had a leading lady and no director or vice versa and I was beginning to think that probably nothing was ever going to happen when Barker wrote to say they had definitely got Kaye Ballard for the lead. Once again I felt excited; I thought Kaye Ballard was a fantastic comedienne and a wonderful singer too. Physically she was not my ideal Chrysanthemum but I knew she would do something extraordinary with the part and she wouldn't be afraid to give it a sexy, Mae West touch that neither of the others had done. I knew Kay slightly from when she came to London in 1950 with the American revue, 'Touch and Go' and bowled us over with her brilliant comedy. Friends introduced us and she came to Halsey Street a few times, as did some of the other Americans in the cast. When the show closed she stayed on in London for a while and we very much wanted her for our Rayne Storm Productions revue, 'On The Tiles', that was to star Hermione Baddeley and came to such a catastrophic end before it had even begun.

I can't remember who the director was at this point, or even if there was one, but Barker and Schuler had already started looking for backers and with a group of well rehearsed singers and musicians, they flew to Dallas, Texas to audition the show to some rich businessmen who were there for an important conference. They felt pretty sure that they would raise the money they needed, but, and wasn't it just 'Chrysanthemum''s luck, on landing at Dallas Airport they were greeted with the news that President J. F. Kennedy had just been assassinated driving into the town. There was nothing else for it; they didn't even leave the airport, they just got on the next plane back to New York. After that things went very quiet and I somehow had the feeling that the heart had gone out of it.

When their option on 'Chrysanthemum' expired Barker asked us if we would renew it free of charge. Max Kester of Fosters Agency was not happy about this. He said if they couldn't afford a few hundred dollars for an option how were they going to find enough money to put the show on. So the option was dropped and we never heard from Howard Barker or Robert Schuler again.

Some years later I had a letter from my friend, Paul Horner (with whom I had written material for the Stanley Baxter TV shows) who was then living in Hollywood where he had become a friend of, and written songs with Peggy Lee. One evening he was accompanying her at a concert at the Hollywood Bowl and also appearing on the programme was Patrice Munsel. He happened to mention my name to her and she told him how much she had loved 'Chrysanthemum' and what a tragedy it was that it never got to Broadway. And that ends the story of 'Chrysanthemum' in the incarnation in which we knew it, but it was about to undergo a strange metamorphosis.

At the beginning of 1968 I was in Sydney, Australia, where I spent six months writing sketches and lyrics for a popular TV show, and one night I went to the cinema to see, 'Thoroughly Modern Millie'. As I watched the film the strangest feeling of déjà vu swept over me: It was set in the 1920s not 1913; they were dancing the Charleston not the Turkey Trot; the scene was San Francisco's Chinatown not Limehouse; but Julie Andrews' modern Millie was very much an American Chrysanthemum and Mary Tyler Moore's Dorothy had a lot in common with Mary Ann – having to be rescued from evil white slave traffickers by our plucky little heroine; and Beatrice Lillie's wonderfully sinister Mrs. Meers was a dead ringer for Ma Carroty, hypodermic syringe at the ready, chatting up of her young victims: "All alone in the world, dear?" bore an uncanny resemblance to Ma Carroty's: "Are you by yourself, dear?" There was even a Chinese laundryman like Ching Loo. I thought I might be hallucinating but friends who knew the show also commented on the close similarities. I have often been asked why we didn't sue, but what chance would an almost penniless British writer have against the might of 20th Century Fox, who I am sure would be able to persuade a jury that the similarities were purely coincidental. Personally I don't believe they were.

Several years on, 'Thoroughly Modern Millie' was adapted as a stage musical and became a big Broadway hit. I often thought that but for a few little quirks of fortune that could have been 'Chrysanthemum's fate. Now that is definitely my last word on the subject!

————

By the spring of 1962 having survived another bad foggy winter Denis' health was in a bad state. Walking any distance had become a major problem. No more could he stroll up to Kensington Gardens on a sunny day or if the weather was bleak down to the Victoria and Albert Museum where many a winter's afternoon had been pleasantly spent. Now after only a few hundred yards he would be breathless and need to use the puffer, which I noticed was becoming less and less effective. Apart from the much looked forward to afternoon drives he took with Barbara Back, when she could spare the time and he was feeling up to it, he had hardly left the flat all winter. Tommy's weekend invitations he no longer accepted; he feared he wouldn't be able to cope with the socialising required, especially if there were other guests there.

Denis had good days and bad days, some were very good and some very bad, and you couldn't tell in advance what sort it was going to be, which made planning ahead almost impossible. I was always having to ring people up and put them off. Sometimes on a very good day we would take a taxi to a cinema and catch a film he wanted to see; or if Bumble invited him to dinner he would be brave and go. I sometimes accompanied him but he also went alone. He felt at ease in Bumble's flat; it had a very relaxing atmosphere, and he enjoyed the company of their mutual old friends: Bunny Roger, Elizabeth Welch, Edward Burra... A couple of times Vivien Leigh was there and they got on very well together. Sadly, I never met her. Vivien always insisted that Bumble oversee her stage and film costumes, even when she had not designed them. She had implicit faith in Bumble's taste and couturier knowledge, and over the years they had become very close friends. During the spectacular break up of her marriage to Olivier, with the whole of Fleet Street hounding her, Bumble's flat became her hideaway. When a snooping reporter came sniffing at the door Bumble professed no knowledge of the star's whereabouts and coolly sent him on his way. To thank her for those helpful words in his newspaper the next day he described her as, 'Vivien Leigh's faithful old dresser.' Bumble was not amused – not as much as we were.

When the weather started to get warmer I sometimes noticed from our window an attractive looking woman pushing a wheelchair with a large, bearded man in it up Queens Gate towards the park, and an hour or so later pass again the other way. I recognised the man as Michael Flanders, half of the brilliant comedy song partnership, 'Flanders and Swann', who were enjoying great popularity in the theatre, on radio and television, and had recently had a successful season on Broadway. At Oxford, Flanders, handsome, athletic, standing over six foot tall and with a fine, deep voice acted in many plays, and it was thought by some that he might be the next Olivier or Donat. He left Oxford in 1941 to join the RNVR, and in 1943 while on service contracted Poliomyelitis; consequently he was to spend the rest of his life in a wheelchair.

While at Oxford he and a clever young composer called Donald Swann got together and wrote some witty revue material; later they would contribute to many smart West End revues. It was a very brave decision of theirs to perform their own songs in public. You might suppose that with one man seated at a piano and the other in a wheelchair it would make for a very static evening's entertainment, but not a bit of it: Flanders manoeuvred his chair about with great dexterity, and with their strong, very individual personalities and brilliantly written material they fully animated any stage they were on. I saw their very first show, 'At The Drop Of A Hat', at the New

Lindsey Theatre in 1956 – the same year 'Chrysanthemum' was on there (oh, dear, I said I wouldn't mention that word again).

Watching Flanders go by one day I thought how nice it would be if Denis could get up to the park and see the flowers that were now springing up all over. I suggested that we too got a wheelchair but he wouldn't hear of it. I don't think he could quite see himself as a wheeled about invalid; but as the days got sunnier and he thought more about those spring flowers the idea became more acceptable, and it wasn't long before we took a taxi down to a medical and orthopaedic appliance shop in the Brompton Road, near Harrods, where one could hire wheelchairs. We chose one we thought most suitable and I pushed him home in it. It was not as easy going as I had anticipated, having seen the effortless way Flanders seemed to glide past our window. Lifting it onto and down from high kerbs was hard work and my admiration for Claudia Flanders, whose load was far heavier than mine, increased enormously.

And so began our almost daily visits to the park and it was wonderful to see the pleasure Denis got from these outings. He had always been a very keen gardener and seemed to know the name of every plant. His magnificent garden in Cairo with its myriad of exotically scented flowers he had created himself and tended with the help of his cook/gardener, Mahommed. On one of our perambulations down the flower walk in Kensington Gardens we happened to cross paths with the Flanders and as I had seen pram pushing nannies often do I nodded politely as we passed. I wanted to say, "Thank you, not only for your wonderful songs but also because you are responsible for Denis being here in the park today," but I could just imagine their expressions had I done so.

One afternoon Benny Goodman came to tea and brought us an LP recording of Richard Rodgers' new musical, 'No Strings', that had just opened on Broadway and to which he had attended the first night. The Goodmans and Rodgers were next door neighbours on Long Island and close friends of many years. When Oscar Hammerstein the second died in 1960 Rodgers lost the second of his two life long collaborators, the first being Lorenz Hart who died in 1943. Deciding to go it alone he wrote both the music and words to 'No Strings', and a very professional job he made of it. Later he would work with Stephen Sondheim on, 'Do I Hear A Waltz?', but it was not a happy collaboration and they never repeated it. Benny thought 'No Strings' was a terrific show and what particularly intrigued him was that the orchestra, instead of being in the pit, was on the stage as part of the action, and, like the title, had no strings to it.

Benny had come to England to stay at the country home of his good friends and great fans, Lord and Lady Londonderry. He still loved to travel and had recently been in Moscow, where he bought some paintings by modern artists whose work he admired. Alice no longer travelled with him; she seldom ventured beyond the garden of their Long Island home. Denis and she occasionally corresponded but she had more or less become a recluse. Alice had kept open an account she had at Coutts Bank in London; on deciding she would no longer need it and knowing that through ill health Denis had not been able to work for some time she had what money was in it transferred to his account at the Westminster Bank. It was not a great sum, just a few hundred pounds, but it was very welcome and Denis was most touched by the kind gesture of a once close friend.

Denis' condition permitting, Maude still came around at 6 o'clock for her preevening date drink. He enjoyed her company and liked to hear all the gossip from the films on which she was working. Her escort for the evening no longer came in for a dry martini; Denis did not have the energy to lay on the charm he always felt obliged to when meeting strangers; so with their car or taxi waiting in the courtyard they would ring the bell and Maude having knocked back her drink, would hurry out to join them.

That summer most of Denis' old friends came to see him, some several times, others once or twice. Bumble was a regular visitor; also Graham; then there was Robin, Moura; Katusha; Dilkusha; Mathew, who brought with him a clever young painter he had discovered, who lived on a Chelsea houseboat, and Denis bought one of his pictures; Elizabeth came a couple of times with gifts from Roche, her favourite French shop in Soho, once it was escargots freshly arrived from Paris, the next time a wonderfully ripe Camembert; Joy flitted in on one of her fleeting visits to England; and one evening Brian dropped by with an extremely handsome young guardsman he had just picked up and wanted to show off before they returned to his Knightsbridge flat for an hour or so's conviviality; whenever they were in London Irene and Harold would come to see how he was, but they seldom left Norfolk that summer – Irene had not been well herself; some of my friends, around my own age, who Denis liked also came, although I usually saw them away from the flat; it was a refreshing break to get out for a few hours, and anyway, most of them smoked like chimneys and like my mother found it difficult to socialise for long without a lighted cigarette between their fingers. Now, forty five years on, as I recall some of their names, Hanns … Ginny … Johnny H … Hattie … Johnny W … Diana … Richard … Frazer … Ken … it's sad to think that all those bright, individual personalities are no more.

All at once autumn was upon us. I don't recall autumns in South Africa. As I remember it the seasons just merged into one another and either it was hot and sunny or cold and wet. But autumn in London holds a strange potency for me. When the bright flowers have all gone and the park is sepia coloured, when the watery rays of the sun have lost their warmth and the scent of burning leaves permeates the misty afternoon air, I wallow in the sweet melancholic sadness of the dying season. It's what I call my Chekhov mood.

That autumn was especially poignant for both of us. Nothing was said but we knew that when the weather turned our visits to the park would have to cease, and then there would be just winter ahead with its inevitable fogs and smogs that Denis so dreaded.

At the beginning of October there were some beautiful sunny days and we took full advantage of them, never knowing which might be the last; and as we sat in a quiet clearing among the trees, hardly talking, just soaking in the last of the year's warmth, I sensed a cloud of deep despondency settling on Denis. I could see him thinking, 'this is as good as it's going to be – a few more afternoons like this, perhaps, and then the long confinement in a flat that was already beginning to feel like a condemned cell. Yes, this was as good as it was going to be.'

In mid October the fogs started and Denis's breathing became badly affected. In frustration and fury at his condition he became morose and ill-tempered and at times took his anger out on me. There were days when I could do nothing right. He wouldn't say what he wanted to eat but whatever I gave him was wrong and often remained untouched. I really didn't know what to do. And in his rages he could say cruel things. Laziness was blamed for my not achieving as much with my life as he felt he should have done with his. He always thought I was more talented than I actually was. His encouragement and praise of my work was invaluable, it gave me the confidence that I needed, and I doubt if I would have achieved half as much had not some of his knowledge and sophistication rubbed off on me, but I was never going to write the brilliant comedy he was expecting. Yes, I had a certain talent for writing and acting and most of my life I have made a sort of living from both, but I knew my limitations and accepted them – he couldn't or wouldn't. He expected so much more of me and I was sorry to have to disappoint him.

In the jaundiced state he was in he saw his own life as worthless, an utter failure, what had begun with promise had dwindled away to nothing. This was rubbish, he had done some amazing things that anyone would be proud of, until ill-health turned up like a spectre at the feast. In his youth Denis was the golden boy; apart from his weak chest – a condition both he and Irene had inherited from their father – everything seemed to be going his way. At their home in Fairlight, East Sussex, Marie converted an Elizabethan barn into a beautiful theatre as a play thing for her blue eyed little boy, and when still in his teens he staged several Shakespearian productions that were highly regarded by the audiences that came over from nearby Rye, home then to many writers and painters. His good friends there were Ellen Terry's actress daughter, Edith Craig and the artists, Paul Nash, Edward Burra and R.G. Eves. Another distinguished resident and sometime mayor of the town was the novelist, E.F. Benson, whose wonderful 'Mapp and Lucia' stories were set in the fictitious town of Tilling that was unmistakeably Rye. Benson lived at Lamb House, once the home of Henry James, and for a short while Edith Wharton resided there. Denis remembered as a small boy meeting Henry James in the local shop and being given a penny by him, plus a lengthy dissertation on how the coin might be most efficaciously spent.

When he was in his early twenties his Fairlight production of Beaumont and Fletcher's, 'The Knight Of The Burning Pestle' so impressed Lance Seifking, a producer at the BBC, that a glowing report of his capabilities was given to Sir John Reith, the Head of Broadcasting, and in due course he was invited to join the Corporation. The studios were then situated at Savoy Hill, just south of The Strand, and there in extremely cramped conditions, they remained until Broadcasting House, No 1. Portland Place was built in 1932.

Denis's first job with the BBC was to create a sound effects department and for a while he went around banging things together to hear what they sounded like. But soon making noises for plays gave way to actually producing them, and over the next few years he did some amazingly innovative and audacious productions as well as introducing the British listeners to exciting new writers and composers from Europe and America. He was responsible for them first hearing the work of Bertolt Brecht and Kurt Weil in his own English translation of, 'The Threepenny Opera'; and he took part in the first play ever to be broadcast on television: Pirandello's 'The Man With A Flower In His Mouth'. Hermione Gingold in her autobiography, 'How To Grow Old Disgracefully' (published by Victor Gollancz Ltd) recalls with humour those early days at Savoy Hill, a passage of which I would now like to quote, and as she sometimes forgot to pay me when using my material I think we can call it quits: 'Sir John Reith was the BBC's formidable general manager, as the director general was then called, and Denis Freeman was head of Drama. Denis used to do some quite exciting and avant-garde plays, including one called 'Les Maries de la Tour Eiffel' by Jean Cocteau, in which I played the part of a telegram. The play was scored for two whips, a washboard, a whistle, and an iron that was banged down on a piece of tin. Rehearsals were going splendidly, if noisily, when suddenly Sir John walked in and said, "What is this?" Looking round at the whip and washboard he asked, "Is this supposed to go on the air?"

"Oh, yes," said Denis. "It's a play by Jean Cocteau."

"It is NOT going on the air," said Sir John, and walked out. That was the end of that.'

On the light entertainment side among Denis' successful discoveries were Harry Roy and his Band; Young Ella Logan, just down from Glasgow, who would go on to be a Broadway star; and a fairly unknown young American comedy duo who had been traipsing around the English provinces doing twice nightly variety: George Burns and Gracie Allen. Denis found their wacky style of comedy hilarious, and after they had done a few broadcasts for him, so did the BBC audiences. Riding high on their radio success they returned to America and straight away started making it in the big time.

Working for the BBC under Sir John was rather like being in the army. The rules were strict and rigidly enforced. Although they could not be seen by the listeners, all male members of staff had to wear suits with ties during the day and dinner jackets at night; their social life was carefully monitored; divorce was a dismissible offence, and sex without a wedding ring was completely taboo. By the mid 1930s Denis, thoroughly fed up with having his personal life so restricted, and wildly jealous of Joy and other irresponsible friends who were having the time of their lives in the hot spots of Berlin and Paris (they didn't need to work for a living, he did), resigned from the BBC and became a freelance producer. For the rest of the decade, as well as having fun toing and froing across the channel in both reputable and disreputable company, he also produced some excellent plays and revues in the West End. 'Spread It Abroad' was considered by some with knowledge on the subject to be the best revue of the 1930's.

In 1940, having escaped from France, he wrote a best selling book about it, and after the war he was awarded the *Croix de Guerre* for his bravery while driving ambulances at the front.

His war years in Cairo were an undoubted success. Working with the Free French in liaising between them and the British, both highly suspicious of one another, was of great diplomatic importance, and in Cairo society his charming, witty presence was in constant demand.

And then on returning to Britain, with me in tow, the future indeed looked bright until his wretched lungs began to play up and sap him of his strength and creative ability. If I am going to be perfectly honest about this, and tell it the way it really was, you will have to be told of another factor, besides his health, that contributed to his not getting the recognition and reward his talents so richly deserved, and it was self inflicted. Inherited from their monstrous mother, I have no doubt, both Denis and Irene had a small but indelible streak of self destruction in their characters. When things were going really well for them and the band began to play, instead of getting up and leading the dance they would shoot themselves in the foot. Denis had masses of friends, few enemies, but those few were carefully chosen, and you can be sure they were the very people who could have been the most helpful to his career. I shall name but two: H.M. Tennent and J. Arthur Rank – the two most important producers of plays and films in Britain of the day. It was possible to survive without them, but as Denis learned to his cost it wasn't easy.

In that summer of '62 Stevie Smith had published a book of selected poems that Denis admired, and he kept a copy beside his bed. One poem he particularly identified with was called, 'Not Waving but Drowning', and in the morbid state his mind was in he strongly empathised with the last two lines of the poem:

'I was much too far out all my life
And not waving but drowning.'

He also read the poems of Christina Rossetti that dwelt on the melancholy theme of mortality:

'When I am dead, my dearest,
Sing no sad songs for me...'

And:

'Remember me when I am far away,
Gone far away into the silent land...'

The deep despair that had taken hold of him was pitiful to see, and there was nothing I could do to alleviate it.

On Monday the 22nd of October a real pea-souper of a fog descended upon London and I became seriously concerned for his health. By Tuesday morning it had developed into a thick, acrid smog that deadened all the usual sounds of the city – it was a deathly silence; and so dense was the smog that traffic had to crawl through the streets, the drivers hardly able to see in front of their vehicles; and no matter how tightly doors and windows were kept shut, and curtains drawn, that horrible, yellow gas-like substance managed to seep its way into every room. Seeing Denis literally fighting for breath I rang Patrick and told him to come at once. He came as soon as he could, took one look at him and said, "You can't stay another day in this smog. We must get you out of London straight away." He made a couple of hurried phone calls and told me there was a bed waiting for Denis at a chest hospital in Surrey, not far from Woking, and to get him there without delay. I rang the car hire firm we sometimes used and told them we needed a car immediately. While waiting for it to arrive I got him into some warm outer garments and packed a small bag with his toiletries and a clean pair of pyjamas. He sat in the front seat of the car where he could be more upright, to assist his breathing, than in the back. I told the driver to hurry as it was an emergency, but under the circumstances of the weather he couldn't; so cautiously, at a snail's pace, we crawled out of London unable to see anything through that hideous, evil smelling smog.

Once we had left the outskirts of the city conditions improved, there was still fog about but it was nothing compared to what we had left behind. On arrival at the hospital Denis was put in a wheelchair and taken off to be seen by a doctor. I was told to go to a waiting room and there I sat for what seemed like ages. I was beginning to wonder if they had forgotten about me when a nurse came in and said I could now see him, but I was not to stay long as he had been sedated and needed to rest. His bed was about a quarter of the way down a crowded ward on the left hand side; I sat on a chair beside him and when I touched his hand he looked at me and smiled, but I could see he was in no condition to talk. I said I had better leave and he nodded. "I'll see you tomorrow," I said, but he shook his head. "No," he said, "it's too far and the car's expensive. Leave it till the day after when I'll be feeling better." I said, "All right. Get them to ring me if there's anything you want. Now try to rest." As I hurried out it was all I could do to hold back the tears.

The journey back to London was long and tedious and I felt thoroughly exhausted and numb. I realised later that I should have telephoned Irene and told her he was in hospital but my thoughts were so much in turmoil that it never entered my mind.

At 9 o'clock the next morning I rang to ask how he was and was told by a nurse he had had a quiet night and was in a stable condition. I decided I would ring again at 5 o'clock, and was on the point of doing so when the telephone rang. It was Patrick to say I should go to the hospital immediately. He was going to ring Irene and tell her the same thing. I rang the car hire firm and told them of my urgent need, and, as luck had it, I didn't have long to wait. It was the same driver as yesterday, a charming, very sympathetic man, but I had no desire for conversation; I just sat there silently wishing him to drive faster. The smog was not as dense as the day before and in the country the fog was quite light, so we accomplished the journey in a shorter time, although in the anguished state I was in it seemed much longer. I told the driver not to wait and hurried in.

Denis had been moved to a small side room on the right of the entrance to the ward. There was one bed in it and a couple of chairs. He was in an oxygen tent and heavily sedated. I sat on his right and watched him as he drifted intermittently between consciousness and sleep. During one of his brief spells of awareness I said his name and he looked at me and smiled. I leaned forward, took his hand in mine and tried to say comforting things, although whatever I said seemed to have a hollow ring to it. He started to say something affectionate to me but his words trailed away unfinished as he drifted back into sleep. Some time later, during one of his more lucid moments I told him we could no longer live in London, the fogs had become too much of a threat, I said we would go and live in Brighton. It was typical of Denis that, with hardly any breath left in his lungs and his brain befuddled by morphine, he was still able to say quite plainly, "Don't like the people in Brighton." He was going to be difficult to the very end. That spirit of defiance had not deserted him. He then drifted off again and shortly afterwards slipped into a deep slumber. A nurse came in at regular intervals to check his pulse and do whatever was necessary, and on one occasion he was given an injection, but he didn't stir.

A couple of hours later Irene and Harold arrived. They had had a dreadful journey down from Norfolk, driving through thick fog most of the way. Irene was upset that Denis did not know she was there, and she kept hoping he would wake up and see her, but he slept soundly on. Irene and I sat either side of him and there we kept our all night vigil. Harold came and went with cups of tea or coffee and at one point he brought us each a sandwich. I didn't feel remotely hungry but he insisted I eat it, so I did. Denis didn't stir once and I began to wonder if perhaps he was in a coma. Dawn broke and I could hear the birds outside singing in the trees. It was just after 8.30 when the head nurse came in and told us we would have to vacate the room for a short while as the nurses needed some time alone with Denis. She suggested that we went and had breakfast at a nearby country hotel; she assured us that he would not wake up while we were gone. I didn't want to leave the hospital but Harold insisted we went, so we did.

I suppose I must have eaten something, I don't remember anything about it, I was in a complete state of shock. I do remember lots of strong black coffee and some brandy and my impatience to get back to Denis. As soon as breakfast was over we returned to the hospital and as we hurried to the ward the head nurse came out to meet us. I knew straight away what she was going to say. She told us that Denis had died at approximately 9.35 having never regained consciousness. She then asked us if we would like to see him and Irene and I both said we would.

The oxygen tent had gone and Denis was now laid out with a white sheet covering him up to his neck. He had been washed and his hair neatly combed. His face wore an expression of calm tranquillity, very different to the pain and anxiety that had masked those features for so long. He looked younger, he was only fifty nine but illness had aged his face considerably. I stood for a couple of minutes looking at what was left of the man with whom I had spent eighteen and a half unforgettable years, good and bad, and all I could see was the sad, worn out detritus of a once beautiful human being. Denis was no longer there. Denis had gone. I left.

Irene had to go to the Registrar's office and complete all the paperwork that accompanies the death of a close relative. She was given the name of a firm of undertakers in Woking where we then drove, and there arranged for Denis to be cremated. The funeral would take place four days later, on Monday the 29th of October at the Woking Crematorium. It was already the afternoon by then so we had something to eat and drink in a pub before driving back to London and the flat.

I dreaded going in and seeing Denis' things just as he had left them two days before. Irene would stay with me for the next three days to help me sort out and decide what to do with his clothes and other personal effects. Harold asked if he could have Denis' Croix de Guerre which I gave him. He went back to Norfolk and would return for the funeral and to take Irene home.

I hate funerals. I don't suppose there are many who actually enjoy them, although these days they do seem to draw a crowd, especially if the deceased has any sort of celebrity. But I have no feeling for them whatsoever and unless by not attending I might offend a partner or close relative I stay away. When I die I am quite content to think that my remains might be put in a refuse sack and taken away with the rubbish. Irene felt rather as I do and we decided it would be a simple funeral with no flowers, eulogies or music. We would have been quite happy to have no service at all, but that was going to be a problem, so some anonymous vicar with a dull voice mumbled a few meaningless words about someone of whom he knew nothing, pressed a button and the coffin slipped away; but none of this had anything to do with Denis – he had long since gone.

Bumble, a staunch Roman Catholic, came. She had rung up to see how Denis was only to be told he had died. Maude knew about the funeral but didn't wish to attend, which I quite understood. Robin also found out by a chance phone call and offered to drive Irene and me to the crematorium, which we gratefully accepted. On hearing about it afterwards from Bumble, Brian rang me to ask why he had not been told. He was extremely cross, and that was the last time I ever heard from him.

On leaving the crematorium we made for the nearest pub and had several stiff drinks. I couldn't bear the thought of returning to the flat alone for the first time so Bumble invited me to stay at her place, which I did for two nights; I spent the next three nights at Johnny White's flat; then Robin and Andy took me to their house in Northamptonshire for the weekend, a beautiful Palladian building designed by Inigo Jones, where I went for long walks by myself, feeling completely lost. I was thirty eight years old and had never lived alone. First I had my family, then the camaraderie of the Entertainment Unit and then eighteen and a half years of stimulating companionship with Denis, who was always there when I needed him. Peggy Ramsay had got it right, I was always in awe of him.

When we drove back to London on Monday morning I had already made up my mind to pull myself together and stop wallowing in self pity – for that's what it was. Denis was out of his misery and we should be glad of that. I returned to the flat ready to sort myself out and prepare for the second, and scarily unpredictable, half of my life which I couldn't help feeling was going to be down hill all the way. I would never find anyone else to share my life the way Denis had. All I could see ahead was a lot of meaningless little affairs that would soon fizzle out, and enough alcohol to dull the senses. Thirty eight is not a good age in the gay world, where youth holds the ticket to the ball.

My first concern was to get shot of Alexandra Court. We still had two and a half years to go on our lease and, as I was a sitting tenant, the landlords couldn't get rid of me. We were well aware that when the lease expired the rent would be considerably increased and we would probably have to leave, so the landlords and I came to a mutual agreement: I would vacate the flat by the 30th of November in exchange for them forgoing the quarterly rent in advance that had been due since the beginning of October. I had no idea where I would go, I just wanted to get away from a place that held so many unhappy memories for me. Back into storage went the contents of the flat except for my clothes, typewriter and make-up box. I did sell quite a few things that I thought I would never need again: an 18th century black Wedgewood tea service with several extra Wedgewood tea pots, several Leeds and salt glaze plates, jugs and bowls and some Art Nouveau vases. Spinks bought a few of the Egyptian and Greek antiquities but they were not of much value, the best objects having been taken by friends who wanted something of Denis' to remember him by. In all it was a few hundred pounds which I felt I might need where I was going, although where that may be I still had no idea.

Midday on Saturday the 30th of November I walked out of Alexandra Court for the last time, having made no arrangements as to where I would stay. That was typical of me. Denis often called me 'a foolish virgin', the first half of that was probably true, but somehow I had always landed on my feet. So there I was with my belongings in a public phone box on South Kensington Station ringing an old friend of mine, Bruce Copp who had a basement flat in St Georges Square, Pimlico, where he sometimes let his spare room to a friend. I was lucky, he was in, and luckier still, there was no friend in the spare room. He said I could have it if I liked. I said I liked. I had known Bruce for some years. When we first met he was managing the restaurant at the Players Theatre and also had a flat above Hattie and John in Eardley Crescent. We became good friends and Denis liked him too.

On my first evening at St Georges Square, with heavy snow falling, I walked dramatically along the Embankment to Vauxhall Bridge, stood half way across it and threw my key to Alexandra Court into the river. This was my very theatrical way of saying, 'the past is over – let the future, whatever it brings, begin!!!'

The winter of 62-63 was the coldest on record since 46-47, when the whole of Britain froze and there were lengthy power cuts every day. I can remember rehearsing a play at Blackpool in an overcoat, gloves and woolly hat, on a stage with the dock doors open so we could see what we were doing as we acted in front of a beautiful backdrop of falling snow. And at the digs where Pat Moran and I were staying, so cold were my feet that I put them rather too close to the coal fire and the plastic soles of both my shoes melted.

Bruce's flat had no central heating, the rooms were heated by paraffin stoves and the one in my room gave off noxious fumes and very little heat. I either sat huddled before it in my overcoat or lay on the bed covered by blankets. I spent very little time there; about midday I would go to the Salisbury in St Martins Lane, meet actor friends and warm up on Guinness or wine. I spent most evenings at The Establishment Club in Soho, a club that Peter Cook had newly opened, which specialised in satirical cabaret. Bruce managed the restaurant and bar and I always had a warm welcome there. Many brilliant performers I saw doing their stuff on that little stage. I even caught one of the few appearances of the great Lenny Bruce before he was arrested and deported by the Home Office for heroin addiction.

I also went to the theatre quite a lot and the plays I remember particularly were Brenda Bruce in Samuel Beckett's, 'Happy Days' at the Royal Court – Beckett's bleak depiction of the human condition suited my mood very well then; Richard Johnson in John Whiting's, 'The Devils'; and Peter Brook's remarkable production of 'King Lear' starring Paul Schofoeld, which reinforced my belief that he was our finest actor.

Christmas was looming, the thought of which I dreaded. Unhappy memories of the last one were still with me. I had the stomach for none of it: the ersatz joviality, the clichéd sentiment, the peace and good will to all men until Boxing Day, the endless hackneyed Christmas songs, the expensive and useless presents, the pretence that the turkey was not over or under cooked – Ebenezer Scrooge had nothing on me that year. Friends had invited me to Christmas dinner, and Hattie's all day party was on again, but for once I had no real reason to be in London so I flew to Paris, the city that held many happy memories for me – and I couldn't have made a bigger mistake.

Cecil Robson and my few other friends who lived there were all away for the holidays; the streets and cafes of the left bank seemed strangely deserted; and the weather was far worse than in London. The icy winds that swept across from the Urals made walking in the streets a painful experience, and the ice and snow piled high on the pavements also made it a hazardous one. At the small hotel where I was staying in the Rue Bonaparte the meagre bars of central heating in my room remained barely tepid and the only way I found of keeping warm was by sitting in the Café de Flore and Les Deux Magots drinking endless cups of coffee and the occasional cognac, and at the inflated prices these venues were now charging it proved to be a very expensive way of keeping warm. The cafés were mostly empty, because of the atrocious weather I supposed, and the few who did venture in looked very uninteresting – not a painter or an existentialist among them. What had become of that Mecca of the arts, the Rive Gauche? Apart from the waiters who served me I spoke to no one at all; and in the gay bars I visited, the scenes of many a happy encounter in the past not one interested glance came my way. Standing at the bar knocking back the fine a'l'eau and feeling very sorry for myself the words of a Compton & Green lyric came to mind: 'The party's over, it's time to call it a day…'; and as I trudged through the snow, back to my lonely, freezing little hotel room I gave myself a stern lecture. "Neville," I said in a firm voice, "facts have to be faced. It appears to be abundantly clear to everyone except yourself that you have passed your sell by date." "The party's over," I sang in a tragic, maudlin voice, "it's all over, my friend." And then I remembered how Hattie, by leaving out the comma, gave a completely different interpretation to the last line: "It's all over my friend," she sang indignantly.

Christmas morning it was still snowing heavily, the streets were more or less deserted and most of the restaurants remained closed. After searching a while I found one open in Saint-Germain-des-Pres and there I lunched on a rare Filet de Boeuf Forestiere and a bottle of fine Burgundy, both perfect I am sure, but from neither did I I derive one iota of pleasure. I felt utterly alone and unwanted; a word that came to mind was, 'superfluous'. This was one of my four worst Christmases.

I returned to London on Boxing Day feeling almost happy to be back in my paraffin fumed basement room. Paris, the city where, apart from Cairo, I had had the most exciting times of my life, had been a total disaster.

I saw New Year in at The Establishment Club with Bruce, Johnny Heawood and a few other friends. During the evening Hattie made a brief appearance with her new handsome lover. She and John had parted. As we toasted in the New Year with champagne I wondered what shocks 1963 might have in store for me. I didn't have long to wonder. Early in January they came, there were two of them and both in letter form.

The first was from Peggy to say her list of clients had grown too large and she was having to unload some of them, and I was one of those. I was terribly upset, I had grown very fond of her over the years, and also, from a purely selfish point of view, having her as my agent did no harm to my reputation as a writer. The second letter, much more of a bolt out of the blue, came from Maude, and stated in quite blunt terms that she had loaned Denis a few hundred pounds some time before and she now wanted it back. I was absolutely flabbergasted. It was complete news to me that Denis had borrowed money from her. He had never mentioned it to me. I also felt hurt at the unfriendly tone of the letter. I was on the point of writing back that I would return the money as soon as I was able when a mutual friend, Julia McDermott, stopped me. Maude, she said, had been extremely upset that Denis, whom she considered her closest friend, had not mentioned her in his will. The reason he had not done so was because he left no will and the reason for that was because there was nothing to leave except for twenty five pounds in his Westminster Bank account and the effects of our flat. I had offered Maude the chance to choose something of his as a memento, as I had done with a few others, and Bumble, rather greedily I thought, took the two finest Tanagra figures and a couple of beautiful little brass studded Regency chairs, but Maude took nothing. Julia then told me that Maude in her naivety believed that the four prints we had of Degas ballet dancers, inherited from Marie, were the original drawings and worth a lot of money. I couldn't disabuse her without revealing my source of information. Still smarting from the tone of her letter I replied in an equally cool manner saying I felt myself under no obligation to pay a debt incurred by another and about which I had no knowledge whatsoever. Nevertheless, should a lucrative job come my way in the foreseeable future I would be only too happy to give her what she claimed was hers. There was no reply, and we didn't speak again for over thirty years.

The meeting came about when my partner, Jeremy (not yet in the story), had become an actors' agent and was doing a deal with Maude on the casting of a film. She invited him for drinks at her smart new flat in Upper Brook Street, Mayfair (old Mrs. Spector had long since died), and having heard we were an item she suggested he brought me along. With a certain amount of trepidation I went. We were given champagne and she couldn't have been more charming and polite, although I thought I sensed at times a slight chill behind the smile. Denis' name was never mentioned. Apart from the occasional glimpse of her across a crowded auditorium on a first night I never saw Maude again. I still believe she was slightly in love with Denis and because of my closeness to him, jealous of me.

Suddenly a little joy re-entered my life. Joy was back in town and staying with the ballet critic, Richard Buckle in his large, sprawling flat on the top floor of a building in

Long Acre, its windows overlooking Covent Garden Market. And there I was invited to several meals and lots of jolly parties. Buckle lived a very Bohemian existence, fascinating people came and went all the time, and besides Joy, staying at the flat was Kenneth Tynan's ex wife, Elaine Dundy who had written the successful novel 'The Dud Avocado'. Buckle was in the process of getting an exhibition together to celebrate the 400th year of William Shakespeare's birth at Stratford upon Avon and his flat was teeming with students from the Royal College of Art who were assisting him with designs. Among them was a good looking, fair haired young man called Eddy, whose whole demeanour I found provocatively sexy. To my surprise and absolute delight his response was favourable and straight away we took off on a delightful little carnal diversion that continued for some weeks. It ended when I started to take it seriously and that was not what he wanted, he was still young and keen to play the field. He was also very ambitious and looking for a bigger fish than me: he probably found one in the Long Acre flat. Still, it was most pleasurable while it lasted and did wonders for my flagging morale. It was just what the doctor ordered.

And something else very nice happened around that time. Johnny White had a mews flat in South Kensington (the mews is no longer there, having become part of the Lycee Francaise) and there, almost every Saturday night actors and actresses from West End shows and Croydon Rep, where Johnny was a member of the company, would turn up with bottles of cheap wine and sometimes party until dawn – not without occasional complaints from killjoy neighbours. They were very innocent parties: people would play the piano and sing or put on a record and dance; drugs were not yet on the scene and there was never any louche behaviour; it was just a group of like minded people letting off steam after their final performance of the week.

Two regulars were Martin Crump and Maurice Libby, a most affable couple. Hearing that I needed somewhere to live (Bruce's room being merely a stopgap) they told me a friend of theirs was about to vacate a cheap but cheerful little flat in Knightsbridge and suggested that I meet him. We were both invited to dinner at their flat where I took an instant dislike to the young man, an interior decorator who had just opened a shop in the Kings Road, Chelsea and was moving to a smart, much larger flat close to it. His main topic of conversation was the grand country houses where it seemed he was in constant demand as a guest. Eventually we got him onto the subject of the flat. It was an attic where the maids would once have slept in a tall elegant Georgian house in Brompton Square owned by a peer of the realm. As he resided mainly at his stately country home and only spent a few days a week in London he had no use for the two top floors of the house, and, being of a charitable nature, he allowed impecunious young artists and scholars to stay there for a mere pittance. The attic flat was semi-furnished and no rent was charged; one was asked to contribute something towards the household expenses, that was all, and this came to the vast sum of seven pounds, ten shillings a month. It was really just a token so one didn't feel like a pauper. By this arrangement one was a guest in the house and could not claim to be a sitting tenant and unable to be got rid of should he desire it. All this sounded too good to be true and I was waiting for the catch. It came quite soon. When he mentioned the landlord's name, Lord Faringdon, I said, "Ah, Gavin, I know him well." Instantly his face froze and he abruptly changed the subject. I realized then he was hoping to get money from whoever took on the flat without Gavin knowing about it. He left immediately after dinner, the subject of the flat not having been mentioned again. I knew I would have to work fast. I did know Gavin but not really well, we had met at cocktail parties and the occasional dinner at a friend's house. It was his boyfriend, a very cultured and witty young American from Chicago, with whom I was on easier conversational terms. Denis, of course, had known Gavin since the 1920s, when he was one of the bright young things. Yes, I knew Gavin, but not well enough to ring him up and ask if I could have a flat in his house. But I knew someone who could do that for me. Robin was a good friend of his and often dined at Brompton Square. I rang him the next morning and asked him if he would broach Gavin on the subject. He did so straight away and rang back to say Gavin had no idea the young man in the attic was leaving, he had said nothing to him about it, but if that was the case I could certainly have the flat. And that was that. I had fallen on my feet again. Good luck had come my way.

At the end of January, when the snobbish and greedy young interior decorator had decamped to his spacious new dwelling in Chelsea (achieved by more than a flair for fabrics, I imagine), I received a phone call from Douglas, Gavin's butler come cook come housekeeper, to say I could come to view the flat the following Sunday at midday when the house would be empty and he could spare me some time. I thought there was a tone of condescension in his voice, even a little hostility, but I put it down to an over heated imagination.

So, on Sunday at exactly noon, through a light flurry of snow, I made my way up Brompton Square looking at the numbers of the tall elegant houses as I went, each façade in perfect preservation – this was real grandeur! I found the right house and rang the bell. In his own time Douglas came up from his quarters in the basement beside the kitchen and opened the door. If you are now expecting me to describe an immaculately turned out butler with the manner of a Jeeves you are in for a disappointment. He was wearing shabby slippers, jeans, a plaid shirt and a baggy old cardigan. His face was unshaven and I doubt if he had even bothered to wash or comb his hair. As for the Jeeves manner, his coarse, slightly sinister features wore a fixed forbidding half smile, and without saying a word he let me know exactly what our relative positions in the household were to be. He was definitely in charge, and would administer only to the master and his guests, of which I was not one. I was merely one of his lordship's eccentric deeds of charity that from time to time occupied the two top floors of the house, an area that in his scheme of things did not exist, so there was never any need to go up there – except to read letters and rifle through drawers when one was out. As he silently led me up the several flights of stairs I thought that with a good shave and wearing the right drag Douglas would make a very credible Mrs. Danvers.

When we reached the penultimate floor and paused for breath before the final ascent I was informed that the rooms on that floor were occupied by one of his lordship's former protégées, now a famous face on television. He was a Canadian called Robert McKenzie, one of the BBC's top political commentators, particularly famous for his election broadcasts, where he had introduced an apparatus called a 'Swingometer' that kept the viewers informed as to how the voting was going. He was a poor young student newly arrived from Canada to study at the London School of Economics when he met Gavin and was offered a temporary roof over his head. Now, all these years later, he was still there. McKenzie had done very well for himself with his broadcasting, writing for newspapers and magazines and lecturing at universities, and with some of the money accrued bought himself a cottage in the country where he spent his weekends with friends. But he had never made any effort to leave Brompton Square, where surrounded by his books and other comforts he felt completely at home. Another reason for staying could have been that it was practically rent free – and perhaps Gavin had even forgotten he was up there.

The attic flat was very cosy. The ceilings were low and apart from the living room everywhere else was small – no space to swing a cat, but then I didn't have one so that was all right. There were two bedrooms, a kitchen, bathroom and lavatory, and the size they were it was going to be easy to keep warm. A great added attraction was an enchanting little roof garden with flower boxes around the railings and a couple of handsome stone Greek heads. When the boxes were full of sweet scented flowers this was going to be the perfect place to spend summer days and warm summer evenings. The view was superb: to my left was the large, glistening white dome of the Brompton Oratory; beyond it, to the right, the classic domes and gothic towers of the South Kensington museums; below me a beautiful tree lined garden, once the graveyard of Holy Trinity; above it and to the right, peeping over the rooftops, the many church spires of Kensington. I could gaze at that view for hours on end, and as I was not overlooked by anybody I need not even wear clothes. This was going to be a little paradise, and for the foreseeable future it was mine.

The flat was sparsely furnished and felt very impersonal; the previous occupant had obviously filled it with his own stuff and taken it with him. Douglas verified this. It now looked very bare, so when I had got onto slightly better terms with him and he saw I was prepared to toe his line he agreed to turn a blind eye to my bringing in some of my own things. The flat being the size it was, I couldn't have anything large, so I settled for a small chaise-longue, a round French Empire table with ormolu, some chairs, a cabinet in which to display the antique artefacts, books, pictures, a couple of Persian hangings, and on my bed the tiger cat rug that Major Myles Bourke had given to Denis when he visited Pretoria in 1944. By the time I had finished, the soulless, almost bare attic had been transformed into a really attractive, cosy little home where, loneliness permitting, I could be happy.

The real reason why Douglas had turned a blind eye to my furnishing the flat was because he did a bit of antique dealing on the side and wanted to see what I had in store and, if he wished to, buy some of it off me at his own price. I realised this was a sort of blackmail but I was in no position to refuse his offers. He carried off a beautiful Biedermeier sofa for a fraction of its value, a large mirror with a lovely carved frame and several other things. Not knowing when or if ever I would be needing the rest of the stuff, and the cost of storing it rising all the time, I let Douglas put it into auction for me and take what he considered was a fair percentage for his pains.

A year or two later, without a word of warning, Douglas had suddenly gone and his place was taken by Harry, a much older and gentler man with boot black dyed hair. I never discovered what had happened. One idea that crossed my mind was that perhaps some pieces from the many unused sets of fine silver, china and porcelain, all packed away in basement cupboards and seemingly forgotten, had found their way onto the market. This was pure speculation on my part. I wouldn't have put it past Douglas but I can't say that was what happened. Whatever the reason, he certainly left under a cloud.

Robert McKenzie and I never socialised. We once had a drink together and discovered we had nothing in common. He wasn't interested in the arts and I cared less than nothing about the workings of 'Swingometers' and such.

Gavin and I had few conversations, it was usually just a greeting as we passed on the stairs. I was invited down to drinks three or four times (his lovely American friend had returned to live in Chicago and had been replaced by a rather humourless looking Englishman who wore striped suits and probably did something in the city), and I was asked to dinner twice; the first time, after I had just arrived, it was with Robin; the next time with Bumble; and once he and his friend came up to the attic for drinks when Joy was there. He looked a little surprised at what I had done to the place but said nothing.

Before we move on I would like to tell you a little more about Gavin Faringdon. He was a socialist peer, a great supporter of the Labour Party and was on close terms with several of its leading figures. He was also a keen member of the Fabian Society and they sometimes dined at the house. On one of these nights I passed Lady Violet Bonham Carter and a group on the stairs as they came down from the first floor drawing room to the dining room. On another occasion, far more embarrassing, it was the Chinese Ambassador and party who had come for supper after a Gala Performance at Covent Garden, the women in their finest evening dresses and jewels, the men in white tie and tails and I in sandals, jeans and a tee-shirt. What they thought I can't imagine. But it wouldn't have worried Gavin, being of the aristocracy he felt himself above such things as idle gossip.

Although never close friends, Denis had known Gavin since the early 1920s when he was one of the more outrageous of the bright young things and had acquired a certain notoriety in London society. It was said that the character of 'Miles' in the Evelyn Waugh novel 'Vile Bodies' was based partly on Gavin. His parents, exasperated at his continuous wild behaviour, decided enough was enough, it was time for him to marry and settle down, so, in 1926 a suitable bride was sought. Her name was Honour, she had three older sisters, all married to dukes, and her dragon of a mother was determined that she too would have a title. Gavin was only an honourable then, but one day he would be a lord, and that was better than nothing. They had a very grand wedding at St. Martins in the Field in Trafalgar Square with the cream of English society present, and all would have been in the best possible taste had not some wicked prankster sent a wedding invitation to the entire cast of, 'Blackbirds', an all black American revue that was taking London by storm, and there seated in the stately pews between dukes and duchesses in their sedate wedding attire were these jazzily dressed, exuberant young singers and dancers from Harlem. The scene could have come straight out of a Ronald Firbank novel. Snobbish London society tittered over it for months afterwards.

When Gavin failed to consummate the marriage, Honour's dragon mother, determined her daughter should produce a son and heir, whisked her off to Rome and got an annulment from the Pope. Another, more suitable, husband was then found; he sadly didn't have a title but he had the next best thing, money, and soon, to everyone's relief, a beautiful bouncing baby boy was born.

In the 1930s Honour and Denis became good friends along with Alice, yet to meet Benny Goodman, and the three of them kept up their tightly knit friendship until the 1950s when Honour died in a gruesome car accident in Portugal. Both Denis and Alice were bereaved and always continued to mention her in their letters to each other.

In the late 1940s I was invited, along with Denis, to a soiree at Honour's beautiful house in St. John's Wood to hear Francis Poulenc, who had especially come over from Paris for the occasion, play and sing his new and yet unperformed Opera-Comique. It was a very exciting evening. Two of the other guests at the soiree were Gavin and his American friend.

One last anecdote concerning Gavin: when his father died and he inherited the title, while making his maiden speech at the House of Lords he almost brought the house down with laughter when instead of addressing the assembly as, '"My lords,' he called them, 'My dears'.

When that seemingly endless white winter finally turned grey with slush and spring made a belated entrance in green I took long, solitary walks in the park, and as I trod certain familiar paths memories returned of those last, sad Autumn afternoons with Denis trapped in his wheelchair, his eyes deep wells of despair, and I felt hollow inside. He was the only person who had ever really known me, and when he went, so, I felt, did my identity. I was now just as others saw me, and I wasn't quite sure who that was. I felt like a boat that had broken loose from its mooring and was drifting aimlessly on a strange, uncharted sea; or to put it less poetically, I was thoroughly fucked up.

I saw friends a lot, I would visit them and they would come to me; and I had several one night stands with strangers I met in bars and clubs, about which, thanks to the alcohol, I remembered nothing. I was killing time and most of those nights I was glad to have time dead.

My roof garden had become a little haven for me, I spent a great deal of time out there, and while the daffodils in the flower boxes gave way to tulips, and they to Nemesia and geraniums (I was no gardener, kind friends advised) I was being gainfully employed by the BBC, writing comedy sketches for the Stanley Baxter and Dick Emery shows. I also wrote a few more lyrics for Jimmy Phillips at KPM, but with Rock and Roll taking over that source soon dried up. Peter Bridge, who was preparing a lavish new revue called, 'Six of One', to star Dora Bryan at the Adelphi Theatre, asked me to contribute some material to the show. Chappell & Co Ltd would publish, 'I Was Passing By', written by Robb and me, and sung in the revue by Dennis Lotus. And every now and then a letter would come from Bob Schuler and Howard Barker telling me their latest choice of star and director for the Broadway production of, 'Chrysanthemum'. There, I've said the word again and I promised I wouldn't. That, I swear, was definitely the last time, and let me seal it with an oath made by Mary Ann in the show (I didn't say I wouldn't mention her name): "Cross my heart and hope to die!"

With the burgeoning of spring and the days getting hotter the ice in my heart started to crack and melt a bit, and I began to feel little twinges of what Cole Porter once described as, 'the urge to merge with the splurge of spring.' I had a slight urge but there was no one with whom I seriously wished to merge, let alone splurge; and being the pessimist I was, and with another horrendous birthday hovering just a few months away, I was firmly convinced there would never be anyone again who would seriously want to merge with me. The good thing about being a pessimist is that you don't get any disappointments, and if something nice does happen you are in for an unexpected surprise – and such a surprise was about to come my way!

On Friday the 14th of July, the eve of my thirty ninth birthday, I was invited to a party by Richard Price and Fraser Kerr at their flat in Marylebone. It was a jolly gathering and I knew a lot of the guests. Fraser at that time was a member of the BBC Repertory Company so there were quite a few radio people present: John Tydeman, Head of Radio Drama, and his boyfriend, who was known as the Irish dancing master; Glyn Dearman, a radio producer; Jessie Mathews who had just taken over as Mrs. Dale in the daily weekday serial, 'Mrs. Dale's Diary'; Richard and Fraser's next door neighbour, the lovely young actress, Sally Home and her boyfriend who was soon to be her husband, actor, George Baker; and among the oldies were Henry Kendal, Bobby Andrews (Ivor Novello's devoted companion of 35 years); Norah Blaney, half of the vaudeville act, 'Farrar and Blaney' (Gwen Farrar I have already written about) who made it to America and The Ziegfeld Follies; Dorothy Summers had been in the long running Tommy Handley radio series, 'ITMA' and as Mrs. Mopp was famous for the catch phrase, "Can I do you now, sir?" Sometimes at a party, after a drink or two, Dorothy could be persuaded to evoke Mrs. Mopp's immortal line and everybody would fall about laughing. To my certain knowledge she did it twice that evening.

Quite soon after my arrival I was introduced to a handsome young man who had also come on his own. He was a twenty four year old actor called Jeremy Conway who had recently been in a play with Richard at the Royalty Theatre. The play had starred Anton Walbrook whose stage swan song it sadly turned out to be. I thought Jeremy was extremely attractive and I was intrigued by his bright, intelligent conversation, and the passion he had for the theatre also excited me. The longer we talked the more attractive he became, and he can't have found me too boring because he never made any attempt to move away, and with new guests arriving all the time he had ample opportunity to. Like the good, dutiful guests we both were, we now and then separated to talk to others but then somehow always gravitated back to each other again. It was as if a magnet was drawing us together.

In a flash the party was over, it was already my birthday, most of the guests had departed and Jeremy and I were still deep in conversation. Not wanting to outstay our welcome we decided we too should leave, and stepping out onto the pavement I screwed up enough courage to ask if he would like to come home with me. He said he would.

We spent a heavenly night together but it was all too brief, he had to get up and leave terribly early as he was spending the weekend with his parents at their home in Berkshire and needed first to go to his flat in Regents Park to change his clothes and meet a friend who was going to drive him down. While he was getting ready to go I wondered if I would ever see him again and the thought saddened me. Then, just as he was leaving, he paused at the door. It was a pregnant pause and I took it as my cue. I asked if we could meet again and he said, "Yes".

The meeting took place late in the afternoon on the following Tuesday at the Classic Cinema in Baker Street where Hitchcock's 'Strangers on a Train' was showing. He had never seen it and I was quite keen to see it again. After the film we went back to his flat where he had prepared a delicious stew. I was to discover he was also a brilliant cook (I wonder what Mrs. Beeton was like in bed?). We spent another blissful night together and didn't get up until lunch time. From then on for some weeks it was his place or mine every night. All that to'ing and fro'ing across London each day got pretty exhausting, but for me it was well worth it. I kept waiting for him to say he had had enough but he never did, and when the relationship seemed to be secure enough I suggested that he moved in with me and he happily accepted the offer. I told Gavin I had a friend coming to stay, I didn't say for how long because in all honesty I didn't know myself, and he didn't seem to mind.

So Jeremy came to stay – that was almost forty three years ago and he still hasn't left. It is February 2007, he turned sixty eight in January and I will be eighty three in July. We now live in our own house in Fulham with two dogs and a cat. We also have a house in Wiltshire with a large garden and a pond full of Japanese koi. It's almost unbelievable how the years have flown. It seems like only yesterday he came to live with me in Brompton Square. I really feel that mine has been a charmed life. As I have said before, nothing I planned ever went accordingly, everything good that happened was purely by chance, and somehow I always landed on my feet. If that's not a charmed life, I don't know what is? How many people can claim to have had two such long lasting, meaningful relationships in their lives? The first endured for eighteen and a half years, and after the trauma of Denis' death, when all I could see ahead was a lonely old age, blow me if another didn't come along and, so far, come July, run for forty three years – we may outrun 'The Mousetrap' yet. Of course we have had our little differences, he leaves lids off jars and I sometimes forget to record 'Coronation

Street', but somehow we manage to rise above it and merrily roll along. What is the secret? I think it is the love we both share for the theatre, a passion that hasn't waned for either of us. We have had our share of dud shows, slept through some and walked out of others but we have never become jaded. We are always waiting to be astonished and some nights we are. Both of us are still in the business: Jeremy is one of London's leading theatrical agents, and I do my vicars and butlers and funny old men in films. I suppose it's sad that I never made it to the National Theatre or the RSC as an actor, or that I didn't manage to write the great comedy, or even another, 'Thoroughly Modern Millie', but I mustn't be too greedy, for, all things considered, I do believe, and I don't see how anyone can contradict me, that I have been one of the luckiest people on the planet. Curtain…applause….the Ivy!

POSTSCRIPT

On the morning of May the 11th 2007 at Fulham Town Hall Registry Office, with our friends Sheila Wilson and Adam Robertson as witnesses, Jeremy and I became civil partners. There – I thought you'd like a tidy finish.

Printed in the United Kingdom
by Lightning Source UK Ltd.
132097UK00001B/47-58/P